RELIGIOUS
EXPERIENCE
AND THE
NEW WOMAN

RELIGIOUS EXPERIENCE AND THE NEW WOMAN

The Life of Lily Dougall

Joanna Dean

INDIANA
University Press
Bloomington & Indianapolis

This book is a publication of

Indiana University Press
601 North Morton Street
Bloomington, IN 47404-3797 USA

http://iupress.indiana.edu

Telephone orders 800-842-6796
Fax orders 812-855-7931
Orders by e-mail iuporder@indiana.edu

The paper used in this publication meets the minimum
requirements of American National Standard for Information
Sciences—Permanence of Paper for Printed Library
Materials, ANSI Z39.48–1984.

Manufactured in the United States of America

Library of Congress Cataloging-in-Publication Data

Dean, Joanna (Joanna Elizabeth)
  Religious experience and the new woman : the life of
Lily Dougall / Joanna Dean.
     p. cm.
  Includes bibliographical references (p.   ) and index.
  ISBN 0-253-34814-5 (cloth : alk. paper)
  1. Dougall, L. (Lily), 1858–1923. 2. Modernism
(Christian theology)—Anglican Communion. I. Title.
  BX5199.D68D43 2007
  230'.3092—dc22
                                                2006016495

1 2 3 4 5 12 11 10 09 08 07

For Ankaret and John Dean

Contents

Acknowledgments

This book has been years in the making and I have accumulated numerous debts along the way. The first is to the communities of women who have fostered the project in its many manifestations: my fellow graduate students, especially Janet Friskney, Beverly Boutilier, Erika Koenig-Sheridan, Diane Dodd, and Leona Crabb; the group of writers who gathered around Janet Lunn, especially Dilys Leman, and the reading group of women's historians in Ottawa.

My second debt is to the community of scholars at Carleton University: Brian McKillop, who has been a thoughtful mentor, and Marilyn Barber, Deborah Gorham, Pamela Walker, Susan Whitney, Mark Philips, Sandra Campbell, and James Opp for their advice. Historians at home and further afield have found time from their busy schedules to comment on my work: Marguerite Van Die, William Westfall, Pamela Walker, Marilyn Barber, Susan Whitney, Barbara Freeman, Michael Brierley, Paul Mackenzie, Ann Taves and two anonymous readers. James Stayer introduced me to the intellectual puzzles of religious history when I was an undergraduate.

I have learned a great deal from the small group of people fascinated by Lily Dougall: Michael Brierley, whose insights as an Anglican minister were invaluable; book collector John Whitefoot, who is still searching for the elusive second edition of *The Earthly Purgatory;* Louise Armstrong, who researched Cutts End; local historian of Cumnor, Peggy Inman, who tracked down wills and contributed photographs; and Lorraine Vander Hoef, whose work will shed new light on Dougall's life. The careful research of Lorraine McMullen, who sadly passed away before completing her own biography of Lily Dougall, has been of great value. At an early stage in my research, philosopher Dorothy Emmet made me dinner and reminisced about Lily Dougall.

I would also like to acknowledge the assistance of librarians and archivists. Library and Archives Canada introduced me to Dougall: I spent a rapt afternoon in the depths of the archives reading Sophie Earp's loving biography of Lily, when I should have been researching a guide to women's papers in their collection. Colin Harris made the modern reading room at the Bodleian feel like home. The librarians at St. Paul's University in Ottawa welcomed me to their theological treasure trove, and archivists at the McCord Museum of Canadian History shared my delight when we found photos of Lily and Sophie. Callista Kelly and staff at Carleton's interlibrary loan office were endlessly patient.

The Social Sciences and Humanities Research Council funded the early stages of my research. Heather Sherratt's sensitive editing of early drafts persists in this final form. The editors at Indiana University Press—Michael Lundell, Elisabeth Marsh, Joyce Rappaport, and Dawn Ollila—have been everything an author could hope for. All remaining errors are, of course, my responsibility.

Finally, my family: my children, who grew up with this book and suffered the absent attentions of a mother whose mind was often in England with Lily Dougall; my husband, David Wilson, whose steady love and support have allowed me to survive the vagaries of an academic career; my in-laws, Arthur and Cicely Wilson; my English relatives who welcomed me to Oxford (and taught me to punt); and my parents, John and Ankaret Dean, who encouraged me to think for myself and to whom this book is dedicated.

RELIGIOUS
EXPERIENCE
AND THE
NEW WOMAN

Introduction

THERE ARE TWO MEMORIALS to Lily Dougall in her parish church. An elegant marble tablet inside the church describes her literary career:

> In grateful memory of Lily Dougall, author of
> *Pro Christo et Ecclesia* and other adventures in religious
> thought, also of *Beggars All* and other stories, who
> lived and wrote at Cutts End, Cumnor 1911–1923
>
> *Whatever is true is God's way of revealing Himself* L.D.

A long, flat stone in the graveyard outside limns her personal life: her birth in Montreal, Canada, in 1858, her long relationship with Sophie Earp, who lies buried with her, and her death in Cumnor, England. Under Lily's name, deep in the turf, is an inscription: "He Satisfieth the Longing Soul." The marble tablet speaks of Dougall's position at the leading edge of theological reform, and the shared gravestone suggests the female world and experiential roots from which her theology sprang.

The memorials are framed by St. Michael's, a twelfth-century church that embodies Anglican tradition: it is set in the center of Cumnor, now a prosperous suburb of Oxford, with the vicarage to one side and the ruins of the old manor house on the other. The church's interior is filled with the comfortable clutter of medieval gargoyles, Victorian monuments, and last week's Sunday school notices. In the churchyard new stones and ancient vie for space in muddled rows, the vicar can be seen puttering along the turf path with an old wheelbarrow, and children run between the graves. There is a sense of permanence and continuity.

The two memorials test this comfortable complacency. The rough-cut gravestone—a long slab of stone about five feet long and eight

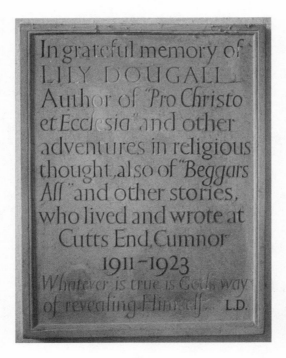

In grateful memory of
LILY DOUGALL
Author of "Pro Christo
et Ecclesia" and other
adventures in religious
thought, also of "Beggars
All" and other stories,
who lived and wrote at
Cutts End, Cumnor
1911–1923
Whatever is true is God's way
of revealing Himself.   L.D.

Memorial to Lily Dougall, St. Michael's Parish Church, Cumnor, England. *Courtesy Geoffrey Beard.*

inches wide—is like no other in the crowded churchyard. It is set in a corner created by the transept of the church, slightly apart from the other stones, and might be mistaken for a fallen section of the church wall, until one sees the inscriptions buried in the turf down each long side. The tablet, mounted high just inside the transept, was designed by artist-craftsman Eric Gill. Like others in the Arts and Crafts movement, Gill rejected the vulgarity of the industrial world for the authenticity of craftwork; he worked within a quasi-medieval Catholic craft guild. His tablet, like the gravestone, and like Dougall's Arts and Crafts home just across the field, appeals to the authenticity of the past in a way that is inherently modern.[1] The decision to remember Dougall with such unusual memorials was a deliberate one: a decision that in death, as in life, she would be distinguished from the mundane and the orthodox.

At the time of her death, Lily Dougall was a prominent member of the defiant Anglican modernist movement, and it is likely that it was her modernist friends who chose the memorials. Modernists had pressed Anglican tolerance year by year at a series of public conferences until finally in 1921, only two years before Dougall's death, a debate over the divinity of Christ precipitated the creation of the Commission on

Doctrine of the Church of England. The quotation on the tablet, "Whatever is true is God's way of revealing Himself," [2] was taken from one of Dougall's religious essays and offers an implicit challenge to the Commission. It summarizes the modernist position: there can be no limits on free thought, because all truth leads to God.

The term *modernism* has always carried a political edge: it was coined in the early twentieth century by the papacy in condemnation of Roman Catholic liberalism, and the adoption of the label by Anglicans marked a departure from the dry Broad Church movement into combative ecclesiastical debate. In North America, religious modernism is best known as the antithesis of militant fundamentalism. But Dougall's interests were broader, her sympathies wider, and her religious feeling deeper than this party label might suggest. The quotation on the gravestone points to the experiential faith that underlay Dougall's modernism. "He Satisfieth the Longing Soul," [3] is taken from the Psalms and refers to the bedrock of Dougall's theology: the personal experience of God.

Intellectual freedom and religious faith are usually understood as mutually incompatible; historians caught up in the binary logic of secularization have generally assumed that faith has been the casualty of free thought. Dougall's life suggests otherwise: the two components of her thought operated as a dialectic, each balancing and fueling the other. It was only because her experiential faith satisfied her "longing soul" that Dougall felt free to pursue biblical criticism, philosophical idealism, and psychology. These intellectual pursuits broadened her understanding of the experience of faith; over time, the experiential evangelicalism of her childhood expanded to incorporate elements of incarnational Anglo-Catholicism, Quaker inner light, and modernist mysticism. What is intriguing is the ease with which these elements combined to create a religious outlook that was profoundly spiritual and also fiercely combatively independent and liberal.

A TRANSATLANTIC LIFE

How did a North American woman come to be remembered in an Oxford church with such memorials? Lily Dougall was the brilliant and rebellious younger daughter of one of Canada's leading evangelicals, newspaper publisher John Dougall.[4] After a difficult adolescence in Montreal and New York City, she escaped to study in Edinburgh and then the south of England, where she found a supportive intellectual community with the new generation of women university graduates. Sophie Earp, one of the earliest graduates of Newnham College, Cambridge, became her companion. With Earp's assistance, Dougall began to publish short stories in magazines such as *Chambers* and *Longmans*, and in 1891 she published her first novel, *Beggars All*.[5] The novel posed Star, a young American living in Britain, with a bizarre moral dilemma. She is unable to support her crippled sister and widowed mother after the death of her father, and they are slowly starving on the stinting charity of their church. In desperation, she answers a marital advertisement and marries a man who will support them, virtually prostituting herself on behalf of her family. She then discovers that her new husband is a Robin Hood, stealing from the rich to support the poor, and has to decide whether to stay with him. The audacity of Star's response to the advertisement, her marital quandary, and the novel's condemnation of religious philanthropy caused a buzz in literary London, and *Beggars All* became a bestseller.

Subsequent novels placed assertive young women in equally improbable situations. One escapes a remote Quebec lumber camp (and the marital intentions of an older man) by hiding in her father's coffin; she rises out of the coffin at a train station, in a feminist resurrection, and goes on to establish herself in business. Another Canadian immigrant spurns a respectable minister for his rebellious younger brother, a butcher. A third independent young woman, a stereotypical New Woman, escapes rape in a lumber camp in the Rocky Mountains by pretending she is the Madonna. Dougall's characters are, as was Dougall herself, well read and argumentative young women who engage in vigorous debate with narrow-minded ministers, challenge overbearing suitors, and think for themselves.

The memorial tablet describes these novels simply as "stories," but, as the plots suggest, the novels served as entertaining vehicles for the latest in transatlantic ideas: liberal theology, New Woman feminism, idealist philosophy, and early psychology. Dougall's upper-middle-class readers took their philosophy light, spiked with ghosts, sexual danger, and romance, but if she presented complex ideas with a quirky wit, her understanding of the intellectual climate was solid and her explication sound. She cultivated the friendship of prominent men like Henry Sidgwick, William Wallace, Edward Caird, William James, J. R. Illingworth, and Frederic Myers, badgered them with questions and asked them to review her manuscripts. Unfortunately we will never know how Oxford's pre-eminent philosopher, Edward Caird, felt about his idealism being expounded in *The Zeit-Geist*—in a Canadian swamp by a reformed drunk recovering from attempted murder in the arms of his lover.

In 1900 Dougall wrote her first theological work, *Pro Christo et Ecclesia*, a stinging attack upon the church: Dougall compared Anglican and Nonconformist Churches to the Jewish sects that crucified Christ, and asked whether modern sectarians were not also enemies of Christ.[6] *Pro Christo et Ecclesia* was a lyrical exposition of the ideas of Christian socialist F. D. Maurice and it found an enthusiastic readership among the growing numbers of Christian socialists in Britain and North America. The book was published anonymously; most readers assumed that it was written by a cleric, and the anonymous "author of *Pro Christo et Ecclesia*" established a popular following as she published a series of controversial essays: *Christus Futurus* (1907), *Absente Reo* (1910), *Voluntas Dei* (1912), and *The Practice of Christianity* (1913). These religious essays were too light and too controversial to be considered theological studies. The wording on the memorial tablet is carefully chosen: they were "adventures in religious thought."

In 1903, after crossing the Atlantic almost annually, Dougall settled with Earp in England. When they moved close to Oxford in 1911, Dougall gradually dropped her anonymity and spoke at conventions, ran discussion groups, and published articles in liberal journals such as *The Modern Churchman* and *The Hibbert Journal*. She found intellectual company with the growing group of modernist Anglo-Catholics at the university. With Canon B. H. Streeter she created a theological think tank, the Cumnor Group, and edited a series of influential books, *Concerning Prayer* (1916), *Immortality* (1917), and *The Spirit* (1920) with contributions from eminent psychologists, biblical scholars, clerics, and philosophers.[7] She also became a leader in the Guild of Health, a group that tapped the energy of therapeutic healing movements, for whom she wrote *The Christian Doctrine of Health* (1916); and she joined the Anglican Fellowship, an elite Anglican reform movement. Many of her young associates, including such men as R. G. Collingwood and William Temple, went on to establish themselves as intellectual leaders of the subsequent generation. At the time of her death, Dougall was in the midst of speaking engagements with several articles underway. B. H. Streeter and Sophie Earp edited a posthumous work, and made plans for a commemorative book of selected letters. They died, however, before completing the book, and as theological tides began to turn against liberalism Dougall was quickly forgotten.

CONTEXTS FOR RELIGIOUS EXPERIENCE

Lily Dougall's work might be approached from any number of angles; this is a study of her ideas, but it is also, following a feminist understanding of the interplay of life and mind, an introduction to Dougall's life. The full complexity of her life will be left for later biographers; here

I will be exploring the ways in which her experiences as a woman at the turn of the century informed her ideas about religion. To paraphrase feminist theologian Carol P. Christ, I will be asking how her faith was rooted in her experience, her time and place, and her body.[8]

In rooting her faith in her life, I am, ironically, challenging the basis of Lily Dougall's theology. Dougall understood her experience of God to exist outside of time and beyond history. Like many liberals at the turn of the century, Dougall turned to personal religious experience when she could no longer accept the authority of a literal Bible. The experience of God offered the only remaining foundation for faith after intellectual speculation had swept away the old authorities of the Bible and the Church; as she explained: "The only rock on which [Christians] can rest is the personal experience of God's voice in their hearts."[9] Scholars have since identified religious experience as "the common core" of faith. They have traced a long genealogy in the mystic traditions and identified a mystic core underlying every religion from Hinduism to Catholicism.[10] As Catherine Albanese has observed, we now largely accept that the idea that "spirituality" exists independent of creed or Bible, and we commonly distinguish "spirituality" from the intellectual and structural apparatus referred to as "religion."[11] Feminist theologians in particular have appealed to the "the life of the spirit," going, as Nelle Morton says, "deep in the experience itself," in opposition to the patriarchal creeds and theologies of religious traditions.[12]

Contextualists have questioned the purity of this "core" of religious experience. They argue that we do not travel unencumbered into the depths, that we cannot so simply slip the bonds of gender, place, and time. Following Wittgenstein, contextualists suggest that the central experience of faith is mediated by language and culture, and so is subject to the influence of time and place. Steven Katz argues that the mystic's encounter is shaped by his or her expectations of the divine: "the experience itself as well as the form in which it is reported is shaped by concepts which the mystic brings to, and shapes, his experience."[13]

This study will be firmly contextualist. It will locate Lily Dougall's experiential faith in her North American evangelical childhood, in her transatlantic female community, and in the philosophic currents she encountered in Edinburgh and Oxford. Biography is the ideal vehicle for the exploration of an experiential faith, precisely because it foregrounds the personal, and makes evident the particular context within which religious faith is experienced. Through Lily Dougall, this study will set the very idea of the "common core" of religion into cultural and historical context, and show how this idea of a common spiritual core was a response to the cultural needs of a particular place and time.

As the study of Dougall's thought will reveal, liberals like Dougall turned to personal religious experience in response to the collapse of biblical authority. They constructed an experiential theology out of evangelical piety, recovered mystical tradition, idealist philosophy, and the new psychology of religion.

The language we use to understand experiential faith is important: terms such as *piety, spirituality,* and *mysticism* are notoriously slippery and value laden. While *piety* accurately describes the emphasis upon the inner experience of God, it also suggests a suspension of reason, an emotive irrationality suspicious of critical thought. *Mysticism* smacks of spiritual athleticism and exclusivity. *Spirituality* has become a popular term, but it is broad and amorphous, and is built upon many of the assumptions that I hope to challenge. This study will refer to "experiential faith," by which I mean a faith built upon the religious experience. *Experiential* is a word that arises from the nineteenth-century context, and it travels comfortably with Dougall from the evangelical piety of her Montreal family to the mystical and incarnational theology of her modernist friends. Yet it is free of the modern uses and definitional debates that accompany such words as *mysticism* or *spiritual*.[14]

The ensuing chapters locate Dougall's theology in the cultural context of the late nineteenth and early twentieth century. They take a chronological approach to her life and work, and are divided into three parts. Part 1 describes the origins of Dougall's experiential theology in her family's holiness faith. We observe her as a young woman in a highly charged evangelical community in Montreal and New York City, vacillating between the pulls of evangelical faith and liberal thought, moving from an emotive liberal evangelicalism to the intellectual freedom of Broad Church Episcopalianism, and then briefly back to the holiness movement. The struggle is a spiritual one, but it is also familial. It is only upon her mother's death that Dougall is able to completely break free of her family's evangelicalism.

Part 2 describes Dougall's growing prominence as a novelist and religious essayist and the support provided by a community of university-educated women in Britain and North America, and particularly in her lifelong loving relationship with Sophie Earp. Dougall initially progresses along a path charted by historians of idealism, from a dreamy romanticism through to the Oxford idealism of Edward Caird, but she is unable to accept the spiritual aridity of absolute idealism, the next step in the idealist arc. In her maturity we find her moving to a more relational personal idealism under the influence of J. R. Illingworth. Again, I argue, the social context has a bearing: personal idealism, dismissed by philosophers and overlooked by historians, reflects the close world of Dougall's female culture. It was a theology cum philosophy that stressed the interrelationship of all, and reflected Dougall's world of interlocking friendships.

Part 3 describes Dougall's public role in the Anglican modernist movement and emphasizes the centrality of a mystical faith in this combative theological environment. She was recognized as a spiritual leader among modernists, one of a series of North Americans who brought a reinvigorated spirituality to the academic British church. At the close of her life, in a second rejection of the isolated religious experience, she turned away from the individualist mysticism of modernists like Evelyn Underhill, and turned to the fellowship of the Cumnor Group, the Student Christian Movement, and the Anglican Fellowship. Her mature emphasis was upon a relationship with God, rather than a mystical dissolution into the One, and she insisted that this relationship was best understood and experienced in the context of relations with other people, in Christian fellowship.

The emphasis throughout this text is on the grounding that Dougall found in religious experience. The authority of religious experience served as her rock in a changing time; as she boasted, "no sane man doubts his experience." [15] In the epilogue, however, I describe the threat posed to Dougall's faith by the new science of psychology. For many years, as Ann Taves has observed, the science of psychology operated in parallel to the theology of religious experience. [16] Dougall was an enthusiastic member of the British Society for Psychical Research; she met with Frederic Myers and William James; and at Myers's suggestion, she incorporated their theories into an early novel, *The Mormon Prophet*. Later she invited psychologists to contribute to her Cumnor volumes. By the end of her life, however, the threat posed by psychology was becoming apparent. As she observed: "Religious experiences are now described in psychological terms, religious values are largely psychological values." [17] The epilogue argues that the interpretive framework offered by psychology was ultimately an insidious one that undermined the only remaining "rock" supporting the faith of liberal Protestants.

GENDERING RELIGIOUS EXPERIENCE

Gender must be the central context in any interpretation of Lily Dougall's intellectual life. The basic premise of all feminist theology, Carol P. Christ and Judith Plaskow explain, is that "the vision of the theologian is affected by the particularities of his or her experience as male or female." [18] This is not to say that all women experience faith in

the same way, or that a woman's faith is essentially different from that
of a man, but as long as women's lives differ from those of men, then a
different theology will arise from these experiences. Ann Braude has
applied this idea historically, and suggested in a much-quoted article that
the twentieth century saw a "reorientation of liturgy and theology based
on women's experience." [19] The examination of Lily Dougall's work,
especially in the context of her extensive relations with other university-
educated women, suggests that this was true, but it also suggests that
the process was more conflicted than Braude has anticipated.

The best way to understand these conflicts is to turn to the father of
liberal theology, Freidrich Schleiermacher, who laid out a deeply gendered trajectory in his *coincidentia oppositorium*. Schleiermacher's coincidence of opposites is a dialectic in which male rationality encounters
female piety and moves to a higher liberal faith. Assumptions about female
piety existed long before Schleiermacher's formulations (Augustine associated piety with his mother's milk) but his dialectic gave them new liberal life: F. D. Maurice, Phillips Brooks, and numerous other liberal men
describe the spiritual center found in the static and irrational piety of
their mothers, wives, and sisters. Crisis-of-faith novels typically describe
a young man faced with the barren alternatives of a rigid orthodoxy or
skeptical rationality; his faith is renewed by a woman's piety and he
attains the maturity of a liberal experiential theology. Feminist critics
have observed that the *coincidentia oppositorium* consigns women to a
static role as mediators of male experience.[20] As such critics point out,
men move dialectically between the core of religious experience and the
evolving world of theology and church doctrine, but women are largely
confined to the experiential. They are simultaneously given voice and
silenced: women have special access to the "life of the spirit," but this
spirituality is a static and passive well that has been severed from history
and thought. Lily Dougall struggled with this legacy, and we struggle
with it again in trying to understand her life and her work.

Schleiermacher's dialectical play between static spirituality and
evolving theology informs modern scholarship. Scholarly work on
mysticism is based upon the idea that the mystical "common core" is
the permanent ground upon which historical change and transformation takes place. Sociologists allow that faith dies, but not that it can
change; secularization is, by definition, the death of faith.[21] Church
historians similarly assume that faith is at its core inalterable: the expression of faith may change, the language in which it is spoken and the rit-
uals that accompany it may alter, but the underlying faith is unchanging.
The argument often becomes circular: faith is by definition that part that
has not changed. Further, this religious experience is assumed to be

inherently incommunicable, or "ineffable," to use the language of mystical studies. As Schleiermacher said, "it can scarcely be described, so little does it properly exist." [22] Church historian Owen Chadwick concluded that this experience was beyond the purview of the historian: "These inward movements are too profound for those who experience them to articulate successfully. They can give hints and suggestions and poetic phrases. Biographer and historian can hardly pass beyond such little lights." [23] Chadwick and a generation of historians avoided the ineffable depths and the uncomfortable intimacy of experiential faith; they focused instead upon the measurable outward signs of religion, and provided a sociological accounting of the church.

The implications of this for women have been significant. Women, as pure conduits of an ahistorical spirituality, have frequently been left outside religious history as we study the development of the masculine realms of theology and ecclesiastical reform. This erasure of the feminized spiritual has been perpetuated by feminist historians who, concerned to establish the intellectual credibility and active agency of their subjects, have been embarrassed by evidence of piety; women's historians have been, as Braude has said, "squeamish" about religious faith. [24] We have focused upon active religious women such as social workers, missionaries, and fund-raisers, and have only recently started to examine the contemplative components of women's lives. If piety appears in the historical record, it is commonly described as the vestigial trace of an earlier outlook; a pious woman is, by definition, a traditional woman. A woman's experiential faith is assumed to be the same faith that informed her mother's life, and historical development is assumed to lie in the loss of this faith, rather than in its growth or alteration.

Contextualists are returning history to the study of mysticism, and their approaches offer some guidance to the historian interested in bringing religious experience within the purview of history. The sweeping surveys of mysticism as a "common core" are being replaced by the close particularity of historical studies, and text, as the site of the mediation between the experience and the context, has become central. There are numerous biographies of mystics, like Teresa of Avila, that are personal in focus, textual in analysis, and attentive to the historical and cultural context. [25] Bernard McGinn, author of the highly respected multivolume work *The Foundations of Mysticism*, advocates a "historico-contextual" approach. His work is thickly historical, and he defines mysticism not as the fleeting experience but much more broadly as the "practice of the presence of God." [26] The emphasis is on "spirituality as an experience rooted in a particular community's history rather than as a dimension of human existence as such." [27] It is the community of thought that is important.

Michel de Certeau's analysis of mysticism as an arena of discourse in *Mystic Fable* offers some important insights. He also offers a cautionary note, one that may explain why the study of the history of spirituality has not progressed further.[28] De Certeau argues that mysticism is fundamentally incompatible with history: the power of the mystical experience lies in its ability to break with the chronology of time. "These events which must be nothing but arrivals from an (impossible) eternity or a (postponed) end, continually contradict the time produced by historiography." He concludes, "Historiography begins at the point where the mourning of the *voice* begins."[29] This is the question underlying this and any contextual study of religious experience: are we, in situating faith, murdering it? Are we, by historicizing and contextualizing an experience, severing it from supernatural origins? Are we perhaps mourning that which we have already lost? Is it a sign that Lily Dougall's liberal faith has lost its power that we are now pinning it upon historical time?

This study arises from a fascination with the spiritual, but it is not a celebration of feminized spirituality. In many ways it is an examination of the crippling effects of such a spirituality: the gendering of liberal theology offered Lily Dougall a voice but also silenced her, and this is in large part a study of silences. During Dougall's youth, theology was considered to be beyond a woman's intellectual ability; even F. D. Maurice, a proponent of women's education, drew the line at women studying theology. Women were denied theological training, and denied pulpits or lecterns from which to preach. Women like Dougall found a way around these proscriptions, by reading the materials in their fathers' libraries, arguing with brothers, debating with guests at the dinner table, and discussing ideas among themselves. As women's historians have long realized, they presented their ideas anonymously and through such acceptable feminine forms as tracts and novels. Dougall published stories as Ernest Dunns, novels as the genderless L. Dougall, and her religious essays anonymously. She expressed her ideas through metaphor and plot, through humor and dialogue. "I don't think you are as tall as Lovereen," wrote liberal cleric T. B. Kilpatrick, on reading a draft of her first novel, "but you are quite as capable of talking metaphysics behind a row of peas."[30] The young Lily, as was the case with the autobiographical Lovereen, found that her ideas were best received if expressed lightly, in an oblique, self-deprecating manner. Mermaids swan about in her novels, the Madonna materializes, and ghosts appear. The devices titillated readers, but they also allowed Dougall to raise metaphysical questions without appearing overly serious. The novels allowed Dougall to talk metaphysics behind a row of peas; theology as female foolishness, an entertaining form of speculation that might be indulged. The result is a distorted theological discourse that must be interpreted aslant, with close attention to the gaps and erasures, to things not said, and to the use of metaphor and symbol. Feminist literary critics have delighted in the interpretive puzzles offered by women's writing. Dougall's first autobiographical novel, "Lovereen," lends itself to this kind of decoding: Chapter 3 of this study shows how Dougall divided her youthful self into two characters in this novel, a rational young man and a mystical young woman, in order to fit Schleiermacher's *coincidentia oppositorium*.

Literary detective work is, like Dougall's novels, entertaining, but Dougall's light literary voice cripples her religious essays. They are characterized by a charming sort of bravado, a very feminine form of self-assertion that includes its own retraction. *Pro Christo et Ecclesia* and *Absente Reo* are hard-hitting attacks upon ecclesiastical rivalry and clerical hypocrisy, but their tone is light, their language lyrical. Consequently, the essays charmed rather than convinced their readers. The tone was a sign of Lily Dougall's own sense of intellectual unworthiness. There was a subtle current of self-deprecation running through the work beneath the bravado, an inability to take herself, or her ideas, entirely seriously. At the end of her life, particularly after she moved to Oxford, her books and speeches were undermined by apologetic prefaces, self-deprecating introductions, and frequent references to illustrious mentors.

This has led some to dismiss her work. At the beginning of the research for this book, I sought out one of the few individuals who remembered Lily Dougall, British philosopher Dorothy Emmet. Emmet as a young girl had met Dougall, and she recalled that Dougall was a pleasant hostess and a popular writer, but not a figure to be taken seriously.[31] Emmet was not entirely incorrect, for Dougall's work lacks the intellectual rigor of Emmet's own philosophy. This book, however, speaks to the importance of taking Dougall seriously, for the sake of her ideas, for the purpose of understanding the religious outlook of her thousands of readers, and also to understand the subtle ways that women's ideas about religion were distorted in a theological world that relegated women to an experiential wasteland.

SPIRITUALITY AND RELIGIOUS EXPERIENCE

Lily Dougall's combative, iconoclastic memorials have lost their power to shock; they now operate as part of the eclectic mix of St. Michael's Church, absorbed in the larger tradition that they once sought to challenge. Very few of the faithful would question her claim:

"Whatever is true is God's way of revealing Himself," and it is now common for even the orthodox to seek God beyond the walls of the church. This, then, is perhaps the point: Dougall's generation laid the groundwork for our generation's understanding of spirituality.[32] The distinctions that she drew at the turn of the nineteenth century between the living religious experience and the tired theology of the churches have become accepted wisdom at the turn of the twentieth century.

This study of Dougall's life and work might have celebrated her as the progenitor of modern faith. Instead, I have suggested that this is a troubled legacy, one plagued by deeply gendered constructions of faith, and a too easy recourse into emotive spirituality. I have chosen to problematize the distinctions between spirituality and religion, and work toward a contextual history for spirituality. There can be no single history of spirituality. This is the history specific to Lily Dougall, her friends, and her readers in North America and Britain. Other currents of experiential religious thought, some of which Dougall acknowledged, like Westernized Buddhism, some of which she borrowed from, like the Quaker inner light, and some of which she rejected, like mental science, also have contributed to our modern understanding. Spirituality was specific to a place and time. The modern concept of universal spirituality has been constructed over the last century, and is the product of various competing and highly contested currents of thought.

PART I

COMING OF AGE
IN CANADA

1

An Evangelical Childhood

Lɪʟʏ Dᴏᴜɢᴀʟʟ ᴡᴀꜱ ʙᴏʀɴ on April 16, 1858. As the granddaughter of Canadian sugar magnate John Redpath, and the daughter of a prominent Montreal publisher and importer, John Dougall, she should have had a protected and comfortable childhood.[1] Her parents, however, sacrificed the family's prosperity and health for their evangelical faith, and Lily's youth was overshadowed by a failed attempt to establish a temperance newspaper in New York City. The family crisis ensuing from this venture, and the liberal experiential faith that informed it, laid a conflicted basis for Lily Dougall's adult faith.

This chapter draws upon family papers to understand the potent religious environment of Lily's youth. John Dougall's evangelicalism is best described as the cultivation of heightened religious experience: he held prayer meetings at work, preached on the docks, and traveled to religious revivals in order to live in constant communion with God. Lingering elements of Calvinist doctrine girded the religious experience. Over time members of the family embraced the holiness theology of the "second blessing." Hannah Whitall Smith taught evangelicals to aspire to higher consecration by "resting in God." Lily considered her older sister Janet to be a perfectly consecrated soul, but diaries reveal her brother John struggled unsuccessfully to attain whole consecration. Fundamentalist Benjamin Breckinridge Warfield dismissed holiness as a feminine mysticism that fuelled female independence, presumption, and pride; examination of the roots of holiness in the work of Thomas Upham suggests that holiness did, paradoxically, offer women like Janet Dougall a form of self assertion through active, willing acquiescence in God's love.

Lily Dougall grew up on her grandfather's estate in the heart of Montreal. When John Redpath built an imposing mansion, Terrace Bank, on the forested edge of the Montreal mountain, he gave his eldest daughter the old farmhouse on the property, Ivy Green. Lily grew up surrounded by a large extended family including her older siblings, the children of her grandfather's second marriage, and numerous cousins. She later described an idyllic childhood, playing in the orchards and woods with Willie (likely William Wood Redpath, her grandfather's youngest son).

The Redpaths were Free Church Presbyterians. They took their religious obligations seriously, as part of their business leadership. Lily's father, John Dougall, however, placed religion before business. Shortly after arriving from Scotland in 1826 to set up a dry goods wholesale business, Dougall was converted by an American Presbyterian and temperance advocate, Joseph Stiff Christmas; he became a founding member of the Montreal Temperance Society in 1832 and editor of the society's journal in 1835.[2] His piety was renewed in 1838 by Dr. Edward Norris Kirk, of Boston, and when he married Elizabeth Redpath in 1840, they left the Presbyterian Church, because it "worshipped rumsellers," and instead joined a Congregational church, the Zion Church. In 1846, twelve years before Lily's birth, John Dougall's religious and business interests merged in the weekly *Montreal Witness*. The newspaper became his pulpit, from which he preached nonsectarian temperance evangelicalism. It may have depleted his wholesale business: Dougall and his partner, his brother James, struggled with debt in the late 1840s and 1850s, and declared bankruptcy for four years from 1865.[3]

A draft advertising sheet described the evangelical *Witness* as a "missing link between the Church and the world. . . . It has nailed its colors to the mast as a catholic evangelical newspaper opposing firmly but courageously Romanism, Ritualism, and rationalism and supporting to its utmost all good causes such as those represented by the great catholic religious societies and YMCA."[4] The evangelicalism was initially a fiery Calvinism; as J. I. Cooper noted in a study of the early years of the *Witness*, "the attitudes of the Godhead which appear to have appealed most strongly were those of judgment and vengeance. . . . [M]oral fervor and gloom were present in about equal quantities."[5] It was virulently anti-Catholic; John Dougall supported the French Canadian Missionary Society and fought an ongoing battle with the Roman Catholic Church, "that system of Godless superstition."[6]

Over the years, the *Witness*'s evangelicalism became less urgent and the commercial and political news gained in importance. The paper's stated purpose in 1868 was more muted: to "promote evangelical religion, sound morality and useful knowledge."[7] Despite a restrictive advertising policy (the *Witness* did not endorse patent medicines, liquor, or tobacco) the newspaper became a commercial success, spawning a

Lily Dougall and William Woods Redpath, 1861. Photograph by William Notman. *Courtesy Notman Photographic Archives, McCord Museum of Canadian History, I-2666.1.*

publishing empire that eventually included a semi-weekly, a weekly, as well as a daily edition; a literary monthly, *The New Dominion Monthly;* a Sunday School paper, the *Sabbath Reader;* an inexpensive semi-monthly temperance review, *The Canadian Messenger* or *The Northern Messenger* (from 1865); the French Protestant *L'Aurore;* and from 1901 (under Lily Dougall's editorial control) the international review, *World Wide.* In 1870, when his Montreal daily had the second highest circulation in Canada, John Dougall moved to New York to start another paper, the *New York Witness.*[8]

His timing was unfortunate. The panic of 1873 soon knocked the bottom out of the New York economy, and although he had an anonymous financial backer—a Mr. Remington of Ilion, New York—the paper barely survived, moving from crisis to crisis.[9] This venture dominated Lily's youth and put tremendous emotional and financial strain on the family. The paper finally failed; as a grandson put it, the daily *New York Witness* "died of galloping consumption of family money."[10] The

Ivy Green. Lily Dougall grew up in the original farmhouse on her grandfather's estate, a gift from John Redpath to his eldest daughter, Elizabeth Dougall. *Courtesy Redpath Sugar Museum.*

Montreal Witness, placed under a ban by the Roman Catholic Church in 1875, also suffered flagging circulation and declining revenue.[11] Years later, after the death of her mother, Lily Dougall wrote repeatedly to her father to reassure him: "I wish you would not grieve over our New York troubles which are past, or be anxious about our money for the future. If we lost health and money in the conflict, we gained what is of far more value than either."[12]

The family losses in money and health were significant, however, and were to color Lily's feelings about evangelical faith. A small collection of letters provides insight into the family dynamics.[13] It appears that Elizabeth Dougall shared her husband's faith, if not his energy, but their children struggled with the consequences of his religious commitment. In her unpublished autobiographical novel, "Lovereen: A Canadian Story," Lily Dougall described the difficulties of a young girl, Lovereen Walford, whose father neglects business and social conventions in order to evangelize. The manuscript describes an emotionally intense, somewhat overbearing man. He is compared by an aunt

Terrace Bank, c. 1880. The home of Lily Dougall's grandfather, John Redpath. *Courtesy Notman Photographic Archives, McCord Museum of Canadian History, II-133286.*

to a neighboring volcano: "in the first place she could not remove him and his preaching; in the second she had no doubt that he was placed there by Providence to perform that function and in the third she was under constant apprehension of an abnormal irruption of his religious zeal which in result would overwhelm himself and his relatives in the hot lava of the world's scorn." The aunt concludes, no doubt reflecting some of Lily Dougall's own feelings about her father: "It is perhaps a misfortune that enthusiasts must be left independent in action while they can never be alone in the suffering their action may entail." [14]

The financial strain appears to have been borne by the oldest children, John Redpath Dougall (1841–1934), James Duncan Dougall (1843–1914), and Janet Dougall (1845–1904), who remained in Montreal to run the original family businesses. The younger John Dougall took over editorial duties at the *Montreal Witness,* Janet worked as an editor, and James carried on the family's other commercial ventures. These adult children, in their late twenties at the start of the New York venture, initially saw themselves as willing martyrs to the cause of evangelicalism. As James wrote in an optimistic moment in 1876,

> It is marvellous to me how both Father and me get on from day to day and from week to week always writhing [?] on the edge of anxiety and despair. . . . I am sure that if any of the ancient worthies had to come back to earth again and be subject as before to temptation and weakness he would prefer to be placed in some position where he would *have* to feel day by day and hour by hour his dependence upon God and that is just the position which our Father in his infinite love has chosen for us.[15]

But over time this willing martyrdom became strained. James in particular, who had a wife and young children to support, was driven to distraction as he watched the family money and reputation disappear. Having invested $11,000, in 1878 he wrote,

> How many months of anxiety have I had for want of that money lest my whole life should be ruined at the outset? How much hard work have I had to go through to keep the businesses here floating without it? I say nothing of the money sent from the *Witness* here as that was your own yet but for me in all probability the lack of it would have caused the failure of the paper here.[16]

He and his wife, Laure, were forced to move to a smaller house, and she bought a sewing machine. They were not poor by any means, but they were hard-pressed to keep up with their extended family and Montreal acquaintances.

Letters suggest a drop in social standing over these years. John Dougall's evangelicalism was aimed at the working classes. He preached on street corners in the dockyards and poorer districts of the city, and an employee noted, "the best feature of the *Witness* is that the *common* man can read it and understand it, and the *common people* take it." [17] Lily's older sister, Janet, was praised for remaining with her small Congregational church when she might have joined a "more fashionable church." [18] Over time, family members found themselves excluded from Montreal social life. By 1886, Lily's brother John wrote, "Our social sphere grows smaller all the time. We cannot now be said to have any. Mrs. Alfred Savage had [a party?] and asked all our circle and not us." [19]

John Dougall seems at times to have been almost oblivious to his family's difficulties in his secure belief that the Lord would care for his own. As the crisis deepened, his faith in God came into conflict with business imperatives. He wrote to Lily's mother, Elizabeth: "I trust the Lord will smile upon us and our offering—he did so on Abel but allowed him to be slain. Whatever he does is best." [20] James was less willing to leave business in the hands of the Lord and became more openly critical of his father's methods. He was embarrassed by his father's repeated petitions to his subscribers for yet more donations: "Can it be His will that his servants should go into debt for the requirements of this work while their Master is able to provide everything?"[21] As John Dougall's backer gradually withdrew from the *New York Witness,* and the situation became more desperate, he began to contemplate more extreme measures to keep the paper afloat. James wrote to him, insisting that the debts be cleared, even at the cost of an opportunity to evangelize.[22] In a rambling and emotional letter, he warned his father that the evangelical purpose was in conflict with business ethics:

> Your argument that the *New York Witness* is the Lord's business and must be left to his management is inanswerable [sic] I think if it can be shown that any other kind of guidance is promised than the dealings of providence as understood by the aid of the Holy Spirit but if that is the guidance we are taught to expect then we come back to where we were before that. You must judge for yourself how to act seeking the divine guidance and in view of all the circumstances in which we are placed. The question then comes up Is it lawful to do anything in the Lord's name which would be wrong if done in your own? [sic][23]

He was rebuked by his mother for speaking out and in later years he resorted to such short aphorisms as "Trust in providence *and* keep your powder dry."[24]

Janet and her brother John were less overtly critical of their father's choices; they remained single, and their main concern seems to have been the welfare of the younger family members who had moved with their parents to Brooklyn. Lily and two other sisters, Mary Helen (Polly) and Susan (Susie), were frequently ill. "The whole family save James and Jessie [Janet] seem weak and with little promise of Life in this world," their brother John wrote in his diary in 1870.[25] On February 27, 1872, after months of illness, Polly died at age twenty-four when Lily was thirteen.[26] Polly's death heightened the family's concerns for Lily and Susan's health.[27] Lily suffered nervous collapses in 1877 and 1878, and returned temporarily to Montreal. In 1878, Susan also broke down and entered a hospital in Dansville, New York, where over ten months she slowly regained her strength. Lily's mother, Elizabeth Dougall, was also frequently ill.

The illnesses are not identified. It appears that the younger daughters inherited their mother's predisposition to debilitating asthma, a chronic disease that had significant psychosomatic components.[28] The breakdowns in Polly, Susan, Lily, and Elizabeth's health were clearly associated with the stress of the New York venture. Commenting on Susan's slow improvement, Janet said she had been in failing health for ten years—a period of time that roughly coincides with their father's New York venture.[29] Letters point to the inadequacies of the Dougalls' housing in Brooklyn and their relative poverty, as her brother John put it, "the change in climate and circumstance." A letter from Lily's father several years later said he had been wrong to assume she had malaria, and acknowledged that she had been "overtaxed." [30] Reading between the lines, it is obvious that the young girls were also struggling with the emotional demands of their invalid mother and overbearing father.[31] The move to New York placed them in claustrophobically close quarters with their parents, cut off from the supportive social world of the Redpath kin.

What was the faith that informed the family's sacrifices? Family letters reveal a potent mix of experiential faith and evangelical outreach, girded by a Presbyterian Calvinism and heightened by a holiness interiority. The sense of the presence of God was central. Lily Dougall's depiction of the father in "Lovereen" is of a man alive to God. As the fictional figure explains: "There is only one thing that mars our lives, and that is that we do not live, as we ought every day in conscious communion with God." [32] A young woman who has fallen under his spell says ecstatically: "Your father says that people can never study the Bible too much, that when they study it a great deal Jesus often gives them a wonderful sense of His presence, so that they feel He is with them all the time, just as if they could see Him. That must be very beautiful." [33] The young girl Lovereen recalls leaving a chair out when she was a child, in order to imagine Christ sitting beside her in his robes. "I used to say the questions that troubled me and try to listen in the depth of my soul to see what answer He would give me. . . ." [34] God's presence was vivid and constant.

It appears that this sense of the presence of God was heightened by holiness teaching. Holiness was an American variant of the Methodist doctrine of Christian perfection, popularized by Phoebe Palmer, who brought the teaching to Canada in a series of widely publicized revivals in the 1850s. Holiness or perfectionism attracted evangelicals from Congregational, Presbyterian, and Baptist churches, as well as Quakers, who retained their denominational affiliation while identifying with the larger movement. With holiness, the highest point of evangelical experience shifted from conversion—the moment of crisis when a Christian, typically an adolescent, accepts Christ—to the second blessing. Conversion was no longer the dramatic high point of a Christian life. Lily recalled her own conversion as a gradual and imperceptible experience: "*I* for instance, as a child, was converted—at least I suppose I was, not at any definite time and place, but still the course of my childhood, so to speak, ran to that end." [35] She appears to have experienced the Christian education described in Horace Bushnell's *Christian Nurture* (1847), led through prayers at her mother's knee and Sunday School to a gradual knowledge of God. As the emphasis shifted, conversion remained necessary, but no longer sufficient: notes taken from Bible classes by Lily's brother, John Redpath Dougall, put it succinctly, "Without conversion nothing is done, after conversion a great deal is needed."

As the second blessing became the primary preoccupation of the believer, daily life took on a heightened experiential dimension—a sense of living in conscious communion with God. Phoebe Palmer described the second blessing as an instantaneous spiritual baptism of the Holy Ghost, but by 1858, the year of Lily's birth, Presbyterian William E. Boardman described a more gradual process of constant "infillings" of the Holy Spirit in *The Higher Christian Life.* John Dougall wrote to Lily's mother from a religious meeting: "I have not got what I came for yet— some assurance of the divine favor and support and a fresh baptism of the Spirit. There is little doubt that the Holy Spirit is here but I am not conscious of any special blessing received from the brethren's addresses or prayers, though these have been able and earnest." [36] The Dougalls cultivated a sense of God's continual presence through a range of religious practices: private devotions, family prayer, lay preaching, church services and revivals. In addition family members were expected to testify publicly to their faith by preaching: the elder John Dougall held numerous small prayer meetings, such as the fifteen minute prayer meeting at lunch time at the *Witness* offices, and he preached among the poor in dockyards and street corners.[37] It appears that public praying came as easily as breathing to him. As an employee at the *New York Daily Witness* testified at John Dougall's funeral service in 1886:

> He taught me one thing, and that was how to pray. We were in trouble one time and I went to see him before he went to Philadelphia. He said, "Let us pray about it." I did not know before what prayer was; he simply told God who we were and what we wanted, and asked Him to grant it if it was His will, for Christ's sake and that was the end of the worry.[38]

For Lily's father, God was ever present and prayer was, quite simply, "the end of the worry."

Ian Bradley has described evangelical faith as a series of vivid personal experiences rather than a logical system of beliefs, but there were, of course, theological underpinnings.[39] A Calvinist theology, from John

Dougall's Presbyterian youth in Scotland and Elizabeth Dougall's Canadian childhood, girded their faith. Although the Dougalls had joined the Congregational Church on their marriage, the family ties to Presbyterianism remained strong, and elements of Calvinist teaching— the doctrine of eternal damnation, the image of a punitive God, and the doctrine of original sin or the total depravity of mankind—were an integral part of Lily's childhood. Among the very few childhood mementos in her personal papers was a copy of the sermon preached at her Presbyterian maternal grandfather's funeral in 1869 when she was an impressionable eleven-year-old. The words remind us of the continuing power of the Calvinist image of a wrathful God:

> Those of you who are God's people know what it was to have been bound with fetters laid upon your souls, enslaved of lust, misled, deceived, benighted, and befouled of sin. Your souls remember the wormswood and the gall, the gloom, the misery, and the horrors of the prison house and the grave in which you lay. But oh!, the joy, the thrill of unutterable happiness which you experienced when by the Lord's hand the fetters were shattered, and your sins and iniquities were cast into the sea . . . at one time you looked upon the Almighty with dark suspicion and dread. His holiness, justice, and power inspired you with terror. . . .[40]

The sermon continues at length about the corresponding joys of salvation, and concludes by enumerating John Redpath's numerous philanthropic and community services—proof, to the extent that there could be any proof, of his place among the elect. The few extant letters from Elizabeth Dougall reveal that the Devil was a force in her life. She spoke of the Devil as if he were locked in a struggle for a person's soul: "The Evil one has to be ordered off we cry to the Lord to undertake for us to keep him off seeking earnestly that the Holy Spirit be with us and Jesus with us Satan departs and the Spirit prays." [41]

Fears about eternal damnation appear in family letters about the conversion of an uncle, Elizabeth's brother. In 1881, John Dougall wrote to a friend, "My wife and I cry for the conversion of her brother John James Redpath." [42] In April 1883, Lily's sister Janet wrote Susan, "Laure goes to see J J [John James] as often as she can, he seems to be in a very softened mood, Says he cannot believe, thinks he would need to go through what Saul of Tarsus did to be converted." [43] Two weeks later, Lily's Aunt Jane wrote to Elizabeth, mourning the death of their sister Helen. "I know as soon as you are able you will write to poor John Oh may this solemn warning be blessed to him poor fellow how long has he been an object of solicitude to us how wondrously God has preserved his life which by his own efforts he has sought to destroy surely *he* [?] before the end comes [*sic*]." [44] Their urgency would suggest that the idea of hellfire was still powerful.

These Calvinist elements were not overturned so much as gradually outmoded. John Dougall's emphasis upon religious freedom eased such theological transitions. He was an active member of the Evangelical Alliance, a transatlantic organization committed to the pursuit of religious liberty. The Alliance argued that religious truth was the product of the individual conscience and a private matter between the individual and God. [45] The result was a release from dogmatic sectarianism in a common faith. As one of the founding members of the Canadian Evangelical Alliance was reported to have said in 1846: "Dogmatic theology has been a source of great weakness. He lamented to think what talents and time have been wasted in dogmatical theology when the world was perishing." [46] This religious freedom had its limits. It was not understood as freedom to do without religion, but as freedom to express faith without impediment. As an Evangelical Alliance leader, Philip Schaff, put it, "It is freedom *in* religion not freedom *from* religion." [47] The authority of the literal Bible was not questioned.

Lily Dougall later attributed her theological liberalism to her father's influence, recalling, along classic gender lines, "the faith in God I imbibed from my mother and the love of freedom I derived from my father." [48] But John Dougall's liberalism was very different from the Broad Church liberal theology that she was to embrace. Her liberalism led her to try to rework the intellectual scaffolding upon which her faith rested; John Dougall simply rejected the scaffolding as unnecessary. He felt it was enough to rest upon the authority of scripture and the experience of the Holy Spirit. The result was a heightened faith, with a diminished theology and a looser sense of denominational affiliation.

The Congregational Church provided a comfortable home for liberal evangelicals like the Dougalls. The Church was a leading force in the formulation of liberal theology in North America. Congregationalists placed authority at the level of the congregation, which had traditionally been beholden to no other authority but that of scripture. As Frank Hugh Foster recalled in 1939: "It has been their great good fortune to be free churches, free from ecclesiastical control and free in the association of like-minded men zealous for truth and determined to know it ever more perfectly." [49]

Although family members were active within their church, their greater loyalty was to a common broader cause, a cause manifested in Sunday School parades, urban revivals by Moody and Sankey, and YMCA meetings that transcended denominational barriers. [50] The community of believers was both wider than the church, encompassing all evangelical Protestants, and narrower, including only those who were saved.[51] The *Montreal Witness* proudly "acknowledged no sect but Christianity," and when John Dougall left Montreal to start the New York paper he carried a letter of support from Presbyterian, Wesleyan, Anglican, and Congregationalist ministers and the leaders of the Protestant School Board, the French Missionary Society, and the YMCA.[52]

How did this evangelicalism translate into the second generation? Lily Dougall's two closest siblings were John Redpath Dougall and Janet Dougall. Lily considered Janet to have had almost perfect faith. John was her mentor; a graduate of McGill University (B.A. 1860, M.A. 1867), he became her confidante during difficult teenage years when she did not dare share her religious doubts with her mother. Both siblings became widely known and respected for their social reform work, much as the historiography of the Social Gospel has led us to expect of second-generation evangelicals.[53] John was active in the Young Men's Christian Association (YMCA), the French Canadian Missionary Society, and the Congregational Church. Janet worked on the family newspapers, was a founder and longstanding vice president of the Montreal Women's Christian Temperance Union (WCTU), the president of the Hochelaga County WCTU, and president of the Calvary Congregational Church Women's Missionary Society.[54] At her death in 1904 she was eulogized for her good works, and a row of WCTU workers sat together in her funeral as a tribute.

The historical literature assumes that this reform activity led to a diminished spirituality, but this does not seem to be true of the second generation of the Dougall family. On a voyage in 1870, Lily's brother John wrote in a journal, "A week at sea has passed I have been at two sermons in cabin, four open meetings in steerage, 2 meetings in the forecastle and have spoken on prayer at five of these meetings."[55] He described going to prayer meetings as well as YMCA meetings held for the purpose of converting young men. John made it clear that his activism was in service to his faith: "Such [YMCA] meetings are encouraging, but only a means to an end, a weak means to a mighty end."[56]

Janet's faith was central to her work. A newspaper clipping in the Dougall files reported that Janet had spoken at a meeting of the National American WCTU in 1886. She reminded them of the centrality of the Spirit: "Miss Dougall, asked to tell by what means they had been so successful in enlisting the churches on their side in Montreal said she never liked to hear temperance people talk as if their work was outside the churches; how much Christ loved his Church which he had purchased with His precious blood."[57]

It appears that the faith of the Dougall family was renewed in the 1870s by Hannah Whitall Smith, who brought holiness to a second generation of evangelicals through articles in *Christian's Pathway to Power,* later published in the bestselling *The Christian's Secret of a Happy Life* (1875). John Dougall made references in his diaries to whole consecration and higher life from the 1870s. He noted that a friend loaned him a copy of *Pathway to Power* in 1875, and in 1877 Lily referred to her older brother's "rules for happy living." [58] Like William Boardman, Smith taught evangelicals to look beyond the first experience of God's grace in the conversion, to a "second blessing" of the Holy Spirit. She described an ongoing state of consecration in which the Christian surrendered their whole self to God. Evangelicals were taught to stop striving, and rest in God, in complete faith.

Janet appears to have been successful in this. In her speech to the WCTU she described the glow of the presence of the Lord when she crept into "God's secret place." Lily later described Janet as having had almost perfect faith, to have been "a truly consecrated soul." [59] Janet's obituary describes her as holding "[l]ittle praying groups in church in mission hall, and private homes . . . having more faith in little bands of consecrated workers than in large crowds of less consecrated individuals." [60]

John's diaries reveal a more anguished pursuit of holiness. Holiness has been described as providing a release from the pressures of a Calvinist creed, but the occasional entries in John's small brown diary reveal an ongoing struggle to attain the security of a heightened religious experience. John programmed an hour of private prayer, with invocation, record, means, prayer, reading scripture, reading other devotional material, and finally more prayer, although, if the diary is to be believed, the plan was honored more in the breach than in the observance. [61] In 1870, as a man in his late thirties, he regretted time spent skating: "A week of pleasure has past but am I any nearer God? How strange that the hours for devotion are so scarce I was on whole hour on the ice but not one at devotion and my soul must be starving. I find family worship a great help since I had it myself but it cannot long be good for me or anyone else unless the mind be fed in private." [62] Entries in 1873 lament: "I pray constantly for holiness and the Holy Spirit, but no answer seems to come." [63] His hour of daily prayer included personal holiness in a list petitions of religious causes and individuals: "*I have much to pray for today* Holiness, Purity, McGibbon, Short, Moore, my SS Class especially Annie Graham, Coleman, Witness, NY Witness, Davis, Zion Church, Shaftesbury Hall." [64] Two years later, he still castigated himself for failing to find an hour each day for private devotions: "Going to get an hour for seeking the Lord every afternoon, and as much as possible of the noon hour for prayer, will see how it succeeds. . . . Mother says in prayer every word should be distinctly enunciated. This is a good rule." [65] Two months later he had made little progress: "No amount of perfunctory service brings one near to God. Oh God what will? I have never in all these years found the key of thy secret place except when burning with the blush of sin. Hast thou no other cleanlier doorway? What shall I do what shall I accept or believe that I may get out of this vile region into the upper air of thy love and joy?" [66]

John's anguish was a matter of personality—he also despaired at the decline in the family's social standing—but it may also been a matter of gender dynamics. Women played a significant role in John's spiritual life, both, it appears, as temptations and as spiritual guides. (He was a very eligible bachelor at this time, and never did marry.) A Miss Barnjum, who with her mother and brother operated the St. George's Home for Inebriates, was particularly active. She chastised him for inconsistent conduct; said special prayers for him; advised him to stay away from a married woman; and allowed him (or not) to walk her home. He did not always take her advice: "Miss Barnjum had plenty to say about rest in God, but nothing new to me." [67] A Miss McPherson lent him holiness articles. Another unnamed female friend, observing his "dissatisfied look," described "her recent happy religious experience in being able to lay her head on His shoulder like a baby and rest perfectly." [68] He despaired: "How often have I said all that. I came home and kneeled down and told Jesus that He knew how often I had tried to do that, how often I thought I had until startled out of it by sin, by a fall permitted to let me see that I was asleep. . . ." [69] Men played a role: "I had a very pleasant talk with [Fred] Barnjum at Alexanders about the higher life . . . that is complete consecration. Lord whatever thou wilt!" [70] But the overriding sense, from these diaries at least, and from Lily Dougall's descriptions of her mother and sister as near saints, is that holiness was a feminized spirituality.

The legacy of holiness is a mixed one, and it has not yet received sustained feminist analysis, but it appears that the movement may have, paradoxically, offered women a strengthened sense of self through submission to God's will. The best analysis of its feminist potential, ironically, lies in the work of one of the original fundamentalists, Princeton theologian Benjamin Breckinridge Warfield, who argued that holiness posed a threat to male authority.[71] "[A] great deal of the perfectionism which vexed the American churches through the first three quarters of the nineteenth century was mystically coloured," Warfield wrote, condemning it as an "irrational feminine mysticism." [72] Warfield pointed to the work of holiness writer Thomas Upham, a Congregationalist professor of mental and moral philosophy. As Upham's titles reveal—*Elements of Mental Philosophy, embracing two departments of the intellect and the sensibilities* (1831); *Outlines of Imperfect and Disordered Mental Action* (1840); *Principles of the Interior or Hidden Life* (1843); *Treatise on Divine Union: Designed to point out some of the intimate relations between God and Man in the higher forms of religious experience* (1852)—he moved between the interpretive frames of mental philosophy and Quietist mysticism. He had been introduced to Phoebe Palmer's holiness by his wife, who received special permission for him to attend Palmer's women's Tuesday meetings, and he developed an interest in Quietism, a Roman Catholic doctrine of possible perfection in a mystic union with God. Like John Wesley, whose biography of Madame Guyon had appeared in 1776, Upham adapted Quietism for a Protestant audience.[73] His books were widely read: *Principles of the Interior or Hidden Life* went into eighteen editions and an 1847 biography of Madame Guyon went into thirty-seven.[74] In a description that utilized evangelical language as well as the incipient psychology in mental philosophy, Upham argued that Guyon replaced Catholic works with an inner faith:

> No sound was heard but that of "the still small voice" which speaks inwardly and effectually. There was no dream, no vision, no audible message. Her change was characterized, not by experience, not by revelations imparted from without and known only as existing from without, but by affections inspired by the Holy Ghost from within and constituting, from the time of their origin, a part of the inward consciousness.[75]

The Holy Ghost operated not through miracle, but from within as part of a transformed "inward consciousness."

The radical potential of Quietism is the paradoxical power of all mysticism; by renouncing her own will, the Quietist effectively claims divine authority for her action. As Upham said of Madame Guyon: "Something within her, told her that God's providence, which searches through all space and reaches all hearts, had designated her, not merely as a subject of forgiveness, but as a subject of *sanctifying* grace; not merely as a sinner to be saved, but as a living Temple in which His own Godhead should dwell."[76] This concept of the Godhead within provided a strong sense of self: "[Madame Guyon], however warm-hearted and diffusive may have been her charity to others, felt that there were duties to *herself*."[77] Quietist mysticism fueled an individualist faith that was disruptive of established (masculine) power. As Warfield noted, this theology unsettled women's customary respect for authority. Quietist nuns, he wrote, were "very independent towards their superiors and directors, very full of presumption and pride. . . . They attended preaching as little as they could saying that it distracted them, and they needed nothing but God. . . . They conceived of so lively and so inconvenient an appetite for prayer they neglected their most necessary duties."[78] Guyon's battle had been with Catholic hierarchies, but the heat of Warfield's dismissal suggests the power of this theology against all forms of religious authority: "And this is the characteristic mental attitude of the mystic—a truly morbid preoccupation with his own subjective states and experiences. He looks within to find God, he says: it is with difficulty, apparently, that he finds anything there but himself."[79]

Warfield went on to invoke a classic charge against self-directed women: that Guyon neglected her maternal duties. "Madame Guyon's freedom of soul, it seems, was unlikely to be shackled by domestic affections, which were but partially sanctified. . . . It would seem quite dangerous to live within the reach of the only partially sanctified emotions of a saint."[80] We might read this inward turning very differently: what Warfield saw as the dangers of Quietist mysticism might be read as its potential for middle-class holiness converts, some of whom were literally "shackled by domestic affections." It provided them with a sense of self as a "living Temple," rather than as a sinner to be saved. Mystical theology offered women the opportunity to step outside masculine ecclesiastical hierarchies and claim a higher divine authority.

A subsequent generation of women writers, including Harriet Beecher Stowe and Hannah Whitall Smith, popularized Upham's message (and even his titles—Smith published her own *Interior Life* in 1886).[81] Smith disavowed philosophical speculation and made a virtue of her innocence of theology: "This is not a theological book," she stated at the outset of *The Christian's Secret;* "I frankly confess I have never studied Theology and do not understand its methods or its terms. But the Lord has taught me experimentally and practically, certain lessons out of his Word, which have greatly helped me in my Christian life, and have made it a very happy one. . . ."[82] But as Warfield noted, Smith extolled the power of the human (feminine) will, and as he astutely observed: "It is anything but a passive will that Mrs. Smith has in mind; . . . behind that passivity we are intensely active, instituting and maintaining it."[83] In 1878, Smith herself explained, drawing upon her Quaker background, "A Quaker concern [God's inward directive] was to my mind clothed with even more authority than the Bible, for the Bible was God's voice of long ago while the 'concern' was His voice at the present moment and as such was of far greater present voice." This statement had gendered connotations: "Not even the most tyrannical 'man-friend' even if he wanted to, would ever dare to curtail the liberty of his womankind, if they could only say they 'felt a concern' for any course of action."[84]

Smith's message has had an ambiguous legacy. Although it was enthusiastically received by some Broad Church liberals in England in the 1870s, leading to the Higher Life movement, holiness increasingly moved in conservative directions and, as Debra Campbell has observed, Smith's teaching has been cited for antifeminist purposes.[85] Lily had little patience with her brother's "rules for happy living." She struggled with the contradictions, as we shall see in the next chapter, and finally broke free of both holiness and her family. The message had great potential, however, for a generation of women unable or unwilling to make demands on their own behalf; as Nancy Cott has observed, "submission of self could be a form of self-assertion."[86] As John's numerous feminine advisors had realized, in the acquiescence to God's power lay the potential for an assertion of one's own sense of spiritual self.

Janet Dougall was a "truly consecrated soul" in Lily's eyes. She was also remarkably independent. She studied at Vassar and worked as an editor and appears to have found strength in her experiential faith. Her family newspaper reported that she told the National (American) WCTU in 1886 that "she had been so wonderfully led and supported all through her work by her Heavenly Father that it seemed to her as if she had done nothing but let Him carry her." The one thing she had to do was to creep into God's secret place and stay there: "[W]e temperance workers should make it a rule never to leave the place of prayer till we feel the glow of the conscious presence of the Lord."[87] Hers was a feminized spiritual community; her praying circles, her single state, and the row of female WCTU workers at her funeral suggest a sense of sisterhood. The similarity to the image of a Catholic nun is irresistible (and probably inconceivable to the evangelical Janet): when she joined the church, a woman friend sent a hymn celebrating a marital relationship with God: "O happy hand that seals my vows . . . I am my Lord's and he is mine."[88] Lily Dougall's model of "complete consecration" was a strongly feminine one.

The evangelical Congregationalism of Lily Dougall's childhood was, then, a potent experiential faith, girded by the stern echoes of a gradually fading Calvinist Presbyterianism. Three themes stand out: a liberal attitude to doctrine and creed, the primacy of the experience of faith, and a feminized interiority. It was a legacy that framed Lily Dougall's life, even as she tore herself away from it.

2

"Lovereen": An Untold Story

LILY DOUGALL HAD A STRONG and ambivalent reaction to her family's faith. She publicly acknowledged her debt to their teaching, and stressed the spirituality of their "life" rather than the doctrines they held. She dedicated her first book of fiction to her sister and a book of theology to her brothers, noting that they "live the life of which I speak."[1] At the height of her career, when she was widely respected for her religious writing, she again acknowledged her family's example: "I should never dare to write these books out of my own experience. It is because my people have lived *the life* in the midst of all the turmoil and discouragement of journalism and their other manifold activities, because I have so long observed the inner joy and beauty of the spiritual life they lead, that I dare give it such literary expression as I can."[2]

This tribute was, however, a mature response, the product of her youthful fight to distance herself from her family's piety. From her teens until almost the age of thirty she struggled between the demands of her parents' faith and the lure of the wider world, swinging from fervent piety to liberal doubt, moving physically from New York to Edinburgh, from her evangelical home to the academic world, and suffering two breakdowns. This chapter examines Dougall's protracted departure from her family's evangelical faith through the family letters and through an unpublished autobiographical novel, "Lovereen: A Canadian Story."

Lily suffered her first breakdown in May 1877, seven years after she moved to New York, five years after her sister Polly's death, and, perhaps most significantly, two years after she left her parents' Congregational faith to join the Episcopalian Church. Her older brother John extricated her from her parents' home. As James's wife, Laure, explained to Elizabeth: "John was thinking it would be perhaps better for Lily to come [to Montreal] now while Jessie [Janet] is away, I am sure I should like to have her come now if she could. John was thinking it would do her good to come soon. The house is so clean now that she would not have to fear anything."[3] When Lily suffered a second nervous collapse in the fall of 1878—"Dr. Katz said it was a very uncommon case of nerves and she did not know what to recommend except outdoor life and good nourishment"—Janet tried to keep her in Montreal again, explaining diplomatically to her mother,

[Lily] has been pretty anxious about you thinking I suppose every day that the east wind blew and that she did not have a letter that her proper place was in Brooklyn. I have thought that perhaps she might stay here until I went down to Brooklyn in October and that as she would not be needed while I was there she might remain here until my five or six weeks visit was nearly over. Of course this plan depends upon your health remaining good until say the middle of October which experience hardly leads us to expect and we would need to feel quite sure that we would hear if you were ill or we could not feel easy.[4]

The exact nature of Lily's difficulties is not made clear in the family letters. It was in part physical: Lily had struggled with asthma all of her life. Susan became ill at the same time. Her breakdown was also, the letters seem to suggest, a psychological reaction to the emotional climate of her parents' new home, heightened by adolescence and the straitened circumstances in New York. Family members fondly describe Lily's high spirits. In her letters to her parents, Lily is frequently explaining herself: "We do not really have more company than most people have. Aunt Maggie, Aunt Ada, or Barrie [?] from what I hear have quite as much. It is because you are so very quiet on Felix St. that it seems a great deal."[5] She justified her purchases of clothing: "I have spent one hundred dollars which seems dreadful but you know that I was pretty badly off for garments when I came. I have accounted for every penny of it."[6] She is defensive, and rarely critical of her parents' ethics. Only once does her frustration at her restricted life spill out, in a letter to her mother, when she says, "Not that it makes much difference being of age in a world where one must do just what seems right and nothing else."[7]

Lily had a keen sense of humor, and there is little doubt that she was frustrated by the earnest young evangelicals who gathered around her parents.[8] She liked to tease and provoke. In an apologetic letter to a young member of the Plymouth Brethren, Lily apologized for "a sort of mischievous delight I took in shocking you and my good cousins." She then explained: "the remark I made about dancing was rather in dislike of what seemed to me the impropriety of the games than in favour of dancing, because I never dance." [9] In an early novella, *Rosemary for Remembrance* (1896), Dougall describes a young girl, Annabel, who is the "very mischief incarnate." She has a quick wit and a fertile imagination, and teases a self-righteous suitor mercilessly with her tall stories. Annabel tells her amused family one night,

> "He took me out into a lonely place, into a very lonely place, away up the river in an old cockleshell of a boat and there"—Annabel paused and amused herself by closing one eye and looking at the rosy glow through the chink of her fingers.
> "Well what there?" they cried.
> "There he lectured me," she said, shaking her head slowly.
> They all laughed again.
> "He told me," she continued, speaking quite seriously, but half preoccupied in watching the effect of the firelight upon her little hands—"he told me that he was grieved and distressed to observe that I sometimes said what was not quite true." [10]

The others break into laughter. They are amused by Annabel's clever telling of the story—her tale of seduction in a lonely place—but also by the dull suitor's inability to appreciate Annabel's flights of imagination. The story goes on to show that Annabel's tall tales exhibit a better grasp of reality than his grim literalism.

In the world of heartfelt evangelicalism, especially among the earnest members of her father's set, Dougall's imagination was a liability. Theater, novels, and the arts were considered the products of a corrupt world. As her brother John wrote in his diary, "I have not been living to Him of late; may I now be weaned from the world." [11] The Dougalls had a very ambivalent attitude to novel writing: though they published fiction in their newspapers and put out a literary paper, *The New Dominion Monthly*, after 1867, there were limits to the acceptability of fiction, especially when written by a family member. Both of Lily's brothers considered the enjoyment of fiction to be a weakness: James said in a letter, "the reading of ordinary novels or the skimming over of any book does not cultivate the imagination but rather depresses and weakens." [12] In his diary, John compared his reading of fiction to his flirting with young women. [13] Their *Montreal Witness* repeatedly ran articles condemning fiction. An article in 1868 argued that some literature could be uplifting, but "where, however, incident and plot form the staple of the narrative, the effect is evil, only evil and that continually. . . . What class of writers, taken as a whole, were so immoral as novelists?" [14] An editorial written in 1871, when Lily was thirteen, compared fiction to alcohol, a highly charged metaphor for a temperance paper. Fiction had its uses, but these had to be placed within narrow limits: "The rage for novels in our day is something astonishing. . . . It is in literature what ardent spirits are among drinks; and seems to affect the mind much as alcohol does the body." [15] The writer goes on to describe "dissipating and pernicious" sensationalist Sunday School literature: "Like 'light wines' such religious fiction often creates the appetite for something stronger." The young Lily, whose taste ran to the fantastic, would have been severely curbed by these strictures. At a low point, at age twenty-seven, Lily wrote to her friend Janie Couper: "I have fought for years with my imagination, and now I see that for me the narrow path is one of wise sober thought. Oh think how narrow this way is. To lay down all one's day dreams and self indulgent fantasies at His feet: to walk on in life's sometimes dull path without them." [16] Her sentiments were wildly shared among children of evangelicals. Elisabeth Jay describes "the numerous accounts of an Evangelical childhood where the imagination was starved or forced to find strange or pathetic outlets," and cites George Eliot's letters: "My imagination is an enemy that must be cast down. . . ." [17]

Even after she moved to Britain, Dougall hid her imaginative writing from her family. When she showed "Lovereen" to friends, she said, "I have not said anything to Auntie about it. It would distress her greatly to hear of such goings on." [18] She hesitated to publish her first stories, and initially published under a male pseudonym.[19] Her caution was warranted; her father was critical and her beloved aunt sent a "very severe" letter to her protesting against the language in her first published story. When Dougall defended herself—she had put the expressions "Mon Dieu" and "Holy Mary" in the mouth of a French man—her aunt said that she should give up writing if it involved breaking the second commandment.[20]

It is revealing that when the familial and economic situation became too difficult in Brooklyn, the young girls retreated to the extended family in Montreal. The older siblings, John, Janet, and James, engineered recuperative retreats, removing Lily and Susie for weeks at a time from the parental home. In 1878, Janet wrote: "John fears that the association of Brooklyn would bring back the nervous depressed condition under which [Lily] laboured last winter [1877–1878] which she can hardly speak of without horror." [21] Lily expressed a great deal of guilt and anxiety each time she left her mother's side to pursue her own interests. Elizabeth Dougall appears to have been a loving but demanding woman, who used her invalidism and her substantial financial assets to control her children.[22] John and Janet placated Elizabeth Dougall, and offered themselves and a reluctant young niece as substitute companions.[23]

John wrote to his father suggesting Lily return to Montreal, even if it left Elizabeth "bereft of all her girls":

> Nothing would please us more than to get Lily back. She was the life of the house and accomplished easily what is a burden to Janet who has to husband her strength. Janet would I think be much the better of having Lily here while I think mother was if anything better when they were all away but mother longs to have them with her and it does seem cruel to her that she should be bereft of all her girls. Jessie [Janet] could not go down for a month now. She always comes back the worse for her trip and she has not at present any strength to spare although I hope gradually gaining ground. It is very strange to me that you and mother should find yourselves better able to stand the change of climate and circumstances than any of us younger ones but so it seems. Lily might come as soon as the spring give signs of coming say in Feb. and stay till it is fairly in so as to avoid the worst of the weather.[24]

It was John who finally engineered a complete escape from the family home. At John's initiative Lily traveled with him to Edinburgh in the summer of 1880, and stayed with her doting aunt, Jane Redpath, until September 1881, studying and traveling.[25] This was a period of intellectual awakening, as Dougall immersed herself in cultural activities and religious controversies. She went to Shakespearean readings and studied art and geometry at the School of Design.[26] Women were not admitted to the University of Edinburgh at this time, but the Edinburgh Ladies Educational Association offered a form of an extramural arts department for women, drawing upon the faculty of the University of Edinburgh, with lectures leading to a "higher certificate" for women.[27] Dougall attended David Masson's lectures in English literature and Henry Calderwood's class in Moral Philosophy and received First Class certificates in both subjects.[28]

The freedoms and luxuries she experienced in Edinburgh were exhilarating. She later wrote, "Auntie keeps the most royal castle of indolence that can be imagined. She has cupboards full of nice books, a fire in August and a drawing room full of lounges and easy chairs."[29] On her return to Canada in the fall of 1881, however, Lily again took on the role of the dutiful daughter. For two years she devoted herself to nursing her mother. They lived in claustrophobically close quarters, sharing a bed at one rest home and spending most of each day together.[30] Lily then experienced a religious awakening in 1882 and 1883.[31] Letters suggest she turned to the holiness teaching of Hannah Whitall Smith: "I studied that book early last spring [1883], and at the time I did enter into the life it speaks of, and experienced not only the peace, but the evident growth in spiritual life which I had so long been longing for."[32]

This teaching was not new to Lily (as we have seen, John had been struggling to attain holiness since the 1870s), but it may have met a need in her confined life with her mother. Smith's book, *The Christian's Secret of a Happy Life* (1875), was addressed primarily to women burdened by family responsibilities.[33]

Lily Dougall's venture into holiness was brief. In *The Christian's Secret of a Happy Life*, Smith taught joy through surrender of self and trust in God, but self-abnegation was unsuited for someone with Dougall's lively temperament. When she moved to Montreal for the summer of 1883, "full of a new peace and determined to show by my life that there was a present and eternal calm to be found in Christ," her turn to holiness led to depression and despair. She explained in a letter written to her friend Janie Couper the following February,

> According to my theory I should be *willing* to give up all earthly joy and desire only that God should be glorified in me, and I found that I loved earthly things and longed for them just as much as before, and the result was a despondency which ended in the return of all my old doubts. I passed a most miserable summer, and by the time you came in the autumn I had only got as far out of the slough of despond as to endeavour to do right and forget my doubts in hard work.[34]

The attempt to give up "earthly joy and desire" was a failure.

Elizabeth Dougall died on November 9, 1883. Her death might have brought Lily a release. As Lily wrote to a friend, "It has always been my dream that when mother did not need me any more then I could study and educate myself for something. This has consoled me in all the years I have been obliged to spend without study." Obviously, however, her family's expectations were different, as she noted, "Now I am tied with all the bondage of housekeeping in a most difficult household with nothing before me but a daily round of market and servants and the necessary sociabilities. This has been a great heartbreak to me."[35] Dougall later wrote to a close friend with similar difficulties: "Dear Katie, I often think the hardest position on earth is the position of a girl at home with all the cares of a family and household upon her shoulders, and yet no power to guide the ship, or to arrange matters as she would have them. It does not seem to me that any fight which men have with the world can be as hard to bear as the numberless petty trials that surround a girl in that position."[36]

Lily's letters reveal that in December 1883 she turned inward again to Smith's "life hid with Christ in God":

> Dear J [Janie Couper]——you will expect me in this letter to say something to you about the loss of my mother, and I have nothing to say about it to you or anyone else. I have no thoughts about her death that

are not all bound up and hidden away with that part of my life which is hid with Christ in God. When I am sure that *all* my life is hidden with Him then that will be *perfect* rest. Many times a day the tears come, and I do not know why. I have no regret, no desire: God has supplied all my need, even my need of my mother.[37]

There is a growing strain of despair and martyrdom in her letters. Dougall's language echoed the cadences of the holiness movement, and instead of the actively critical tone of her earlier letters, she adopted an earnest passivity:

How good God was to teach me something about Himself before this trouble came. My daily life is just full of the work that I naturally dislike most; all the servants to manage; all this house to put in order. . . . I know it is good for me I am sure that I needed just this, and I am learning each day, more and more that God supplies *all* our need—yes, *all*, all my need of my mother (loving and tender and sympathetic as she was the Lord is infinitely more loving and more sympathetic)—all my need of courage in speaking to the servants I think he makes the servants conscientious and gentle. Indeed there is nothing in the world that I want; He has given me and will give me, all that I want. Perhaps you think this letter is a contradiction. . . .[38]

Hannah Whitall Smith had advised women with burdens to give them to Christ to carry: "She abandoned her whole self to the Lord, with all that she was and all that she had, and believing that He took that which she had committed to Him, she ceased to fret and worry, and her life became all sunshine in the gladness of belonging to Him."[39] Dougall's life, however, did not become "all sunshine." Ten days later she told Janie that she hoped to die.[40] Two weeks later she collapsed under the strain: "I have been obliged to ask Miss E. to take the housekeeping for a week or two and give up the attempt to do anything. I am so sorry for this. O I cannot help believing that if I had more faith, I should not have broken down."[41]

Lily's father was initially unsympathetic. She went away to Andover, Massachusetts (the home of Congregational liberalism), to study at the Abbott Academy, and then, unable to work, was told by a doctor to take six months to recover. After the doctor's diagnosis, her father wrote contritely: "My own dear wee pet, Please forgive and forget your father's ungracious letters written in ignorance of the weak state of your health. . . . I now realise that you were overtaxed, mind and body, just as you were several years in Brooklyn."[42] He allowed her to take the time to recover, and after a vacation in Old Orchard, Maine, and North Conway, New Hampshire, in October she returned to her sympathetic aunt in Edinburgh.

Lily Dougall never returned to her father's home on a permanent basis after 1883, nor did she try again to submit herself entirely to a holiness faith. She explained to Janie, "This life of God is something deeper and wider and fuller than Mrs. [Hannah Whitall] Smith's definition of it, or than our grasp of it, and we must not limit it by our theories."[43] Instead, she established a productive life in Britain, ostensibly acting as companion to her aunt in Edinburgh, who "made a special pet of Lily," but in fact taking frequent advantage of her asthma to study in warmer regions.[44] Supporting herself with an inheritance from her mother, supplemented reluctantly by her father, she engaged in a self-directed course of work, studying Greek, mathematics, and Latin at St. Boniface in Ventnor on the Isle of Wight, taking correspondence courses from St. George's Hall in Edinburgh, and then studying Greek in Cheltenham with a tutor.[45] She wrote examinations, passing English in Edinburgh in 1886, and passing Greek, moral philosophy, and logic and metaphysics in Cheltenham in 1887, and received the Lady Literate in Arts (LLA), through the University of St. Andrews, a diploma equivalent to the M.A. open to women who had pursued private study.[46]

Lily had asked her father to fund her studies in order to make her self-sufficient as a teacher.[47] It was a sensible goal—the vast majority of women with higher education at this time went on to a career in teaching.[48] But Dougall saw teaching mainly as a career to fall back upon; her real goal was to become a writer. Her focus on Greek reveals a sustained interest in biblical criticism. Hers was an ambitious education for a woman: as a friend, B. H. Streeter, noted: "Towards the end of the period [Dougall] acquired a sufficient knowledge of Greek to be able to read the New Testament in the original language—an ability which at that time few women possessed."[49] As an interesting point of comparison, Elizabeth Cady Stanton had to limit her famous work of feminist biblical criticism, *The Woman's Bible* (1895), to social and political commentary because none of the contributors had expertise in Greek or Hebrew. Stanton commented defensively in the introduction: "Whatever the Bible may be made to do in Greek or Hebrew, in plain English it does not exalt and dignify women."[50]

Five years after leaving home, Dougall tried to make sense of this difficult and prolonged maturation in her autobiographical work of fiction, "Lovereen, A Canadian Novel." The novel describes the conflict between a young girl and her evangelical father, Mr. Walford, a wool-clothing manufacturer who sacrifices his family's financial and physical health to his evangelical mission. He is blind to his family's difficulties, irrational in his beliefs, and crass in his evangelizing. Lovereen, his daughter, is by contrast a sensitive and artistic girl who is embarrassed by her father's religious fervor and chafes at the restrictions of an evangelical life. Through the course of the lengthy three-volume novel—each volume is made up of almost 500 manuscript pages—Lovereen struggles with his evangelicalism, enters a prolonged depression, and emerges with a more liberal faith. This high theme is interwoven with a melodramatic romance involving shrieking ghosts, mysterious disappearances, and imbecilic aristocrats.[51]

The novel provides the emotional background to the Dougall family letters. Sophie Earp, who became Dougall's lifelong partner, assisted her with the manuscript and said, "because it is essentially [Dougall's] own life and her own problems which are depicted, it affords real insight into her girlish character and standpoint."[52] Dougall seems to have initially been unconscious of the feelings expressed in her novel, particularly toward her father. When another friend, cleric T. B. Kilpatrick, wrote disparagingly about the character of Mr. Walford as presented in an early draft, Dougall defended Walford. Confused, Kilpatrick responded, "When I wrote as I did I had no idea but that I was reproducing your own view, and I am considerably surprised at the admiration you and Miss Earp feel for him. . . . I am a little perplexed. There are still two vols to come, and he may yet display a nobility which you know him to possess. . . ."[53] One volume later Kilpatrick was still confused but more wary. He wrote, "I don't lie and will not speak of Mr. W."[54] Six months later, perhaps encouraged by Dougall to be open, he wrote, "As to Mr. Walford—it is almost pathetic to see you trying to make him out a fine character . . . I don't quarrel with the representation you give. It is probably true to life."[55]

Lily describes the young Lovereen shrinking from her father's emotional displays of religiosity: "[Lovereen felt] a nervous objection to talking seriously with her father upon any subject akin to religion, for she knew any heart to heart expression of interest in his work was sure to lead him to speak about her own religious responsibility . . . Her heart was too sensitive to bear the touch of his handling. . . ."[56] She was embarrassed by his public declamations: "Who but her father, who, at least, of men who were not otherwise vulgar would have conversed on the subject of another man's spiritual state through a railway carriage window in a crowded station?"[57] Walford preaches to the working class and he associates with, as Lovereen's aunt put it, "all those horrid country ministers . . . Baptists and what-not."[58] Lovereen is scathing about the evangelical girls with whom she was expected to keep company:

> I do argue for the distinction between person and person which recognises the fact that some are on our own level of thought and some are

John Dougall, Lily
Dougall's father, 1861.
*Courtesy Notman
Photographic Archives,
McCord Museum of Canadian
History, I-1929.1.*

not . . . Father is constantly urging me to make friends with this one or
that one because they are morally worthy—their moral worth is not the
question, they must be able to understand me and I them. What have I
in common with the daughters of the country parson? In this country
such girls have no ideas beyond the multitudinous babies of their
mother's nursery and their father's shirts and dinners. It is not their fault
that their ideas are cramped but on what common ground can I meet
them? Their wildest dream of excitement is their possession of a new
gown or the reading of one of Scott's novels or perhaps if maturer
thoughts have entered the gentle breast, the addresses of some unctuous
member of the "Young Men's Christian Association." [59]

Nor had she patience for the young Andover theology students who
gather at her father's house. "I like all these men in a class, as I like
sheep, but it would be difficult to have any strong preference for one
sheep over another." [60]

Lovereen also found her father's earnest asceticism stifling: "[Lovereen's] father watched over her most carefully and, in accordance with the spirit which distinguishes Puritanism and all its modern modifications, she was not permitted even moderate indulgence in those pleasures which in their abuse might prove harmful. Dancing, the theatre and novels were proscribed." [61] When friends plan a ball for Lovereen, her father refuses to let her attend, and she watches through the window as her friends dance. Her "evil angel" tells her that "to be good means to be miserable." [62] Lovereen complains to her friend Paul,

> That is just exactly what is the whole trouble with everything. I ought not to take any satisfaction in my new frock, but I do; I never had a stylish frock before and it gives me much pleasure to think how grand I look. I ought, of course, to be willing to lie here like mother, in the cheapest shabbiest way, and devote all my strength to taking care of father, in order that he may preach at meetings. Instead of that I want to go to a boarding school, and then marry a rich man, and wear satin gowns and drive in a carriage. That's what makes me want to die. All that is good I detest; all that is wicked I like. I ought to be good, and love good things, like mother, but now she is dead, there is no use. . . . I am wicked, and I can't help it, and that is all there is to say.[63]

Paul reassures her: "Perhaps it is not wrong, after all, for you to like fine frocks and such things." [64] Dancing, taken up secretly by Lovereen, signifies all the pleasures and beauties of God's world that were denied by evangelical Christians. (Dougall's later novels toy with sexual tension, and it is not unreasonable to suggest that Dougall was also protesting against the suppressed sexuality of an evangelical life when she describes Lovereen's joy in the physicality of the dance.)

The character Lovereen is also denied the opportunity to go abroad with friends for further education. Her father refuses to allow her to learn "false creeds," and insists that she stay home to act as his housekeeper. When her friends return from two years of study in England, the young Lovereen is more envious of their education than their new dresses: "Their minds, well-furnished with instruction on many subjects and enlivened by the variety of scene were sweet and fresh as a running stream, while hers, turned constantly in and on itself, for lack of objects to arrest her attention, felt like a stagnant pool . . . She now abruptly asked what gain, either of her own or of others, had corresponded with her loss?" [65]

Lovereen experiences a protracted crisis, caught in the nexus of family obligations with no clear alternative path. She swings from a bold liberalism to a submissive faith. When she is feeling confident,

Lovereen tries to rework her religion—"dared to make theories of religion for herself setting up reason alone as the judge of duty, and judging her conduct by its unaided light." [66]—but is unable to continue alone in the "path of reason" and retreats to her parents' faith: "whenever the shadows of trouble fell on her she was afraid to walk in the path of her own theories and ran back to the track which her father and mother had beaten for her." [67] The internal battle is expressed in physical illness and "long periods of listless indifference and almost of despair." [68] Her protracted illness, Dougall notes, was "the final struggle of her spirit to free itself from the control of the conscience, which her education had created." [69] Isolated from her friends and alienated from her father, she gradually finds her own faith: "her spirit was forced to view its own unbelief face to face and grapple with it. Little by little she found the rest of a certain and unchangeable faith, which is to feel the hand of God." [70] Lovereen explains to her uncomprehending father,

I cannot go [to be a missionary] because I cannot think as you do. I have tried till I have worn myself out with trying. I know now, looking back, that it was that that made me ill. I was so accustomed to see all religion in your way of seeing it that when I could not see it that way I was afraid it was all untrue; but now I know that was foolish. Then too I thought that perhaps your way was true and that because I thought differently I had deserted God and He me. Now I know better—that God is helping me as he is you.

It did not occur to him to ask how she came by the knowledge. He supposed that belief in a helping God went without saying, and was the possession of all sober minds. Such a belief seemed to him no resting place, but only the foundation upon which religion was built. He was like a mariner who, being accustomed only to elaborately constructed steam-engines, could not brook the thought of being in the ocean with only sail and helm; he had never known what it was to be afloat without either.[71]

When Walford leaves for the mission fields Lovereen stays behind to make a new life with her childhood friend, now lover, the liberal and critical Paul.

"Lovereen" was never published. The initial reason was that the manuscript was too long, and although Dougall tried after the success of *Beggars All* (1891) to revise it, she never finished the revisions and turned to other work. She may have realized in the course of the revisions how revealing and conflicted the work was. She said she had misgivings about "Lovereen": "I have not felt very sure of a lot of things in it. . . . I have my doubts about the righteousness of some things which cannot be easily altered. . . ."[72] Dougall's description of Mr. Walford belongs in what Elizabeth Jay has the described as a genre of "anti-evangelical" novels. Jay and Valentine Cunningham have observed that evangelicals were frequently depicted as opportunistic social climbers or naive purveyors of religious cant.[73] They were caricatured for their self-congratulatory tone and presumptions of special providence, and their habit of *ex tempore* preaching. Even though Lily Dougall's second draft is kinder to Walford—she removed, for example, his dalliance with the wife of the Anglo-Catholic minister—her condemnation of all that her parents, and, now, her brothers, stood for is strong. The anti-evangelical novel, as a genre, culminated in Samuel Butler's *The Way of All Flesh* (1903) and Edmund Gosse's *Father and Son, A Study of Two Temperaments* (1907). As Elizabeth Jay notes, "Butler had drawn upon all the various tools of the anti-Evangelical Victorian novelists and fashioned a myth which gained not only literary transmission but the status of historical evidence."[74] Gosse first published his book anonymously and Butler, who was twenty years older than Dougall, had his published posthumously, probably for the same reasons Dougall found it impossible to publish her first novel. She still loved her family and it would have been cruel to expose them to her criticisms, even if these feelings were widely shared in the broader literary world. The manuscript of "Lovereen," a confused and lengthy document of female doubt, remained buried among Dougall's papers.

3
Gendering the Crisis of Faith

W E MUST BE ON GUARD against reading Lily Dougall's description of Lovereen's difficult youth too literally. Students of life writing have argued that the truth often lies in the elisions, in words not said and characters not developed, and Dougall's autobiographical manuscript is no exception—the gaps provide more insight into Lily Dougall's life than the story itself. To begin with, what happened to Lily's mother? Why does Lovereen's mother, Mrs. Walford, die early in the novel, and why are all of young Lovereen's difficulties centered on her father? More significantly, what happens to Lily Dougall's intellect? Why does Lovereen not study Greek? Finally (and here lies an answer, as well as a question) who is Paul?

The religious crisis in literature, from its origins in Thomas Carlyle's *Sartor Resartus* (1833–1834), J. A. Froude's *Nemesis of Faith* (1849), and J. H. Newman's *Loss and Gain* (1848), has been a masculine one, closely tied to the religious maturation and vocational difficulties of young college men. By the end of the century, when Dougall was writing "Lovereen," the genre followed a predictable pattern:

> The emphasis falls on one central character, around whose spiritual biography the plot is built. The novel traces his doubts, loss of faith, and his search for a new religious position, unorthodox and undogmatic, or for some substitute "religion." The chief problems are the inspiration of the Bible, the presence of pain and evil in the universe, and the divinity of Christ; solutions are found in Pantheism, Universalism, and a belief in "Brotherhood," "true Christianity," the "living Jesus of the Gospels." [1]

It was not simply that the models were masculine or that the narratives drew upon the male—and upper-class—trajectory of university education and clerical careers, but that the very nature of the crisis was conceived of in ways that conformed to a masculine sense of religious identity. Women were assumed to lack the capacity for theological reflection or rational doubt, and the role they played in this masculine narrative was usually the secondary role of spiritual resource. The crisis-of-faith narrative frequently describes the young man's recourse to the piety of a spiritual mother, sister, or friend.

Lily Dougall, like other women authors, struggled to situate her own doubts within the narrative. "Resisting the shape of male autobiography is only the beginning," argues Gail Twersky Reimer. "The female autobiographer must also resist cultural pressure to remain silent." [2] To fully understand Dougall's youth, we need to look past the sweet young girl Lovereen to her alter ego, the critical Paul. Through Paul's scholarly interest in biblical criticism, his flirtation with Catholicism, and his attraction to a historic church, we can trace Lily Dougall's intellectual development. Dougall's need to speak through a male character suggests the depth of her own discomfort, as a woman, with the skeptical workings of her own intellect.

The first sign in the family records of Dougall's disaffection with her parents' faith was her surprising decision at the age of seventeen to be confirmed in the Episcopal Church near New York.[3] A confirmation is a serious declaration of purpose, and although Dougall remained a member of the Anglican communion for the rest of her life, she never discussed her reasons for this momentous decision. The move from Congregationalism to Episcopalianism was not an unusual one. Of thirty writers described by Ann Douglas in *The Feminization of American Culture*, ten had converted from Congregationalism to the Episcopal Church.[4] But the decision is difficult to reconcile with John Dougall's public disparagement of Canadian Anglicans; Dougall could have found a liberal theology within Congregationalism in the New Theology of Horace Bushnell.[5] None of the other Dougall children appear to have left the Congregational fold; family members attended her confirmation, and her brother John only commented dryly that the service was "interesting." Sophie Earp later reflected that Dougall's defection to the Episcopalian Church did not represent a fundamental rift between Dougall and her family.[6] But Earp made no mention of Dougall's subsequent nervous illnesses and repeated holidays from the parental home, she edited the apologetic portions from one of John Dougall's letters, and she attributed the family difficulties to outside pressures. There was clearly a rift in the family, and it does seem to date from the time of Dougall's confirmation.

It is easy to imagine the attraction of the Episcopalian Church for a young girl who had been bored by the earnest young preachers and confined by the asceticism of her father's evangelicalism. As Dougall explains in "Lovereen," the Episcopalian Church was the most "fashionable" church in New England.[7] Among the New York Episcopalians, Dougall would have found an upper-middle-class community similar to that of her extended family in Montreal. She did not have to give up the pleasures and beauties of the world in order to be a good Anglican. The service was aesthetically pleasing; as she explained in a letter in 1880: "The more I see of the English church, in contrast to other church services, the more I feel in sympathy to it. . . . It is 'all the people saying, Amen'; the grandeur of the building, the bells, everything was more as we would desire our Lord to be worshipped. It is like the palm branches and the Hosannas that the children sing."[8] The metaphorical symbolism of the sacraments, the dignity of the service, and the language of the liturgy appealed to her artistic sensibility. But the beauty of the service was not the central reason for her turn to the Episcopalian Church. "I love the church service," she explained once, "but it is not that. . . ."[9] Earp suggested that the attraction lay in the freedom and toleration of the Broad Church movement.[10] The Broad Church was a liberal Anglican movement characterized by a critical attitude to the Bible and a comprehensive understanding of religious faith.

It is likely that Dougall was introduced to this liberal movement through the popular American Broad Churchman, Phillips Brooks (1835–1893) who was particularly influential during Dougall's adolescence in the 1870s. Dougall made no reference to his sermons, but in the year before her confirmation, 1874, Brooks and other Broad Churchmen organized the first Church Congress in New York City, "to see what can be done to keep or make the Church liberal and free."[11] Brooks was, like Dougall, born a Congregationalist. His parents became evangelical Episcopalians, and when he adopted a more liberal theology he retained the emotional center of his evangelical childhood. Brooks, however, understood the incarnation as God's presence in the world; rather than praying with Lily's brother to be weaned from the world, he embraced God in the world.

The Broad Church also provided intellectually satisfying answers to Dougall's growing questions about the Bible. Evangelicals like Lily's father clung more tightly to a literal Bible as they rejected creed, theology, and clerical authority. An early *Witness* article explained: "Human literature is like the clouds that sometimes gild but much more frequently darken the mountain summit whilst the Word of God is like the sublime and changeless mountain."[12] Broad Churchmen, however, followed Coleridge, and behind him the German critics, treating the Bible as another, perhaps higher, form of human literature. Coleridge had written: "I take up this work [the Bible] with the purpose to read it for the first time as I should read any other work,—as least as far as I can or dare. . . ." [13] This critical approach was a sharp departure from evangelical faith in a literal Bible, though Coleridge's critical reading did not necessarily strip the Bible of any sacred meaning. Coleridge's conclusion at least had been reassuring: "I have found words for my inmost thoughts, songs for my joy, utterances for my hidden griefs and pleadings for my shame and my feebleness? In short whatever *finds* me, bears witness for itself that it has proceeded from a Holy Spirit. . . ." [14] This interpretation gave Broad Church clerics wide latitude for a critical, historical study of the Bible.

Dougall began to read the Bible critically shortly after her confirmation. "I have been reading the Bible," she wrote to her older brother John in late February 1877, "beginning in the beginning and trying to disabuse my mind of all its former ideas concerning it, to find out what it really says." [15] This led inevitably to difficult questions, and by March she was asking: "What do you think about the Garden of Eden? It certainly is, taking it either as fact, allegory or fiction, what we would call now a queer story." [16] Lily hid her questions from her mother, "It would be simply wrong to disturb Mother's peace of mind by suggesting my doubts to her." (She was probably wise: another of her siblings had recently written to their mother, enthusiastically describing a sermon on the authority of Scripture: "I am very glad of it for there never was a time I think when such preaching was more needed Only I wish he had four or five times as large an audience.")[17]

Lily turned instead to John, apologizing for her preoccupation with metaphysics: "I put these questions to you, because there is no one else I can speak to on the subject." [18] John was a graduate of McGill; he had served the university as a senior representative Fellow in Arts and was instrumental in the organization of the Congregational College. He took little pleasure in his studies, however, and his diaries show that his concern was in finding holiness, rather than sorting out the truth.[19] When Lily plied him with questions, he responded with holiness maxims. In one letter, she remarked to him, "I am afraid I have not made my argument plain, and you will not at all see the connection to your rules for happy living." Lily, in contrast, had little interest in "happy living" and insisted on the pursuit of truth. She pointed out that the good life must be an examined life: "for if everything that we are and have and do is entirely for the higher education of our souls, it is of much more importance that we should not only do right but do it in the right way." [20]

The Broad Church also offered Dougall an alternative to the Calvinist doctrines of original sin, predestination, and eternal torment; like

John   Redpath   Dougall,
Lily Dougall's brother, 1881.
*Courtesy Notman Photographic
Archives, McCord Museum of
Canadian History, II-60708.1.*

many liberals she found these doctrines, quite simply, unfair.[21] On
February 23, 1877, she told John it was "impossible to believe that any
soul should through sin die eternally, unless perhaps the one unpardon-
able sin is that of rejecting an understood, and believed in, Saviour." [22]
Some Congregationalists mitigated the concept of eternal damnation with
the idea of a probationary salvation, wherein the sinful worked their
redemption after death, but Dougall was skeptical about this: "And if
there is still probation after death, where may we affix a limit to it?" A
few weeks later she is bluntly critical about the doctrine of everlasting
punishment: "Human life must be a very light thing, a *very* light thing,
if we believe that thousands of human souls are created yearly merely
to die." [23] We do not have John's response to these letters, and have
to assume he was a sympathetic audience for Lily's doubts, but with
his father at least he hewed the orthodox line: when a Canadian
Presbyterian minister, D. J. MacDonnell, was charged with heresy in
1876 for expressing doubts from the pulpit about everlasting punishment, John reported to his father that he quietly supported the orthodox view through the Montreal papers.[24] Broad Church theologian

F. D. Maurice offered another interpretation. He argues that eternity was an alternative reality, another dimension in time, rather than a future state. He had been removed from King's College, London, as a result in 1853. While there is no evidence that Lily Dougall had read (or understood) his Johannine sense of eternity, it is likely she knew something of it. She later described Maurice as one of the mountain peaks of her youth.[25] Historian Colin Brown observed that Maurice was most influential in the United States during these very years: "the principles [Maurice] enunciated and insights which flashed forth from his writings provided one of the most important influences on religious and social thought in the United States during the years after Maurice's death in 1872."[26]

John may not have shared Lily's concerns but he did engineer her escape to the University of Edinburgh, where she met leading liberals. One of her professors, Henry Calderwood, likely introduced her to the work of Friedrich Schleiermacher, the father of liberal theology.[27] In Scotland, the questions she had posed to older brother were directed at a range of academics and ministers. As she wrote her father, "I remember that you told me once that it was always best to make a man talk on the subject he knows most about. I have found this to be a most invaluable plan, for it pleases the man, and I pick up a great deal of information that I never would be bothered reading in books."[28] She quizzed clergymen about ecclesiastical hierarchy, shocked an old couple with her ignorance of the Shorter Catechism, and stalled young men with theological questions. "So I ask the students to explain Scotch theology when they disturb us when we are sketching, and I really have got quite good notion of Geology from the said Mr. Smith. I tell you about them because I have really nothing else to write about. They are quite harmless young men."[29] Dougall's light tone in her letters disguises her serious interests. The information she gleaned from these men met her central questions about church and faith. Geology, of course, was the subject that toppled the faith of many believers in a literal Bible.

Her visit to Scotland coincided with the heresy trial of Robertson Smith, "the turning point in the mind of Victorian Scotland."[30] Smith held the Hebrew chair in the Free Church College in Aberdeen. When he denied the historicity of Deuteronomy in the *Encyclopaedia Britannica*, a protracted dispute ensued and Smith was finally deposed from his chair. Dougall attended the hearings; her description in a letter to her father is fascinating. Her tone is light and she predicates her comments with a feminine disclaimer: "I have not been able to *study* [Smith's] views. Of course, I am not capable of forming an opinion as to their truth, and I have none." But she delivers a cutting assessment of Smith's critics. Of the principal of Free College, she wrote, "Dr. Rainy's argument was this: Prof. Smith has bothered the church for five years; he has been impertinent to me and to others; away with this turbulent fellow and we will carefully consider afterwards whether his views are correct or not." Of another party she wrote: "Mr. Wilson briefly expressed the argument thus: 'If my neighbour digs in his own cellar, he may *say* he is not shaking my foundations, but when my walls are beginning to crack I have a right to stop him.' . . . I do not wonder that Mr. Wilson is panic stricken if he rests on no firmer foundation than that."[31] Dougall's own foundations, evidently, stood firm, and the experience, combined with her university lectures, reinforced her growing liberalism.[32]

When we turn to Dougall's autobiographical "Lovereen," we find this intellectual development has been erased. There is scant evidence of Lily's intellect in the fictional Lovereen. Although much is made in the novel of the battle in Lovereen's mind between reason and faith, Lovereen is described as having an artistic, rather than intellectual, temperament. As Dougall's clerical friend T. B. Kilpatrick observed, Lovereen is a dreamer who dabbles in "metaphysics":

> I don't think you are as tall as Lovereen, but you are quite as capable of talking metaphysics behind a row of peas. . . . Lovereen is so completely yourself I daren't criticise her. Dreamy, speculative, slightly inactive; decidedly odd; profoundly religious, after an Oriental rather than an Western type; constitutionally unable to appreciate an historic religion; instinctively preferring a formless, luminous and beautiful mist to any basis of fact . . .[33]

Lovereen was stereotypically female: inactive, dreamy, preferring a formless "Oriental" mist to any historic religion. She was proudly anti-intellectual: "Oh I know nothing about theology, I care nothing for the revision of creeds."[34] Her reaction to her parents' faith, as we saw in the last chapter, is presented largely as an emotional rebellion against a narrow outlook on life, the opposite of the surrender and self-abasement required by a holiness faith, but hardly the stuff of a new theology. Lovereen was argumentative but her ideas were unformed: "She read much in a desultory way; she thought more; she formed crude opinions, and her mind had that quality of originality which ill satisfies conventional expectations."[35] She had none of Lily Dougall's drive or ambition and, most important, none of her interest in academic pursuits. Lovereen could not read Greek.

These "masculine" aspects of Dougall's personality are transposed onto Lovereen's childhood friend, Paul. Paul is a brother figure throughout much of the novel, and emerges as a suitor in the conclusion. He is engaged in the kind of scholarly endeavor and intellectual debate that Dougall herself enjoyed but was considered inappropriate for a woman. "Paul had become a great student . . . study, always a delight for its own sake, had stored his mind with the best part of a student's harvest—patient insight into the meaning of things, and an ardent desire to go on and learn more of all that might be learned." [36] It is not Lovereen who pursues biblical criticism (she dryly tells an enthusiastic friend, "I know what is in it")[37] but Paul:

> The one thing which in his whole life he had learned to do thoroughly was to study a book, and he began with a will to study this one, sitting at it early in the morning and late at night, the English dictionary on his knees and his Greek lexicon and great commentaries from Mr. Walford's library spread out before him on the table. He began at the beginning and worked on verse by verse, toilsomely looking up all the references, making notes of compared authorities and computing the chronology.[38]

Through Paul, Dougall defends biblical criticism. He explains to the High Church missionary: "For instance, by scientific methods of studying history, the *history* of the doctrine of the Atonement can be traced. But to know the history of an idea—how it came to be—does not in the least explain it away, as so many suppose." [39] Paul considers going on to university to pursue a scholarly career as a biblical critic.

Why did Dougall need to speak through a male character? The answer lies in part in the narrative structure. The literary crisis of faith was a male genre, built around the vocational crisis of young men. Lovereen's familial ties, her housekeeping obligations, and her protracted nervous illness simply did not fit this narrative structure. The answer also lies in the proscriptions against intelligent, critical, and skeptical young women. Lovereen is repeatedly criticized by her aunts for being overly serious: one observes, "She has been so much alone with older and serious people and she has read so much that positively she sometimes talks just like a book; of course it shows she has very good mind and all that but it is not exactly what is admired in a young girl—*men* for instance always dislike that sort of thing." [40] Another aunt, Mrs. Maxwell, thought: "[T]he girl was too silent, and when she did speak, too opinionated; she was too old in her thoughts and manners, and, at the same time she was childishly unsophisticated when caprice made her playful. In short she was not the least like Mrs. Maxwell herself, or any other girl that lady had known." Others describe her as "headstrong and foolish," "born serious" with "a slight shade of peculiarity" over all she does. When she is invited to a dinner party with visiting British aristocrats, she engages a skeptical doctor in debate about religious enthusiasm. In frustration at his sophistry, she bursts out: "I do not know how to answer you, but I am certain you are talking great nonsense."[41] Her aunts are horrified.

Lily Dougall as a narrator is dismissive of these meddling aunts. Her description of one of them, the wife of the Anglican rector, is the first in a series of scathing portrayals of clerical wives: "nature had not endowed her largely, either as to mind or heart."[42] When the aunt tells Lovereen to pay more attention to her neighbors, Dougall allows the girl a sharp riposte: " '[B]ut it would take so long, one has so many neighbours,' said Lovereen, forgetting for the moment the extremely literal character of her aunt's mind." Nevertheless, Dougall did feel constrained by popular opinion, and just as she had made light of her own theological interests in her letter to her father, she brushes off the young girl's inquiries in a curiously ambivalent passage: "[Lovereen's] own desire to discuss and question seemed to her for the moment like a wanton game compared with his [Paul's] way of looking at such things, although she had no knowledge of what his way was. It was perhaps a proof of her own earnestness that she could suddenly doubt it and tell herself that she had never been in earnest, that she had been playing with religious doubts."[43] Lovereen could not take her own doubts seriously; nor could Dougall, as her creator, give Lovereen's doubts the same intellectual weight as Paul's.

The cultural proscriptions against women engaging in theological speculation, particularly in disbelief, were strong. An article, "Agnosticism and Women," published in the influential British monthly *Nineteenth Century*, when Dougall was twenty-two, argues that it is impossible for women to become agnostic without losing their femininity. Novels reinforced this message: Elizabeth Jay has observed that late-nineteenth-century novels assumed that the capacity for sustained intellectual skepticism was incompatible with femininity. Women internalized this and rarely wrote intellectual, spiritual autobiographies or their secular counterparts.

Paul, then, is a convenient device. He appears in the manuscript irregularly, usually when Dougall needs to discuss problems that appeared incongruous for a young girl. Other women writers employed similar devices. T. B. Kilpatrick compared "Lovereen" to three recent novels written by women, Mary Ward's *Robert Elsmere* (1888), Margaret Deland's *John Ward, Preacher* (1888), and Olive Schreiner's *The Story of an African Farm* (1883).[44] These women novelists all speak through a man when they discuss the intellectual dimensions of the loss of faith. *The Story of an African Farm* is most similar to "Lovereen" in structure: the novel centers on the tragic life of the free-spirited Lyndall, but it is a male alter-ego, a brother figure, Waldo, who pursues the implications of the loss of faith. Shreiner later acknowledged that both Waldo and Lyndall were herself. We can probably assume the same of Dougall—through Lovereen and Paul she explored different aspects of her own character and faith.[45]

Paul undergoes the classic crisis of faith: a sudden disillusionment based upon higher criticism, the open rejection of childhood teachings, the public and dramatic departure from evangelicalism, and the turn to social reform. He had set out upon an evangelical career, under the tutelage of Mr. Walford, Lovereen's preacher father, in which he was paid to study in the winter and evangelize in the summer. He was skeptical about this mission from the start, saying, "I don't see any use in sending a fellow who isn't good to tell other people to be good, but if you want me to do it, I'll do the best I can."[46] But he perseveres until he runs into the classic stumbling block of biblical literalists, the story of Jonah and the whale. He convinces Walford to let him reorient his evangelizing toward a social gospel, by starting a "ragged school," a night school for men, and a summer savings club for winter fuel, but then finally breaks with Walford, and plans to become a high school teacher. The director of a Roman Catholic college, presented as the wisest, most cultured, and most tolerant religious leader in the community, is able to tell Paul the secret of Paul's own paternity, and, in a neatly parallel development, offers him the security of the Catholic Church. He offers Paul a place in a French college so he can devote his life to higher criticism.[47] Paul is tempted—his ideal is "to help in the knowledge of the world"[48]—but he finally decides to take over his uncle's grocery store. He needs the money to support Lovereen (who has refused to follow her father to the mission fields) and pay the medical bills of the young daughter of the impoverished High Church missionary. This unlikely conclusion is echoed in later books (Dougall's protagonists marry grocers, butchers, and thieves), but here it serves to show that the freethinking Paul, unlike the two missionaries, puts people ahead of religious doctrine.

Lovereen, as we saw in Chapter 2, experiences a more protracted crisis, trapped in a web of family obligations. Her crisis is closely tied to the career of a single daughter: the tyranny of household responsibilities and the imposition of a restrictive role upon a woman. Dougall simplified her own struggle for fiction: Lovereen's difficulties climb directly toward a crisis and are resolved neatly in the conclusion, whereas Dougall struggled in and out of illness and despair over a number of years. Lovereen's final faith is a vague and pantheistic one that can be distilled into a simple phrase: "that God is, that he blesses all who seek Him, through whatever form or creed or parable they seek." Toward the end of the novel, Lovereen tells Paul,

> I think that perhaps we are not meant to know anything about God but just that his light is always behind our clouds; the more to our feeble sight is actually less. The more religion tries to explain God, the more our thought of Him becomes small, comes to be merely a force by which we regulate our conduct rightly, we can live more effectively. . . . It seems to me that life becomes so much holier if we realise that God is in all things, that his life flows through us as through all nature.[49]

This position reflects Philips Brooks's incarnational theology; through Lovereen, Dougall is arguing that evangelicals were shutting themselves off from much of God in denying his earthly creation. As Lovereen puts it to her father: "It is your temperament to want to contract all life within religion and it is mine to want to spread religion over all life. You think that whatever is not godly is wrong; I think that whatever is not wrong is godly."[50] At a turning point in the novel, Lovereen realizes the gulf that lies between them: she has slipped home from a ball, and hears him singing: "Oh let no earthborn cloud arise / To hide Thee from thy Servant's eyes." She prays "No No teach us to see *Thee* in all things."[51]

Kilpatrick, a liberal Presbyterian, was alarmed by Lovereen's "formless mist." He identified Lovereen as a representative of Higher Life, the movement sparked by Hannah Whitall Smith in England.[52] Kilpatrick noted, on reading a draft of the first volumes, "the net result is the despair of Christianity; for Lovereen is not a Christian, though she owes to Christianity all that is noble and true in her."[53] Paul, on the other hand, receives Kilpatrick's strongest endorsement, as the "Christianity of Christ."[54] After weathering his crisis, Paul becomes an apologist for the Broad Church. Paul dismisses Lovereen's pantheism: "You have wandered into the realm of beautiful poetry." He claims that this would be a dangerous reversion to primitive faith, and argues that the doubter should remain within the safe confines of an historic church: "a visible Church, a holy, organic unity alone entrusted with the continuous mission of the gospels."[55] In contrast to Lovereen, who blithely argues, "It doesn't matter what other people think—this is the way of thinking that is true for me," Paul plans to work toward a corporate rethinking:

> There is a very great difference between making our own what we can find to live by in the common creed, acquiescing in the rest and if we must wait for more light looking for it to come through the growth of the Church—there is all the difference in the world between this, and setting up a creed of our own, looking for it to grow like a little particular ladder between our souls and heaven.[56]

The historic church offered a community and history that grounded the flights of biblical criticism. The two elements, biblical criticism and historic church, balanced each other; the freedom of the higher critics testing and expanding the base of the historic church, and the comprehensive security of that historic body grounding and securing the flights of criticism. The tension and balance is a Mauricean one. F. D. Maurice's most influential book, *Kingdom of Christ,* is addressed to a Quaker friend, and is structured as an extended argument for Quakers to bring the inner light into the safe confines of a liberalized Anglican Church.

Paul's interest in a historic church is so strong that the High Church Anglican, Mr. Myers, worries that Paul will convert to Roman Catholicism.[57] Paul instead turns briefly to Myers's High Church Anglo-Catholicism, thinking that it offers a compromise: a "dogma free from superstition of Rome, in which our minds may rest and by which we feel ourselves an integral part of the great historic Church of all ages."[58] He attends a talk on "Church Doctrine" by Myers:

> Paul, who went to the first lecture under the impression that there was little to be said in favour of the High Church movement which a sensible mind could accept, found that in comparison to this slighting [?] estimate the arguments were weighty and the foundations strong [Dougall crossed out "the foundations strong"]. His strong young mind was given a new ideal to feed upon—that of a religion not purely spiritual, but which claimed to meet man perfectly in his two fold nature as a being who was not, and could not be, purely spiritual. . . . And this religion was of a form not antagonistic to Paul's reason as the precepts of Rome which he had set aside.[59]

Paul, however, dislikes Myers's intolerance, and his feelings are vindicated when Myers takes advantage of an invitation from the Nonconformists to lecture about the "apostolic succession and the gifts that come to us in an unbroken stream of soul healing thus proceeding from the Lord in whom we all adore." He tells them that those outside the Anglican Church could not receive the fullness of Divine grace. Myers's speech has the effect of "an explosive war shell," and he is chased through town by a mob throwing eggs.[60] Paul's attraction to Anglo Catholicism and final rejection are classically Broad Church; they follow F. D. Maurice's Tractarian leanings and his departure over Pusey's teaching on baptism.

Lovereen and Paul, then, represent two sides of Dougall's religious thought. Lovereen, in accordance with gendered notions of religious experience, represents the incarnational, mystical side, the "formless mist," and Paul the more intellectual and critical side of Dougall's character. The dialectical play of the two identities is introduced in romantic scenes. The novel concludes with the reconciliation of these views, Schleiermacher's coincidence of opposites, when Lovereen and Paul decide to marry and Lovereen's amorphous spirituality is contained within Paul's concept of the historic church. Theologians have commented upon the contradictions between Maurice's conservative emphasis on the historic Anglican Church and his radically mystical understanding of eternity. For Lily Dougall, however, these two elements balanced each other: Maurice's theology offered the security and community of a historic church and the freedom to explore a deeply felt spirituality.

If the creation of Paul accounts for Lovereen's intellectual vacuum, how do we account for the absence of a mother figure in Dougall's manuscript? Mrs. Walford, Lovereen's mother, is described as a saintly woman, a victim of her husband's zealous evangelizing: "Mary Walford . . . was a lovely and selfless character. She was of Puritan descent and held deep religious convictions. She could take great pleasure in the pleasures of the others but her own pleasure consisted chiefly in prayer and praise to God and self-sacrifice to the beings given to her love." [61] This saintly mother dies before the novel opens, allowing all of the young girl's difficulties to be focused on the father.[62]

How are we to account for the absence of the mother in this narrative? In her analysis of Canadian autobiography, Helen Buss suggests that the masculine narrative, constructed as a movement away from the mother to an individual separate rationality, is fundamentally unsuited to women, for whom the movement has been a cyclical one of ongoing relationship. Whereas masculine development is individualist, women's development is communal and relational. Buss cites Bella Brodzki, "the daughter's text, variously, seeks to reject, reconstruct and reclaim—to locate and recontextualize—the mother's message." [63] Removing the mother from "Lovereen" enabled Dougall to develop the novel in conformity with the classic masculine autobiographical narrative.

This elision also allowed her to avoid dealing with the complex feelings toward her demanding, powerful, and loving mother. Although Dougall suggests that a saintly mother could cast a shadow over her children's lives, "chilling the gaiety of their waking hours and sleeping dreams," [64] she erased any conflict in the fictional relationship, describing "the sixteen years in which Walford's wife and daughter had lived together in passionate reciprocal love and oneness of feeling, even when the girl had differed from her mother in thought." [65] Devout mothers are the stuff of evangelical iconography: in 1846 Lily's father had printed an inspirational article on mothers in the *Montreal Witness:* "On a mother's love. It conquers all. It is identified in the mind with its first

Elizabeth (Redpath) Dougall, Lily Dougall's mother, 1861. *Courtesy Notman Photographic Archives, McCord Museum of Canadian History, I-1924.1.*

knowledge of God. She is contemplated as with God. Next to the divine efficiency, her influence is all pervading and most powerful."[66] Some forty years later, Lily repeated this elision of God and mother in her letters, her poems, and her fiction. She wrote, on her mother's death, "God supplies *all* our need—yes, *all*, all my need of my mother: (loving and tender and sympathetic as she was, the Lord is infinitely more loving and sympathetic.)"[67] And she speaks in her fiction through Lovereen, who recalls, "Yet her mother had told her with her last breath that . . . [in] the all pervading presence of Divine Love she would find a love as intimate and as tender."[68] A book of poetry, written shortly after her mother's death, repeatedly elides mother and deity:

> The child, with fears in unnamed darkness faints
> Finds bliss in climbing to his mother's bed
> So would I creep, caressed and comforted
> Within thy will Lord God Omnipotent

One poem develops the parallels:

> Thou teachest still the lesson thou has taught—
> To know what thing is love, and in me wrought
> The question, Can the Infinite be less?[69]

The question is a revealing one. "Can the Infinite be less?" Can the Infinite be understood apart from a mother's love and power?

A passage in the introductory chapter of "Lovereen" suggests a reading similar to Brodzki's. Dougall describes the flowers dying in a November garden, and suggests lyrically that each generation's faith grows anew from the death of the earlier faith:

> There is no apparently unbroken progress in the way in which the generations rise nearer to God. The parents make the best of their life's summer, and the fruit and flower of their lives, in deed and hope and thought, will often seem to fail and fall, and blossom of their children's lives to spring up in fresh form from the decadence; yet it is from the life of the summer, not because of its death, that the new life of spring comes.[70]

The imagery, we shall see, is the imagery that informs the liberal Anglican movement. The husk of the old faith dies, and the new springs from the germ of life within. Dougall suggests here that her adult quest was, as Brodzki suggests, to reject, then reconstruct and reclaim, the deep faith taught at her mother's knee. Unlike the straight masculine trajectory in independence (and even that trajectory is, of course, a fiction), Dougall's life would suggest a circling, a return, and renewal springing from a deep and continuing web of relationships. After her mother's death, Lily moved to England and found new relationships, egalitarian and liberal, that allowed her to reclaim and recast the faith she learned at her mother's knee.

PART II

A THEOLOGY OF RELATIONSHIPS

4
"She Was Always a Queer Child"

I feel very sorry for you, my dear John, that you are a
man. I do not think men enjoy themselves much; they
have not the slightest conception how much women find to
enjoy.

Lily Dougall[1]

ONE RELATIONSHIP STANDS OUT above all others in Lily Dougall's life:
Sophie Earp lived with Dougall for most of her adult life and is buried
with her under a single gravestone. Earp was a graduate of Newnham
College, Cambridge, and first among a large number of well-educated,
single women friends who supported and encouraged Dougall. Of all
the contexts in which Dougall lived, this community of women was
probably most important, for her relations with women informed her
fiction, her theology, and her sense of her relationship with God.

This may be the most difficult context for those of us living in the
twenty-first century to properly understand. Lily Dougall's relationship
with Earp lasted from 1887 until 1923, when Dougall died. Or we
might say it lasted until 1928, the year of Sophie's death, because
Sophie kept the relationship alive in the pages of her manuscript, "The
Selected Letters of Lily Dougall." The second date would be an appro-
priate one, because 1928 marked two watershed moments in the history of women in Britain: in 1928 British women won full suffrage and
in 1928 obscenity trials over Radclyffe Hall's lesbian novel, *The Well
of Loneliness*, irrevocably changed our understanding of women's love
for one another. The two events are related: the image of the degenerate, predatory lesbian was used to undermine women's colleges and
marginalize women's battles for political autonomy.

I will argue that to understand Lily's love for Sophie we need to
imagine a period when same-sex relationships were not primarily about
sexual desire but were informed by a shared sense of moral womanhood.

This is not to say that the relationship was not erotically charged. Lily Dougall's papers reveal a loving, exclusive, playful relationship. (That they do not reveal more is probably due to Sophie's censorship; in this case the silence speaks volumes, and there is certainly no need to assume that theirs was a chaste romantic friendship, even if there are no grounds to suggest that it was anything more.) Dougall's novels, however, suggest that she understood sexuality to be male, and violent. Women's power lay in their ability to rise above the "selfishness" of men, rather than in the expression of their own sexual desires. The novels reveal a preoccupation with violent heterosexuality: the strong young women featured in the novels repeatedly flee rape, usually in the form of an imposed marriage. The overarching theme is the avoidance of what Adrienne Rich has called compulsory heterosexuality, and the assertion of female power and independence.[2] In the conclusion, I tie this aversion to masculine power to Dougall's anticlericalism. I argue that Liberal theology offered Dougall a model for female independence, in its rationalism, its search for first principles, and its dismissal of tradition and hierarchy.

Lily and Sophie met in Cheltenham, where Sophie was lecturing at the Cheltenham Ladies' College, on October 28, 1887, and they moved in together in January 1888. The relationship was a close one. Lily explained to her friends, "[A]ltogether it is very like being married. . . . We have such cozy little breakfasts and dinners and suppers, and make each other toast, and pet each other generally."[3] It was also playfully intellectual. Lily told a friend, shortly after meeting Sophie,

> If you want to know what I look like in this gown, Sophie says that I look exactly like the "Beaver in the Snark," I can't tell you why, but she sees the likeness so strongly that she seldom calls me anything else. Of course, it follows that she is the "Butcher" and when she explains any of the grand things she learned in her Cambridge tripos, we call it "explaining the Jub-Jub."[4]

The nicknames were revealing. Earp was well educated: she had studied moral philosophy at Newnham College at Cambridge, and been granted a second-class degree, or tripos. In Lewis Carroll's *Hunting the Snark*, the Butcher pontificates upon mathematics and natural science to the receptive Beaver, and

> The Butcher would gladly have talked till next day,
> But he felt that the lesson must end,
> And he wept with delight in attempting to say
> He considered the Beaver his friend.

While the Beaver confessed, with affectionate looks
More eloquent even than tears,
It had learned in ten minutes far more than all books
Would have taught it in seventy years.

They returned hand-in-hand, and the Bellman, unmanned
(For a moment) with noble emotion,
Said "This amply repays all the wearisome days
We have spent on the billowy ocean!"

Such friends, as the Beaver and Butcher became,
Have seldom if ever been known;
In winter or summer, 'twas always the same—
You could never meet either alone.

And when quarrels arose—as one frequently finds
Quarrels will, spite of every endeavour—
The song of the Jub-Jub recurred to their minds,
And cemented their friendship for ever.[5]

Lily also sometimes referred to Sophie as Dodo, another reference to Lewis Carroll.

Sophie, who was later described as a woman with an "energetic— it might almost be said, masterful—individuality," sustained Dougall.[6] She took on a supporting role, acting as an advisor, editor, and sounding board, and relieving Dougall of much of the tedium of secretarial and editorial work and domestic chores. As their friend B. H. Streeter noted after Dougall's death: "But for Miss Earp, Miss Dougall, who was physically frail, would not have accomplished one fourth of what she actually did."[7] Sophie was also an active partner in the intellectual process. Lily explained: "[Sophie] understands me and I her, better than I have sometimes believed possible."[8] The relationship was a fruitful one for Lily and clearly a happy one for Sophie. They spent a year in Europe, largely in Lausanne, Switzerland, from September 1888 to late August 1889. Lily worked on "Lovereen"; Sophie took dictation. It was a period Lily was later to recall as "that happy Swiss life when we starved, feasted, despaired and were happy."[9]

Diaries and biographical papers suggest that the relationship with Sophie became more difficult to maintain after 1890 as Lily was torn by continuing obligations to her aunt in Edinburgh and Sophie held a position as lecturer in political economy at Midland Institute in Birmingham.[10] Sophie continued to handle much of Lily's literary correspondence.[11] They continued to meet for intense periods of work and holidays, but there were long absences and suggestions of strife. There were other close relationships. An excerpt from Dougall's diary in 1891 reads: "My

Lily Dougall, 1891. *Courtesy Notman Photographic Archives, McCord Museum of Canadian History, II-95873.1.*

Sophie Earp, 1891. This photograph was taken directly after the photo of Lily Dougall on the previous page. *Courtesy Notman Photographic Archives, McCord Museum of Canadian History, II-95879.1.*

Do [Sophie] went to Nottham [Nottingham?] I was very sad and then Woolly lived with me." [12] Sophie appears to have been replaced, at least in her role as assistant, by a Miss McGillivray between 1893 to 1895.[13] In July 1895, Sophie noted: "Drifting apart." [14] Lily returned to Montreal frequently in the summers, and when her aunt died in August 1897, leaving a substantial legacy, she decided to return to Canada permanently.[15] Separation appears to have strengthened the relationship. Diary notes for April 8, 1898, read, "Long love letter," and in September of that year she wrote to Sophie: "How much I want you I can sometimes never tell; no one else seems to do instead." [16] In 1899, Lily returned to England to spend the spring and summer with Sophie; she spent another winter in Montreal, moved back to England in the spring of 1900, to return to North America in 1901. In a letter to a mutual friend that winter, Lily announced that "a plan that I have been working for, for years—that of living with my great friend and working steadily with her, can now be carried out. . . ." [17] In 1903 this peripatetic life ended when they found a home together in Exmouth. They lived together until Lily died.

Sophie managed Lily's life. She acted as social convener and household organizer, but most important, she provided Lily with editorial assistance and advice. The manuscript for "Lovereen" is peppered with her comments, and by 1893 she was overseeing all of Lily's manuscripts. They became a team, and Lily frequently described their work as a shared project: "[I]t is three years since we have had any luck. . . ." she despaired in 1898.[18] On January 12, 1909 Sophie wrote, "B. [Beaver] came to Melbourne. We are revising *Christus Futurus* for the second edition." [19] They worked so closely that editors and literary agents found it a confusing partnership, and wondered where to address their queries. On one occasion Lily provided Sophie with two different responses to her agent, and left the selection up to Sophie, saying "If you don't like either of these notes to Watt concoct one. . . ." [20]

Lily was known to have "a genius for friendship," and Sophie was the central figure in a wide circle of women friends and acquaintances.[21] Family letters refer to her childhood friends Katie and Agnes Drummond (her cousins) and Janie Couper, who visited her in Britain, and her British diaries document a constant stream of engagements and numerous shared excursions and holidays with women friends and relatives. Letters suggest a supportive female culture, with a heady sense of broken barriers and new privileges. When she had tea with Miss M. R. Walker, Dougall wrote her brother: "We had tea in the little parlour, and expressed to each other our innocent delight in being independent young maidens who could enjoy ourselves just as we pleased within the narrow limits of our circumstances." She went on: "I feel very sorry for you, my dear John, that you are a man. I do not think men enjoy themselves much; they have not the slightest conception how much women find to enjoy." [22] Sixteen years later, she has a male narrator express surprise at women's capacity for friendship: "I've never been able to explain to myself the way that women attach themselves so easily to women." [23]

Dougall's was the first generation in England to gain admission to higher education, and her new friends were drawn largely from the growing circle of academic and literary women. [24] These women were unlikely to marry. An 1895 article in *Nineteenth Century* pointed out that only 208 of the 1,468 British women with a university education had married. A larger number, 680, became teachers. American women university graduates had a similar disinclination for marriage, [25] many finding employment and independence as teachers. Sophie found employment at the Midland Institute, and M. R. Walker became the headmistress of St. George's School and Training College. Another friend, Hilda Oakeley, was the head of the new Women's College connected to McGill University when she met Dougall. When they returned to England, Oakeley became a reader in philosophy at King's College, London, and they stayed in close contact. [26]

In 1894, this generation took on literary identity when a series of articles in the *Nineteenth Century* was picked up in the American press, and the title of an article in the *North American Review,* "The New Woman," encapsulated the identity of the single, independent woman. [27] The New Woman crystallized growing fears surrounding female independence, for it had not only been Dougall's highly educated cohorts who had remained single. The numbers of single women in the United States had been rising and, in the generation born in the decade after Dougall, between 1865 and 1875, an unprecedented 11 percent remained single. [28] The New Woman was characterized as assertive and modern and caricatured riding bicycles and smoking cigarettes. More than one hundred books of fiction, including Dougall's *Madonna of a Day,* contributed to a heated debate about these women, resisting some elements of the New Woman and celebrating others.

Lily and Sophie were typical New Women, and keen participants in the bicycle craze; their bicycles symbolized independence and physical strength. More important, however, was their participation in the intellectual community created by the numbers of single women. These friends broadened Dougall's horizons and provided access to the British intellectual world. Earp showed Dougall's early fiction to Henry Sidgwick, the Knightsbridge Professor of Moral Philosophy at Cambridge. [29] A writer friend, "Sarah Tytler" (Henrietta Keddie) introduced Dougall to the idealist philosopher William Wallace. Oakeley took Dougall with her to a London philosophical society, the Aristotelians.[30] These friends provided her with support for her literary ambitions and allowed Lily to resist the prohibitions of her family and her elderly aunt. Their advice on reading "Lovereen" was typically enthusiastic: "The book is splendid" said one; another wrote, "L. has like the smell of a baby," and a third friend, writing in an intimate slang, wrote to "My Dear Beautiful Clever Beaver, . . . a Work teeming with 'ideas' like the Tale of the Beaver simply fills [me] with 'wonder, love and praise.' " [31]

How can we define Lily Dougall's relationships with other women, particularly her relationship with Sophie Earp? Should we identify this as a lesbian relationship? Need we define it? In 1975, Carroll Smith-Rosenberg described the "romantic friendships" that flourished in the literate middle classes: nineteenth-century women found female companions with whom they shared their lives, and sometimes their beds. They used words of endearment and even passionate love, and described their relationships as marriages. The romantic friendship allowed women a great deal of latitude in the physical expression of their love.[32] Sex was conceived of as male penetration, so, as Esther Newton argued, "what 'pure' women did with each other, no matter how good it felt, could not be conceived as sexual within the terms of the dominant nineteenth-century paradigm."[33] Smith-Rosenberg, however, emphasized the emotional elements, and described relations modeled on familial, especially mother-daughter, bonds. Lillian Faderman was even more definitive in her 1981 study and has noted recently that "friends had difficulty accepting my insistence that most female love relationships before the twentieth century were probably not genital."[34]

Dougall's generation of New Women replicated this "female world of love and ritual" in the institutional settings of colleges, romantic friendships were destabilized after World War I, with rising cultural anxiety about the New Woman and a new emphasis upon sexual expression.[35] Sexologists like Richard Krafft-Ebing and Havelock Ellis categorized same-sex love as a degenerate pathology. Members of an emerging lesbian subculture, drawn from a second generation of modernist New Women, born in the 1870s and 1880s, began to construct a new lesbian identity: sexual, modern, independent, and masculine in dress. Radclyffe Hall combined the image of sexology's "congenital invert" with the mannish lesbian to create the prototype of the modern lesbian in her novel, *The Well of Loneliness* (1928). The novel was charged with obscenity and the ensuing trials attracted wide public interest. The playful fluid and shifting lesbian identity froze, casting the modern lesbian in Hall's own much-photographed image. The public began to identify women's love for other women with sexology's degenerate and predatory lesbian.

In the 1980s, Smith-Rosenberg blamed this modernist generation of New Women for undermining the advances of an earlier generation of feminists.[36] Sexology has received more nuanced treatment in recent work, and historians have described the construction of the modern lesbian identity as a flawed, but liberatory assertion of an autonomous sexuality. They point to new evidence, such as Anne Lister's heated homoerotic diaries, to demonstrate that nineteenth-century relations were sexual and argue that reticence should not be interpreted as absence of sexual desire, and indeed might be considered an "erotics of unnaming."[37] Terry Castle, who calls romantic friendship "depressingly chaste," has insisted on the historical presence of lesbian desire—"the incorrigibly lascivious surge toward the body of another woman." Castle points out that women did not need the findings of sexologists to identify and act on their desires, and asked, "why is it so difficult to see the lesbian—even when she is there, quite plainly, in front of us?"[38]

This critique points to the need for an acknowledgement of eroticism in relationships like the one between Dougall and Earp, although whether we need to "see the lesbian" is more debatable. Despite attempts by Adrienne Rich and others to broaden it, the term bears the marks of era in which it emerged and, as Rich herself notes, has a clinical tone and an emphasis on genital sexuality that limits our understanding of women's eroticism. The retroactive application imposes a modern identity politics on a more multivalent past. Dougall and Earp's love could no more be a "romantic friendship" in the asexual terms of the mid-nineteenth century, than it could be a "lesbian" relationship in the highly sexualized terms of post-1928 modern lesbian identity. It was something in between. Martha Vicinus observes: "The polymorphous, even amorphous, sexuality of women is an invitation to multiple interpretive strategies . . . Many lesbian histories, contradictory, complicated, and perhaps uncomfortable, can be told."[39] The early twentieth century was a period of indeterminacy and flux, as Laura Doan has shown in *Fashioning Sapphism: The Origins of Modern English Lesbian Culture*, and there is evidence for a surprising degree of tolerance of same-sex relationships prior to 1928.[40]

Doan is describing a subculture of younger, more bohemian women, but Martha Vicinus's work on some of Dougall's Anglican peers suggests that even here a variety of relations were accommodated within the prevailing heterosexual norms. Vicinus describes the reluctant acquiescence of the Archbishop of Canterbury, Edward

Benson, to his wife's decision to share her bed with a female lover from the late 1880s to her death in 1918.[41] And two of Dougall's friends at Oxford, Charlotte Anne Moberley and Eleanor Jourdain, the principal and vice principal of St. Hugh's College, lived together in a relationship described by a friend as that of "husband and wife" for 23 years.[42] Their shared vision of Marie Antoinette—which occurred, significantly, shortly after Moberley and Jourdain first met in 1901—published to some ridicule as *An Adventure* (1911), has been described by Terry Castle as a homoerotic or lesbian legitimation fantasy.[43] It is likely that a multitude of such relationships existed within Dougall's world of scholarly single women; she did not have to choose one specific lesbian identity (or a similarly limited heterosexuality), but could model her relationship with Earp on any one of a wide range of women-identified relationships.

There were, and always had been, bounds, rarely articulated, within which such relationships were accepted. Women policed themselves: in "Stray Thoughts for Girls" (1893), L. H. M. Soulsby, the headmistress of Oxford High School, and one of Lily Dougall's associates, warned her female students not to let their attachments to each other outweigh family ties.[44] As the findings of sexology percolated from doctors' offices, and women's love became identified with the abnormal "congenital invert," there was growing need for silence.[45] Dougall's working relationships with psychologists like James Hadfield, a lecturer in psychopathology and mental hygiene, would have meant she was cognizant of the pathology of "sexual inversion." By the 1920s, when Sophie prepared Lily's papers for posterity, it is likely she felt the need to protect their privacy. At some point before her death in 1928, Sophie transcribed most of their letters and diaries, while preparing "The Selected Letters of Lily Dougall," and probably destroyed the originals.

Vicinus has reminded us of the adroitness with which women deflected public gaze: "They managed to be open and closed, to keep a secret and to tell it to anyone who might be listening."[46] Sophie's affection for Lily is obvious in her text in "The Selected Letters" and Lily's love is clear in the letters Sophie chose to include: "How much I want you I can sometimes never tell; no one else seems to do instead"[47] and "[Sophie] understands me and I her, better than I have sometimes believed possible."[48] Their love was, perhaps, too obvious for Canon Streeter, who was supposed to edit but never did complete his half of the manuscript after Sophie's death in 1928, when public debates about lesbianism were at their height. But the papers suggest there was more. In one diary entry Lily exults, "Oh be joyful, my Do [Sophie] came back." [49] A few of their notes, scribbled on letters to the publisher, escaped Sophie's culling. In September 1893 a lonely Sophie wrote: "Thank you darling for that sweet pretty picture I found in my room. I like it very much for itself and because it comes from you. And then it is a sign of you coming here. I suppose you judge that at present you can get on just as well where you are. . . ." [50] An 1895 note from Lily concludes, "I love you very much. So tired. B." [51] An excerpt from Lily's diary, transcribed by Earp but not included in the "Selected Letters," provides a rare glimpse of a playful, physical love: "Do [Sophie] had a fight after supper and butter B's [Lily's] nose. B hurt Do's arm. Do made B asthmatical. . . ." [52] We might read more into some of the material. What was it that Lily "could not tell" when she wrote, "How much I want you I can sometimes never tell"? But this is speculation, and we are largely left with the view of the relationship that Sophie has created.

Dougall's novels provide further, independent, insight into her feelings for women. We might read Dougall's love for Earp in her descriptions of the physical strength and beauty of the leading women characters (one of whom is called Sophia; two of whom were educated at Cambridge, and all of whom are strong, argumentative, and independent). But these descriptions are not erotic. The power of Dougall's female characters lies in their ability to rise above the base passions of the men, rather than in the expression of their own desires. It is coercive heterosexuality that dominates many of these novels: under such romantic titles as *The Mermaid: A Love Tale* (1895) lie melodramatic tales of narrow escapes from heterosexual violence. [53]

Dougall's career as a novelist lasted seventeen years. Between 1891 and 1908, she published ten novels and a number of short stories. She never found a publisher for "Lovereen," despite her friends' enthusiasm, but published short stories in magazines such as *Temple Bar, Longmans,* and *Atlantic,* and broke into the literary world in 1891 with a best seller, *Beggars All: A Novel.* [54] *Beggars All* is a clever romance with a quirky moral twist. A well-born young woman, Star, answers a matrimonial advertisement and marries a stranger in order to save her invalid sister and widowed mother from desperate poverty. She then discovers that her husband has taken morality into his own hands and provides for the poor by stealing from the rich. The book, as her agent said, was "a decided success." [55] The horror of Star's marriage to a stranger skirted the limits of acceptable controversy. Dougall posed Star, who by the end of the novel loves her husband but cannot condone his thievery, with an intriguing moral dilemma. A friend recalled: "It was the kind of book that everyone talked about, and enjoyed that kind of vogue that causes certain folk to feel 'out of it' if obliged to confess that they have not yet read the book." [56]

Her second novel was less successful. *What Necessity Knows* (1893) is set in Canada and traces the fortunes of two young women, Sissy and Sophia.[57] Sissy is a Canadian girl living in a remote lumber camp who escapes marriage to an older man, Bates, by hiding in her father's coffin as it is transported to the train station. She rises from the coffin, wrapped in a winding sheet, in a feminist resurrection to find a new life as "Eliza," eventually taking a position as a hotel manager. Sophia, a member of the British gentry who has moved to Canada to live in genteel poverty, spurns an ambitious minister to marry his younger brother, a butcher. The novel culminates in the dramatic midnight rescue of Sophia's younger sister who has climbed a hilltop to witness the second coming. The novel did not meet expectations; the plot, spun out over three volumes, was unwieldy, and the escape in the coffin and the marriage to a butcher seemed to stretch the credibility of romance readers. Critics objected to moralizing elements in the book.

Dougall then wrote four shorter novels that were published in quick succession in 1895: *A Question of Faith; The Madonna of a Day: A Study; The Mermaid: A Love Tale;* and *The Zeit-Geist.*[58] They were light romances with theological overtones and odd undercurrents of heterosexual violence. *A Question of Faith* describes the difficulties of a Girton graduate, Alice, who has to deceive her fiancé when a man extorts a promise from her to assist his fugitive son. *The Mermaid* is the unlikely tale of a contemplative woman, Madame Le Maître, who does good works on a remote island (and swims in a mermaid costume). *The Madonna of a Day* is the story of a New Woman, Mary, who fends off rape in a lumber camp by assuming the guise of the Madonna. *The Zeit-Geist* is the story of a reformed alcoholic who expounds idealist philosophy. Dougall suffered an acute crisis of confidence after publishing these works, and struggled with feelings of depression and inadequacy for three years before she published another novel. Dougall's depression seems to have been related to her temporary relocation to Montreal, an intellectual backwater in comparison to Oxford, and the loss of Sophie's companionship. *The Mormon Prophet* (1899) was a fictionalized but carefully researched account of the Mormon movement from the eyes of a young convert. It culminates in the protagonist's dramatic escape from the Mormon leader, Joseph Smith, who wants to enter into a bigamous marriage with her.[59]

Dougall began to publish religious essays in 1900. Perhaps because she had this new outlet, the moral elements are more muted in her subsequent novels. The preoccupation with heterosexual violence is also reduced; perhaps because Dougall, who was forty-two in 1900, had passed marriageable age, or possibly because she had finally established a permanent home with Earp. *The Earthly Purgatory: A Novel* (1904) was published in serial form in *Temple Bar* and then in one volume in Britain and in the United States, where it was called *The Summit House Mystery*.[60] The book is a light and melodramatic mystery, with, as the first title indicates, the usual mix of serious moral intent. The plot revolves around a single woman living in isolation with her younger sister who bears the scandal and shame of a murder committed by her dissolute father. A dramatic sequence of events, involving bludgeoned bodies, false identities, letters left in trees, and fortuitous accidents, result in her father being left under her care, completely paralyzed, in an earthly purgatory that will presumably bring about his final redemption. The moral elements are largely implied rather than stated, and the mystery well constructed, so that the book was popular on both sides of the Atlantic. A second mystery story, *The Spanish Dowry* (1906), with the full panoply of ghosts, buried treasure, mysterious nuns, and a befuddled and elitist Anglican minister, eschewed serious issues. Dougall's last fictional work, *The Paths of the Righteous* (1908), is a thinly disguised tract on behalf of religious tolerance. Dougall attempted one final fictional explication of her ideas, but this didactic manuscript, "Corchestor of the Future," was refused by Macmillan.[61]

The leading women in Dougall's novels are strong figures, as their names suggest: Star, Sophia (or wisdom), and Madame Le Maître (the master). They are often well educated: Alice and Mary had both studied at Girton.[62] They frequently have a healthy sense of their own superiority, which Dougall's readers sometimes found disconcerting in a woman, and her friends noted "was deliciously characteristic of the distinguished author herself."[63] They are ambitious—as Sissy tells Sophia, "I want so much—I want so much."[64] They are often physically strong: Sissy "was a large, strong young woman," who "had a sense of power within her"; Oriane in *The Paths of the Righteous* is "tall and strong and vigorous," and Sophia casually packs a pistol in her belt as she goes to rescue her younger sister.[65] The women in the short stories are similar: in one, a "statuesque" woman rescues and carries a "bantam" man home when he twists his ankle. In another, a young man falls for a farmer's niece, a tall, strong gymnast trained in New York; when she chases him, he breaks a leg.[66] Women overshadow the men in the novels; indeed, Henry Sidgwick's complaint regarding *The Mormon Prophet*—"the chief criticism I should make is that the hero—if Joseph Smith may be so styled—plays so decidedly 'second fiddle' to the heroine"—might be made of most of Dougall's books.[67] Even though Dougall pruned the women down in order to fit the genre—reducing Sophia's age to meet the expectations of romance readers—her admiration for their strength and power is evident.[68]

Familial bonds are central in the early work. Lily's relations with her mother had been intense; the poems written after her mother's death are passionate:

> I had a mother for a few short years
> Who taught me what love was; for that O God
> I thank Thee though for want of love I die.
> To love is to live with open soul towards whom we love, that all
> they may desire
> Of help, or tenderness or trust or prayer
> Of lighter playfulness or smiles or tears
> Is theirs as it is ours, and only ours
> As it reflects from them.[69]

In *Beggars All*, she describes the saintly death of a mother in terms that echo these grief-stricken poems. In "Lovereen" we can see how this love, which was not entirely lacking in erotic power, is transferred to women friends. Dougall describes not only the "passionate reciprocal love and oneness of feeling" between Lovereen and her mother, but also the physical intimacy when Elsie pulls her mother down onto a narrow couch and lies, "picking at her buttons."[70] She describes a similar physical intimacy between Flora and Lovereen: "[Lovereen] went to sleep that night in Flora's arms, soothed by her kisses and gentle assurances of unbroken friendship."[71]

There are some hints about Lovereen's sexuality. Paul recalls, "I played with her every day for years; she was just like another boy." In an early draft, the doctor notes that she "was rather a tomboy." This was edited to read "was always a queer child."[72] Her first suitor, fresh from Paris, describes her as "odd, decidedly odd."[73] It is Marian, however, the forty-year-old single woman in *Beggars All*, who comes closest of all of Dougall's characters to a modern lesbian identity. Dougall tells us, repeatedly, that Marian has never loved a man: "She sympathized with women, not with men." One hundred pages later, the text states, "Marian did not like men," and again, two hundred pages further: "Marian did not like men and was unaccustomed to them."[74] But Dougall's description of Marian is not a celebration; she draws on all the stereotypes (and possibly her own fears) about the life of the lonely older spinster. *Beggars All* is, as the title suggests, a cautionary tale about the economic difficulties of single women: Star is forced to sell herself in marriage to support her family, and Marian's years as a teacher have left her "not with the modest independence that the same toil and economy would have given a man, but without means of support." She is forced to become a housekeeper for a tyrannical uncle. When a young girl tells her mother in the novel that "old maids are good and nice," the mother emphasizes economic realities. "They are so common now that a sentiment has risen up in favour of the state, and I would not disparage it; but a lady's health rarely stands the strain of self-supporting labour and dependence on the whims and fancies of others is not enviable. Romantic stories of maiden ladies doing good are pleasant reading, but unless they have means, they are not at liberty to do much. . . ." [75]

Loneliness deformed Marian: "She was much more than she looked—a woman of strong natural feelings, in whose heart these emotions, by reasons of having no outlet, warred with one another and with overruling reason, producing strange fancies and morbid hopes and fears." [76] Dougall concludes that Marian needs someone to love, and forgetting momentarily that Marian does not like men, she suggests that a child, a woman "friend," or a "man's love" would fulfill her: "a woman friend would have lit her neutral tinted days with sunshine, as a man's love might have flushed them into a roseate glow." [77] Eventually Marian finds this fulfillment with Star. When Star declares her love, Marian replies: "I, too, love you; indeed, you do not know how much happier you have made me. It is of no use, I think, to *talk* about friendship. It is only when we *feel* how much it means that we know." [78] Dougall brackets this love with Star's growing love for her thieving husband; the novel concludes ambiguously with Star and Marian together, waiting for the errant husband to return.

In subsequent novels there is only the occasional suggestion of the pleasure Dougall found in her relationship with Earp. This, like Marian's happiness with Star, is often undercut by an impending marital relationship. Mary is traveling with an older woman friend at the outset of *Madonna of a Day,* but Dougall is careful to include a crowd of admiring young men at the train station, and the story centers on Mary's subsequent isolation among the rough men in the mountains. When she returns from the wilderness, a male cousin displaces Mary's woman companion, and seems destined to become a somewhat uninspiring marriage partner. Madame Le Maître's experience of the perfect human relationship was her schoolgirl friendship—"I was perfectly happy when I was with her and she was with me; it was a marriage" [79]—but she lives in fear of an abusive husband, and marries a gentle doctor at the conclusion of the novel. One reviewer noted of *The Mermaid:* "It all ends in the most bourgeois and blissful way." [80]

The comment could be made of most of Dougall's novels. (One perceptive reviewer observed that none of the short stories in Dougall's collection, *A Dozen Ways of Love*, is a conventional love story.)[81] Her strong young women generally conform to the conventions of the romantic novel and marry. Sissy dismisses marriage in *What Necessity Knows*:

> "Most women are much happier married." Sophia said this with ortho-dox propriety, although she did not altogether believe it.
> "Yes, when they can't fend for themselves, poor things. But to be for-ever tied to a house and a man, never to do just what one liked! I'm going to take pattern by you, Miss Sophia, and not get married."[82]

But Dougall brings the novel to a conventional conclusion by marry-ing both women off. Sophia finds love with the minister's younger brother, and Sissy decides, after her dramatic escape in a coffin, to marry Bates, but he is by now an older and weaker man, and she has by this time established her independence: "She was mistress now and he slave."[83] The marriages are anticlimactic conclusions to the power-ful identities the women have established as single women, and in both marriages the women are dominant figures. Many of Dougall's women enter passionless marriages with wise older men and gentle brotherlike men. Lovereen marries the brotherlike Paul. Alice turns to a gentle, and somewhat asexual, father figure. Madame Le Maître, con-veniently widowed, is wiser and stronger than her new lover, the young doctor.[84] Susannah is briefly married to a gentle Quaker in *The Mormon Prophet*; after escaping Joseph Smith she marries a bookish cousin.

Other marriages are more disturbing. Flora in "Lovereen" marries the degenerate son of a dissolute British aristocrat, an imbecile who has fits. Lovereen asks herself as Flora leaves on her honeymoon with the groom—and his nurse—"Would this first bitter discovery of her bridal journey be only the fore runner of a life of hidden miseries?"[85] Star's marriage is simply prostitution, albeit for the best of reasons: "I *sold myself* when I married him."[86] Alice's engagement is loveless: she and a cousin have to marry to receive their inheritance.

A subtext of truly violent heterosexual relations further under-mines the romantic plot. Sissy was only the first of several characters to make a dramatic escape from marriage. Bates was not a villain, but he was a controlling older man, and as Dougall notes, he had intended to make Sissy a "slave-wife."[87] The other men are classic villains. Madame Le Maître in *The Mermaid* fears sexual assault upon her seafaring hus-band's return, and is saved only by his sudden drowning. Susannah flees a bigamous marriage to Mormon leader Joseph Smith. Mary in *The Madonna of a Day* fends off a camp of "Chinamen," rough lumbermen, and finally their debauched leader, "a man who had early worked his way through all the vices of society," whose nickname, "Old Harry" refers to the devil. (At least two of the novels make reference to men beating their wives.)[88]

The most revealing of these stories of heterosexual violence is *The Madonna of a Day*. The book is a contradictory (and perhaps hurriedly written) response to the transatlantic debate over the New Woman. Mary is New Woman, university-educated, brash, agnostic, and emancipated, who disputes the stereotype even as she lives it: "I have been three years at Girton, and I've lived in town for a year or two and I've traveled around the world and I can assure you the 'New Woman' is a pure myth." Her cleverness proves inadequate, however, when she sleepwalks off a train on Christmas Eve in the wilds of the British Columbian mountains and finds herself alone with a rough gang of men. She narrowly avoids a brutal rape only because the lumbermen mistake her, speechless in a blue cape, for a vision of the Madonna. Their leader, a man whose expression "bore the creeping shadow of low brutality and cunning," [89] discovers Mary's cigarette case (which identifies her as a modern and impious woman) and tells her she must marry him, or the men will attack her: "They would not touch my wife, or speak against her, but . . . they said if you were not my wife, they would have their revenge." He implies that they will rape her: " 'Revenge,' I think, 'is the best term for what they threatened; if I told you their threats your hair would turn grey—and it would be a pity to turn such pretty hair grey.' " She appeals to the chivalry of a cynical dwarf, and he helps her escape, only to be disillusioned when they return to civilization and she abandons her feminine piety, saying, "Now what I want is a good stiff brandy and soda and then half a dozen cigarettes." [90]

Mary is chastened by this experience: mystical visions in the mountains have given her a sense of a higher reality, and she realizes as the dwarf descends into debauchery that she has failed him. Mary is still critical of Christian orthodoxy: she takes up "St. Paul upon the theme of women and hurl[s] it at her companions." [91] But Mary has learned a lesson in the mountains and Dougall has her realize her "true" womanly duty in the conclusion of the novel: "All those other men . . . could be turned into any sort of beautiful thing that one chose, if there were women to do it, and the women were angels." [92] The conclusion is a conservative one: that Mary's lack of piety has left her vulnerable to the men's "selfishness." The New Woman abandons the power of moral womanhood at her peril.

What are we to make of these "romances"? Dougall delivers the culturally mandated romance plot but does so half-heartedly, with per-functory marriages to compliant men. We might read these marriages as pointing to a new future when men and women could marry as equals, if the unions were not so lacking in passion, and if there were not so many ambiguities. Star's husband is a thief. Flora's is an imbecile. Lovereen and Sophia's are butchers. The suspicion that these marriages were concessions to popular taste is confirmed by a curious twelve-page summary found in her papers, "Synopsis of *Earthly Purgatory*." The synopsis slightly alters the story by marrying off the two couples at the end "to give it a happier ending." [93] Dougall's description of an awkward courtship in "Lovereen," her most unguarded story, provides further insight. Throughout the novel, Lovereen has been learning to dance. Her dancing, perfected alone in her bedroom, is described as hypnotic, pagan, and sexual: "all the motion of the natural world—the swirl and rush of the water, the swoop of the birds, and the wind in the forest trees—became as threaded for the web of her dance . . . she hid the thing as a maiden hides a guilty love." (The word *guilty* has been crossed out and replaced with *secret*.)[94] Lovereen is caught dancing by her first suitor, the cosmopolitan Gilbert, who wishes to marry her and display her talents in a Paris salon (Paris was understood to be the center of sexual license, as Dougall makes clear in the text). On the last page of the manuscript, Lovereen chooses to dance for Paul, in the culmination of what is a painfully self-conscious courtship:

> To talk and think of plans for life was nothing new to them, but to realise that they were lovers—that was very new. Lovereen felt shy; she walked away a few steps and turned from him. Paul followed her only with his eyes—which were alight with the glad joy of absolute possession. . . .
> "Paul," she said, turning with an effort and coming nearer to him, "I would like to show you something. At least it's not a thing, it's something I can do. I want you to see it." This very shyly.
> [She bangs her cymbals and dances for him.]
> Paul sat breathless. Lovereen—his own Lovereen—seemed suddenly to have become identified with that part of things which we call nature. He saw her dance; beyond, below the slope, the tree tops began at the same moment to sway with the breeze of sunrise. . . . Her low breathless song was only part of the hum of the wind—just as she was part of the morning. . . .
> "I am so glad you like it. I will dance for you often." . . .
> "O, Paul," she said, "you are good, You shall lead me and I shall follow."
> The first long ray from the suns bright disc touched them just there. Paul turned her face toward it.
> "No, love, no," he said. "The Light shall lead, and we shall walk hand in hand." [95]

The moment is suitably egalitarian, but curiously lacking in erotic tension. Paul does not join Lovereen in the dance. Lovereen's dancing appears to represent her awakening sexuality. It is only partly directed at Paul, and he, as I observed in the last chapter, plays a curious role in the text. In the first part of the book, he represents the masculine intellectual drives that Lily could not write into a young woman like Lovereen; in this conclusion he might represent Sophie. Lily's pet name for Sophie was Butcher—and Paul makes the unlikely decision to give up a scholarly career to take up his uncle's work as grocer and butcher. This is not the only time she makes a male lover a butcher: in *What Necessity Knows* Sophia's decision to spurn a minister for a butcher is a central plot device.

The concluding marriages of most of the women in Dougall's novels are alternatives to a more coercive heterosexuality; marriages are places where women find financial security, social acceptance, and companionship within a culture of compulsory heterosexuality. They also offer a narrative retreat from the possibility of same-sex love. Patricia Smith has described "lesbian panic," the consequence when lesbian authors cannot confront their own desire, and retreat mid-text from the implications of the scenes they have created; the concept can be usefully applied to Dougall's fiction.[96] Immediately after Marian and Star announce their love for each other, in *Beggars All,* Star reconciles with her husband, and the ambiguity continues to the conclusion when their loving companionship is undercut by the expectation of the husband's eventual return. In *The Madonna of a Day* Dougall inserts a doting male cousin between Mary and her older female companion. She makes the two women in *The Earthly Purgatory* sisters. Over time, as women's relations became pathologized by sexologists, we can trace a retreat in Dougall's novels, from Flora and Lovereen's innocent intimacy, and Marian's declarations of love, to the indisputably asexual relationship of two sisters in *The Earthly Purgatory.* Was this a retreat from a plot line Dougall could not write? From the "impossibility" of same-sex love?

Dougall's novels do not suggest an asexual (or to use Terry Castle's terms, a "boringly chaste") woman. They are the work of a woman who is fascinated by sexuality: by the play of power in marriage and the potential for violence in heterosexual relations. The story they tell is of a woman breaking with the conventions of compulsory heterosexuality, and exulting in her independence and freedom. If my reading of the dance is correct, Dougall was also exulting in the discovery of an autonomous eroticism. It is only the evidence in Lily's papers that suggests that this eroticism found an object in Sophie—and Sophie ensured that their privacy would be protected.

The literature on modern lesbian identity exists in a different scholarly universe from that on theological liberalism.[97] In *The Madonna of a Day*, Dougall draws the connections between sexuality and religion. Mary says modern women should be respected for their lack of hypocrisy in their relations with men and their relations with God: "She may make good honest friendships with men instead of flirting with them in a ballroom; and if she doesn't believe in religion she can stay at home instead of continuing to keep up a respectable sham."[98] The novel's disturbing conclusion is that women who abandon the "respectable sham" of religion are vulnerable to male sexual violence. Mary says that she was victimized because the lumbermen were backward and associated her "new-fangled notions" with the loss of virtue, but the missionary argues that she was helpless against their sexual demands if she did not believe in a higher ideal: "It is this holy ideal reflected in good women that men worship in such sort that they can subdue selfishness in its presence. Without it . . . you are nothing more than an object of selfish delight . . . and nothing can save you from becoming the victim of man's selfishness because he is stronger than you." Earp reiterates this conclusion in a letter to a reviewer in *The Queen*. Earp argues that honesty alone would not have saved Mary:

> Mary was obliged to abandon her own ideal: it was too low to serve here: a little vulgarity more or less—even a good deal less—would not have saved her. . . . Is not the dominating reflection with which the story leaves us this. That to be one's honest self (is not enough to make a good woman) (is not a rule which will suffice to live by).[99]

It appears that Dougall was to select her choice of concluding phrases. This appeal to a higher ideal does not, however, mean recourse to false piety, or to the formal pieties of the church. Mary had been vehement about this: "I don't believe in the little humdrum rules and regulations that men make for women. . . . It is only since we began to shake ourselves free from the superstitions of religion that we have *begun* to have laws that are just for women." She insists that our ideals arise from the "developing moral consciousness of the world, not sent down from heaven," and she argues that these ideals have progressed since Christ's day and must be separated from the superstitions of that era. A missionary (speaking, it appears, for Dougall) argues that this moral consciousness is "the outcome of man's dealing with the spirit of God, is indeed that very kingdom of Heaven which is within us," but he wisely decides not to press the point. They agree that most Christians are misled by leaders who "teach that piety consists in some old rule of life, rather than in that attitude of the soul which ever seeks fresh wisdom from above." [100]

The first point is that women need recourse to a higher power. The second point is that this power cannot be found in church orthodoxy. Although Dougall's novels were strongly spiritual: "a profound realization," one critic wrote, "of the unseen forces and unknown currents which mould the life of man," [101] they were critical, even hostile to the masculine authority of the church. Dougall's challenges to ecclesiastical authority were indirect at first, expressed in oblique comments, in tangential references, and in silences in her fiction. Her opinions were frequently revealed by what was not said, rather than by any openly critical statement, by the very absence of clerical authority in novels that centered on moral and spiritual dilemmas. Ministers simply do not figure in the extended discussions of faith and belief. Instead, the moral and spiritual leaders are either well-educated young women or older men—often visionary lay evangelicals.

The narrator of "Lovereen," for example, is dismissive of preachers: "They were a motley collection, both young and old, some of them were of gentle birth and superior minds; for the most part they had little to recommend them except their strict religious views and the diligence with which they adhered to their work." [102] Nor were Anglicans worthy of respect: the minister is complacent and the Tractarian priest is "weak and fanatical." [103] In *Beggars All*, a Baptist preacher is a moral figure, but he has left the church to work as a servant, and the most spiritual character is an older woman. The spurned minister in *What Necessity Knows* is portrayed as a social climber, more concerned about maintaining his social position than about religious or moral values. Similarly, in *The Mermaid*, the minister is a poor shadow beside Madame Le Maître. In *Madonna of a Day*, a missionary rather than a minister speaks for Christianity; he does not speak with authority, but rather with the voice of experience as a worker in the church. In *The Zeit-Geist*, Dougall writes of the minister, "His heart was better than his head, as is the case of all small-minded souls that have come into conscious contact with God, but his opinions ruled his official conduct." [104] Even the evangelical preacher, whose personal faith gives him a closer relationship with God, is imprisoned by his creeds: "The hard outline of his creed had grown luminous, fringed with the divine light from beyond, as the bars of prison windows grow dazzling and fade when the prisoner looks at the sun." [105] Another rather inconsequential minister figures in *The Spanish Dowry:*

> The rector was always running about the village, and holding services and preaching. He was so good that he lived up to his ideals, and so lacking

in goodness that his ideals were such as he could live up to. The climax of importance in the village was the rector's wife. . . . [who] always wore a bonnet with a high feather which was, indeed, the very type and summary of her attitude towards all mankind. . . . [I]t was obvious she conceived of the Infinite as being something very fashionable and aristocratic.[106]

Dougall is at her most condescending with her portrayal of the weak and vindictive Anglican minister and the self-satisfied Nonconformist in *Paths of the Righteous*. Harold Anson, who knew her at the end of her life, recalled Dougall's cutting comments about parish priests. He commented: "She had naturally, I think, a rather sharp and mordant critical facility, which she made great efforts to keep under control." [107]

Dougall rarely describes her characters attending church. Religious experiences take place in fields and forests or among the mountains. Nor do the other accoutrements of religious institutions figure in her work. There is not much evidence of Sunday School, mission work, charitable organizations, or the multitude of social service agencies that were emerging from women's work in the church. In *Beggars All*, Dougall is highly critical of religious philanthropy. She depicts the humiliation and desperate poverty of a family forced to rely upon their chapel's charity, and the immorality of a man raised without love in an orphanage. Dougall argues that true charity must be offered as part of a personal relationship, rooted in a personal spirituality, and must be part of wider social reform. Her position bypasses the role of the church as an intermediary, by calling for more personal charity and a more political reform.

This anticlericalism is the natural corollary of the gender relations in Dougall's novels. It is no surprise that Lily Dougall's independent young women would have little patience for pompous ministers; no surprise that young women who had found the strength to escape abusive men were also rejecting restrictive religious precepts. But for those who might miss the connections between ecclesiastical authority and women's oppression, Dougall spells it out clearly in one early story, "Thrift," published in *Temple Bar*.

In "Thrift," a dying woman tells a priest that years ago she murdered her husband by leading him, blind drunk, to a hole in the ice, in order to build a better life for their children. The woman is not making a confession to the priest, rather she is making an accusation and telling the Catholic Church that it erred in pressing her to marry. A Catholic priest had tricked her as a young girl into marrying a widower with five children. "Marry, and marry, and marry—that's what you priests in my young days were for ever preaching to us poor folk." "I hear that you priests are at it yet. 'Marry, and marry, and marry.' . . . I thought before I died I'd just let ye know how one such marriage turned out." [108]

Lily Dougall's dismissal of clerical authority was not unusual. Canadian novels written by women at the turn of the century often presented ministers—the embodiment of the institutional church— as fools, hypocrites, and villains. Joanna Wood described the rapture of "the little Methodist parson" in her 1898 novel, *Judith Moore: or, Fashioning a Pipe:* "he had once dreamed of a loftier destiny than the life of a Methodist preacher, but that was long past; still it was sweet to recall so vividly the season when his spirit had wings." [109] Even wives, daughters, and cousins of clergymen, such as Agnes Maule Machar, Marshall Saunders, L. M. Montgomery, and Alice Chown were critical of the church.[110] Suffrage advocates like Flora MacDonald Denison and Frances Marion Beynon were scathing: Beynon described the church as the "leading hound in the pack of social tyrannies which try to drive the fine free souls of men to uniformity of thought." [111] These women were all liberals or radicals, whether measured theologically or in terms of their gender politics, and most worked within female net- works.[112] Dougall's anticlericalism, then, was not unusual among Canadian women novelists, and seems to be linked to gender affilia- tion. It is not that these women had lost their faith in God, just that their God was best found outside the church and away from ministers. Revelation, in their novels, comes from sunsets and forests, and divine truth is ascertained by a mystical apprehension in the natural order, rather than by God breaking through that order with miracles. Dougall's bite was sharper, and her understanding of philosophical and theological developments more acute, but the underlying direction of her thought was widely shared.

The Broad Church movement provided a route past masculine cleri- cal authority. The Broad Church was at heart a battle for the reconfigu- ration of power and authority; reformers were fighting for the voice of the rational individual against the traditional authority of the church. It was a struggle with multiple resonances for the woman movement.

5
Personal Idealism

That busy mart of mind, where men may sell
their lore their dreams; where folly for a song
may run and buy ideas all day long;
where all the world delights to hear and tell.[1]

Lily Dougall

SOPHIE EARP RECALLED THAT Dougall spent early 1894 in Oxford "making connections and forming friendships, which increased and became ever more important in her life from this time on."[2] She returned to Oxford in 1895 and, again, for an extended stay, in 1896, and even after she moved back to North America in 1897, she made trips to Oxford in 1899 and 1900. In 1902, feeling lonely in Canada, she said "everything draws and draws at my heart strings—the sea, the English shore, the friendship, the work, Oxford—Is there need to say more? the last word includes so much. Since I *cannot* live in Canada, Oxford is nearer home than anywhere else."[3] Finally, in 1911, Dougall moved permanently to Cumnor, just outside Oxford. She stayed there until her death in 1923.

What was the attraction to Oxford? The presence of other educated women was important: the university town offered a strong female academic community and, not coincidentally, an active community of liberal Anglicans. But the central attraction was likely the intellectual climate, created in part by these women, which in the 1890s was imbued with Edward Caird's idealist philosophy.[4] Increasingly from 1894, Dougall's novels became lighthearted vehicles for an idealist philosophy. Idealism provided respectable intellectual grounding for Dougall's immanent faith: a philosophical frame for Lovereen's faith that "God is in all things, that his life flows through us as through all nature."[5] Idealism also provided Dougall an explanation for the variety of religious expression in her North American youth, and her differences with her family's evangelicalism: religious belief was an evolutionary expression of the Hegelian world spirit coming to consciousness.

Idealism has been described by historians as a spiritual cul-de-sac, the first step toward a secular outlook, but Dougall did not blindly follow the philosophers down a blind alley. When the abstractions of absolute idealism threatened the personal elements of faith, Dougall turned to the relational philosophy of personal idealism. Personal idealism was a philosophy that reconciled Dougall's deep sense of a relationship with God with idealist thought, and conformed to the interlocking friendships of her female community.

It is not a simple matter to trace the philosophical currents in Lily Dougall's novels. As we have seen, Dougall had learned as a young girl to approach ideas sideways. Early letters show her deploying elaborate strategies to head off criticism; she toyed with ideas, asserting them, but at the same time denying and undermining their import. She stated opinions and retracted them at once, slipping away from any assertion of authority with light and apparently easy humor. Reporting to her father on the most controversial issue in the Scottish Church, Robertson Smith's heresy trial, she parried: "I have not been able to *study* [Smith's] views. Of course, I am not capable of forming an opinion as to their truth, and I have none." [6] In an early novella, *Rosemary for Remembrance,* Dougall described her own playful philosophizing. The central character, Annabel, perplexes a pompous visiting artist by refusing to take him or his ideas seriously. She teases him by spinning tall stories and pokes fun at his need for literal truth. The suitor decides against proposing to her, concluding, "No man wishes to be constantly surprised by his wife's theories, or to feel that at any moment he may become the victim of her love of fun." [7] The story, as Lorraine McMullen has pointed out, is clearly autobiographical, and it includes a fascinating defense of the play of imagination. When the suitor accuses Annabel of "telling falsehoods," she replies,

> You are an artist. You know that if two men sit down to paint the same thing, the one will fill his canvas with cold browns and neutral tints, while the other will have a hundred bright colours in little dashes here and there. Is it that one man is untrue, or is it that, with a keener eye, he sees more truth than the other? [8]

The suitor's idea of truth is dismissed as mere "verbal accuracy"; she points out that a painter might better capture the truth of a scene than a photographer and concludes, "to reverence truth is to see beyond the

Hilda Diana Oakeley, 1900. Lily Dougall's close friend Hilda Diana Oakeley (1867–1950) had studied at Somerville College, Oxford, but was denied a degree as a woman. When she came to McGill University, Montreal, to teach philosophy and act as warden of the new women's college, Royal Victoria College, she was given a B.A. and M.A., and was the first woman to be granted an honorary degree at McGill. She subsequently taught philosophy at King's College, London, England. *Courtesy Notman Photographic Archives, McCord Museum of Canadian History, II-133286.1.*

outside of things—to try to see the Power that makes them what they are. . . ." [9] Dougall is saying that Annabel, in playing with the truth, and painting it bright, comes closer to a higher reality than her didactic suitor.

Unlike Annabel's fictional suitor, Lily Dougall's new British friends were delighted by intelligent foolishness—"talking metaphysics," as T. B. Kilpatrick had put it, "behind a row of peas." [10] Mary Walker recalled, "[Lily] would turn from the study of Jevon's *Logic* to repeat with glee verses from *Alice in Wonderland*." [11] Earp commented,

Lily Dougall, as I remember her then—nearly forty years ago—showed the same combination of high seriousness and irrepressible humor which has always struck her friends. In most people, who distinctly possess both qualities, one or the other seems to predominate; but in her one felt the one was as natural and fundamental as the other. She could turn from the whole-hearted enjoyment of a witty saying or a comical situation to the equally whole-hearted consideration of a problem of conduct or of theology or *vice versa* with the utmost ease, and with no sense of incongruity. [12]

With their support, Dougall felt comfortable writing both "high seriousness and irrepressible humour" into her fiction. She speaks through metaphor and melodrama: mermaids offer transcendence, Madonnas offer redemption, and coal gas flames offer revelation. Oxford ideas arise in the unschooled backwoods of Canada, and Hegel speaks through drunkards. The genre allowed her to voice metaphysical interests without taking herself too seriously and without losing her femininity. It was not simply that the melodrama was a mask for a didactic metaphysics, for Dougall clearly delighted in the play of metaphor and understood herself, like Annabel, to be painting "in a hundred bright colors" that told of a higher truth than "verbal accuracy."

This playful philosophizing can leave the modern reader in the uncomfortable position of Annabel's perplexed suitor. Because Dougall assumes her reader to be fairly well educated and familiar with the late-nineteenth-century intellectual landscape, she rarely identifies the source of her ideas. Thomas Carlyle is never mentioned, but his ideas are central to Dougall's work. When Paul explains to Lovereen that he does not question spiritual truth—"What needs investigation is the form in which this spiritual truth comes *clothed* to us"—he is paraphrasing Carlyle's *Sartor Resartus* (1833–1834) a book Dougall probably read when she took classes in Edinburgh from Carlyle's disciple, David Masson, if not before.[13] Lovereen extends the metaphor, developing Paul's thoughts in a typically pantheistic direction: "The facts men dispute about are only the garment He wore for the time; but everything is just as much this garment—the sunlight on the snow, the wind in the trees, the beautiful thoughts that come to our minds."[14] Carlyle's *Sartor Resartus* (the "Tailor Retailored") describes the "Philosophy of Clothes" in which the externals of religion, the clothing, are discarded for the central core of faith:

> Church clothes are, in our vocabulary, the Forms, the *Vestures,* under which men have at various times embodied and represented for themselves the Religious Principle. . . . [I]n our era of the World, those same Church clothes have gone sorrowfully out at elbows: nay, for worse, many of them have become mere hollow Shapes, or Masks, under which no living Figure or Spirit any longer dwells; but only spiders and unclean beetles, in horrid accumulation, drive their trade; the Mask still glares on you with its glass eyes, in ghastly affectation of Life—some generation and a half after Religion has quite withdrawn from it, and in unnoticed nooks is weaving for herself new Vestures, wherewith to reappear, and bless, our sons and grandsons.[15]

Carlyle's idealist metaphor—that the creeds of the church are only so much worn clothing that hides the life of the Spirit—runs through "Lovereen" and much of Dougall's later work.[16]

Dougall wrote her most philosophical novel, *The Zeit-Geist*, in 1894, on board ship to Canada after her first visit to Oxford. It appears that she was reading Edward Caird's latest work, *The Evolution of Religion* (1893). Later that summer, as she struggled with the contradictions between her family's evangelicalism and her own liberal ideas at a Christian Alliance summer camp, the full implications of idealist thought dawned on her. She wrote to Sophie Earp,

> I can't ever say what that book of Caird's has been to me. It has united things that seem hopelessly separate (although one felt that there must be a union some place) and it has given everything a place and a satisfactory place, in the big whole of things. I never felt how really satisfying Caird's solution was, until I thought his book quietly over in the very midst of these great meetings.[17]

On her return to Oxford in 1895, Dougall became acquainted with Caird and his wife. Caird was known for his habitual reserve, and Dougall tells a delightful story of her first encounter with him at a dinner, when, misunderstanding the introduction to the "Master of Balliol," she took Caird for an elderly relative of her hostess, and only discovered his true identity after a few hours of conversation. She seems to have charmed both Caird and William Wallace, White's Professor of Philosophy at Merton College, and over the next months she cultivated a relationship with them, walking and boating with both men and their wives.[18] The social aspects facilitated more intellectual ambitions; just as she had plied Edinburgh acquaintances with questions, she now turned to these eminent philosophers. They were intimidating company: "I felt like Thackeray's snob walking on Piccadilly with a duke on either arm, or rather, I should like to have felt like that; I only felt sleepy and unable to converse. I think I am the stupidest person in conversation I ever met."[19] A letter from Caird, dated May 4, 1896, indicates that she considered sitting in on his lectures at Oxford. He was an advocate of women's education, and welcomed her, saying, "I suppose you will not mind being the only lady present," but she moved back to Montreal that fall, and does not appear to have taken him up on the offer.[20]

Caird's *Evolution of Religion* was in effect a philosophical elaboration of Carlyle's metaphor of old clothes:

> The history of religion is but the history of the different symbols which have successively risen into prominence and then worn themselves out to make way for better, or which, to use the fundamental metaphor of Carlyle, have been cast aside like old clothes, that humanity might reinvest itself in the garment of a new faith.[21]

Caird described the evolution of religious ideas in dialectical Hegelian terms: each successive phase of thought represented another stage in the self-consciousness of what Hegel called Spirit and Caird interpreted as God. God was "a self-revealing Spirit, whose revelation reaches its culmination in the intellectual and moral life of man." [22] Caird's use of evolution to account for the varied and changing forms of religious faith allowed Dougall to reconcile her liberal ideas with the Calvinism of her grandparent's generation. Her parents' Calvinist theology was the outworn clothing within which the spirit had appeared to an earlier generation. His formulations gave, as Dougall put it, "everything a place and a satisfactory place, in the big whole of things." [23]

Idealism provided a philosophical grounding for Dougall's immanent faith. An idealist God was no longer transcendent, an unknowable ideal, but was realizing himself through nature and through man. Taken too far (or for some theologians simply taken this far) idealism could become pantheism. An immanent God lost his identity, and became indistinguishable from the natural world and from man. A further implication of the immanent God working through history is that the miraculous becomes redundant. A miracle, if understood as a break in the natural process, or an intervention by God in natural law, is unnecessary in a world in which the natural law itself is the working through of God's purpose. God expresses himself through the working out of the natural law and has no need to break through it. Similarly, revelation is a continuous process, part of the ongoing self-consciousness of Spirit. Rather than God's voice breaking into the natural world, revelation is part of that world coming to realize itself. This had implications for the understanding of Christ. Instead of the emphasis on the atonement—a momentous turning point in man's relation with God—the emphasis shifted to creation and incarnation. Christ became understood as the highest moment of man's self-consciousness. He was the realization of the potential for God in all men.

Idealist philosophy gave Dougall new confidence. She developed her ideas in a series of mystical and almost pantheistic novels published in quick succession in 1895: *Question of Faith, The Mermaid, The Madonna of a Day,* and *The Zeit-Geist.* Her purpose is most apparent in *The Zeit-Geist.* [24] Dougall gave drafts of the novel to both Caird and William Wallace, and Wallace discussed it with her at some length. It would be interesting to know what Caird made of the novel, for Dougall had not lost her sense of humor, and on one level the story was stock melodrama. The setting is a dank swamp, filled with the standing corpses of drowned trees. The main characters are Bart Toyner, an alcoholic who is only saved from the bottle by his newfound evangelical faith; Ann Markham, the beautiful beer-brewer he loves; and her father, a murderer. The plot involves midnight assignations in the swamp, ghostly appari- tions, Bart's near-death at the hands of the murderer, and his rescue by Ann.

Bart's experience of an immanent God is both bizarre and pro- found. (It is significant that in this, Dougall's most philosophical novel, she created a main character who, like Paul in "Lovereen," might be taken more seriously than a woman.) He is hit on the head by the mur- derer and lies unconscious in the swamp for two days. Ann takes him to an Edenic cabin in the woods, where he experiences a form of heightened consciousness:

> [H]is heart in its waking felt after something else around and beneath and above him, everywhere, something that meant light and comfort and rest and love, something that was very strong, that was strength; he himself, Bart Toyner, was part of this strength and rested in it with a rest and refreshing . . . it came to him he had made a great mistake . . . he had thought, he had actually thought that God was only part of things; that he, Bart Toyner could turn away from God; that God's power was only with him when he supposed himself to be obedient to Him! Yes, he had thought this; but now he knew that God was all and in all.[25]

Although it was precipitated by a bump on the head, Bart's was a mys- tical experience. Dougall had read widely among mystics as a young girl, and she now drew upon Johannes Eckhart, the father of German mysticism, to describe Bart's appreciation of spiritual reality as the "eter- nal now": "Bart looked around upon the trees and flowers and upon her with happy eyes that had no hint of past or future in them. Something of the secret of all peace—the *Eternal Now* remained with him as long as the weakness of the injury remained." [26]

The new God that Bart discovered in the swamp is, of course, an ide- alist one. Edward Caird had described God as an "an ultimate unity which underlies and embraces 'all thinking objects, all objects of all thought.' " [27] Dougall wrote that God is in everything, that "nothing is ever outside of Him." Individuals are expressions of his reality: "our minds are just bits of His mind." "The life that was in them all was all of God, every impulse, every act." [28] Bart's experience in the swamp serves as a (somewhat improbable) example of the emerging self-consciousness of the Hegelian world Spirit. "[Toyner's] was a life which shows that a man cut off from all contact with his brother thinkers may still be worked on by the great oversoul of thought. . . ." [29] Bart is supposed to have come upon these truths alone, after "years of desultory browsing in popular science and the one year of gospel and prayer" (as well as the abovementioned bump on the head).[30] Without education, or even contact with modern thinkers, Bart had stumbled upon all the truths of idealist philosophy. "No one had told him about the Pantheism which obliterates moral distinctions, or told him of the subjective ideal which sweeps aside material delight. He only felt after the realities expressed by these phrases and dimly perceived that the truth lies midway in between, and that truth is the mind of God and can only be lived not spoken."[31] As one skeptical reviewer noted: "The hero's acquaintance with men and with books—the latter limited, it would appear, to the Bible, 'paper-covered infidel books, and popular books on modern science,'—is when his surroundings, parentage and education are taken into account, by no means sufficient to make proba-ble the splendid theories and practices to which he eventually attains."[32] Neither Caird nor Hegel is mentioned in the novel. Hegel's influence is suggested by the title, but as most reviewers missed the point, one assumes that few readers recognized it.[33]

The novel was given prominence as the first in a new series of "pocket novels," called *The Zeit-Geist Library*, but it met mixed reviews. *The Inquirer* noted that the book represented "the spirit that animates the best work and thought of present-day leaders, preachers, writers and philanthropists."[34] *Church Times*, a conservative Anglican journal (which Dougall later parodied as the *Church Chimes*), took offense at the pantheism of the novel: "This book is intensely purposeful and intensely dull. It shows how a man may attain to Pantheism and a firm belief in the Indefinite and Pervasive by the simple process of being knocked on the head and left in a swamp to die."[35] Other reviewers described the book as "a religious tract," "a sermon," "a study in religious psychology," "a theological disquisition of mystical flavour," "a heavy web of theol-ogy," and "a theological treatise."[36] It fell between two stools, neither convincing as fiction or sound theology. One reviewer mused, "We are at a loss as to how to classify this little book. It is not a story exactly—it is not a theological essay—nor would it be quite true to call it a com-bination of the two."[37] A more perceptive reviewer noted: "But Toyner, throughout, is mainly a peg on which to hang doctrine, and we have a feeling that his experiences are mainly devised to provide the oppor-tunity for his preachings which are long, eloquent and sometimes obscure."[38]

In *The Mermaid*, Dougall presents an even more jarring juxtaposi-tion of melodrama and theology. The story intrigued reviewers, who described it as eccentric, outlandish, original, and weird, but sales were low. One reviewer summarized the plot: "How the Mermaid first intro-duced herself as the heroine of a sea myth, and thereafter proved to be a gracious lady, whose influence raised the rather sluggish and

commonplace, though educated, Dr. Caius Simpson to the appreciation of things transcendental." [39] The book is a romance: Caius falls in
love with a reclusive woman, Madame Le Maître, and is bewitched by
the appearance of a mermaid, who, it transpires, is Le Maître swim-
ming in costume. After many plot twists, including the brief reappearance and fortuitous accidental death of the abusive Monsieur Le
Maître, Caius wins her heart. But the book is also theology: throughout the long and convoluted novel, the mermaid symbolizes another
reality, the breakthrough of the transcendent into the daily world. Scott
Swanson observes that the final destruction of the mermaid costume in
The Mermaid is compared with the rending of the curtain in the holy
temple in Matthew 27:51. Upon its rending, the natural and supernatural worlds become one. [40]

The third novel published in 1895, *The Madonna of a Day*, also toys
with bizarre but transformative spiritual experiences. A remote camp
of rough lumbermen is transformed when Mary appears on Christmas
Eve. They believe she is a Madonna; they are wrong, but the experience
wakes a higher sensibility in the men. A degraded dwarf is temporarily
reformed in response to her apparent piety and womanly vulnerability.
For her part, Mary has a spiritual experience when, in a moment of
extremity, she sees a distant mountain and a burning light. (The light,
like the Madonna, turns out to be a natural phenomenon—a coal gas
leak kept lit by the men.)

Dougall's subjects find the divine in the strangest places: in mermaids,
Madonnas, and burning lights. Frequently they discover that these occurrences are false revelations, that the mermaid is a swimmer, the Madonna
a New Woman, and the light nothing but a coal gas leak. But the discovery of the mundane reality behind the visions does not diminish their
power. The visions work their changes in the lives of those around them:
through the vision of the mermaid, Caius meets a reclusive contemplative woman; through the false Madonna, the ugly dwarf realizes (temporarily) a truer ideal; and through the coal gas the Madonna herself has
insight into a higher reality. Dougall's provocative message is an idealist
one (although Edward Caird might not recognize his paternity). She is
suggesting that God does not work through extraordinary miracles,
whether these be biblical miracles or mermaids, Virgin mothers or false
Madonnas. Rather, God is present in the world and works through natural law. God is realized through mystical flashes of insight, momentary
breakthroughs that Dougall understood as the workings of a romantic
Higher Reason, and part of the rational framework of Platonic idealism.

The moral elements are more muted in Dougall's subsequent novels, *The Earthly Purgatory*, or *The Summit House Mystery* (published under

different titles in the United States and Britain; 1904–1905) and *The Spanish Dowry* (1906).[41] Her last novel, *The Paths of the Righteous* (1908), was, however, sent back by her publisher for revision. George Macmillan suggested that particular care had to be taken with religious books, and said: "You have to a considerable extent sacrificed your story to your purpose which we take to be a plea for liberal thought and practice in religious matters." He finally decided to publish it regardless of profitability, but his initial assessment proved accurate and sales of the book were disappointing.[42] Dougall attempted one final fictional explication of her ideas. Her manuscript, *Corchestor of the Future,* was refused by Macmillan for a familiar reason, her importation of theology into fiction. Their reader had judged that the book would have the same fate as its predecessor, to be "praised by the papers but not eagerly read by the public." George Macmillan wrote sympathetically, "To this definite criticism [the reader] adds this comment, with which I am inclined to agree, that in his opinion you would have a better chance as a writer of fiction if you would refrain from introducing current topics whether in theology or politics. This may seem a hard saying for I imagine that it is these questions which interest you most."[43] Macmillan was correct in his assessment of Dougall's interests, and she subsequently focused on religious writing.

Although Edward Caird's concept of an idealist God solved a number of philosophical difficulties, Dougall was troubled by the potential loss of a personal God—the childhood friend beside her always. An immanent abstract God, who is everywhere, is by the same token effectively nowhere. If "our minds are just bits of his mind" and our souls attain their ultimate expression through dissolution in the eternal Spirit, then the relationship between man and God is lost. Dougall observed that Caird's rational approach to prayer left out this "childlike element":

> Don't you think that people like Prof. Caird, and all the modern people who *reason* about prayer, are apt to find their only mental power to believe in its efficacy to consist in submerging the individual will entirely (obliterating it) and while in *one sense* this is what God works out in the heart, in another sense, it borders on fatalism and does truly eliminate all the childlike element from prayer—the one element that is so pronounced in all Bible teaching about prayer and is so utterly at variance with our ideas of the possible.[44]

The question of petitional prayer raises the difficulty in an acute form, for it implies a direct and personal relationship with a responsive and interventionist God. Dougall had never been able to give up her faith in petitional prayer. As she told Earp, "I have never been able to shake off the certainty of the reality of a spiritual power to which I could turn for help." [45] In March 1891, worried about the prospects for publishing *Beggars All,* she prayed directly for success. In her diary she wrote,

> March 11 Had told S. [Sophie Earp] could not pray for what wanted most. Asked how [tried?] for that day and next and next.
> March 13 At night seemed to have answer that book would be successful.
> March 19 [Small picture of a bird] from Do [a pet name for Earp]. Longman [a British publisher] had taken book.[46]

She explained further in a letter to Earp:

> I have been trying to hope about it and pray about it in the right way, but all my want about it seems selfish—just your pleasure and mine, not the highest best thing one should desire—that His will should be done. I don't know how to say the thoughts I think, but I think so many, and I feel as if I were growing into a new way of looking at life a little bit, or perhaps a big bit—I hardly know. I used to think the highest was to be content that God's will should be done with one's self and one's work. Now I felt as if there was something false about it, if one cannot pray most about what one desires most. Do you really desire most that our work should honour Him? Or that it should succeed?[47]

Earp balked at this idea of a direct response to prayer, and Dougall conceded that as a person progressed spiritually, he or she should ask for less selfish earthly good.[48] But Dougall could not abandon petitional prayer. "I have found lately that if I only take my questions and doubts very simply to Him, as if he were as near as He was to Martha and Mary, they are transformed and made right in some way." [49]

Richard Ostrander has observed that many liberals simply ignored the theological inconsistencies to retain a belief in petitional prayer.[50] Dougall confronted the dilemma when writing *The Zeit-Geist,* and turned to William Wallace for advice as to how to handle it:

> I told him as well as I could that my difficulty lay in knowing how far Toyner could go towards pantheism, and yet with good sense retain his belief in a God with whom he could hold communication. "Yes," said Mr. W. "I was wondering myself how far he could go." This was not very encouraging. He had a very shy, reserved manner, but Miss Keddie had told me he would have. He began telling me a little in what sense Hegel was a pantheist, but this was not practical enough for me. I explained to him that my difficulty was that I did not know whether, to a man who

held the personality of God, such phrases as "God is in all things"; "the devils live and move in God"; were good sense. He said that he thought 'the all" could not be considered external to God in any sense in which a man's actions could not be external to himself—i.e. he seemed to look upon the view that the self and not-self—the universe, whatever you may call it—was *not a thing made* by God, but a *present action of His,* as necessary to thought. That came pretty near what I wanted.[51]

In defining the question in terms of the "personality" of God, Lily Dougall was following a school of thought derived originally from German philosopher, Rudolph Hermann Lotze (1817–1881).[52] Lotze argued that the human individual was created by God but, once created, exists independent of God. As Dougall later put it, "pantheistic thought identifies the life of the universe with God; . . . it appears saner to regard life as the not-God, which came from God and is being trained by Him to form with Himself a new unity."[53] Reality is pluralistic—a society of persons in which God is the source and ground of all being, but also the ideal personality.[54] This approach later took form in a school of philosophy known in Britain as personal idealism and in United States as personalism.[55]

The roots of Dougall's personal idealism probably lay in the United States with Phillips Brooks. Brooks, who had been introduced to Lotze's work while Brooks was on a sabbatical trip to Germany in 1882, found in his ideas the potential for "holding both together, the personality of God and the divine life of the universe."[56] Dougall had referred to a "universe of unseen Personalities" in "Lovereen" and emphasized the "personal" nature of God's love as early as 1892.[57] But American personalism was slow to take hold in the universities in America, and it appears to have been Dougall's acquaintance with philosophical personal idealists in England that influenced her subsequent work.[58] Scottish theologian James Iverach, whose advice Dougall sought about her early fiction, was an early personal idealist.[59] And after writing *The Zeit-Geist,* Dougall became acquainted with such leading personal idealists as J. R. Illingworth, Hastings Rashdall, and Henry Scott Holland, collaborated on a book with A. S. Pringle Pattison in 1919, and worked on committees with the young William Temple. C. C. J. Webb published commentaries on her religious writing and attended her funeral.[60]

For Dougall, personal idealism functioned as a way to retain the personal God of her childhood within an idealist framework, to hold together, as Brooks had put it, the "personality of God and the divine life of the universe."[61] Personal idealists identified the loss of the individual personality as a problem in absolute idealism.[62] If the aim of all life was the merging of the soul in the absolute, then the individual self was lost. Similarly, God became all, losing his eminence and individuality.

The central experience of worship, the sense of relationship between God and the worshipper, was lost in the unity of all. As Dougall explained in 1916, following an argument developed by Hastings Rashdall: "There is a good deal of vague belief that union between God and man implies unity or Pantheism, God being in fact the All and there being nothing but God. This view, however, leaves no room for faith, because true faith, like true love, of which indeed it is but one aspect, involves an object other than the self that loves and trusts." [63] Just before her death in 1923, she wrote along similar lines:

> God came to be thought of, not as the object of knowledge, but as universal intelligence interpenetrating human understanding. Modern philosophy is thus liable to lose sight of the distinction between Deity and humanity which is essential to the religion of Christ because love can only exist between distant natures, and man's love to God and God's love to man form the basis of Christian fellowship. [64]

Some distance between man and God was essential to retain a relationship.

A further implication of personalist thought, one that would be very influential in Dougall's later religious essays, was that the human personality was understood as "a poor and broken reflection" of the divine personality. [65] Illingworth had quoted Lotze, "Perfect personality is in God only; to all finite minds there is allotted but a pale copy thereof." [66] Dougall, like Illingworth, became slightly defensive about the implicit anthropomorphism in this line of thought. She wrote, "It may seem as though, by basing our capacity to know the goodness of God on some experience of goodness in human beings, we make God after our own likeness, thinking him merely a magnified man." This, however, is only one "aspect of His being, the one we can best know" and she insisted on the necessity of the "larger whole, totally inconceivable to us." [67] She rarely refers to this larger whole in her books, however; the continuing emphasis was upon the parallels between humanity and God. God is compared to a father, a gardener, and an artist. Dougall's argument is frequently circular, moving from the ideal man, to God, back to prescriptions for humanity. Even in her final book she wrote: "We have some reason to believe that what we know of our own nature, which is summed in what we call personality, gives us the best glimpse of God." [68]

Human relationships are similarly "broken reflections" of the highest relationship, that of union with God. "God is thus the very Ideal and Reality, the perfection and completion, of all that imperfectly attracts us in any human being." [69] Therefore, our love for God is like our love for a friend or lover, on a higher level. As Dougall wrote in the 1908 novel

Paths of the Righteous: "In the mystic's true vision of God all earthly loves become as shadows of one Reality, and there is nothing real but Love," and in 1916, "the message of the Incarnation, the Cross, the Resurrection, is this—that God is man's eternal lover." [70] But this is not the submissive relationship described in evangelical theology. Nor is it an exclusive relationship with God. Dougall's characters are free, independent beings; they are moving to a closer union with God, but do this by developing their own individual powers rather than renouncing their will. And rather than focusing on the single relationship with God they are highly aware of their relations with others and their mutual pursuit of a higher order.

The arguments of personal idealists have been dismissed by philosophers—even C. C. J. Webb in 1937 described personal idealism as a weltanschauung rather than a philosophy—but they were popular and filled the needs of people faced with the barren choice between scientific materialism and abstractions of absolute idealism.[71] Personal idealism allowed the subjective a place in theology, and as Dougall's intellectual development suggests it allowed the emotive and experiential elements of holiness and evangelical thought to continue to find a place within the liberal camp. It did so, however, without demanding the submission of individual will and the abdication of reason. Because the individual personality was an expression of the higher personality that was God, and because God's purpose was to be achieved through the development, rather then the denial, of this personality, personal idealism encouraged individual development and growth.

The emphasis in personalism on multiple relationships was particularly compatible with the interlocking world of relationships within which many middle-class women lived at the turn of the century. Relationships in personalism were egalitarian; all human souls were on one plane. More importantly, these were not independent individuals but, as Rashdall explains, a *community* of persons, an interlocking web of relationships, with a common origin and a higher purpose in God. As we have seen, Lily Dougall lived within a network of relationships, with Sophie Earp, with friends, and with a large extended family. Hastings Rashdall's description of the world of pluralist personal idealism would have been very familiar:

[T]he world is neither a single Being, nor many co-ordinate and independent Beings, but a One Mind who gave rise to many. We may of course, if we choose, describe the whole collection of these beings as One Reality, with enough capital letters to express the unaction which that numeral appears to carry with it for some minds; but after all the Reality, whether eternally or only at one particular stage of its development, is a community of persons.[72]

Personal idealism conformed to the new social reality of Dougall's life. The Calvinist emphasis on submission to a judgmental God had reinforced the patriarchal aspects of her childhood home. She rejected this God as she rebelled against the submissive role of the unmarried daughter. Dougall's mature theology was informed by the independence and mutuality of her adult relationships. Feminist scholars such as Carol Gilligan and Nancy Choderow have described the relational world of women and compared it to the drive for autonomy that characterizes a male world view.[73] This personalist theology, with its emphasis on egalitarian relationships, conforms closely to the world that Gilligan describes as prototypically female. We do not have to subscribe to essentialist notions of a "female world" to observe the extent to which personal idealism conformed to Dougall's particular social reality.

6

Christian Socialism: "The Kingdom of God within Us and around Us"

JUST AS DOUGALL APPEARED poised for success, with the publication of four novels within one year, she suffered a crisis of confidence. She retreated from Oxford to North America, and began to experiment with nonfiction, testing the waters first with a carefully researched piece of historical fiction, *The Mormon Prophet* (1899). Her first work of nonfiction, published anonymously as *Pro Christo et Ecclesia* (1900), won immediate acclaim among liberal thinkers in Britain; as a critic for *The Churchman* wrote in 1910: "The author of *Pro Christo et Ecclesia* has already established a sort of vogue. Who he [sic] is we do not know. . . ." [1] Dougall returned to Britain, wrote her last novels, *The Earthly Purgatory* (1904), *The Spanish Dowry* (1906), and the *Paths of the Righteous* (1908), and turned to religious writing with *Christus Futurus* (published in the United States as *The Christ that Is to Be*) (1907), *Absente Reo* (1910), *Voluntas Dei* (1912), and *The Practice of Christianity* (1913). [2]

Dougall's early religious essays are best interpreted as lyrical applications of F. D. Maurice's Christian socialism. [3] Historians have represented social reform as a departure from experiential faith; they argue that reformers abandoned an otherworldly religious vision for the realization of the Kingdom of God on earth. Dougall's interest in social reform, however, was grounded by a mystical sense of communion with God. In *Christus Futurus*, Dougall revised the Lord's Prayer to read, instead of "Thy Kingdom come," "Thy Kingdom be within and around us." [4] Her translation is a deliberate departure from the Greek that suggests a kingdom that is both within, in the form of a mystical experience of God, and around, in the form of the battle for social justice.

Dougall's visits to Oxford in 1894 and then over the winter of 1895–1896 had been exhilarating, but the lofty intellectual company was intimidating. She left Oxford in June and stayed in North America in the fall of 1896, researching *The Mormon Prophet*. In December 1896, her aunt became ill and Dougall traveled to Edinburgh to nurse her until she died in August 1897. Then Dougall returned to Canada to assist in caring for her numerous nieces and nephews. She set up a home in Montreal, and made connections with the other literary people, organizing a series of successful Jane Austen readings involving faculty from McGill University. She reluctantly embarked on a busy social life, dining, for example, with Lord and Lady Strathcona when they entertained the new Governor General and his wife, the Earl and Countess of Minto. "The time and thought and fag are what I grudge," she wrote, "but what am I here for . . . I would rather be amending my preface, but the fact always stares me in the face that I have no reason for being in Montreal if I don't 'do' society as far as I can on behalf of the family." [5] She stayed in North America, with trips back to England in 1899 and 1900, until 1902.

Dougall's writing, which had been surging ahead with the simultaneous publication of *The Zeit-Geist, Madonna of a Day, The Mermaid,* and *A Question of Faith,* came to a halt. She published only a collection of her short stories, *A Dozen Ways of Love,* in 1897, and although she started work on her next book in the fall of 1896, she struggled with feelings of depression and inadequacy for three years, and the *Mormon Prophet* was not completed until 1899.[6] Montreal was an intellectual backwater in comparison to Oxford, and, although she grew close to Hilda Oakeley, the head of the new women's college attached to McGill, Dougall missed the supportive and stimulating company of other progressive and intellectual women. She was affected by the distance—both physical and, apparently, emotional—between her and Earp.

While in Canada, Dougall became involved in a new publishing venture with her brothers as the editor of *World Wide, a Weekly Reprint of Articles from Leading Journals and Reviews Reflecting the Current Thought on Both Hemispheres.*[7] *World Wide* contained a selection of articles reprinted from leading British and American newspapers: political analysis and commentary, literary news and reviews, scientific reports, and, of course, liberal theological news.[8] It was aimed at the same audience as her novels, those well-educated and well-informed members of the middle and upper classes who were interested in cultural, political, and religious questions. Theology was a minor element in the review, overshadowed by politics and literature, but each issue usually contained at least one article by or about a liberal theologian, a review of a new book, or a sermon by Horace Bushnell or Phillips Brooks.

The return to North America slowly bolstered Dougall's ego. She was lionized in Boston, as she wrote Earp: "It has helped me in this way, that I have got back some of the self-confidence about writing that I have been without for some time." [9] Similarly, a positive response by an American publisher, Appleton, to *The Mormon Prophet,* in the spring of 1898, lifted her spirits temporarily—"I have been so oppressed for years with the fear that it was not worth doing, or that I had lost the art of doing it, that it is like a new lease on life." [10] She began to work on her first book of theology, *Pro Christo et Ecclesia* (1900), taking an earlier manuscript, "Theological Dramas" and revising it steadily over the summer of 1899.[11] Dougall did not even tell Earp about the project until September, and then swore her to secrecy. It was not an easy task:

> I am inclined to be terribly depressed about my work, but I try to resist that, as it can do no good, and I am far too useless physically to do anything else, so I may as well keep on. . . . It is three years since we have had any luck and the difficulty is all in this wretched brain of mine which won't work. I have such a lot of things sketched out in my mind that I want to do, but a whole day goes in getting a few things down, and then I am dissatisfied with the quality and tired out. Under these circumstances it seems folly to compete with people who can use their wits.[12]

She struggled against ill health, social demands, and her own insecurities: "sometimes I feel [the essays] are all rubbish, sometimes I feel quite inflated at their brilliancy; but they are dull work compared to a story, and nothing but dogged determination to get them off my mind would have kept me at them." [13] She finally finished the book in the autumn, by secluding herself in a deserted Quebec cabin.

As her letters indicate, Dougall was nervous about publishing her ideas. She had initially written them as a drama, and only gradually revised them into a theological essay. She relied upon Earp's criticism and Cambridge credentials to support her. "My chief comfort in the worry of deciding what to write has been that you will be very competent to criticise this sort of thing—the ethic, the logic, generally whether any part is worth saying or not." [14] She did not trust the book entirely to Earp's critical judgment, however, and, in a manner that was to become a pattern for her theological works, she ran at least parts of the book past the critical eye of the liberal founder and first principal of the newly established Congregationalist theological college at Oxford, Mansfield College, Dr. A. M. Fairbairn.[15]

The transition to religious writing was not an easy one. Melodramatic fiction had provided Dougall an acceptably feminine vehicle for her metaphysical speculations. Now she was venturing into a masculine and academic realm. It was not simply that Dougall lacked education; as a woman, she was considered to lack the faculty of understanding essential for theology. Christian socialist F. D. Maurice (who was, iron-ically, a champion of women's education) had argued that women cul-tivate the feelings that "embrace and comprehend the truth" and men cultivate the understanding. "Our faculty is worth nothing without theirs," he claimed, but it was the male faculty that underlay theology: "There probably does not exist a female in England who, in any proper sense of the word, can be said to possess a knowledge of theology . . . merely an edifying proof that women, unless it shall be thought expe-dient to give them a scientific education, never can become theolo-gians."[16] Reviewers of her fiction had often assumed that "L. Dougall" was a man; those who knew better commented on her "masculine" command of theology.[17]

Dougall adopted different strategies to overcome this prejudice against women theologians. She sometimes made a virtue of theologi-cal innocence. Hannah Whitall Smith had argued that women could not do theology: "but remember that God sometimes reveals, even to Babes, secrets that he has hidden from the wise and prudent."[18] Women, like babies, could be pure vehicles of God's truth. One of Dougall's pro-tagonists says (while giving spiritual advice to a priest): "I am no the-ologian, I am only a disappointed woman," and Dougall herself assumes the common sense voice of a layperson while lecturing a minister about his duties in *Absente Reo*.[19] Increasingly, however, Dougall wrote with the new-found, and still halting, voice of women academics, who spoke with the authority of their studies. In her religious works, Dougall displayed her knowledge of Latin in her titles, she made learned refer-ences to biblical history, and cited scholars and clerics. It took some time to find this new authoritative voice, however, and a sense of inadequacy continued to plague her.

Dougall published *Pro Christo et Ecclesia* and subsequent religious works anonymously because she felt that her ideas would not be treated seriously if it were known that they were written by a woman, especially a woman novelist. She had hidden her gender before, pub-lishing her first stories under a male pseudonym and her novels as the genderless "L. Dougall." With the religious work, however, she went to some lengths to retain anonymity. Even her publisher did not know her true identity until 1907, but corresponded with her through Mrs. Tyndale of Oxford. In 1911, and again in 1912, Earp mooted the possi-bility of revealing her identity to the public, noting, "We have heard in various quarters that the authorship is known to a number of people and as it has apparently been stated pretty freely that the author is a woman it is of less consequence perhaps if the name is known."[20] It was not, however, until 1917 that Dougall published a religious book under her own name. By this time, significantly, she was publishing her essays with a well-respected group of male clerics and academics.

Pro Christo et Ecclesia was a critical and long-lasting success; a third edition was published in 1913.[21] The book was an eloquent and biting attack on the church, referred to by the reviewer in the Anglican Church organ, *Church Times,* as "that powerful book, *Pro Christo et Ecclesia.*"[22] Dougall's Christ was a liberal reformer battling self-righteous individuals within the religious establishment. "[O]ur Lord waged war to the bitter death with the pious standards of the time. The wrath of the Lamb blazed out against men who were well-meaning, self-sacrificing and devout."[23] Dougall indicted the organized church of the Pharisees, and by implication the churches of the modern world, in the crucifixion: "Jesus Christ was slain because he would not conform to rites and doctrines as a test of spiritual life."[24] The appeal of the book lay in Dougall's confident authority and in her power of expression. She was writing for a growing audience of liberal clerics and lay people who were happy to be convinced that their liberalism brought them closer to Christ's teaching.

The success of *Pro Christo et Ecclesia* tempted Dougall to return to Britain. She had been plagued by ill health in Montreal, and was forced to move to warmer climes, in North Carolina or California, each damp spring. In early 1902, she struggled with another serious bout of illness, and wrote to Hilda Oakeley, justifying the decision to leave her family again and return to Oxford (of all places) for her asthma.[25] Living in Oxford would place Dougall in the center of Anglican thought, in close proximity to the leaders of the growing movement of liberal Anglicanism. Oxford is notoriously damp, however, and Dougall's asthma flared up on her return. A doctor recommended she spend the winter in rooms in Exmouth. Exmouth is in relatively balmy Devon, and like Ventnor, an earlier winter retreat, is a seaside town looking south over the English Channel. She made another attempt to settle in Oxford in the spring, but her asthma returned in the damp climate and she reluctantly returned to Exmouth. Earp resigned from her position at the Midland Institute in 1903, and they found a house, "East Undercliff," where they made a home together from 1903 to 1911. The years in Exmouth were recuperative and quiet. Dougall wrote fewer books, and traveled less, and gradually her health returned.

Pro Christo et Ecclesia had placed Dougall among the leading religious writers of the day, and chapters of her next religious work, *Christus Futurus* (1907), appeared in the leading liberal journals, the *Hibbert Journal* and the *Monthly Review,* before being published in book form.[26] Macmillan published *Christus Futurus* in London and New York (where

Lily Dougall, c. 1903.
Henry J. Morgan, *Types of Canadian Women* (1903).
Courtesy Library and Archives Canada.

they translated the title to *The Christ that is to Be*) and credited it to the anonymous "author of *Pro Christo et Ecclesia.*" The book was not as tightly constructed as her first work, and Dougall, possibly in response to comments made by the publisher's reader, wrote an apologetic preface:

> This book is only a series of successive efforts to think what the gospel of Jesus really is. Each line of thought is unfinished, and there is very much in what is said that, in a mature work, would be more carefully guarded from misconstruction. These fragments are only published in the hope that those who have greater opportunity may find in them something to refine and complete.[27]

When the essays received critical reviews, her publisher blamed the preface: "I think it is not at all improbable that the preface may have given people the idea that *Christus Futurus* was a series of disconnected fragments rather than a consecutive argument. The pity is the preface was ever written." [28] But sales were better than the reviews, and the book sold well—one 1913 letter describes sales of *Christus Futurus* at 2,272—and was revised for a second edition in 1909, and a third edition in 1914.[29]

Subsequent books, *Absente Reo* (1910), *Voluntas Dei* (1912), and *The Practice of Christianity* (1913), were also published anonymously. The books condemned the hypocritical charity, the social snobbery, and the conservatism of the existing church, and called for sweeping social change based upon Christ's teaching. Reviews were fairly positive but sales were uneven and none of the books matched the success of *Pro Christo et Ecclesia*. *Absente Reo* was the most highly regarded. The reviewer in *Church Times* wrote perceptively: "this brilliant writer . . . has much to say on prayer and faith and worship and it is said most beautifully and probes to the very bottom of religious truth. At times he [*sic*] is hurried and one sided but he is always thoughtful and intensely spiritual." The reviewer notes that the church needs to be reminded of deficiencies: "If so it is as well that we should be reminded by one to whom the Presence of God is the joy of life, and this we believe to be true of the author of *Absente Reo*." [30] Over time, with reviews such as this one, the anonymous "author of *Pro Christo et Ecclesia*" built up a reputation as one of the leading writers on religion in the Anglican world.

Dougall makes no direct reference to F. D. Maurice in *Pro Christo et Ecclesia*, but her book presented a lyrical explication of some central tenets of his liberal Anglican theology. Maurice's theology is legendary for its obtuse complexity: "Of all the muddle-headed, intricate, futile persons I have ever studied," Leslie Stephen complained, "[Maurice] was about the most bewildering." [31] Maurice's understanding of the church is particularly difficult. He distinguished between the universal church, which is the manifestation on earth of the "Divine Order," the eternal and unchanging Kingdom of God, and the petty religious world, which is made up of sectarian religious authorities. In Maurice's theology, the Kingdom of God was not a future aspiration but already encompassed all of humanity as alternative mystical reality. Knowledge about this kingdom is unfolding progressively, through the Incarnation, the Resurrection, and finally the Pentecost, when the Holy Spirit gave the disciples and the church, through apostolic succession, perfect knowledge of the reality of the Kingdom of God. Maurice has been criticized for equating the universal church with the Church of England, but, as Torben Christensen has observed, he does not argue that the Church of England offers exclusive access.[32]

In contrast to the universal church, Maurice posed what he called the "religious world": those sectarians who try to control access to God. The sectarian religious world threatened to destroy the universal church, from without by undermining its teachings, and from within by turning the universal church into yet another sect. And so, he argues, every true prophet has to fight the religious world. "So the prophets of old found; so the apostles found; so the reformers found; so it was in the days when our Lord walked upon the earth. All had to contend with the religious world of their day—He most of all." [33] Maurice identified the Jewish sects in Christ's time as displaying all the characteristics of the sectarian religious world. In his own time he identified the evangelicals, and to a lesser extent the Tractarians, as members of this group, and he felt it presented a constant threat to the universality of the Anglican Church.

Dougall's *Pro Christo et Ecclesia* was a lyrical exposition of Maurice's argument. She had been exposed to Maurice's work since her teenage confirmation in the Episcopalian Church. "I only know I had to write [*Pro Christo et Ecclesia*]," she told Earp, "as it seemed the outcome of all the things I have been trying to say for years and could not." [34] Dougall adopted Maurice's description of Christ's battle with the sectarian religious world, and wrote, "The world that hated Jesus was the religious world." [35] She described Christ as a liberal fighting against the Sadducees, "those orthodox and stagnant in belief," and the Pharisees, "those progressive in belief, determined to govern the whole life by an increasing application of religious law and increasing separation from evil doers." [36] Christ was, by implication, a religious liberal, fighting the conservatives among the Tractarians and the evangelicals.[37] As her modernist friend, Canon B. H. Streeter, wrote: "In effect it is an appeal to people inside the churches, who are genuinely religious and believe that they stand for the cause of true religion, whether they may not be standing, like the zealous Pharisees of old, for a religion which resembles Pharisaism more closely than the religion of Christ." [38]

Maurice focused upon the evangelicals in his criticism of the religious world, and Dougall argued that Christ's greatest anger was reserved for their Judaic equivalent, the Pharisees. Dougall's historical approach and metaphorical style allowed her to avoid identifying any particular parties or sects. Although she did mention the modern "Puritans" of Mildmay and Keswick, Dougall generally made vague and sweeping condemnations: "[Christ] said that the impious vices were nearer to God than any conservative religion, or any form of zealous piety which, having its root in a personal or party desire for heavenly favour, imprisons the generous emotions in an assured doctrine of a God whose character is a reflection of human selfishness." [39] Her language could be biting:

> Jesus would have no share in any outward act which was set up as a test of spiritual condition. . . . Even when the ceremony was harmless he replied, "I take my stand outside your way, with those who, you say,

know not the law and are cursed. I neglect your rite, despise your interpretations of Scripture and make my friends among those who ignore
them. See now if you can recognise God's inspiration in another form.
And those Pharisees could not. Let us remember that the devout among
them thanked God for their privileges, that they coupled this gratitude
with an unresting zeal for converts, and with a sense also that there was
something of a redeeming force for the many in the faithfulness of the
few. Had they lived nowadays we might have defended them, saying
how very good they were—"very narrow, bigoted, in fact, but that is
almost a necessary consequence of intensity." Jesus Christ called them
"children of hell." [40]

Sectarians were the "children of Hell" and liberals were Christlike; at
one point Dougall goes so far as to compare Christ to higher critics and
modern philosophers.[41] She turns religious uncertainty into a sign of
truth and argues lyrically that one of the signs of the religious sectarian
is an unfounded sense of assurance: "their assurances had built a wall
round the heart, which is the organ of sight, a wall composed of the
stern fibre of their very conscience." Assurance caused the deadly sin
of pride, and the resulting separatism. Christ, in comparison, offered no
literal answers: "His answers to all questions, of followers or enemies,
are at once like a rift in the heaven above, and a yawning of the earth
beneath. They open the mind to the heights and depths involved in the
matter, before undreamed of, and fill the new sense of ignorance they
create with some new aphorism of limitless significance." Even deep
spirituality offers no doctrinal assurance: "Whatever be the meaning of
that mystical dipping into the unseen world of the soul, the sense of
personal contact and comfort which by psychic law is the inevitable
result of absorbed prayer, it is evident that personal experience can
supply no criterion of opinion." The best that humanity could reach was
"an earnest waiting," "a dim notion," the "ignorance of adoration." [42]
The lack of assurance of the liberal, a lack that might be thought to lead
to doubt and disbelief, became in Dougall's work a cornerstone of faith.
     Dougall was too much of a North American, however, and too
much her father's daughter to entirely accept Maurice's identification
of the Anglican Church with the universal church. She repeatedly criticized Anglican exclusivity in her fiction: this doctrine was the fatal
weakness of her Tractarian minister in "Lovereen," she refers to it in
The Spanish Dowry, and she played out this debate again in her last piece
of fiction, Paths of the Righteous.[43] Rather than identify the universal
church with the Anglican Church Dougall sought the same unity
through an ecumenicism that embraced all Christian churches under
one umbrella. Maurice had provided grounds for this departure in his

criticisms of the Tractarians. When Dougall wrote of the Church in *Pro Christo et Ecclesia*, capitalizing the word, she appears to be describing the entire Christian body of believers, rather than the Anglican Church. The following passage suggests how she drew upon Maurice's understanding of the Church as a vehicle of truth while broadening her sense of the Church to include the "manifold diversity" of Christian thought:

> The blind Church which cannot accept the spiritual religion of Christ in its purity and entirety, until it has read the continuation of its own selfish and material religions into it and out of it once more, is led by ways that it knows not; and we see in the more intimate record of any age of the Church that the divine life quickens successively now one phase of religious thought and another, as if that which had become hackneyed could not be its vehicle. Are we not, therefore, bound to believe that in the manifold diversity of Christian fellowship, in the long stream of thought and sentiment that flows throughout Christian literature, there is room and food for all possibilities, for all limitations of the individual, who is surely safe with God if he will but honestly pray. Just as in natural things, isolate himself as he will, he is still an organic part of the race, moving with it in its development, so when he prays he is lapped around by The Spirit that informs the Church; think what he may, do what he may, he must move with the great march of the world-soul advancing to its God.[44]

A Hegelian sense of the irreversible progress of the world Spirit, "the great march of the world-soul," allows Dougall to place confidence in a broader sense of the universal church. Many Anglican liberals shared Dougall's ecumenical faith that the progressive individuals in every denomination are moving in the same direction. There is, however, sometimes even in Dougall's work, a lingering Mauricean echo in the underlying assumption that the ecumenical unity was, ultimately, an Anglican one.

Pro Christo et Ecclesia appealed to a large and growing audience of Mauricean Christian socialists in Britain and North America. Canon Scott Holland praised the book in *The Commonwealth* for its "singular spiritual insight."[45] Dougall's subsequent theological books were oriented toward these well-educated progressive individuals. The Christian Social Union (CSU), the most moderate and the most popular of Christian socialist organizations, provided a large (and wealthy) audience; by 1900 there were 4,000–6,000 members in Britain, and a substantial number of transatlantic branches, with an additional 1,000 members, including such social reformers as W. D. P. Bliss and Vida Scudder, in the United States.[46] It was upper-class and academic—disparaged as "socialism for bishops"—but Dougall had loved Oxford and was comfortable in this milieu.[47] Her audience, she felt, had never been the "ordinary middle-class reader." [48] Many members were Anglo-Catholic. Dougall's books followed the fortunes of the CSU closely. The CSU was at its height in 1908, and disappeared in Britain after World War I. Dougall's Christian socialist books were correspondingly published in 1907, 1910, 1912, and 1913.

The critical edge of *Pro Christo et Ecclesia* was still present in these books. *Christus Futurus* had, *The Manchester Guardian* noted, "the charm of style, the illuminating flashes of originality and the insistent desire to pierce through religious convention to the very mind of Christ which arrested us in the former volume." [49] They were increasingly aimed, however, at social reform, the "regeneration of corporate humanity." *Christus Futurus* was a series of essays on the realization of the Kingdom of God, as a message of joy and love rather than retribution.

The Practice of Christianity was, in Dougall's words, "a criticism of our present civilization as judged by the Christlike temper of uncompromising faith and hope and charity." In a lyrical, but slightly hectoring tone, Dougall criticized the existing "City of Destruction" in chapters on the penal system, warfare, personal violence, poverty, and competition, and called for the "Pilgrimage of the Soul." Beatrice Webb offered to review the book for the *Statesman;* her review, "A Rational Mysticism," is worth quoting at length.[50] She says that the section titled "City of Destruction" is most original:

> Here our author becomes, perhaps unconsciously, distinctly revolutionary. One by one the typical institutions of the modern State are subjected to the test of Christianity: are they or are they not compatible with the supremacy of love; and one by one these institutions are rejected. There is a scathing chapter on the unabashed sanction of war and preparations for war by the Christian Churches. Our penal system, equally sanctioned by our Church, is shown to be neither scientific in its processes nor religious in its motive. . . . [T]he almsgiving of the rich, with its careless distribution of a surplus which they have not earned, which they do not need, and which they ought not to have accepted, and its equal vulgar insistence on servility or 'gratitude,' is condemned as a mean substitute for an insistence on the essentially Christian principle of the universal Equality of Consumption.[51]

Despite similar positive reviews in *The Commonwealth* and elsewhere, and Earp's efforts to have the book distributed at the Student Volunteer Movement and the Social Service Conference at Swanwick, *The Practice of Christianity* did not prove as popular as *Christus Futurus*.[52]

The most eloquent of these books, *Absente Reo*, was an indictment of Anglican conservatism structured in the form of a series of letters from a layperson to a fictional young minister.[53] Dougall describes the Anglican Church as a decaying and hypocritical institution, closely tied to the privileged and wealthy members of its congregation, focused on the externals of religion, and blind to both social justice and true spirituality. This message was delivered with a provocative and playful tone. One reviewer of *Absente Reo* noted that "the author rides full tilt at clerical narrowness, intellectual unfitness and social conventionality, yet in such a kindly fashion that no offence can be taken." [54] We sense Dougall's delight in preaching to the men who usually preached to her:

> God is life and the fuller life comes only from Him. But this impulse of fuller religion implies independence of hackneyed thought, getting into the mountains of the soul at night time, and meeting there with God, going out a great while before it is day into the solitudes of the spiritual life.
>
> And you—what are you doing? Is not the greater part of your time spent in forcing, as it were, the nose of the laity to the grindstone of hackneyed words, hackneyed ideas, hackneyed responsibilities.[55]

She argued that the church had lost touch with the age, and would not be able to give a definitive answer to the doubts raised by biblical criticism and historicism. Nor would it be able to keep its congregation if it continued to fashion itself in a hierarchical form, and administer charity rather than social justice. "You must preach a new doctrinal argument, a better social life and civil order, a deeper spiritual life, if you are to hold the people." [56]

Dougall criticized the minister (described as a reader of CSU tracts) for failing to support the younger members of the congregation who had a new vision: "When this iron-master's son came home from the university filled with the new conceptions of what the Kingdom of God would mean for young and old, rich and poor, did you frankly side with him?" She continued, "When Mrs. Smith's daughter returned from her training at the slum "settlement" her eyes dazzled with the new vision, did you stand by her and tell all your frightened feminine followers that they must learn what she had to teach? or did you help them to prune her down to their own level?" [57]

The book was surprisingly mystical; the answer to the threats of doubt and social injustice can be found in recourse to the indwelling voice of God. Sophie Earp wrote, "Perhaps the central idea of the book may be said to be the importance of personal illumination rather than the ceremonial forms which accompany that inward illumination and vary with age." [58] One reviewer described her as a mystic, and Dougall told Oakeley that she felt she might have neglected the outer forms of religion in this book, in her attempt to stress the inner life.[59] The mystical component of Dougall's Christian socialism comes as a surprise to those schooled in the recent historiography of practical and efficient social activists. It is frequently argued that with the turn to social reform, the church had lost its mystical dimension. Historians point to the muscular Christianity of Charles Kingsley and the overtly masculinized social gospel of Walter Rauschenbusch, and argue that mysticism became associated with a weak Catholicized femininity. They suggest that the experiential became a private matter, divorced from and existing in some tension with public activism.[60] More attention to the women in the movement might alter this interpretation, for Dougall's was a social reform theology built upon a complex otherworldliness.

It was not that Dougall was unaware of the practicalities of reform. As her health improved, she attended numerous conferences and meetings with Earp and built upon her relationship with Beatrice Webb by attending the latter's Fabian summer school. She wrote to Hilda Oakeley in 1910, describing "arduous" holiday going to Fabian School and a "Destitution Conference" and visiting quarrymen, miners, and farmers. "All these have been visited with a conscientious desire to get to the bottom of things and a sense of stupidity and timidity which made one feel shockingly like a mere sightseer and quite incapable of realising the human toil and distress that ought to evoke tears."[61] She wrote to Beatrice Webb, who had been privately disappointed with the summer school, complimenting her on the optimistic comradeship.[62] Dougall's sympathies lay more with progressive and secular reformers than with those she called self-righteous Christians. As she wrote in *The Practice of Christianity,* "Those who believe in and work for the triumph of the principles of Christ are surely much nearer to the Kingdom—be their name for the Highest Good what it may— than are those who, with the name of Christ perpetually on their lips, despair of earthly progress or hope only in the triumph of the purse or of the sword."[63] Nevertheless, Dougall felt that the real reform must be based upon religious feeling: "I am sure that all the doing in the world is no good, unless it proceeds from, results spontaneously from, a growing aliveness to God," she had written to Sophie in 1892.[64] This was her family's attitude: they had little patience with social reform that did not arise from a changed heart. The protagonist in Dougall's last novel, *Paths of the Righteous,* says on her conversion,

> I don't want to go away and be a hospital nurse or a ministering angel to any set of people, or give jam to the poor, and I'm quite determined to give up my class in Sunday School. I think it's very right to do all those things, but just now for me they don't go deep enough or far enough to

touch either the terrible pain or the terrible joy of life. . . . Good and evil seem so much more real than ever before, and so terribly different from one another; and the good, you know, is so much greater that if people would only bask in it and take it in and grow in it, they would set about the reform of life in a different way. They would go about it gently and effectually as the mushrooms when they lift up stones. Just now we are all running about like ants, and the stones are not rolled away.[65]

Her interest lay in the "terrible pain and terrible joy of life"; touch these and reform would grow, like "mushrooms when they lift up stones." An inveterate meeting goer and letter writer, Dougall argued in *Christus Futurus* that society did not need a "calling of meetings, or much talking, or letters in the newspapers; still less do we want organization of new societies. These may have their place, but they are not essential— each must individually form new purpose."[66]

Mauricean Christian socialism provided a practical and politicized reform built upon this "growing aliveness to God." Maurice's concept of the Kingdom of God suggests a complex trope, a vision of the future grounded in an experiential present. Individuals did not simply work toward a Kingdom of God on earth or anxiously await the second coming. Rather, they were already members of an eternal kingdom, and had only to recognize their existing relationships with God and each other to bring about the Kingdom of God on earth. The concept is a complicated one, built upon Maurice's nonlinear sense of time and his controversial interpretation of the word "eternity." Maurice had argued that eternity could be experienced within time. His was a Johannine sense of eternity as an alternate dimension, derived in part from Coleridge.[67]

Dougall, it appears, had adopted this concept of eternity, and its implications for the Kingdom of God, at the age of nineteen when she attempted to explain herself to a disapproving young member of the premillenialist Plymouth Brethren: "For instance you believe that Christ will come to set up his visible kingdom upon earth perhaps next week, perhaps next year. We believe He is close beside us always, not only as a God and King, but as a friend, and as the Kingdom of Heaven is in men's hearts now, so it will be in the Millenium when all men come to him."[68] Twenty-two years later she described the Kingdom as an existing entity, as well as an emerging, future one: "Jesus taught that we must first find *within* us the Kingdom—the purposes and works of the Spirit—before that Kingdom can be realized in the complex harmony of the external life."[69] As late as 1918, she wrote to the Roman Catholic modernist Maud Petre, "I think in the main I agree with you as far as I understand your meaning with regard to spiritual union. Perhaps I differ slightly in thinking that the spiritual union exists more widely at present than you do, and needs only to be manifested, rather than to be brought into being." [70]

The Kingdom of God was not, then, simply a moral ideal, but an alternative reality that existed outside of time as it was being realized in time. Dougall wrote in *Christus Futurus*, "We turn to the Gospels and find that their main theme is a 'Kingdom' *both present and eternal*, to which Jesus calls all men, of which he is the king. This implies that he still lives in an invisible world of spirit, very near; still calls us to enter and enjoy the Kingdom, to proclaim its power and suffer for its sake." [71] Dougall lived then as a citizen in two kingdoms, the Kingdom of God and the earthly kingdom, and it was the power of the first kingdom that drove reform in the second. In her translation of the Lord's Prayer in *Christus Futurus*, "Thy Kingdom be within and around us," [72] Dougall suggests a kingdom that is simultaneously within, in the form of a mystical experience of God, and around, in the form of the battle for social justice.

The tendency has been to define social reform by its movement away from religious faith, but even a cursory examination of two leading women reformers, Vida Scudder in the United States, and Beatrice Webb in England, reveals that both women led active spiritual lives. Scudder explored a Mauricean Anglican faith through a female devotional group, the Society of the Companions of the Holy Cross. She edited work by mystic St. Catherine of Siena; a review published in Dougall's *World Wide* noted: "Perhaps the keynote of Catherine's success is her perception of and her firm belief in, the actual presence of God in the human beings around her." [73] Biographical work reveals that Beatrice Webb was inspired at least in part by religious motivation, although she understood her religious sensibility as a private and feminine attribute, and kept it apart from her public work. [74]

Dougall's was a mystical vision, but, as Beatrice Webb noted, reviewing *The Practice of Christianity*, it was a rational and militant mysticism: "The mysticism of this book is not the 'Quietism' of the medieval saint. The love sought after is to be militant in its attitude to life." [75] Communion with God came first, but it led inevitably and necessarily to social reform: "Thus the Kingdom of God, when really within men, makes for the Kingdom of God manifested in outward conditions." [76] Maurice was criticized by fellow Christian socialists for his otherworldly focus. Ludlow had challenged him in 1852: "it does seem to me that you are liable to be carried away by Platonistic dreams about an Order, and a Kingdom, and a Beauty, self-realized in their own eternity." [77] The CSU was also criticized for its lack of programmatic reform; the Mauricean defense given by the mystical Bishop Westcott that "it is not the office of the church to propose any social programme but to enforce eternal principles." [78] Dougall was vulnerable to this same criticism. In *Christus Futurus,* she argues explicitly against greater organization, explaining that "those who offer to God the same thoughts, the same desires, the same adoration, have not to hope for union with one another—they are in union with one another, their union is not to become a strength, but is a strength,—a strength which no outward organization, having its own sort of strength, can increase." [79] Her books offered no political or economic analysis, and even her most reformist book, *The Practice of Christianity,* consists of sweeping condemnations of war and selfishness, rather than specific reforms.

Christian socialism ebbed after the Great War. Dougall continued to work for social justice, and before her death was involved in the planning of the 1924 Conference on Christian Politics, Economics, and Citizenship.[80] It appears, however, that the Mauricean fusion of spirit and activism was dissolving, and she turned to more purely spiritual issues with *Concerning Prayer* (1916). Beatrice Webb wrote a long and critical letter about this volume; Dougall was hurt, but argued that Webb was objecting to an old and outdated Christianity. Dougall said that the distinctions between her work and Webb's socialism were largely ones of language, and she complimented Webb for the good work Webb was doing "for what you call humanity and I call the Kingdom of God." She was disappointed that Webb did not see the matter in the same light.[81]

How are we to interpret this parting of the ways between the social reformer and the religious writer? Was Dougall's spirituality only a remnant, one that could be discarded when scientific reformers such as Webb moved forward on the linear trajectory toward the social sciences? This argument assumes that spirituality is static and only science moves forward. From the perspective of Dougall's work, the social reform movement appears as a transitory phase in a dynamic reworking of Christian theology. Liberal Anglicans, as we shall see in the next chapter, became increasingly focused upon a mystical interiority, as the titles of Dougall's subsequent books suggest: *Concerning Prayer, Immortality, The Spirit.* Did the emotive focus of this mystic revival lead reformers like Scudder and Webb to retrospectively divorce themselves from the religious impulse? Scudder reflected in 1937 that she had been torn between her faith and her social reform work, which took place in a largely masculine environment. "My religious position consigned me again to solitude. . . ." she wrote.[82] Webb also felt herself an outcast by 1926: "Like so many other poor souls, I have the consciousness of being a *spiritual outcast.*" [83] When she wrote her autobiography, Webb described the centrality of faith, and the difficulty in reconciling her faith and scientific socialism:

> That is a creed which is only the product of one side of our nature, the purely rational, and ought we persistently refuse authority to that other faculty which George Eliot calls emotive thought? And this, when we allow this faculty to govern us in action; when we secretly recognise it as our guide in our highest moments. Again what is the meaning for our longing for prayer, or our feeling happier and nobler for it? Why should we determine in our minds that the rational faculty should be regarded as the infallible head in our mental constitution? . . . But perhaps the real difficulty is that the emotional faculty, though it gives us a yearning, a longing for, perhaps even a distant consciousness of, something above us, refuses to formulate and to systematise; and even forces us to see moral flaws in all the present religious systems. [84]

Religious faith took a mystical direction in the early twentieth century, and it is this shift, as much as the shifts in scientific social reform, that accounts for the widening gulf between Lily Dougall and Beatrice Webb. In the next chapter, we examine the mystical turn among British progressives at the beginning of the twentieth century.

PART III

ANGLICAN AUTHORITY

7

The Making of a Modernist Mysticism

L<small>ILY</small> D<small>OUGALL'S</small> <small>EMPHASIS</small> on mystical experience in *Absente Reo* (1910) reflected a new self-conscious recognition of a mystic tradition among liberals. For several years, Dougall associated with the leading writers on mysticism: she spoke publicly with Evelyn Underhill; worked closely with Rufus Jones, the American Quaker mystic; borrowed liberally from W. R. Inge, the mystic Dean of St. Paul's; and argued with William James over his explanation of mystic experience. Dougall eventually rejected their frames of reference, just as she had rejected absolute idealism. She turned from "the ecstasy of the mystic vision" to the relational philosophy of personal idealism and the Christian emphasis on fellowship.

This aspect of her life, however short-lived, deserves focused attention. Modernist writers on mysticism not only provided the context within which Dougall lived and wrote, but also set the terms of our modern understanding of religious experience. They constructed many of the conceptual tools with which we now approach religious faith. This chapter will look at the influence of mysticism upon Dougall's life. It will show how recently constructed the mystic "tradition" is and how closely tied it is to liberal theology. Examination of the mysticism of Lily Dougall's associates shows that those liberals and modernists who claimed to reach beyond doctrine, creed, and institution to the "impregnable rock" of faith constructed the mystic tradition from familiar elements of romantic idealism, liberal individualism, and perfectionism.

To understand Dougall's affinity for mysticism, we need to return to her youth and to understand the influence of Quietist mysticism in North America. Quietism has appealed to recurrent generations of Protestant reformers who wished to break with orthodoxy: in 1776 John Wesley wrote a biography of Madame Guyon, in 1849 Thomas

Upham published his biography of Guyon, and in 1905 modernist mystic W. R. Inge wrote the preface for a new edition of Upham's biography.[1] Each writer adapted Guyon's Catholicism for a new Protestant generation. Upham argued that mystical union with God was simply the highest stage of sanctification, the highest stage in a *relationship* with the divine. As he wrote, "It is taken for granted that the subject of this higher experience has passed through the more common forms of religious experience; and has advanced from the incipient state of justification, and from the earlier gradations or steps of sanctification, to that state of *divine union,* in which he can say with a good degree of confidence, 'I and my Father are one.'"[2] These words come close to Madame Guyon's argument that the "soul is not merely hidden in God, but has in God become God,"[3] but Upham's "divine man," unlike the Quietist mystic, never loses his individuality, and never annihilates self in the union with the divine. The distinction is an important one that anticipated the adaptations made by Dougall's modernist cohorts. Upham's holiness faith, although it borrows heavily from Quietism, retains a sense of individuality. The self, that which members of Dougall's generation were to call "personality," is never lost in the divine.

It is likely that Dougall read at least some of Upham's work; she would certainly have been aware of the popularization of his ideas through Horace Bushnell, Harriet Beecher Stowe, and Hannah Whitall Smith. But her family's virulent anti-Papism made her suspicious of Catholic mysticism. She recalled in 1910, "When quite young I once collected as many of the writings of the mystics as I could get, and read and read." She distanced herself from their "fantastic" imagery: "[I] was put off by the 'half metaphysical half imaginative' descriptions by mystics like Eckhart. I remember being worried by the effort to see my soul like an alp, its peak lost in heaven. The 'Spark' at the apex of the soul, one with the uncreated God, vexed me by the picture it raised."[4] Her conclusion, she recalled (with perhaps some modernist hindsight), was to write the mystics off as unhealthy, extreme examples of the normal phenomena of religious experience: "I remember feeling that the notable mystics were perhaps more different from the common devout man in the gift of a fantastical imagination and in love of expression than in having clearer perceptions of things unseen." As she grew up and distanced herself from her family, Dougall began to recognize commonalities between her family's faith and Catholicism. In 1881, when she heard Father Ignatius, an "ascetic, aesthetic fanatic" preach a "powerful Gospel sermon," she told her brother that she had learned "to have a greater respect for the 'poor, benighted, priest-ridden Romanists.' ..."[5]

The turning point in Dougall's openness to Catholicism appears to have come in 1888, with the writing of the manuscript "Lovereen," and is likely due to Sophie Earp's influence.[6] In the novel, Lovereen's alter ego, Paul, is attracted to Catholicism and is fascinated by the Roman Catholic principal, who is the most learned and tolerant character in the novel. Dougall's description of the conversion of Lovereen's father, Mr. Walford, reveals significant changes in her understanding of religious experience:

> It is usually a new discovery to a man when he finds that religion is not anything he can do or believe, but the yielding to an inward power, other than himself, which transforms his deeds and beliefs. . . . [he was] aware that there was a heavenly strength to be had in this life, a power for holy work in the personal presence of the Christ.[7]

Then she (perhaps at Sophie Earp's urging) changed the passage, replacing the phrase "a power for holy work in the personal presence of the Christ" with "which transforms conscious life into a conscious union with God." In this simple shift of language, the Christocentric evangelical experience became mystical: the "presence" became "union," a union, significantly, with God rather than Christ. Religion was, as it had been for her parents, yielding to an inward power rather than a ritual or creed, but Dougall's understanding of this experience—if not the experience itself—had changed.

The Mermaid, written several years later, shows similar ambiguity. Caius's first sight of the mermaid is described in language drawn in part from evangelical conversion narratives, and in part from descriptions of mystical experience:

> In the procession of swift winged hours there is for every man one and another which is big with fate, in that they bring him peculiar opportunity to lose his life, and by that means find it. Such an hour came now to Caius. The losing and finding of life is accomplished in many ways: the first proffer of this kind which Time makes to us is commonly a draught of the wine of joy, and happy is he who loses the remembrance of self therein.[8]

To lose one's life in order to find it is an image familiar to evangelicals, but the situation, even apart from the bizarre appearance of the mermaid, lacks any of the other hallmarks of a conversion narrative. Caius does not experience an extended period of anxiety, a conviction of sin, repentance, and a sudden assurance. The loss of self, however, in a joyous experience of the divine, is characteristic of a mystical experience:

> For it must all have been a dream—a sweet fantastic dream, imposed upon his senses by some influence, outward or inward; but it seemed to

him that at the hour when he seemed to see the maid it might have been given to him to enter the world of dreams, and go on in some existence which was a truer reality than the world in which he now was.[9]

In conformity with both the conversion and the mystical experiences, this moment is a transformative one.

More prosaic visionary moments appear in her other novels when the "Madonna" in *Madonna for a Day* thrills at the sight of a mountain top, the spurned minister in *What Necessity Knows* finds insight at the riverside, and Bates, the Calvinist Scotsman in *What Necessity Knows*, gazes into the sunset: "It was only perhaps a moment—one of those moments for which time has no measurement—that the soul of this man had gone out of him, as it were, into the vastness of the sunset. . . ."[10] These references draw upon a romantic tradition of nature mysticism common among Canadian women writers at the turn of the century. Their work echoes themes made familiar through American transcendentalism. It is closely connected to the anticlericalism described in chapter 4; the turn to nature in many cases is tied to an explicit rejection of a church-based spirituality. Francis Marion Beynon observed that the God she learned about in Sunday School was always angry: "There are good people who claim to have met the God of the big quiet places and the starry heavens in the churches but personally I never have. . . . But I met him in the afternoon in the corner of the pasture field." She describes a passing breeze: "I know God passed me by in that breeze because for a little while I was not afraid of father or mother, or of anything in the world."[11] Beynon's God is explicitly counterposed to the authoritarian father God she was introduced to in church. Similarly, in 1898 Joanna Woods, who had dismissed the "little" Methodist parson, rhapsodized, "For there is some great open secret surely in the universe, that being deciphered will set all our jangling nerves in chime. It is about us, around us, above us; the tiniest leaf tells it, the stars of heaven proclaim it, the water manifests it, and the earth declares it, and yet we do not see it."[12] Flora MacDonald evoked a similar pantheism in *Mary Melville* (1900), when a young man wanders into the pine woods and has a revelation that provides "reasons why things are as they are, and a consciousness of knowledge not written in books, a consciousness of the vast sea of information in nature's huge reservoir, a conscious relationship and sympathy with the giant pines, with the tender undergrowth, with the soft white snow, and even with the hard granite rock."[13]

More orthodox writers also described the power of nature. Marion Keith was a conservative Presbyterian whose theology was treated mercilessly in Lily Dougall's review *World Wide*.[14] She describes the difficulties of a young liberal preacher; his breakthrough comes not in a church or at prayer, but at night, in the woods: "Next he entered the woods, so dark and still, with only the light of a few stars peeping through the branches. . . . The strange, still whisper of the forest, that gave a sense of life, as if the whole dark surrounding were some great breathing creature touched him nearly. He felt awed; the trivial things in life seemed infinitesimal now, in the fact of this mysterious wonder."[15] Agnes Maule Machar describes a young man whose crisis of faith is resolved by the natural beauty of a summer landscape: "With the new, marvellous beauty of the summer landscape, that burst on his gladdened eyes like a revelation, there seemed interfused a higher more subtle influence. How, he knew not—such things pass our knowing—and doubtless many things led up to it; but there and then, it seemed to him that the chilling mists of doubt had almost passed away from his soul." Machar, more aware of the theological subtleties than some of the other authors, was careful to place the "divine Father and Saviour" behind the beauties of nature: "He felt the divine Father and Saviour, the brooding spirit of love and strength, closer and more real than the lovely vision around him. And he felt that he should never lose them more."[16] As these excerpts suggest, however, these pantheistic moments are rarely seen to have any connection with anything that might be referred to as *mysticism*. Their value lies in their independence from the Church.

Nor were Dougall's pantheistic moments connected to a religious past. Bart Toyner's reference to Johannes Eckhart's "eternal now," in *The Zeit-Geist* is one of the few examples in which the reference to mysticism is made explicit in her novels.[17] By 1907, however, Dougall was citing mystical phrases from St. John in *Christus Futurus*: "And the glory which thou has given me I have given unto them; that they may be one, even as we are one; I in them, and thou in me, that they may be perfected into one."[18] (Beatrice Webb's review of this book was appropriately titled "A Rational Mysticism.")[19] By 1910, Dougall has not only recognized something that she calls "mysticism" but, as she told Hilda Oakeley, she saw it as the highest form of faith: "I am sure that mysticism produces the truest sanity."[20] One South African reviewer of *Absente Reo* (1910) commented, "The writer is a mystic, a twentieth-century mystic," and, if his enthusiasm led him to overstate the case, the book marks the high point of Lily Dougall's adoption of the mystic tradition.[21]

What had happened? Dougall, acutely sensitive to shifts in religious thought, was responding to a sudden surge of interest in mysticism. At the beginning of the twentieth century, a flood of books on the topic had appeared, written by modernists including W. R. Inge, Evelyn Underhill, Baron Friedrich von Hugel, and Percy Gardner, and American liberal Quaker Rufus Jones.[22] No longer associated with asceticism, fanaticism, or even, necessarily, Catholicism, mysticism became an acceptable topic for theological debate and public discussion. These books reached a wide audience. Inge's 1899 Bampton lectures, *Christian Mysticism*, went into a sixth edition in 1925. Underhill's *Mysticism, A Study in the Nature and Development of Man's Spiritual Consciousness* (1911) was reprinted ten times, revised in 1930, and is still widely recommended as a primer on the subject.[23] The flood of publications was augmented by reprints of earlier texts. Thomas Upham's work on Madame Guyon, for example, reappeared in a new 1905 English edition edited by W. R. Inge.[24] Most popular was a fifteenth-century classic, Thomas à Kempis's *The Imitation of Christ*. A reviewer of *The Imitation of Christ* in Lily Dougall's *World Wide* observed in 1905: "All this seems very strange, when one considers the writer is, before all things, a monk, a celibate, an ascetic." He concluded that the attraction lay in the monk's "exceptionally vivid account" of religious experience.[25]

This revival of mysticism has been dismissed by historians. Jackson Lears described the Anglo-Catholic mysticism of Vida Scudder and the Buddhism of wealthy Americans as selfish and ultimately futile expressions of a weak and feminine antimodernism: "Eager for liberation from Victorian constraints but lacking firm moral commitments outside the self, many Americans transformed mysticism and aestheticism into therapeutic cults of personal fulfillment."[26] He described the contemplative life as "morbid introspection," neurasthenic, dependent, weak, and ultimately effeminate, ignoring evidence, in Vida Scudder's life at least, of strong active reformism. The work of R. M. Bucke, a Canadian whose work *Cosmic Consciousness* influenced William James, and is still in publication, has similarly been dismissed by Canadian historians as debased supernaturalism.[27]

Michel de Certeau offers a less judgmental approach in his *Mystic Fable*.[28] He looks at sixteenth-century mysticism as a new field of discourse, and asks why that field arose, and what purpose it served. Eric J. Sharpe moves to the heart of the issue with the simple question: "But why did the *word* mysticism, quite apart from any phenomena to which the word might be taken to refer, suddenly become fashionable in the 1890's and the early 1900's?"[29] Sharpe points out there had only been one survey of "mysticism" before 1899, R. A. Vaughan's *Hours with the Mystics* (1856).[30] Who was reading the books on mysticism written by Inge, Underhill, and Jones, and to what end?

Evidence suggests that they were widely read, not by eccentrics, but by the same well-educated public that read Lily Dougall's religious essays. Members of the Bloomsbury set and, more surprisingly, the philosopher Bertrand Russell, seriously considered mysticism. Russell, whose interest was provoked by the mystical Anglicanism of his lover, Ottoline Morrell, explained the fascination with the phenomena of mystical experience as the response to a religious vacuum: "The decay of traditional beliefs has made every religion that rests on dogma precarious, and even impossible, to many whose nature is strongly religious. . . . For right action they are thrown back upon bare morality; and bare morality is very inadequate as a motive for those who hunger and thirst after the infinite." [31] Dougall's language was more lyrical, but she gave a similar explanation. She advised the young minister in *Absente Reo* to overcome the difficulties of biblical criticism by teaching his congregation to turn to the experiential voice of God: "[W]ithout faith in some inward authority men must waver, their ranks must break in the face of such disturbing interpretations [of apocalyptic teachings]. It is the inward authority alone, the voice of God in the soul, that can give peace and contentment in the dark places of necessary doubt concerning traditional beliefs." [32] She extends her argument:

> Not long ago men took Christianity on the valuation of the clergy, or they left it altogether; now men are trying to fit Christianity into the facts of life as they are found in history or as they see them today, and life looks very different to this person and that. In the process of sifting all Christians must fall back upon some rock which is not being assailed, some common ground on which they can find footing, and on it stand to fight their battle. *The only rock on which they can rest is the personal experience of God's voice in their hearts.* It is this and this alone which brings the peace which science and research and social institutions can neither give nor take away.[33]

Her language is drawn directly from the modernist mystic W. R. Inge:

> We cannot shut our eyes to the fact that both the old seats of authority, the infallible Church and the infallible book, are fiercely assailed, and that our faith needs reinforcements. These can only come from the depths of the religious consciousness itself, and if summoned from thence, they will not be found wanting. *The "impregnable rock" is neither an institution nor a book, but a life or experience.*[34]

Religious experience, then, offered a secure source of religious authority for the critical liberal Christian. Through mysticism, liberals could lay claim to a heritage that, whatever its pathological "aberrations," had an uncontested claim to a certain knowledge of God. Inge wrote: "I was convinced very early, and I have never wavered in my conviction, that this testimony of the saints and mystic has far greater evidential value than is usually supposed, and that it may properly take the place of those traditional 'evidences' which for one reason or another have lost their cogency." [35] The reinforcement was an effective one: no less a liberal Protestant than Harry Emerson Fosdick attested to the power of Rufus Jones's mysticism in shoring up his faltering faith as a young man. [36]

The early twentieth century's fascination with mysticism was closely connected to the modernist movements in the Roman Catholic and Anglican Churches. [37] Most of the leading writers on the subject were modernists; their ranks included the two long term presidents of the Modern Churchman's Association, Percy Gardner, president from 1915–1922, and W. R. Inge, president from 1924 to 1934. Baron von Hugel was a Roman Catholic with modernist sympathies, and his student, Evelyn Underhill, was an Anglican by birth, who gave up plans to join Catholicism after the Papal condemnation of modernism. She subsequently returned to the Anglican fold and joined the Modern Churchman's Association. Rufus Jones was the exception—an American and a Quaker—but he shared many of the assumptions of the Anglican modernists. [38]

Unlike William James, who emphasized the bizarre and extreme manifestations of mysticism (the "sick soul") in his 1902 *Varieties of Religious Experience*, Dougall's modernist associates were interested in a "healthy" form of mysticism. Inge, for example, disparaged "the debased supernaturalism which usurps the name of mysticism in Roman Catholic countries." [39] He dismissed the *via negativa* as "the great accident of Christian mysticism," the result of "Asiatic" influence. [40] Dougall similarly disparaged the "pathological" behavior associated with cloistered medieval mystics. [41] She invited Rufus Jones to contribute to a collaborative volume on prayer in 1916; in "Prayer and the Mystic Vision," much of which was written at Dougall's home, he argued that Christians must discard the old negative mysticism that introduced such esoteric elements as the "mystic way" to create a new affirmative mysticism:

> We can best help our age toward a real revival of Mysticism as an elemental aspect of religious life, not by formulating an esoteric "mystic way," not by clinging to the ancient metaphysic to which Mysticism has been allied, but by emphasising the reality of mystical experience, by insisting on its *healthy and moral* character, and by indicating ways in which such dynamic experiences can be fostered, and realised, and put into *practical* application. [42]

By shedding the "ancient metaphysic," the esoterics of mysticism, for a "practical," "healthy" experience, Jones normalized, as much as modernized, the mystical experience. The rich complexity of concepts such as the *via negativa,* are diminished in this practical and sensible mysticism.

These writers described mysticism as a continuum whose lower reaches were accessible to any believer. Inge confessed: "I have never myself had what are usually called mystical experiences. But in truth the typical mystical experience is just prayer. Anyone who has really prayed, and felt that his prayers are heard, knows what mysticism means. . . . The higher stages are for the saints who have given up all to win the pearl of great price." [43]

Jones also defined mysticism broadly as "the type of religion which puts the emphasis on immediate awareness of a relationship with God, a direct and intimate contact with the Divine Presence." [44] In *Absente Reo,* Dougall described mysticism as the experience of heard prayer, familiar to every believer. "The lamp of mysticism," she wrote, "is more or less alight in every religious soul, and therefore in every true prayer, although often unrecognised." [45] In *Christus Futurus,* she described prayer as the opening of a window in man's understanding to "this flood of life, falling like sunshine." Individuals, she said, should withdraw "temporarily from the things of sense in order to find God," [46] but beyond a daily hour of private devotion and prayer, she was not interested in the solitary pursuit of God. As she advised a troubled reader, "about secluding oneself for several days in order to find God, I can only say that personally I should never expect to gain anything that way." [47]

The liberals also wrote the erotic out of the mystical. Inge quoted Schleiermacher's description of the religious experience in *Studies of English Mystics* (1921).[48] His quotation was, however, a selective one, and Schleiermacher's evocation of the maiden's kiss and bridal embrace were removed from the text. This may have been more than a matter of British prudery. The metaphor was increasingly that of a friendship rather than a marital relationship, as in Schleiermacher, or the erotic relationship found in some medieval mystics. For modernists, the loss of individual will and control in a passionate relationship with God has been replaced by a measured friendship.

The mystic tradition identified by Inge and Jones was congruent with the philosophic idealism of Dougall's Oxford years. Their books frequently consist of compilations and interpretations of Neoplatonic Christian mysticism.[49] In *Christian Mysticism,* Inge distinguished between those mystics who blind themselves to the world of the senses, and the objective or symbolical mystics, typified by the Cambridge Platonists, who work through higher reason.[50] This was an eminently rational mysticism. At times, however, the selective revision of the mystic tradition verged on caricature. Inge's account of the characteristic features of Western mysticism, drawn from an eleventh-century mystic, Amalric, is remarkably modern: "its strong belief in Divine immanence, not only in the Church, but in the individual, its uncompromising rationalism, contempt for ecclesiastical forms, and tendency to evolutionary optimism."[51] Amalric, despite a few "perversions," has in Inge's description anticipated liberal Protestantism, even to its evolutionary optimism. Inge's description of Meister Eckhart might be applied to Lily Dougall: "intellectually he is drawn toward a semipantheistic idealism, his heart makes him an Evangelical Christian."[52]

This interest in mysticism was also a product of encounters between east and west in the British Empire.[53] In his 1893 Gifford lectures, Max Müller compared Eckhardt's mysticism and Eastern religion, and concluded that the goal of all religion is the same, unity with God.[54] Mysticism had come to be considered the common core underlying all traditions. As Dougall wrote, "Since the world began there has been but one inward and spiritual faith, which has in each of its various stages found many outward and visible expressions. . . ."[55] Dougall's peers understood other traditions as different routes to the same truth. This was not toleration so much as a form of religious imperialism. By stating that all religion was one, but at the same time claiming the right to define that one truth and arguing, as Müller did, that its highest expression is found in Christianity, liberals could appear to accept other faiths while at the same time overriding any threats to or contradictions with Christianity.[56] By 1913, Lily Dougall thought that Christianity was the highest existing form of religious faith, if not the final or ultimate form that religion would take.[57] Her friend, B. H. Streeter, took this concept further when he published *The Message of Sadhu Sundar Singh: A Study in Mysticism or Practical Religion* (1922), a breezy biography of a Christian mystic from India. Theologically, Singh was a liberal; devotionally, he practiced an exotic and foreign kind of mysticism, tamed just enough for British consumption. Streeter was coy about describing Singh's visions and fasts: "To him, the mystic way is not the *via negativa* of self-conscious renunciation but just a simple quiet life of Prayer and self-sacrificing Service."[58] Ten years later, after Dougall's death, Streeter wrote another book in which the imperialist tendencies of this line of thought are made even clearer. In *The Buddha and the Christ* (1932), he argued that "Where the Buddha was most himself, there he was most like Christ."[59] The implications were unmistakable: another modernist cited his work to show that Buddhism was evolving in the direction of Christianity.[60] This mysticism was a form of religious imperialism which incorporated all of the major religious traditions, claiming to find their essence in a modern and Western mystical experience.

Inge and Jones are not widely read today; they spoke to and for their own generation. Evelyn Underhill's work has had more staying power, but her work shows even more clearly the modern adaptation of mystical "tradition." Underhill was by birth an Anglican; she toyed with the occult and then studied under Baron von Hugel, a modernist Roman Catholic, and was about to convert to Rome before the Papal condemnation of modernism. She returned to the Anglican fold in 1921, and subsequently appeared with Dougall at modernist conferences. In *Mysticism*, written in 1911, she deliberately excised Christian language. As she told her researcher, "I want most passages in metaphysical rather than definitely Christian language; i.e. references by name to Our Lord, the Blessed Virgin etc., or bits flavored with scraps of Scripture aren't much good; but those in which the same things are called the Eternal, the All, the Divine Love, etc. etc. will be useful." [61] Christian terminology smacked of narrow orthodoxy, so Underhill sought a mysticism expressed in more universal terms. Her correspondence shows that she was more interested in using the mystics to establish her own ideas about mystical experience, than in understanding theirs. "It is a study of mystical method and doctrine, *not* of specific mystics: so that bits bearing upon my points are more useful than bits showing *their* peculiar characteristics." [62] A second book, *Mystic Way* (1913), written under von Hugel's influence, was explicitly Christian.

It is significant that when Lily Dougall and Evelyn Underhill were invited to speak at a Church Congress in 1920, it was Underhill who spoke on mysticism, and Dougall, who was almost a generation older, spoke on the Spirit.[63] In the years after writing *Absente Reo*, Dougall returned to the language of her childhood, referring increasingly to the Spirit in her writing and work. She published a number of articles on the Spirit, including "The Spirit in the Church" and "The Spirit and the Life," and contributed to a collaborative volume, *The Spirit: God and His Relation to Man* (1919).[64] W. R. Inge suggested that the difference between the terms was only a matter of language: he referred to Emerson's description of the Oversoul, which Inge equated with "regular mystical theology," and said that "Christians have generally preferred the word Spirit." [65] The word *Spirit* might be equated with transcendental or mystical interpretations of the divine, but there were important differences. The Spirit was a Christian concept, clearly located in the historic church. The Spirit was experienced individually, but also could be shared, as in the Pentecost, in a fellowship of prayer. Dougall's mature emphasis upon the Spirit reflects a significant divergence from modernist mysticism, a divergence with intellectual roots in personal idealism.

Dougall moved to Oxford in 1911, the year after publishing *Absente Reo*. It was a time of growing tension between mysticism and personal idealism, and over time she aligned herself with personal idealists, men like Hastings Rashdall, J. R. Illingworth, and A. S. Pringle Pattison.[66] The differences between mystics and personal idealists had not initially divided the liberal Anglican world. W. R. Inge paid tribute to Rashdall as an early reader of *Christian Mysticism* (1899). Inge responded with alarm, however, to articles, including Rashdall's, in *Personal Idealism* (1902) and criticized personal idealists with some vehemence in *Personal Idealism and Mysticism* (1907).[67] As he explained in his memoirs, "by over-estimating the separateness of individual personality, they neglected the doctrine of the mystical union with the glorified Christ, which seemed to me at once the most blessed and the most verifiable part of the Christian revelation."[68]

Many modernists appear to have sided with Inge. Rashdall's doubts about mystical experience appear to have placed him in a minority position—even his short presidency of the Modern Churchman's Association, from 1922 to 1924, symbolically sandwiched him between the two mystics, Gardner and Inge.[69] Rashdall pointed out that the indwelling of the Divine in the human soul was contradictory to personal idealists' belief in the complete independence of individual consciousness, and he argued that emphasis on the mystical could prove morally dangerous by minimizing individual responsibility. Finally, as a Kantian, Rashdall had little sympathy for an epistemology based on religious experience.[70]

In *Absente Reo* (1910) Dougall had casually mixed the two approaches, the mystical idea of loss of self, and the personalist emphasis on relationship:

> The mystical element in prayer is perhaps constituted by the loss of sense of self in communion, and may perhaps be defined as participation in God's side of man's communion with Him. Consciously and with effort, or unconsciously and involuntarily, man's soul often seems to go over the line of its own urgency toward God and become absorbed in God's urgency manward. Of course, when we come to analyse it, this is a common experience of all affection, all friendship; an identification with the other self is involved.[71]

The language is mystical, with the loss of sense of self, and in the soul's absorption in God's urgency, but, like the personal idealists, Dougall compared the relationship to a friendship. After she moved into Rashdall's orbit, Dougall became more careful to define the limits of mystical experience. In *Voluntas Dei* (1912) she emphasized the relationship with, rather than dissolution in, the Divine:

> All spiritual activities seem to rise from man's consciousness that when he is most alone, in the sense of having retired within himself from the things of sense, he is in company with another spirit. . . .
>
> The self if it finds God, certainly finds Him within, in the sense that it is within that the self speaks to God and God speaks to the self. This belief is not pantheistic; there is no identity of the self with God. Identity would put an end to all communication, for, as we have seen, all true union depends on difference. . . .
>
> Difference, personality, selfhood are necessary to a high degree of unity. We have no conception of real unity that does not depend upon difference. . . .
>
> Communion of God and man may be described as "telepathic." Union of man with God does not mean identity. True union depends on community of kind and difference in identity.[72]

Dougall still understood the height of religious experience to be union with God.[73] But it was a union predicated upon difference, upon the independent and separate identity of the believer. And it was a union grounded in fellowship with other believers.

In a brief "author's note" to *Voluntas Dei*, Dougall thanks "a friend . . . involved in important philosophic work" who read the book in manuscript. This was most likely J. R. Illingworth. Illingworth was an Oxford don who had retreated to a small parish just outside Oxford, where he wrote a series of influential books, including *Personality: Human and Divine* (1894) and *Divine Immanence* (1898). Dougall became his neighbor in 1911 when she moved to Cumnor, and she invited him to tea to meet the American philosopher Josiah Royce, in April 1913.[74] By May, she was consulting with Illingworth for her responses to a survey for the Free Church Commission.[75] She visited the reclusive philosopher and helped with his parish work until his death in 1915. In her responses to the Free Church Commission, made with Illingworth's assistance, she argued that the best way of seeking God is in the safe company of other seekers:

> [T]he best way, and the only full way, of opening the life to God, of seeking His wisdom and hearing His voice is to be found in the assemblies, little or big, of God-seeking and God-loving people. It is for this that human beings are endowed with the collective power of evoking the collective intelligence and emotion and soul-energy. This is the highest use of this power, and it is a perversion of life—a sort of insanity—when the religious soul does not desire so to use it. The assembly need not be large, it

need not be small, but it must be like-minded in humility, in love and in turning from past failure to future victory.[76]

Dougall later suggested the Society of Friends, with their emphasis on the inner light contained within their strong sense of community, as a model for a renewed spiritual fellowship.

The logic of personal idealists such as Rashdall and Illingworth (and as we shall see in Chapter 9, the excesses of the mental science movement) led Dougall to reject the mystical flight of the "alone to the alone." Dougall spent the last years of her life promoting a heightened spirituality within the safe Quaker-like fellowship of such groups as the Student Christian Movement, the Anglican Fellowship, the Guild of Health, and the Cumnor School.

8

Fellowship

WHEN DOUGALL MOVED BACK to Oxford in 1911, she created an intimate conference center in her home in Cumnor.[1] The house was situated on a hill overlooking Oxford, within an easy bicycle ride of the quadrangles of the university, but slightly removed in a beautiful rural setting. Here she held innumerable discussions and conferences over the next decade for organizations focused on spiritual fellowship such as the Anglican Fellowship, The Guild of Health, the Cumnor Group, and the Student Christian Movement (SCM). Modernist Bishop E. W. Barnes recalled in an obituary of Lily Dougall written for *The Times:*

> These gatherings had a charm peculiar to themselves, because of Miss Dougall's personal charm and religious insight. Frail in physique and a little hesitant in speech, she was none the less the unifying centre of her various conferences. They were stimulating and strenuous, because conversation, argument, illustration and repartee went on unceasingly. The gravest issues were discussed with sincerity and frankness; and the hostess was ever ready to prevent over-seriousness or *ennui* by flashes of subacid fun.[2]

Dougall's emphasis on fellowship was, as we have seen, a reaction to "the flight of the alone to the alone" that characterized modernist mysticism: "There are two distinct conceptions of the ultimate future of man"; she wrote, "the one seems founded upon the ecstasy of mystic vision, the other upon the experience of the excellence of fellowship or friendship." [3] *Fellowship* was a much used term at the turn of the century: an essay published in Dougall's *The Spirit* by C. A. Anderson Scott provides a sense of Dougall's understanding of the word. Scott argued that biblical references to the fellowship of Christ are not simply references to a sense of companionship, but describe a new order, "the fellowship," created at Pentecost. Through the fellowship, he argued, using terms drawn from personal idealism, individual believers came closer to God: "It was in relationship with one another that men continuously realized their relationship to Christ and to God through Him." Saintliness, he argued, "is a social phenomenon." [4] The fellowship also advanced the modernist pursuit of the truth: "the Fellowship is to have its proper and expected result in the progressive discovery of spiritual truth." [5] Fellowship was intellectually grounded in personal idealism, theologically grounded in the Christian concept of the Pentecost and the Mauricean concept of the Universal Church, and perhaps most importantly for Dougall, socially grounded in the relational world of women intellectuals. [6] It was expressed in Dougall's life through three organizations: the SCM, the Anglican Fellowship, and the Cumnor Group.

The Student Christian Movement (SCM) lies at the organizational heart of these groups. Dougall probably first became known to SCM leaders at a 1911 conference on religious doubt when her *Christus Futurus* was included in a list of recommended readings. [7] Over time she became a mentor, as Tissington Tatlow, the General Secretary, explained in his history of the SCM:

> [*Christus Futurus*] was published anonymously at first, but later it became known that the author was Miss Lily Dougall, who published more than one book with the Student Movement and became our friend and benefactor in many ways. She was a woman of learning, with an original and sympathetic mind. She found herself thoroughly at home in the atmosphere of Student Movement conferences and might invariably be seen with a group of students around her, discussing all kinds of theological questions. A memory cherished by Student Movement secretaries in office at the time was a secretaries meeting lasting for several days, held at her beautiful house at Cumnor. [8]

The SCM's origins, like Dougall's own intellectual origins, lay in the University of Edinburgh where liberal evangelist Henry Drummond led a series of popular revivals for students between 1885 and 1894. [9] Drummond is not taken seriously as a religious thinker today, but he was widely read at the end of the nineteenth century and his simple solutions to complex theological issues were reassuring. His *Lowell Lectures on the Ascent of Man* (1894) might be considered a popular rendition of Caird's *Evolution of Religion*. It is likely that Dougall had seen Drummond on one of her visits to her aunt in Edinburgh; at least one other Canadian writer educated in that city, Marshall Saunders, was enthralled by his preaching, and Lady Aberdeen, the influential wife of the Governor General in Canada, was a close friend and promoter of Drummond's work. [10] Dougall paraphrased *The Ascent of Man* in *The Zeit-Geist* and prefaced the novel with a quote from Drummond's earlier *Natural Law in a Spiritual World* (1884): "If nature is the garment of God, it is woven without a seam throughout." [11] The main character, Bart Toyner, bears a curious resemblance to Drummond; it may be coincidental but it seems not unlikely that Dougall might have modeled her charismatic hero upon the liberal revivalist. [12]

Drummond, like Dougall, was a transatlantic figure. He had been inspired by D. L. Moody, and *The Ascent of Man* had its origins in a series of lectures given in North America in 1893. The transatlantic streams diverged when Moody's followers in the United States moved toward fundamentalism, and the SCM evolved in a liberal direction set by Drummond. By 1900, the British student movement was broadening into an ecumenical organization, with growing and controversial connections to liberal Anglo-Catholicism. "A common complaint," Tatlow recalled in 1933, "was that the Student Movement was being captured by the High Church party." [13] There was particular concern, Tatlow noted, about the presence of Anglo-Catholics at the SCM conferences. He wrote, "Father Kelly's cassock and the appearance of men like Canon Scott Holland and Bishop Gore on the platform caused me no little trouble behind the scenes." [14] Steven Bruce has suggested that SCM leaders abandoned evangelical principles in order to appeal to a wider audience. Tatlow, however, recalled that evangelicals had lost their hold on students. Between 1900 and 1914 he had received "a series of kindly but very mournful letters" from evangelical churchmen who wanted the SCM to remain a stronghold of evangelicalism:

> They regarded the progressive broadening of its platform with distress and constantly suggested the inclusion of men representing their point of view as speakers in the programme of the summer conference. I was constantly trying to persuade the student leaders to accept some of these names, but it happened many times that when some man who was urged upon us as suitable for a course of Bible readings or an address at one of the evening meetings, was given a place on the programme suggested for him, he failed to hold the students. [15]

Over time, the SCM became linked to the Anglican modernist movement. In 1912, the *Modern Churchman* published a positive article on the growth of the SCM; a decade later the SCM was advertising book lists in the modernist journal. [16]

There are intriguing suggestions that it was the women of the SCM who were pressing toward theological liberalism; Tatlow said that it was women students who initiated study circles on apologetics:

> The women students were the first among undergraduates to be concerned with intellectual questions. As questions arose among the women

they were passed on by them to the men in the co-educational universities. . . . It was in the women's colleges that the first study circles on apologetic subjects were started, and women students asked for the first course of apologetic lectures given under the auspices of the Movement.[17]

It was at the promptings of women students, echoed by male theology students, that a 1911 conference on "Doubts and Difficulties," was organized. In his thoughtful M.A. thesis on the origins of the Canadian SCM, Donald Kirkey has argued that in Canada, as well, it was the women who were the more progressive and adventurous theologically.[18]

There is little record of the SCM among Dougall's papers, although she worked closely with various members.[19] A reviewer identified only as T. T. (likely Tissington Tatlow) reviewed *The Practice of Christianity* very positively in *The Student Movement,* and another SCM leader, D. S. Cairns, read over parts of *The Practice of Christianity* and *Christus Futurus* prior to publication.[20] In a private letter to Cairns, Dougall said that the SCM provided a model for renewed Christian fellowship:

> The prayer of fellowship—"the disciples being of one accord in one place"—the spiritual at-one-ment with each other, heightened by the sense of material presence, is, I think, of the essence of Christianity, because it is the human condition to which God can best give the realisation of His own power and presence and the inspiration of His truth. Unfortunately, the spiritual realisation has been too often divorced from companionship in prayer. The ordinary Anglican, who has not been through the education of the Student Christian movement, has no conception of fellowship in prayer that is not *formal.* There probably never was anything more informal than Pentecost; but Pentecost is not a living reality to the Anglicans with whom I work. On the other hand, the inward recollection and concentration of faith—the realisation of God which is re-creative—has been almost absent from the mind of the frequenter of prayer meetings and from prayer meetings; and those who are re-finding it in Christian Science and kindred movements think they can experience its full power without being "of one accord in one place" with others. I am convinced that only when these two ideals are brought into unity will prayer be fully efficacious.[21]

Dougall published her final three books, *God and the Struggle for Existence* (1919), *The Lord of Thought* (1922), and the posthumous *God's Way with Man* (1924) with the student movement.

In 1915, Dougall became involved in a short-lived attempt to bring the SCM energy into the Church through a youthful body named the Anglican Fellowship. For several years before and after the Great War, the Anglican Fellowship attracted the elite of Anglican youth, leaders like

William Temple, later the Archbishop of Canterbury, and Leonard Elliott-Binns, later an eminent historian of British theology. The small group drew its methods, purpose, and much of its membership from the SCM. It was organized by SCM leader, Tissington Tatlow, and the young A. C. Turner as an Anglican version of Malcolm Spencer's Free Church Fellowship. They called a meeting in April 1912, with a number of liberal Anglicans; this was followed by a second larger meeting in October 1912. Finally, a conference took place at Swanwick on July 9–11, 1913.[22] It was described by a member as the "thinking machine" of the church, and was said to exercise considerable influence, but there are very few signs of its existence in Church of England records.[23] Dougall's papers include a number of Anglican Fellowship *Bulletins,* and from them, and others preserved in the Ripon College Library, it is possible to trace the brief history.

The Fellowship was self-consciously reformist. Their initial statement of purpose rings with youthful defiance:

> The Anglican Fellowship is a body of men and women, members of the Church of England, who feeling that the Church does not exercise that leadership in the solution of moral problems which rightly belongs to her, are deeply conscious of their own individual responsibility as members of the Church of England, for many of the failures with which she may be charged. . . .
>
> Members of the Fellowship feel that it is only in fellowship with others that they will be able to justly estimate which problems are and which are not of fundamental importance, or courageously face the difficulties which must confront the church whenever she sets herself to their solution or goes beyond the standards of ordinary public opinion.[24]

The outlook was politically progressive. The first *Bulletin* expressed the concern "especially that we may have and declare the Mind of Christ in relation to the social and labor movements of our day, and the woman's movement."[25] The list of members of 1914 was dominated by academics and clerics but also included members of such progressive organizations as the Christian Socialist Union, men's and women's university settlements, the deaconess movement, the Young Women's Christian Association, and mission organizations.

Ties to modernism were strong. At least fifteen founding members of the Fellowship in 1914 were also active in the Modern Churchman's Union.[26] The Fellowship, however, eschewed theological issues for a common spirituality. An academic tone—"the decadence of thinking"—was to be discouraged, meetings were to avoid becoming intellectual forums or book discussions, groups were instructed to encouraged to practice prayer and silence, and special rules governed the discussions to avoid intellectual sparring.[27] A draft manuscript among Dougall's papers,

"English Modernism," suggests that the association with modernism was controversial:

> These fellowships were certainly not organised for the propagation of Modernism. . . . There can be no doubt that these groups have had a great influence in steadying and liberalising English religious thought; Their influence, on the whole, has been toward Modernism, but perhaps their influence has been most important in checking those extreme innovations in religious speculation and work that are frequently the *bizarre* result of solitary thought and lack of local sympathy.[28]

Her editing of this passage is revealing. After changing the word *Modernism* to *liberalism* in the last sentence, she crossed out the entire phrase "Their influence, on the whole, has been toward Modernism." The article when published in *The Contemporary Review* remained as edited, denying connections with modernism (which, of course, were suggested by their very inclusion in an article on "English Modernism").[29]

Women were encouraged to take leading roles. Unlike the parallel Free Church Fellowship, which initially excluded women, the Anglican Fellowship included a relatively large number of women in its membership and on the organizing committee, including church leaders like Mrs. Creighton and activists like Maude Royden.[30] There were also a large number of women from the new women's colleges, especially St. Hugh's College, the college in whose old building Dougall had lived in 1894. Not only was the head of the college, C. A. E. (Ann) Moberley, and tutors, C. B. Firth (later vice-principal), C. M. Ady, and, possibly, Miss Toynbee, active in the Fellowship, but there were also connections to the governing council.[31] In 1916, the annual conference was held at St. Hugh's, and the next year it was held at a sister college, Lady Margaret Hall, Oxford. Outside observers noted the relatively equal cooperation of women in the Fellowship; women occasionally led discussions and on at least one occasion a woman, Mrs. Streeter, led a devotional meeting.[32] The first committee was made up entirely of men, but they then "co-opted" Miss Fairfield, and after the conference decided to "co-opt" two more women.[33] Once the war started, women took a larger role of necessity. By 1916, the committee was represented by five women, including Dougall, and one man, A. C. Turner, who was subsequently killed in battle.[34]

This female presence does not seem to have greatly influenced the agenda. The *Bulletin* reported that women's issues were at the forefront of the first annual conference:

> [I]t was inevitable in the present circumstances that we should give special attention to the relation of women to the problems before us and of the Church to problems connected with women. So, at the outset, the

needs of women and the anomalies of their present position in the church were before us as constituting a special feature in the situation. The present relations of women to the Church and of the Church to women constitute a danger which it is very difficult, in the present state of affairs, for people to see clearly or discuss reasonably.[35]

However, subsequent discussions of the Anglican women's movement in the *Bulletin* are rather vague, and, despite the presence of Maude Royden (Royden had campaigned for women's right to preach, and created a controversy when she accepted an invitation to regularly preach in the Congregationalist church, City Temple) they avoid such controversial questions as the preaching of women. This may have been a matter of timing: Brian Heeney has argued that women's preaching diminished as an issue with the Great War.[36]

Although a great deal of lip service was paid to the needs of the "common man," the group was elitist. Local groups were initially discouraged and later barred from full membership in order to prevent the wrong kinds of people from joining.[37] In theory, the organizers welcomed free exchange of ideas; in practice, they controlled the direction of these ideas. The Fellowship maintained a level of secrecy—title pages of the *Bulletin* are marked "For private circulation only"—that is puzzling.

The aim of fellowship was not easily defined or achieved, and the Fellowship suffered from lack of direction. The first *Bulletin* proudly announced: "We cannot start with a clear-cut scheme or premeditated plan of campaign. These things must grow out of our meetings and our common work and thought." [38] As the writer candidly noted, however, "we were a very miscellaneous collection of people, and met very much in the dark as to what we were there for, or what was likely to come out of our meeting." [39] Ensuing issues of the *Bulletin* show the organizers grappling with this nebulous purpose. The 1914 conference revealed some loss of direction, and, as the following comments from the *Bulletin* reveal, some impatience:

> [A] condition of mutual bewilderment is not a source of strength if indefinitely prolonged . . . members of the conference themselves began to wonder whether we were really about anything in particular and had not better have stayed home and done our business . . . the question, once raised, was answered on the last evening with an extraordinarily strong conviction that we were there for a very definite and real purpose, even though it might not be easy or even possible at once to define exactly what the purpose was or how it was to be pursued.[40]

The 1915 conference, held in September in Baslow, had only 26 members present, despite a more open membership policy.

Dougall attended the 1913 conference; her name first appears in the records when she joined the Fellowship committee in September 1915.[41] She was active there in 1916, and as a discussion leader until at least 1919,[42] and became part of a close-knit group.[43] Her prominence in the organization is a little surprising. Membership was by invitation only and, as the *Bulletin* had made clear in 1914 in one of a number of vexed discussions about admittance, older people were deliberately excluded: "But it should be remembered that we do not, except for special reasons, invite anyone who cannot definitely be said to belong to the younger generation." [44] At fifty-seven, Dougall could hardly be considered a member of the younger generation, and it is likely she played the same mentoring role in the Fellowship that she did with the SCM.[45]

On the 1915–1916 committee with Dougall were six women, including Maude Royden and Zoë Fairfield, and thirteen men, including such clergy as future Archbishop of Canterbury William Temple; the modernist bishop E. W. Barnes; SCM secretary Percy Dearmer; chair Tissington Tatlow; and secretary A. C. Turner.[46] They were all progressives, active in numerous causes. Maude Royden is best known for the confrontational nature of her suffrage and pacifist politics; she is described as "one of the strongest and most influential personalities of all the religious leaders and teachers of the day." [47] Less well-known is Royden's deep spirituality, and her formation in 1914 of a Fellowship of Prayer, within the Church Congress for Women's Suffrage, and a guild for personal religion in 1919, the "Little Company of Christ." Dougall may have met Royden for the first time at the 1915 conference; Royden's name and address are on Dougall's copy of the *Bulletin*, and she subsequently visited at Cutts End.[48] Zoë Fairfield was the less controversial, if equally dynamic, assistant to the secretary-general in the SCM; she was the editor of a book on suffrage, *Some Aspects of the Women's Movement* (1915).[49]

The most influential voice on the 1915–1916 committee was probably that of A. C. Turner. Turner revitalized the floundering Fellowship by orienting it in a clearly spiritual direction, emphasizing the Incarnation: "What we all want," he said, in an inspirational paper for the August 1915 *Bulletin*, "can only happen as the fruit of a deep and wide spiritual movement of some kind." [50] Dougall was impressed; she wrote E. W. Barnes, "He has some great ideas which I think should go towards making the new epoch. He seems to have a real philosophy of Divine omnipotence. . . ." [51] She immediately invited Turner to Cutts End for a week in September 1915, where, Harold Anson said, she "dragged [an essay, later published in *Concerning Prayer*] from the depths of his singular and persistent reserve." [52]

The 1916 conference featured such popular speakers as Arthur Clutton-Brock, G. K. Chesterton, Harold Anson, Maude Royden, and William Temple. A retreat was held in Swanwick, a series of weekend conferences were organized (for one of which Dougall offered her home, Cutts End), and a number of local groups were established around England, with leaders including Cyril Emmet, Leonard Elliott-Binns, Percy Dearmer, Harold Anson, and C. B. Firth.[53] Their efforts appear to have been successful; forty to fifty people attended the London meetings, and in 1917 eighty members came to the summer conference.

As it emerged from this period, the Fellowship emphasized spirituality within fellowship, rather than reform. This was not understood as mysticism; as C. H. S. Matthews said in the *Bulletin:* "the flight of the alone to the alone is a nightmare. Things are all wrong when there is an absence of the spirit of fellowship. . . ."[54] Yet it drew upon an experiential faith: "its only method is to surrender mind and will in active attendance upon the Spirit of Christ."[55] The key word was Spirit.

Dougall's influence is revealed in the paper "Thoughts Preliminary to the Restatement of the Doctrine of the Holy Spirit," with which she opened the 1917 Swanwick retreat on "The Holy Spirit and the Church." The paper, subsequently published in *The Interpreter,*[56] is anecdotal, and gently provocative and modernist. She had recovered some of the sense of humor that characterized her early work: "I once had a weary discussion with a woman in a hotel who was eager I should admit that a certain Mr. B. was the most spiritual man. Toward the end I discovered that her standard of spirituality was that a man should be very thin and eat little, and have what she called 'liquid eyes.' " Dougall argued for a rethinking of the terms of spirituality. Her argument follows familiar lines. The ideal was an experiential faith—"every Christian soul should train itself to realise the spiritual presence of a personal God and directly offer to Him its thoughts and desires."[57] The danger lay in "tradition" stifling this spirit: "whether the warp and woof of what our tradition offers us as the garment of salvation may not be of the stuff that actually extinguishes the Spirit."[58] Dougall described the narrow doctrines of the Holy Spirit held by the Sacramentalist, who would exclude the Quaker, and the Protestant, who would exclude the Christian Scientist. In their place, she argued for Liberal thinkers or "moderns" who take a broad outlook, "ascribing all that is beneficent in human life to the action of the Spirit, and endeavoring to learn from whatever we find to be beneficent something new concerning the spiritual life."[59] The Holy Spirit may be manifested outside the church in science, in art, in the mental science movement, and even possibly in the teachings of those who are nonreligious or immoral.

The Fellowship report on the retreat was rapturous: "We have long suspected the SCM would turn the ecclesiastical world upside down and it looks as if The Day were not very far off—the day of constructive earth-quake . . . again we know what happened at Pentecost. . . ." Certainty was best found in uncertainty; Dougall had argued in *Pro Christ et Ecclesia* that intellectual assurance led to dogmatism and sectarianism, and called for an earnest waiting, a "mystical dipping into the unseen world of the soul." The Fellowship similarly took pride in their uncertainty and looked to a shared mysticism in the "fellowship of the Holy Spirit." "We settled nothing, except that it is right to be unsettled. . . . [Y]ou can't formulate an adequate doctrine of the Holy Spirit. You simply can't get the final abstraction; but you can experience the fellowship of the Holy Spirit. We were bewildered—and yet we were satisfied." [60] Dougall's paper appears to have been influential: a subsequent "Memo on the Holy Spirit" called for the creation of a "Fellowship of the Holy Spirit" that would unite all those groups, including those outside the church, such as health, women's groups, and socialist movements. [61] The most lasting product, however, was a book, published with another fellowship organized by Dougall, the Cumnor Group.

As Dougall described it, the Cumnor Group or School consisted of "a few writers who meet at the house of one of their number at Cumnor, near Oxford, to discuss subjects of their theological writings. This group gives three days at a time to a meeting, observes regular hours for discussion, and practices the fellowship rules." They published the resulting articles in three popular books, *Concerning Prayer* (1916), *Immortality* (1917), and *The Spirit* (1919) that were widely read by students and clerics. The *Manchester Guardian* reported, on Dougall's death, that "the gatherings at Cumnor [were] known among Liberal Churchmen throughout the English speaking world." [62]

The Cumnor School came into being in 1914 when Dougall and B. H. Streeter met for the first time and immediately planned a collabora-tive work, published as *Concerning Prayer* (1916), drawing upon mutual friends in the Anglican Fellowship. [63] The question of the role Dougall played in these collaborations is an interesting one. Streeter gave her credit for inspiring the series: "Though I acted as editor throughout, the initial idea, not only of this, but of each of the subsequent volumes, was due to Miss Dougall; and the spirit which gave its special character to the group discussions out of which each volume was produced was what it was by reason of the 'atmosphere' which she created." [64] Modernist bishop E. W. Barnes described Dougall as the "unifying centre of her var-ious conferences." [65] Sophie Earp described Lily as the originator of the volumes and Streeter as her collaborator. "With the help of her friend, Canon Streeter," she wrote, "[Dougall] assembled the group who came to be known as the Cumnor School." The idea, she said, was Dougall's: "the wholehearted way in which [Streeter] entered into Lily's schemes and helped her to develop the idea of drawing together a group of people who should together think out and individually set down, their views, made the friendship then begun the most fruitful factor of her life from then on." [66] Harold Anson described the cooperative books as "her books," and described "Miss Dougall's method." [67] He referred to Dougall's work in encouraging A. C. Turner. Hilda Oakeley, Dougall's old friend and a reader in philosophy at King's College London, also gives Dougall credit for setting the tone of intellectual cooperation. [68]

Dougall's role, however, has been overshadowed by that of Streeter, who is generally credited as the editor of the books. [69] Dr. Dorothy Emmet, a philosophy professor and daughter of one of Dougall's collaborators, C. W. Emmet, remembers Dougall as a charming and intelligent woman who played the role of the hostess for a group of learned scholars. [70] The ambiguity is due in part to the collaborative nature of the group writing process; Dougall was the hostess, but this role included a significant intellectual and editorial component. The contributors met for several days at a time, discussed a single topic, and then individually wrote chapters for joint books on the topic. They then met at various stages to criticize one another's contributions. Harold Anson described the process: "[*Concerning Prayer*] gradually took shape, as the result of many conferences. We all produced our papers; they were discussed and pulled to pieces during long morning sessions in her house at Cumnor. After luncheon we went for walks, and in the evening resumed our discussions." [71] Occasionally members of the group would stay and work at Cutts End. [72] Streeter described the cooperative nature of the work in the somewhat self-congratulatory introduction to *Immortality:*

> Intellectual co-operation only achieves its greatest possibilities where its basis is enthusiasm for a common cause and personal friendship; and experience shows that the intellectual activity and receptivity of each is raised to the highest pitch when that fellowship is not in work alone and in discussion, but in jest and prayer as well. . . . As a result of thorough discussion a degree of unity and unanimity has been arrived at which, in view of the very various tastes, training, and experience of the authors, is remarkable, and which encourages them to believe that the conclusions reached are really sound. [73]

(As one reviewer noted, "The Cumnor school of theologians take themselves very seriously.") [74] Other Fellowship members and progressive

Lily Dougall, c. 1920. The Lily Dougall Papers, Box 6. *Courtesy The Bodleian Library, University of Oxford.*

clergy might contribute to the discussions; Maude Royden, for example, appears to have contributed to *Concerning Prayer*, and several academics and clerics, including Barnes, contributed to *Immortality*.[75]

The best description of "Miss Dougall's method" is provided by Harold Anson. It is worth quoting at some length:

> We would meet in Miss Dougall's sitting room about 10 a.m. and have short prayers, partly liturgical and partly unwritten.
>
> Then, generally under Canon Streeter's leadership, one of us would read aloud the article which we had designed for the book, a not unformidable task.
>
> This would be welcomed by Miss Dougall, with a radiant face, and the warmest appreciation. Then the sad task would begin of questioning the author as to what he did exactly mean by that eloquent phrase, prepared by him with such care and, perhaps, self approval. The whole company, always with kindness, and often with much laughter, fell upon the author, and sometimes, in Miss Dougall's case with most urgent seriousness. How *can* that theory be fitted in with Our Lord's teaching? Are we getting away from that high fatherly conception which Jesus held about God? Perhaps the poor author finally felt that the beautiful phrase meant nothing in particular, perhaps it was modified by general consent, perhaps postponed for consideration on another day. Or some problem, unforeseen, would arise and a general discussion would be arranged for the evening. In this way, during two or three days, the book would take shape, each author learning much . . . In the afternoon we would walk . . .; after tea we worked again, and again after supper and then often we talked in our lodgings until well into the night.[76]

This method was not original; as Dougall herself noted in an article on "English Modernism," a series of controversial works of liberal theology had been produced by what became known as the "group method." She explained: "Because Modernism is an attitude of mind, and not a system of doctrine, it makes progress by a new habit of religious group discussion, rather than through an organization for its propagation."[77] The first such book was the controversial *Essays and Reviews* (1860). The second, *Lux Mundi* (1889) originated with the "Holy Party" organized by Dougall's friend, J. R. Illingworth. Illingworth met with a group of friends for several days every year from 1875 in a "Fellowship in the devotion to the Truth," or more light-heartedly, the "Holy Party." Illingworth later hosted the meetings that led to the publication of the third controversial liberal volume, *Foundations: A Statement of Christian Belief in Terms of Modern Thought: By Seven Oxford Men* (1912).[78] It appears that the Cumnor group adopted the Holy Party's method of group discussion, with the addition of Anglican Fellowship rules. Dougall, however, departed from this precedent by bringing together experts from outside the Anglican and clerical fold, including psychologists, literary critics, and Nonconformist preachers, such as her friend from the Free Church Commission, W. F. Lofthouse.[79] Not everyone agreed about the benefits of group work. The Master of the Temple, E. W. Barnes, enjoyed participating "in conversations [on *Immortality*] where seriousness and humor were not deemed mutually exclusive," but he suggested that the results were likely to be conservative.[80] By 1908, however, the collaborative process was so well established that the editor of *Anglican Liberalism by Twelve Churchmen* felt obliged to note, "The Title of this book indicates among the Writers a general community of aim: but each Contributor is responsible for only his own essay."[81]

The first Cumnor volume, *Concerning Prayer,* drew heavily on the membership of the Anglican Fellowship. Rev. W. Micklem and philosopher R. G. Collingwood were the only Anglicans apparently not connected to the Anglican Fellowship. E. R. Bevan and A. C. Turner served on the Fellowship committee with Dougall. C. H. S. Matthews, B. H. Streeter, and Harold Anson had been members in 1914, and Leonard Hodgson subsequently joined the Fellowship.[82] The other two contributors were not Anglicans (Rufus Jones was a Quaker, and Reverend Lofthouse was with the Free Church). The essays are all modern in orientation, emphasizing an immanent God, and critical of the punitive God of the Old Testament. Harold Anson promoted the Guild of Health in "Prayer and Bodily Health"; in "Prayer as Understanding," he distinguished between the Oriental "Sultanic" concept of prayer before an arbitrary God and the scientific reverence of nature. (The chapter led to a rebuke by Archbishop Randall Davidson, who said Anson's teaching would prevent him from offering Anson any responsible position in the church.)[83] In "Prayer and the Mystic Vision," Rufus Jones presented his interpretation of mysticism through a modernist debunking of the *via negativa.* E. R. Bevan defended petitional prayer in "Petition (Some Theoretical Difficulties)." C. H. S. Matthews provided a curious explanation of the Eucharist, "a method of approach from the side of life rather than doctrine and tradition," in which he emphasizes the dramatic value, explains its sacrificial nature as love rather than suffering, and argues that the Eucharist is not essential for every Anglican. R. G. Collingwood (who was later to make his reputation as a philosopher) explained away the Devil.[84] Streeter called for a scientific study of the psychology of worship. Dougall (still writing anonymously) contributed "Repentance and Hope," and "Prayer for the Dead." *Concerning Prayer* was very successful. H. D. A. Major, the leading modernist and member of the Fellowship, gave the book a glowing review in the modernist journal *The Modern Churchman*.[85] After two reprintings, it went into a second edition in 1918, and was still selling in 1938.[86]

Streeter and Dougall immediately set to work on *Immortality*. She called upon two new friends: the writer, Arthur Clutton-Brock, and the modernist biblical critic, Cyril W. Emmet. Emmet took up Dougall's old concern about eternal punishment, proving through linguistic usage that the doctrine was not explicitly taught in the New Testament. J. A. Hadfield provided a scientific perspective. E. W. Barnes, W. S. Bradley, C. H. S. Matthews, W. H. Moberly, and M. S. Earp also participated in the preliminary conferences and contributed memoranda on special points. The group finished *Immortality* in October 1917; Dougall noted that "we have been working at it so incessantly and almost violently."[87] The book sold well to a country devastated by the loss of a generation of young men.[88]

The final volume, *The Spirit*, grew out of the Anglican Fellowship retreat on the Holy Spirit. Streeter noted "[*The Spirit*] owes not a little to that discussion, and still more to the insight into the meaning and possibilities of spiritual fellowship gained at this and at similar gatherings."[89] Hadfield, Clutton-Brock, and Emmet contributed to it with philosopher Andrew Seth Pringle-Pattison (1856–1931) and C. A. Anderson Scott. The book was published in 1919 and reprinted in 1920, 1921, 1922, and 1928. The Archbishop of Canterbury wrote a complimentary letter.[90] In her chapter "God in Action," Dougall distinguished between vital Christians, those who are in pursuit of truth, beauty, and moral righteousness, and nominal Christians, who live in "docile obedience to religious rules." Her vital Christians may include those who deny Christ, but "are one with Him in Spirit." Hadfield argues that a religion's value lies in its ability to tap psychic power, and argued that it must be restated to make it "intellectually possible of acceptance" by modern man.[91]

The Cumnor years were Dougall's most fulfilling. She was at the height of her career, working with a group of younger academics and clerics, and finding a ready audience for her work among the students of the SCM. The emphasis on fellowship was well suited for a woman known to have a "genius for friendship," and the collaborative nature of her later books was an extension of her earlier collaboration with Sophie Earp and consultation with friends and mentors.

In Dougall's earlier religious writing there had been an underlying sense of inadequacy, a deference and hesitancy that undermined her theology. This was most apparent in *Christus Futurus*, when her apologetic preface—"These fragments are only published in the hope that those who have greater opportunity may find in them something to refine and complete"[92]—hurt the reception of the book. The handwritten introduction appended to a draft of a later article titled "Conscience and Authority," was similarly self-deprecatory: "I am well aware that this paper does not set forth this quarrel in a convincing way. . . . I only hope that some who are so much more able than I to think it out will track the question to its lair and deal with it."[93] Subsequent unpublished papers are prefaced with remarks that are almost embarrassing in their apologies. She wrote, for example, "Mr. Spencer [probably Rev. Malcolm Spencer of the SCM] has bidden me to write a short paper on the purpose of the church. It is not a subject on which I have reflected and indeed I am peculiarly ignorant about it; but I presume it is the childlike reflections of innocence that he desires. . . ."[94] In another instance, she stated, "I offer the following myth of creation for you only because our chairman has not been fortunate enough to secure an adequate paper. . . ."[95] Dougall was also self-effacing in private correspondence, suggesting that her theological contributions might have indirect benefits, as "the effort [of thought] even in a slow mind like mine, may start though waves that will over flow in the minds of more able thinkers."[96] The insecurity also surfaced in more subtle ways. She dropped references to friends who were archbishops and eminent theologians, and displayed her knowledge of ancient languages in the titles of her works.[97]

The collaborative nature of the Cumnor volumes helped Dougall to overcome her sense of inadequacy. After she met Streeter, Dougall never again published a book as a single author. She worked as part of a group of theologians, and published with the authority of their credentials and titles. She had always consulted with leading academics, from Edward Caird to William James, but in the collaborative process she was able to discuss her ideas with them, before and after writing her work. In the process, however, Lily Dougall's role disappeared. B. H. Streeter has been given credit for editing the group books, and it has largely been forgotten that it was the charming "hostess" who was mainly responsible for bringing the Cumnor group together, fostering the debates, and ensuring that the books were published.

9

Body and Soul

THE FOURTH ORGANIZATION with which Dougall became involved at this time was the Anglican Guild of Health. The Guild drew upon many of the same progressive Anglicans as the Cumnor Group and the Anglican Fellowship, and Dougall's role with the Guild was a similar one: she wrote pamphlets, articles, and books, and held discussions at her home. At one point, she even proposed renaming the Guild the Fellowship of Faith and Health. Lily Dougall's involvement in the Guild warrants separate discussion, however, because it points to the interplay of religious faith and the body. Lily Dougall struggled with ill health all of her life, and her approach to bodily health was deeply influenced by her youthful exposure to holiness theology and the claim of divine healing to bodily as well as spiritual health. In *Christus Futurus* (1907), she argued that physical as well as spiritual health was God's will; later she turned to the new sciences of psychotherapy to understand the mechanisms of God's action, and the esoteric mental science movements for practical applications. From 1913, disturbed by the intellectual shallowness of mental science, she tried to bring the energies of these movements into the church through the Guild of Health.

Health had been a preoccupation of Lily Dougall's since her childhood. "Anxiety with regard to my health is as innate in me as the faith in God I imbibed from my mother and the love of freedom I derived from my father," she recalled.[1] The three younger Dougall sisters struggled with illness: Mary Helen died in 1872, Susan spent much of 1878 in a rest home, and Lily herself broke down in 1877 and 1878. Their mother, Elizabeth, was frequently an invalid. The Dougall family naturally turned to prayer.[2] In 1879, Susan described a fellow patient who was cured of insanity and feebleness by intensive praying: "I daresay the same wise course would save many and many a one, if their friends could only know how."[3] A few years later, Elizabeth Dougall wrote to Lily's father suggesting that their illnesses had a purpose: "It may be that the bodily ailments, seemingly incurable in our family have been [?] that we might see that the wonderful loving kindness of our Blessed Lord delivering from the power of the Evil one the earthly bodies as well as the souls of his loved ones giving health to the body and deep spiritual life to the soul."[4] Her argument as well as her language suggests the influence of the divine healing movement, in which an atonement theology offered physical health to "earthly bodies" as well as sanctification to the soul, as Lily's mother had put it: "health to the body and deep spiritual life to the soul." In 1874, holiness preacher William E. Boardman had published accounts of Charles Cullis's faith healing; the popularity of divine healing spread with Carrie Judd's *Prayer of Faith* (1880) and Cullis's *More Faith Cures* (1881) and *Other Faith Cures* (1885).[5] As James Opp has shown, narratives of divine healing held special appeal for women, and spread through informal female networks in Canada. Women claimed divine healing, not, Opp explains, as "miraculous recovery, but as a natural state of being, a mode of faith similar to sanctification only applied to the whole body."[6] We cannot know if the Dougalls read these accounts, but a summer retreat favored by the Dougall family, Old Orchard, Maine, became a centre for holiness healing, and in 1885, Lily attended William Boardman's first international Faith Healing and Holiness Conference held in London, England, and offered to send her father a report.[7]

Elizabeth Dougall's letter to her husband suggests the power of this teaching. She recalls: "It seems clearly in answer to prayer that I was raised up last year and I believe it was the same this year although not so marked to myself." Her letter continues, "Perhaps with more perfect faith I might have been raised to perfect health instead of continuing so very weak all summer and ready to be laid down again."[8] Faith healing continued to be an important force within North America through the Christian Alliance, and in Britain in the higher life and Keswick movements.[9] Keswick writer Andrew Murray, for example, published *Divine Healing* in 1900.[10]

It is surprising, then, that Dougall did not turn to prayer to overcome her own chronic ill health. Illness had slowed her studies in 1881 in Edinburgh: "I have been missing a good many of my lectures, and I am a good deal discouraged about it." In 1883, she was forced to abandon studies at the Abbott Academy in Andover, and, in 1885, she almost gave up her studies in Ventnor.[11] Her account of her eventual breakthrough in the winter of 1885–1886 in a letter to her sister, Susan (who was also still struggling with illness while completing a medical degree),[12] echoes the structure of a faith healing narrative even as it points to a different cure:

> I know of a surety that were I in your case, my *chief difficulty* would be *unreal*. I will explain by giving my experience like a man at a "Methodist class." When I went to [study in] Ventnor, everyone said I should not be strong enough to study hard, and I believed it devoutly. I went on working against my doubts and "dragging" on, until, in the middle of the second term I was quite ill, having all the symptoms of a "break-down" about me. I was not willing to give in, so I sent for the doctor.

Her description of the doctor is interesting: "He was more than an ordinary doctor, for he was a scientific man—i.e. a man devoted to science." But his influence, apart from his prescription of bromide, was largely psychological:

> He told me to go on with my work. After that I resolved I should never worry about my health again. Futile resolve! . . . When I found I could not keep my resolution, I determined I would hand over my health *objectively* to the keeping of a good doctor, and allow it no longer to be a matter of subjective consideration. All that spring he told me to go on working, and when I had a headache or could not sleep peacefully, he gave me bromide. His motto was: "Feed, feed, feed."

Dougall's evangelical female relatives warned her to slow down: "Janet wrote warning me; Aunt Jane wrote warning me; Miss Sutton [?] never ceased to warn me; and worst of all my own conscience warned me every hour of the day." But Dougall persisted: "For it is quite possible to have a false conscience, or one that has been artificially produced. But above it all I felt certain I had done right to trust the doctor and not to my own varying feelings. A few days after the exam I was feeling as well as I had ever done in my life." Her difficulties, Dougall realized, had not been physical:

> I am forced to admit that the lion in the path, which so often nearly turned me out of the right way, was not a *real* lion. He was not only chained, but he was a ghost which my own disordered nerves conjured up to affright me, and I feel small hope but that this ghostly lion will stand in my path as long as I live; for looking back I know he was born with me and filled my earliest years with untold fears.[13]

The letter is revealing. Dougall was pursuing an unusual path and family warnings against her studies probably reflect the sense that academic work, especially the study of mathematics and Greek, was unsuitable and hence unhealthy for a woman. Dougall needed the strong support of an outside advisor to bolster her own flagging willpower. Curiously, although she tells the story "like a man in a 'Methodist class,'" and the language echoes faith-healing stories published by Cullis, religious faith plays no role in this narrative.[14] It is Dougall's own willpower rather than her faith that was at stake, and it was a man of science rather than a man of God who supported her. Dougall describes the restrictions of invalidism in the same terms she had earlier used to describe the limiting morality of evangelicalism. Invalidism had produced a "false conscience," an imaginary lion, like the "gruesome spectres" conjured up by evangelicalism.[15] She turned to masculine science to aid her in resisting the warnings of her evangelical female relatives.

Although Dougall was remarkably productive in the decade after her Ventnor experience, her health problems were not entirely overcome; the "ghostly lion" continued to bar her way at times. She chose to live in areas known for their health, Ventnor and Cheltenham. When she returned to Canada (and, significantly, to her family) in 1897, she found she was unable to spend the spring in Montreal, and traveled to North Carolina in 1897, to England in 1899, and California in 1900.[16] On her return to England in 1903, she hoped to live in Oxford, but, as Earp put it, "the asthma intervened." Dougall regained her health in the recuperative quiet of Exmouth with Earp. "Year by year the asthma became less, and though the improvement was slow it was, on the whole, continuous."[17] She still had to be cautious, and when they finally moved to Oxford she found a home high in the Cotswolds. Even so, Harold Anson, who knew her at the end of her life, recalled, "Miss Dougall was a frail woman, constantly oppressed by asthma, and too often very obviously finding breathing a great and distressing difficulty."[18]

It was only as Lily Dougall began to recover that she began to speculate publicly about the interplay of body and spirit. In 1906, after four years with Earp in Exmouth, Dougall published her first article on health in the liberal theological publication, the *Hibbert Journal*.[19] Once again she was at the forefront of ecclesiastical debate, two years ahead of the Anglican bishops who debated spiritual healing at the 1908 Lambeth Conference. "The Salvation of the Body by Faith" was well received. Personal idealist J. R. Illingworth told a friend that there had been a good article published, "on disease not being according to God's will and His consequent readiness to remove it where there is faith—a line of thought I have dwelt on much of late. I think we ought to look on prayer as the normal means of getting healed, whether with or without—but not of course necessarily without—other means."[20] Illingworth, like Dougall, had struggled with poor health; he left Oxford for a quiet country parish (and married a nurse). His praise was surprising, for

Dougall's argument contradicted his own early work. In "The Problem of Pain," Illingworth had argued that pain served God's purpose, whereas Dougall argued that pain, like evil, was not part of God's purpose.[21] But he shared her idea that God worked through the physical as well spiritual world. In *Divine Immanence: An Essay on the Spiritual Significance of Matter* (1898), Illingworth had argued that "while Christ's acts of physical healing are quite subordinate to His spiritual teaching, and are treated by Him as such, yet they are not merely incidental acts of mercy; they are integral parts of His entire work, an essential element in the total impression which He plainly designed to create, that he was Lord of the material as well as of the spiritual order, and came not merely to teach, but to exercise absolute authority over the bodies as well as the souls of men." [22] Illingworth may have contacted Dougall; at any rate, she was a frequent guest when she moved to nearby Cutts End. Dougall consulted with him on other theological matters, and it is likely that he influenced her ideas on healing.

Spiritual healing was a central component of Dougall's next book, *Christus Futurus* (1907). Dougall argued again that suffering and pain were not part of God's plan, and that the faithful should expect physical as well as spiritual health in the coming Kingdom of God. "Jesus taught that health was God's will, that it was an inevitable consequence of right faith." [23] She departed from the miracle-working faith healers, however, by arguing that the power of spiritual healing was not miraculous or supernatural but, like the newly discovered powers of radium, part of the natural order. It was simply a matter of time before science could determine the mechanisms by which healers exercised their power. Even the biblical narratives of Christ's healing powers were not miracles:

> [T]hey were works as strictly conditioned by the natural sequences of cause and effect as any action of our own, the difference being they were conditioned by sequences of which we have only the slightest knowledge. . . . [Christ] could only do them by taking the utmost advantage of the psychic and physical means that the strength of his personality put within his control.[24]

The Christian could, on a more limited scale, exercise the same "natural sequences of cause and effect." To understand these sequences, Dougall turned to the new science of psychology: first to members of the Society of Psychical Research (SPR), who were earnestly and scientifically investigating psychic phenomena and then, as the Great War brought new evidence of mind–body interaction in the form of shell shock, to the new practitioners of neurology and psychotherapy. She explained to her family in 1908 that scientists had identified, in the "subconscious mind," a new locus for the action of mind (and spirit) upon the physical body: "a subconscious but perfectly normal life power which can when it can be evoked cure organic disease, control the nerves and muscles as the conscious mind cannot. . . ." [25]

In *Christus Futurus,* Dougall drew upon the work of Swiss psychotherapist Paul Dubois, the author of *The Psychic Treatment of Nervous Disorders,* and neurologist Alfred Taylor Schofield, to argue that the powers of the unconscious can be applied against illness. [26] Ann Taves has shown that the explanations of psychology frequently operated in tandem with religious interpretations, and, as we shall see in the epilogue, Dougall understood the Society for Psychical Research (SPR) and the early science of psychology to be offering rational grounds for the faith in God. Schofield was the author of a curiously schizophrenic series of books on neurology and faith: *Nerves, in Order and Disorder: A Plea for Mental Therapeutics* (1893); *The Knowledge of God: Its Meaning and Power* (1903); and *With Christ in Palestine: Four Addresses* (1906). The power of the mind over psychological disturbances, or "functional" disorder, was widely accepted, but Dougall argued with Schofield that these powers must also extend over physical, or "organic" disease. Her arguments are weak ones, if lyrically stated. She argues from the example of the healing practiced by the Christian Alliance, from the stories of Jesus healing in the Bible, and from a simple extension of logic: "It is more difficult to believe that while many diseases may be cured by the right mental conditions, there are others over which such mental conditions have no influence, than to believe that all diseases come under the same natural laws, however powerless we may yet be to apply these laws." [27]

If the early science of psychology provided Dougall with a scientific, rational explanation for spiritual healing, mental science movements provided practical application. At the turn of the century, Christian Science had spawned a broad and increasingly feminized movement that went under a diversity of names including Unity School, Mind Cure, and New Thought. [28] As Beryl Satter's work on New Thought has shown, these therapeutic movements were closely connected with progressive and woman movements. [29] New Thought teacher Emma Curtis Hopkins taught a six-step form of contemplation that involved the repetition of affirmations in "the Silence," a meditational frame of mind, and described a mystical merging with the universe, into a center, the "I AM." Hopkins retained only the slightest semblance of Christianity (she claimed her *I Am* was Jesus Christ), but there were connections between New Thought and the early holiness movement in the sense of a transformed self through union with the divine. Like Hannah Whitall Smith, Hopkins emphasized joy and passivity.

Lily Dougall, "having long withstood and derided the literature of the 'mental science' movement as pure rubbish," was finally encouraged to attend their meetings in 1908 by Archdeacon Wilberforce and Percy Dearmer, a modernist Christian socialist.[30] She was fascinated, and described the mental science meetings in a series of letters to her brother:

> These people radiate peace and joy and success in work. All that I have met are workers either in the slums or in professions. After the "silence meeting" where the names or initials of those to be helped are read aloud at intervals, one and another get up to tell that in this, that or the other life the desired change has come. The names are divided into classes: those who need health; those who need conversion to true ideas, and those who need prosperity. The latter class is always large. Nothing else at all is desired from God but that each one mentioned should in his or her own heart be assured that the desire is fulfilled. For example, the leader of the meeting says, "John Smith, know in your heart that in God there is no failure; you live in God and God in you." Then they sing to John Smith: "God is power—pure power—blessed power. That power is yours—*yours*. You live in God and God in you." Then they are perfectly sure that J. S.— wherever or whoever he may be—has been influenced in the right direction, "Almighty Intelligence carrying the message and knowing how to apply it." Day by day John Smith gets the same message.[31]

Dougall claimed to be skeptical, but the movement appealed to her long-standing concerns about her own and her family's health. She was impressed enough at the power of the mental science meetings to take up the offer of a friend who was "one of the all-round Christians in the Mental Science Movement" to take her sister, Susan, "into the silence" which, she noted, "is their paraphrase for prayer." [32]

In another letter, several days later, Dougall described a similar meeting:

> The studio was painted white inside—about 15 or 20 people were there mostly young and very sturdy. Some very [?] dressed and some very plain or poor. The women there between 16 and 30, there was a fashionably dressed youth and two middle-aged men. The artist was an exceedingly pretty girl. She sat down in front of us all and began to read about the man with the withered hand. . . . Her point was that the Pharisees had a withered intelligence just as the man a withered hand. But they would not stretch out their minds when Jesus told them to. She then spoke of the interpenetration of life and matter in the hand. It was not an instrument held by Life, it was not a vessel through which life flowed. There was some kinship between matter and life where the man "reckoned on Jesus" by stretching out his hand. She said all this quite fast in an artless way then she said that we would realise life in silence. Everyone at once sat upright and shut their eyes. They all looked serene

and contented while she recited sentences for meditation at intervals of about five minutes. 1st Be still and know that I am God. 2nd Your bodies are the temples of the Holy Ghost. 3rd God is power. 4th God is goodness and so on through all the attributes which may be common to the divine and human. The moment the hour was over she rose up and everyone went out instantly in various directions. Their manner of departure showed that they had not come for society or out of idleness.[33]

During the same trip, Dougall's Montreal friend Hilda Oakeley, who was now a reader in philosophy at King's College, London, invited her to a "parlour sermon" by an elderly cleric that consisted of a rambling "torrent of musical words" on God as love. Dougall noted that although "none of these people have ever heard of [mental science]," it was "an aspect of the same thing under a different name."[34]

Dougall was defensive about her interest in mental science, carefully telling her family that she had been advised to attend by Anglican clerics, or emphasizing that she had been led to believe the meeting was a health class. In the letters to her family she emphasized the intellectual shallowness of the movement—"it is an intensely practical movement, it has as yet come to no intellectual expression."[35] As she said in later letter, members "write and talk only for the unlearned."[36] She argued, however, that these meetings offered a more practical example of the powers investigated by psychologists. She explained to her family that the "learned and (mostly) scientific people" of the Society for Psychical Research were investigating "(under other names) the powers that the mental scientists with all their eccentricity of expression and effort were trying to bring into direct use . . . The great problem for the psychologist is how to get it to act. The Mental Scientists say yield it to God, trust God with it, and it will act."[37] She described the mental realization practiced by the mental scientists as a "law of spiritual life," working through "the mental image in the human mind."[38]

She argued that mental science constituted an advance upon evangelical prayer meetings. Most prayer books, she noted, require that the Christian must become "perfectly repentant, or perfectly humble, or perfectly submissive, or perfectly consecrated or (most strange of all) perfectly Christ-like—before he is encouraged to believe that God *must* speak to him out of the silence and must fulfil his desires."[39] This, she argued, was a mistake, as in practice it admitted only the arrogant few access to the power of prayer. By contrast, "[Christ's] promises of prayer were cast over the sea of seething humanity without conditions." Mental science was closer to Christ's teaching as "the place of power is not said to depend upon any experience of spiritual depth or height attained by the individual."[40] As she told her family: "However wrong the Mental Science may be in their doctrines, and they have no distinctly formulated doctrines, I am perfectly convinced that they have a great secret which must be added to the ordinary Christian life of this age if that life is not to degenerate." [41]

Dougall suggested that mental science had emerged from the optimistic theology and contemplative practice of the early holiness movement. She argued that the holiness movement had narrowed, "but the impact of this joyful conception of the force of the supernatural grace of the Atonement escaped from these narrow devotees into a larger air, and can be distinctly traced in the theories of 'Christian Science,' 'Higher Thought,' the 'New Theology,' etc. These theories all differ from their prototype, but they beat with the joyful pulse of emancipation." [42] Like holiness believers, the proponents of mental science believed that people were essentially good and needed only to trust in this goodness—and in God—to realize their full potential. [43]

Dougall wrote *Absente Reo* (1910) two years after her initial forays into mental science, when she was still enthusiastic about the movement's potential. She defended "this great wave of thought" against orthodox "caricatures," while acknowledging that it "has as yet not very intelligent expression that I can find. . . ." [44] But by 1916 she was distancing herself from the mind cure movements. In a letter to D. S. Cairns, she said that the healing movement had been dominated by people who "skate gaily on the surface. They do not worship God with their reason; their God is not reasonable, yet they have a secret key which can open great riches of the mind of Christ if they know how to use it." These groups lacked a sense of fellowship: "those who are refinding [inward recollection and concentration of faith] in Christian Science and kindred movements think they can experience its full power without being 'of one accord in one place' with others." [45] Although as late as 1922 Dougall was still speculating publicly that these groups might indeed be tapping divine power, she became increasingly critical of the movement for intellectual shallowness and lack of fellowship. [46]

In *Immortality* (1917), Dougall described the ecstatic vision of the mystic as an immature experience typical of the first apprehension of God. Some mystics overcome this, "but to weaker natures the mistake of mistaking contemplation which has no intellectual content to be the goal of religious life is fatal; and under the delusion we see men and women whose wills become weaker, whose thoughts become more and more shallow, whose virtues are largely negative, and whose prayers seem ineffectual." [47] She calls for a worship that increases individual will and reason, and exalts friendship. In a later article she referred to those groups that, "like a stagnant pool giving off miasma—infest the air with bad moral germs because of a belief in their own infallibility in holding to either traditional notions or novel ideas." [48] An article published posthumously identified New Thought with what was considered irrational Eastern mysticism. Dougall criticized the prayer of the "Oriental Mystery Religions now practised in Christian Science, Theosophy, New Thought" and "any Christian teaching that depreciates the intellectual life." These new schools teach that "God's saving activities can only be fully drawn upon when the needy soul has learned by practice to make the mind vacant and receive what is desired in ecstatic realisation." [49] This form of prayer "is like a flood rising in hot river valleys, making the food fields fertile, but bearing on its tide malodorous things and germs of disease." [50]

In 1913, Dougall became involved in the Anglican Guild of Health, an attempt to bring the energy of mental science into the church. The Guild of Health had originally been organized in 1904 by Percy Dearmer, Conrad Noel, and Rev. B. Lombard. As Noel noted, "The idea was that Christian Science and other health movements outside the Church had been driven into heresy by the Church herself having forgotten to preach spiritual healing and having lost the power to practise it. Hence this revival in the Church of England." [51] It drew a membership of four hundred to monthly meetings and occasional services in London. In 1905, the movement expanded and spread outside London, making its center in Dearmer's parish, and inviting Harold Anson and G. K. Chesterton as speakers, but internal differences led a to decline of members by 1913. [52] Although Dougall initially attended mental science meetings on the encouragement of Dearmer, she does not seem to have played any role in the Guild until 1913, when Dearmer and Anson asked her to assist in the revitalization: "[T]here were a number of men [at the Swanwick Conference on Social Service] who were determined that I should help them to draw up a basis for the new Guild of Health, and we had private confabulations at all hours. I like them very much, especially Mr. [Anson], editor of *The Commonwealth*. We got our minds cleared up on the health subject." [53] She quickly became a key member of the Guild. In 1914, she hosted a conference at Cutts End on "the Relation of Spiritual Health to Bodily Health," and held a subsequent meeting in July 1915. [54] In 1916, she wrote a book for the Guild, *The Christian Doctrine of Health: A Handbook on the Relation of Bodily to Spiritual and Moral Health,* and invited Anson to write an essay, "Prayer and Bodily Health," for *Concerning Prayer* (1916). [55]

The Guild negotiated its position on spiritual healing within a wider Anglican healing movement that spanned the spectrum from the "miracle-mongering" of the Divine Healing Movement led by J. M. Hickson, to the sacramental use of holy oil by the High Church

Guild of St. Raphael.[56] The key difference appears to have concerned the question of miracles: both the Divine Healing Movement and the Guild of St. Raphael emphasized the miraculous nature of the cure and the role of a lay healer or priest, whereas the Guild eschewed dramatic public healing for a gradual improvement in health. The Guild, Anson explained, "aims at not merely removing physical symptoms, but at reconstructing the spiritual basis of life."

It appears there was a strong contemplative element. Evelyn Underhill was a member, and there are references in Guild documents to Baron von Hugel. A private letter written by Dougall to her childhood friend, Katie Drummond, in 1912, reveals the experiential faith behind her public statements: "I find all the health I have comes to me from the belief that health is the will of God, that it is ours as we take it from Him in faith, but I do not always or ever perfectly live up to my privileges." Her description of power of faith draws upon the language of mental science: "I am quite sure that the relief is there for us all, just in so far as we can grasp it. It does not depend on anything more God does for us; it depends on us putting our roots deeper into the Source of our being, as flowers send their roots into his earth and bring up what they need." [57] A letter from Dougall to Presbyterian theologian and Student Christian Movement leader David S. Cairns, written four years later, confirms the importance of this contemplative element, and her sense of responsibility in this regard. She told Cairns that she had been disappointed by the recent Guild of Health meetings at Cumnor, and that they failed to meet the ideal mix of inward contemplation and spiritual fellowship:

> I failed to do this in our little conference, and I take the entire blame onto myself. I had not thought it out, or torn myself from other things to make adequate preparation for the event. I am writing this to you when it seems to me I ought to be writing something else because I want to impart, if I can, my conviction that just beyond our present grasp—not far off in time or in processes of thought—there is something much greater and deeper.[58]

Many of the Anglican clergy, and the more "saintly" of the lay people, were skeptical, Dougall reported to her brother, but the hitherto irreligious, and the medical profession, were responsive.[59] Although the bishops of Winchester, Salisbury, and Worcester acted as patrons to the Guild, Bishop Gore's response to a copy of Dougall's *Christian Doctrine of Health* was guarded:

> I agree with you in the main. At times I doubt. I seem myself to be able (or to conceive easily that I should be more able) to triumph over some

ailments by faith and not over others. Of these others some can be attributed to Satan but not all. Are not these God's work of judgment? Please don't trouble to reply, I agree as to the Church's duty to *fight* disease.[60]

His reaction may in part have been due to the combative modernist terms in which its positions were expressed: a heading in one of Dougall's articles read, "How the Church Came to Neglect our Lord's Commission to the Sick." [61] Or perhaps he recalled Dougall's earlier tone: In *Christus Futurus* Dougall had condemned the Church of England for not following Christ's example as healer, but rather persisting "in wailing that disease is the will of God." [62] A subsequent novel, *Paths of the Righteous* (1908), took aim directly at Anglican bishops. When an artist is injured, his young son runs to the church where a number of bishops are attending a service. He challenges them to follow Christ's example and heal his father, and although a bishop finally agrees to try he can only sit helpless by the dying man's side, evidence of the church's impotence. It is an elderly lay evangelical who is finally able to revive the man.[63]

In 1918, at Lily Dougall's urging, the Guild of Health became ecumenical.[64] The Guild appears to have struggled at this time with attempts to set up study circles (like those in the Anglican Fellowship) and "frequent reversals of policy." [65] It was still closely affiliated with the Anglican Church, and when the Lambeth Conference appointed a committee to look into spiritual healing, a number of Dougall's associates were involved: J. A. Hadfield, B. H. Streeter, Harold Anson, and Dr. Jane Walker. The committee was divided and only reported in 1924.[66]

Dougall's handbook on spiritual healing, *Christian Doctrine of Health* (the manuscript was originally titled "God and the Body"), was probably one of her most influential books. Published in Britain and the United States, it was widely distributed to Guild of Health study groups.[67] It was both a promotional manual, convincing readers of the rational basis of spiritual healing, and a guide with practical advice about how to pray for health, including a chapter on "Child Training." Dougall appealed to the authority of the Bible and the authority of science. She referred to early Gospel tales of healing and then, in chapters titled "What is Health?" "What is Disease?" and "What is Mental Health?" she cited William James and a number of lesser known psychologists and acknowledged in a prominent note the assistance of Dr. Edwin Ash, "formerly of St. Mary's Hospital, London, author of *Mental Self-Help* etc.," and Dr. Jane Walker, a fellow member of the Guild. Perhaps most telling, she cites the *British Medical Journal*, side by side with the Bible, on the title page.[68]

Dougall's practical advice for spiritual healing is couched in terms drawn from the faith healing and mental science movements. She describes God as a creative power welling up and informing from within: "Upon this splendid foundation we ought to ground a belief in the constant outflow of His power to usward, which will be exhibited in our moral and physical health. . . ." Her description of prayer includes elements of the realization or appropriation that is typical of New Thought.[69] "The convinced soul must resolutely live according to his conviction. The bodily state must cease to be an anxiety; the trouble must be cast entirely upon God."[70] The book was, however, a pale reflection of the powerful affirmations of the mental science movement, and it lacked the humor and intelligent iconoclasm of her early critical work. Dougall followed the practice of academic texts by prefacing each chapter with an outline of the argument of the chapter. One of her more illogical summaries, on what is a central point in her argument, is as follows:

1. We must assume health to be always in accordance with God's will, because:
    a. It would be impossible to write a hymn in honour of God's creation and describe the object as diseased and producing diseased progeny after their kind.
    b. It is our duty to devote our whole powers—heart, mind, strength etc.—to the love of God and to bringing about His righteousness on earth, and disease impairs these powers.
    c. All sick people have to be constantly served, and the Christian is not in this world to be served, but to serve.
    d. So many forms of sickness are known to be the result, if not of individual, of racial sin; there is therefore a strong presumption on this ground that all blights and diseases have this origin.
    e. Jesus taught that Disease was Satanic in its origin.[71]

Dougall was aware of the book's flaws, and she apologized to Dr. Ridgeway, the Bishop of Salisbury: "I am fully aware it has many weaknesses, but it was written in response to a real demand, and had to be produced amid a conflict of duties."[72] The year 1916 was a busy one that also saw her first paper delivered at a modernist conference, as well as the production of her first collaborative book, *Concerning Prayer*.

Sales of Dougall's book reflected the public interest in faith healing. A letter from George Macmillan indicates that the book had sold 1,050 copies by 1917. He noted in this and a subsequent letter that later sales were disappointing.[73] When the issue of spiritual healing became controversial again in the 1920s, with a new Lambeth committee appointed and further faith-healing rallies by J. M. Hickson, the Guild of Health published a third revised edition. A revised American edition came out in 1923. At the same time, Dearmer published a new American edition of his 1909 book, *Body and Soul,* and Anson wrote *Spiritual Healing: A Discussion of the Religious Element in Physical Health.*[74] It was only after Lily Dougall's death that her work came to fruition. Hickson's mass spiritual healing meetings in 1924 raised the ire of the Bishop of Durham, Hensley Henson, and the modernist Dean of St. Paul's, W. R. Inge, and galvanized the church. William Temple, the liberal Archbishop of Canterbury, promoted the Guild's work and it reached its greatest influence in the 1930s.[75] Even as the Guild expanded, however, the grounds upon which Dougall had based her work were slipping away. As we shall see in the epilogue, by this time psychology was beginning to undermine the experiential basis of Dougall's theology.

10
Anglican Modernism

> It is sad to see how very widely spread is the assumption that
> no person who is in the least up-to-date dreams of believing
> in the divinity of Christ.[1]
>
> J. R. Illingworth, 1907

LILY DOUGALL EMERGED FROM anonymity through her Fellowship work,
and became known as an Anglican modernist. Anglican modernism was
the second generation of the scholarly Broad Church movement, politicized by the Roman Catholic condemnation of modernism, and infused
with the energy and spirituality of a youthful Anglo-Catholic membership. Modernists publicly questioned the key Christian doctrines: the virgin birth, the physical resurrection, and the divinity of Christ. Their
tactics were frequently confrontational. There has been little historical
analysis of religious modernism; it has largely been defined by its enemies and is usually described as a movement of accommodation with
secular culture. One critic wrote a scoffing prayer for modernists:

> O God, forasmuch as without thee,
> We know nothing whatever about thee,
> Help us all by thy grace,
> To teach the whole race,
> We know nothing whatever about thee.[2]

The metaphors employed by the modernists themselves describe a
movement for renewal within the Church; they describe orthodox faith
in Carlylean terms as so much outworn clothing, or a dry husk of tradition from which a kernel of spirituality is emerging. Mystics such as
W. R. Inge and Percy Gardner sought this spirituality in Neoplatonic
and other forms of mysticism. Anglo-Catholics sought it in the Church,
and brought a renewed sense of the living presence of the Spirit within
the corporate Church into Anglican modernism.

Examination of Lily Dougall's contributions to modernism reveal that she did not believe in the literal truth of the central doctrines any more than any other modernist, but her emphasis lay upon the experience and power of faith. Dougall played a quintessentially feminine role: she found a place in the modernist camp in part because as a woman she expressed the piety that modernists feared they might have lost. She brought a sense of spiritual fellowship, derived from her evangelical childhood, informed by her work with the Student Christian Movement, and influenced by a catholic sense of a corporate Christ, into the elite halls of a disputatious academic movement.

A number of descriptions of the movement were written by the 1920s and 1930s when modernism was the subject of heated debates, and A. M. G. Stephenson provided a comprehensive and thoughtful retrospective in *The Rise and Decline of English Modernism* (1984). More recently, growing recognition of the indebtedness of modern Christianity to modernism has resulted in a number of published and unpublished papers. But there is, as yet, no critical account of the intellectual basis of the movement.[3]

Part of the difficulty in producing a clear history of doctrinal debate is the very comprehensiveness of the Anglican communion. Unlike sectarians who set believers apart—"weaned from the world"—the Church of England was a comprehensive catholic church that laid claim to the world and to all of humanity. This could result in a wide latitude, as the case of Dougall's young associate, William Temple, reveals. When Temple, the son of the liberal Archbishop of Canterbury, Frederick Temple, approached the Bishop of Oxford about ordination in 1906, he was refused because he could not give more than a very tentative assent to the doctrines of the virgin birth and of the bodily resurrection of Christ. Two years later, after consultations with Dougall's fellow liberals, B. H. Streeter and Henry Scott Holland, he approached the archbishop and Randall Davidson found his views to be acceptable.[4] The archbishop's letter to the Bishop of Oxford suggests, however, that Temple may simply have learned to express his doubts in ways that the archbishop, keen to bring his close friend's son into the priesthood, was able to accept.[5] Five years later, Temple was still dancing along the secular line in the sand. He said he believed in the virgin birth, but then dismissed the import of the doctrine: "I cannot in my own mind find any theological significance in it." He said he believed in the physical resurrection, "but if it could be disproved, I don't think it would affect my faith as a whole."[6] Temple was a privileged example, but the fact that he was accepted for ordination and that he eventually became the Archbishop of Canterbury suggests the elastic and inclusive nature of Anglican theology.

The difficulties are compounded by the refusal of liberals to identify themselves as a party. Early attempts at organization in Britain and the United States were short-lived; as American Broad Churchman Rev. D. Samuel D. McConnell (1845–1939) wrote, "The difficulty is it is not a 'party' and never has been. It is a state of mind. The men of that type have always been difficult to organize."[7] F. D. Maurice had, after all, understood himself to be speaking on behalf of the universal Kingdom of God; he condemned sectarians. It was not until 1898 that a lasting body formed, in the Churchman's Union for Liberal Religious Thought.

The early history of the movement can best be traced through scholarly debate. The debate was often heated, but generally the heretical ideas of one generation became accepted in the next, and as young radicals advanced to positions of influence they found themselves reining in the new generation. This process of gradual accommodation was rudely interrupted by the Roman Catholic condemnation of modernism in 1907. Anglican liberals became alarmed at the condemnation of Biblical critic Alfred Loisy's *L'évangile et l'église* (1902) and after 1910, when every Roman Catholic priest was ordered to take the "Oath against Modernism," liberal Anglicans were galvanized into organized action.[8] Anglo-Catholics such as Kirsopp Lake, Alfred Fawkes, and J. F. Bethune Baker assisted in organizing the first modernist conference in Oxford in 1914. Membership in the Churchmen's Union soared from one hundred in 1910 to one thousand in 1914, and Ripon College evolved into a liberal theological college by 1918.[9] The name of their journal, *The Modern Churchman*, founded by H. D. A. Major in 1911, connected the liberal movement with continental modernism, although it was only after a 1919 conference that liberals adopted the modernist label, and the liberal Churchman's Union only formally became the Modern Churchman's Union in 1928.[10] At the same time, liberal Protestants in the United States began to be identified as modernists, largely in reaction to the rise of fundamentalism.

Lily Dougall was drawn into modernism through her friends in the Cumnor Group, her circle of academic women friends, and the personal idealists she met in Oxford.[11] The question of the role of women in the Union is an intriguing one. Some of the most prominent women in the Anglican Church were active in the Union: the lay preacher Maude Royden, novelist Mary Ward, academic Alice Gardner, Dr. Jane Walker, and the writer on mysticism, Evelyn Underhill, contributed to debates. The annual conferences were held at the women's colleges at Oxford and Cambridge, and H. D. A. Major observed that it was the women members of the conference committee who had refused to back down on the controversial subject matter of the 1921 conference.[12] Major's description of the structure of the annual conference committee, however, casts women modernists in a domestic and "self-sacrificing" role.[13] Dougall played no such self-sacrificing role. She was recognized as an intellectual, or perhaps more accurately, as a spiritual leader in the Union.[14] She is the only woman described in any detail in the one historical monograph on the Modern Churchman's Union and among a select few in Major's reminiscences.

Her first public appearance in modernist circles was in 1916, when she delivered the paper "Conscience and Authority" to the third annual modernist conference, held in the women's college, Lady Margaret Hall, in Oxford. Subsequently published in *The Modern Churchman*, the paper was a lyrical contribution to the combative movement. She distinguished between the old legalistic notion of conscience and the living voice of God, comparing the old idea of God to a despotic potentate who keeps men in slavery. The new is less clear—"It goes without saying that to make such a doctrine explicit, coherent and practical, many minds would need to give of their best, and many books would need to be written."[15] The essence of the new is, however, freedom, and Dougall assumes that men, if free, will be drawn inevitably to truth, beauty, and righteousness. The article is one of Dougall's best, clearly and confidently argued, and if it begs many questions, it does so with grace. Dougall spoke again at the 1918 modernist conference, held in August at another women's college, Girton College, Cambridge, the theme of which was "The Psychology of Religious Experience," [16] and a third time at the 1922 conference on "Christianity as a World Religion." [17] By the time of her death in 1923, she was widely known as a leader in the modernist movement, and her name was included by H. D. A. Major in a pantheon of noted academics and philosophers: "A movement which had such leaders as William Sanday, Hastings Rashdall, Lily Dougall, Clutton-Brock, Cyril Emmet, Maurice Pryke, Michael George Glazebrook will not strike those who knew them as lacking in moral or spiritual force." [18]

Historians have frequently described modernism as accommodation with modern secular culture; W. R. Hutchison, looking at the American phenomenon, defined it as "the conscious, intended adaptation of religious ideas to modern culture." [19] The description, even if not intended to be hostile, adopts the interpretive frame of critics of modernist thought. It was evangelicals who drew a sharp distinction between faith and the "world." Liberals did not draw such distinctions: Phillips Brooks embraced the world as God's incarnation. In "Lovereen," Lily Dougall had specifically rejected the separation of secular and spiritual in her parents' theology and argued that God is immanent in the world. As Lovereen told her father: "You want to cut the world—like Cinderella's sisters cut their feet to get them into a little shoe." [20] Dougall argued instead that culture, whether expressed in theater, art, literature, or even (in "Lovereen") in dancing, was an expression of God. Similarly the pursuit of truth, through philosophy or historical criticism of the Bible, was one of many paths to God. Modernists understood themselves to be actively embracing culture, rather than passively accommodating it; historian William McGuire King has aptly described American liberals as theological maximalists and expansionists.[21]

The metaphors employed by Dougall and other Anglican modernists were those of natural growth hampered by the detritus of tradition. The process was one of stripping away the inessentials, the husk, the stubble, the superstructure, for the essential core of faith. Carlyle's metaphor of old clothing shrouding the living spirit was central. Early issues of *The Modern Churchman* featured a quote from Carlyle on the cover: "The old never dies till this happen. Till all the soul of the good that was in it have got itself transferred into the practical New." This was quickly replaced by a quotation from Erasmus, a more respectable figure than the angry, prophetic Carlyle; but a Carlylean imagery and spirit continued to inform the modernist movement. In Carlyle's *Sartor Resartus* creed and liturgy are the decaying vestments that cloak the living spirit of religion; his metaphor had a long life in modernist literature, and we have traced it through Dougall's works.[22]

The imagery of natural growth from within was particularly suited to the evolutionary immanentism of many idealists. The popular work *The Kernel and the Husk* (1886) depicted the dry husk of orthodoxy stripped away to uncover the kernel of life within. Dougall had adapted this image for "Lovereen," when she compared Lovereen's parents' faith to the "decadence" of last year's garden, from which "the blossom of their children's lives [will] spring up in fresh form." [23] The imagery was organic, evolutionary—the "new life" came in "fresh form"; and progress, while not unbroken, was inevitable. The metaphor had wide usage. In Prince Edward Island, novelist L. M. Montgomery wrote in her journal on October 7, 1897,

> I cannot recall just when I ceased to believe implicitly in those teachings—the process was so gradual. My belief in the fine old hell of literal fire and brimstone went first—it and others seemed to drop away like an outgrown husk, so easily that I knew it not until one day it dawned on me that they had been gone a long time. I have not yet formulated any working belief to replace that which I have outgrown. Perhaps it will come in time. These things must *grow,* like everything else.[24]

Like Dougall, Montgomery understood Calvinist teaching as the outgrown husk that only impeded the growth of faith.

Hastings Rashdall, "the greatest and most erudite exponent of English Modernism," used a variant on this metaphor at the first annual meeting of the Churchman's Union: He said the modernists held to the belief in a personal God, belief in personal immortality, and belief in the unique and paramount revelation of God in the historic Christ.[25] As for the rest, "Of the vast superstructure of doctrinal and ritual and ethical tradition which has been built on and around the essential Christianity. . . . There is a great deal of hay and stubble that has simply got to be cleared away."[26] The emphasis was on the clearing away. The metaphors of natural growth explain why Anglican modernists were not preoccupied by modernity, which they took as a given, a natural and inevitable development, but focused on their opponents in the traditional church who threatened to stifle this new growth.[27]

The historical antecedent claimed by Anglican modernists was not, as critics would have it, a Renaissance of rational humanism, but the renewed spirituality of the Reformation, posed against a corrupt and aging church.[28] As Paul Badham has observed, modernism has regarded itself as essentially a positive movement, whose purpose was to affirm rather than deny essential truths.[29] Dougall's collaborative book, *The Spirit*, is prefaced with a quotation from F. D. Maurice: "I cannot but think that the reformation in our day, which I expect to be more deep and searching than that of the sixteenth century, will turn upon the Spirit's presence and life, as that did upon the Justification by the Son." Some years later, R. D. Richardson, in the well-received *Gospel of Modernism*, defined the movement as a new Reformation.[30]

Modernist statements and books were characterized by a challenging, combative, and self-righteous tone. The tone had been established as early as 1860 in the liberal *Essays and Reviews* when Benjamin Jowett wrote, "We are determined not to submit to this abominable system of terrorism, which prevents the statement of plainest facts, and makes true theology or theological education impossible,"[31] but the condemnation of Roman Catholic modernists increased this sense of martyrdom. H. D. A. Major brought a confrontational tone to the newly founded journal *The Modern Churchman*, and to his position (vice principal; principal in 1919) in Ripon College. As Michael Brierley has observed, "[H]is willingness to suffer for what he perceived to be the truth gives the impression that Major was expecting, if not actually looking for, a fight."[32] The report of the first annual conference of the Union in 1914 sounded a note of militant spirituality:

> The feeling that pervaded the Conference was one of invincible hope and prayerful expectation. Its members felt like men "marching into the dawn";

as those about to witness another great advance in the Reformation of
English Christendom. Yet with these high hopes was the solemn realisation
that only fearless truthfulness, spiritual faith, and self-sacrificing love
could cause the movement to prevail; that great aims meant great pains.

"Join us," Hastings Rashdall said, with a self-righteous sense of martyrdom, "and you will be misrepresented, abused and derided."[33]

An Anglo-Catholic incarnational theology coexisted with Ritschlian
liberal Protestantism in the Anglican modernist movement, and distinguished this movement from North American Protestant modernism.[34]
The early years of the English movement were characterized by tension between these two competing theologies. Both liberal Protestant
and Anglo-Catholic modernists rejected creed for a return to the source;
but for liberal Protestants the source lay in the words and actions of the
historic Christ, and for Anglo-Catholics the source lay in the incarnation,
the progressive revelation of God through the church. The differences
lay at the heart of modernism: it was Alfred Loisy's 1902 response to
Adolph Harnack's historic Christ that precipitated the modernist crisis
in the Roman Catholic Church. The idea of the incarnational Christ
had Anglican origins in F. D. Maurice's universal church, and after the
Papal condemnation of modernism it was claimed by Anglo-Catholics
in the Churchman's Union, where it coexisted with the historic Christ
of Ritschlian liberals in ongoing tension.[35] The differences emerged in
public debate, in 1910 when Albert Schweitzer forced the issue in *The
Quest of the Historical Jesus* (1910) by examining the apocalyptic element
in the New Testament and arguing that the historical Christ was
deluded. Hastings Rashdall adopted Schweitzer's position in the pages
of *The Modern Churchman* in 1911. At the first Churchman's conference,
organized in Oxford in 1914, two prominent Anglo-Catholic modernists, F. J. Foakes-Jackson and Kirsopp Lake argued, following Loisy,
that a return to the historic Christ was static, and frequently presentist.
In a book published the following year, Lake adopted Schweitzer's line
of argument:

> Liberal Protestantism thought that historical criticism would remove all
> the misrepresentations of later tradition and reveal the figure of the historic
> Jesus as infallible. Is that hope also to go? Yes I fear so. It is impossible to
> find its fulfillment in Jesus if he conditioned his teaching by Jewish apo-
> calypticism, and believed in what was, after all, an illusory expectation of
> the coming of the Kingdom of God. But is this a tragedy?[36]

By 1921, at the Girton conference, the arguments had become harsher.[37]
The debate continued after the conference when Foakes-Jackson

published an article in the *Hibbert Journal* in which he argued that the Ritschlian modernists wanted to replace Christianity with Jesuanity.[38]

Lily Dougall entered the debate with a book coauthored with Cyril Emmet, *The Lord of Thought* (1922).[39] The issue of Christ's apocalyptic teaching had disturbed her for some time, for it directly contradicted her understanding of God's love and mercy. She seems to have instigated the book and wrote the introductory chapters, laying out her argument. Emmet, a biblical critic who had contributed to two of the Cumnor volumes, provided the scholarly artillery. Letters between the publisher, Hugh Martin, the Literature and Assistant Secretary of the Student Christian Movement, and Dougall suggest some difficulties in writing *The Lord of Thought*. Martin assumed initially that Emmet would only write an introduction; they debated the title until the last moment (*Lord of Thought* was Dougall's idea) and Dougall wrote extensive revisions at the last moment, incurring an expense of forty-two pounds.

Extending arguments she had made earlier in *The Practice of Christianity*, Dougall and Emmet argued that Apocalyptic elements of the New Testament are Jewish doctrines mistakenly attributed to Christ—Dougall arguing from intuition and the peculiar logic of her variant of personal idealism, and Emmet arguing from a textual analysis. More than 1,200 copies were sold in the first year but *The Lord of Thought* was widely criticized, even in *The Modern Churchman*.[40] Probably the most damning criticism came from the modernist scholar of Judaism, Claude Montefiore, who publicly defended his faith from their attacks. In an angry letter to Emmet, Montefiore said Dougall had equated Judaic thought with Apocalyptic literature, and presented it as "that horrid dark background" for Christ's teaching.[41]

Dougall's final position appears in "Orthodox Dualism," a review article in *The Modern Churchman*, written shortly before her death. She describes Canon Oliver Quick's distinctions between liberal Protestants who "take refuge from our metaphysical difficulty by giving attention only to the facts of the manhood of our Lord," the Catholic modernists who turn from the historical Christ to a broader sense of incarnation, and those who "hold that the essential truth of orthodoxy must be retained together with the realisation of Divine immanence." The positive tone of her review suggests that Dougall understood herself to be in this last camp, neither a Ritschlian liberal or an Anglo-Catholic modernist, but a hybrid, for whom the historical Christ is important as a mediator, as the cause through which a mystical incarnation is effected.[42]

Modernists are best known for a series of public skirmishes revolving around the question of miracles, particularly over the divinity of

Christ, the virgin birth, and the resurrection. The arguments were deliberately provocative and the traditionalists responded predictably with
accusations of heresy. Keith Clements, in his aptly titled *Lovers of Discord*,
has said that between 1912 and 1922 "the Church of England was riven
by doctrinal controversy as never before or since. . . ." [43] Dougall tried to
skirt controversy but she sided with the modernist position, if not their
pugnacious expression of their views. One controversy, arising in the year
of Dougall's arrival in Oxford, involved a number of her new associates.
J. M. Thompson, a fellow and dean of Magdalen College and a member
of B. H. Streeter's theological group, caused an uproar by denying the
existence of miracles in the life of Christ. He wrote, deliberately setting the
words in italics: "*Though no miracles accompanied His entry into, or presence in,
or departure from the world; though he did not think or speak otherwise than as a
man; yet in Jesus Christ God is incarnate—discovered and worshipped, as God
alone can be, by the insight of faith.*" [44] There was a public furor. Thompson
was quickly ejected or resigned from Streeter's group, but *The Modern
Churchman* rose in his defense, and he remained an active modernist.

The next debate directly involved Streeter. Streeter's article, "The
Historic Christ," published in *Foundations: A Statement of Christian Belief
in Terms of Modern Thought* (1912) raised doubts about the physical resurrection of Christ and advocated the "subjective vision" theory of the
resurrection:

> The essence of what it is we mean by the hope of the resurrection of the
> body is surely contained in its emphasis on the survival of a full and dis-
> tinct personality. . . . It is suggested that what the disciples saw was a
> series of visions caused by some acute psychological reaction—the hopes
> which He had raised in their hearts, the impression of His personality
> upon them, refusing to submit to the hard fact of His death.[45]

In the resulting outcry, *The Modern Churchman* came to Streeter's defense.
Modernist scholars, such as H. M. Gwatkin, J. F. Bethune Baker,
B. H. Streeter, and Cyril W. Emmet, reacted swiftly and published
responses immediately.[46] William Sanday, the Cambridge biblical scholar,
made a dramatic conversion to the modernist cause. Ronald Knox published his satirical response *Some Loose Stones* (1913). The tension less-
ened slightly when Archbishop Davidson negotiated compromise
among the bishops in 1914 calling for clerical "sincerity" but also
recognition of the need for open inquiry: questioning was acceptable,
but not open disbelief.[47]

In 1915 Hastings Rashdall delivered the Bampton lectures, published in 1919 as *The Idea of Atonement in Christian Theology*. In them,
he criticized the idea of a substitutionary atonement and defended the

Abelardian view that Christ's death "justifies" humanity simply by kindling within humans a love of God. Dean Hensley Henson, who had defended J. M. Thompson in *The Creed in the Pulpit* (1912), was the next very reluctant modernist martyr. Modernists leapt unasked to Henson's defense in 1917 when Henson's suitability for the position of bishop was questioned by Charles Gore. A debate around the first modernist manual, Michael George Glazebrook's *The Faith of a Modern Churchman* (1918), led to a response by his bishop, *Belief and Creed*, to which Glazebrook responded with *The Letter and the Spirit, A Reply to the Bishop of Ely's Criticism* (1920). These debates might have erupted in more controversy but the leading modernists, Major, Rashdall, and Sanday, had agreed to bide their time.[48]

The various skirmishes culminated in the Girton Conference of 1921. Hastings Rashdall's paper was one of the most provocative of a series of liberal papers on Christology. He argued that Christ's divinity was a matter of degree rather than kind, a position he had first raised in *Doctrine and Development* (1898) and reiterated in 1903 at the annual meeting of the Churchman's Union.[49] The public response was heated. Rashdall preached a number of defensive sermons, later published as *Jesus Human and Divine* (1922), and engaged in a public debate with Bishop Gore. The controversy was a bitter one, thought to have hastened his early death in 1924.[50] Major was investigated for heresy, rather reluctantly, by Bishop Burge on the basis of a letters published after Girton in the *Church Times.* Although in his defense Major continued to deny the physical resurrection, Burge, on the advice of a panel of Oxford professors, decided not to proceed with charges. The Archbishop of Canterbury refused to interfere. The debate continued, however, in the Church. Archbishop Davidson appointed a Commission on Doctrine, chaired by William Temple, with a number of modernists including Cyril Emmet and B. H. Streeter, as well as philosophers such as C. C. J. Webb. The purpose of the Commission was to establish limits for doctrinal debate. It did not report until 1938.

Dougall shared the views expressed in the Girton Conference. The existence of miracles, even the miracles of the virgin birth and the physical resurrection of Christ, were not necessary to her faith. In *Christus Futurus* (1907), she suggested Christ's significance lay in his life, rather than in "certain aspects of his prenatal life and his resurrection, to which it is less certain he gave the seal of his own authority."[51] She had been equivocal in *Voluntas Dei* (1912): "Whether then, the doctrine of the divine Fatherhood of Jesus be fact, or only a poetic representation of fact, the idea it symbolises is still true. . . . But he who sees truth and mistakes its form lives more wisely than he who fails entirely to see it."[52] Dougall did not dismiss the centrality of the incarnation and the atonement. She argued that they must be either "corner stones" or "mere illusions."

> If we are to accept Christianity, the doctrines of the Incarnation and the Atonement, which are its warp and woof, must offer the most fundamental explanation of existence as we now apprehend it. . . . If we cannot interpret them to be as much as this, however passionately we may adhere to them, the familiar story . . . will become . . . as it has to many a sincerely religious Modernist, to many a sincere and true-hearted agnostic, a mere mythology.[53]

Dougall retained these doctrines by reinterpreting them. She explained the incarnation as the manifestation of God's participation, as a Bergsonian Creative Intelligence, in the evolutionary process. Similarly the atonement was "the manifestation of the eternal action and passion of the Creator" reconciling humanity by "suffering with it in its waywardness," and the resurrection was "not so much any theory about dead bodies, as the idea of immortal man . . . living on."[54]

In the book written after Girton, *The Lord of Thought* (1922), Dougall was still careful. She had adopted much of Hastings Rashdall's degree Christology, and suggested in a review published at this time that that particular debate was "meaningless."[55] She approached Christ as a human thinker—"I start with the presumption that in Jesus human intellect attained high development."[56] Although she made reference to the divinity of Christ, it is not clear that this divinity separated him from mankind in more than a matter of degree. Christ is extraordinary for the new vision of God that he preaches, but this new vision is the result of his intellect—as "the Lord of Thought"—rather than any special revelation. Her discussion of the resurrection in the concluding summary was remarkable for what it did *not* say, and suggests that she shared Major's conclusions, if not his audacity in trumpeting them to the world:

> To all who know that personal relations are of more account than all the universe besides, belief that God is and is good carries with it belief in the survival of the personality after death. . . . We need not, then, turn first to any transcendental doctrine to explain the belief that death could not hold or change the soul of Jesus. That the friendship of Jesus for his friends was stronger than death, that so ardent and vivid a personality as his must survive, and be no faint reflection, no pale ghost, but more strong and vivid when set free from material conditions, would be a natural belief to men who lived in theocratic habits of thought. . . .
> Turning now to history, we find that something certainly happened after the death of Jesus which gave to the depressed and frightened disciples a tremendous impulse of exalted joy and courage. One day we see them a small despised Galilean sect, all their crude hopes shattered,

bereaved alike of their dearest friend and of the leader whose prestige gave them what little importance they had, disloyal, terrified, broken. Another day, soon after, we see them an indomitable band, strong with sheer joy in the face of persecuting authority setting out with unwavering faith to bring joy and comfort and new power to mankind. This much is historic fact, as is also the large result of it upon the world.

What concerns us further here is that undoubted fact that Jesus of Nazareth was believed by the members of the conquering school of his disciples to be living in the unseen a life of great power and glory, in touch with all who touched him, supplying their spiritual needs; and that through this belief he became, in fact, the most powerful leader whom the Western world has seen.[57]

The evasiveness of this summary, especially in light of the Girton conference, is fascinating. "This much is historic fact," she wrote, implying that any more would be outside of history. Even "that undoubted fact" is a limited one: "that Jesus of Nazareth was *believed* by the members of the conquering school of his disciples to be *living in the unseen* a life of great power and glory. . . ."[58] Christ is only believed to have a spiritual resurrection. Dougall may not have taken the same delight in flouting orthodoxy that Major took, but here we see her presenting at most a very partial view of the resurrection.

Dougall's interpretation is informed by her ongoing belief in spiritualism. Like many members of her generation, she toyed with the idea of communication with the dead.[59] Her discussion of the resurrection in *Immortality* (1917) describes Christ's influence after death as differing only in a matter of degree from the posthumous influence she attributes to saintly humans. She suggests briefly that Christ's reappearance to his disciples may have been the result of telepathy, "but the strength of His spirit and His love were such that He could give clearer and stronger impressions of His presence that other spirits can."[60] The resurrection, then, was like the incarnation, a matter of degree. The phenomena was a natural one, and Christ's resurrection was not a miraculous break from nature but the culmination of a natural process. In 1923, when Dougall published "English Modernism" in *The Contemporary Review,* she said that "all rational Modernists believe that most of the alleged Gospel miracles could have occurred in the natural order."[61]

Why dwell at such length upon the question of the miraculous nature of the virgin birth, the divinity, and the physical resurrection of Christ? The answer is that the question functions as a litmus test for the concept of secularization.[62] Mary Ward's *Robert Elsmere* (1888) was the most widely read fictional representation of the loss of faith. Ward describes Elsmere's crisis of faith, his resignation from the ministry, and his work with a new social movement for the working class of London, the New Brotherhood. He has his moment of reckoning when he realizes that he no longer believes in Christ's divinity.

> *Do I believe in God?* Surely, surely! "Though He slay me yet will I trust in Him!" *Do I believe in Christ?* Yes,—in the teacher, the martyr, the symbol to us Westerns of all things heavenly and abiding, the image and pledge of all the invisible life of the Spirit—with all my soul and all my mind!
>
> "*But in the Man-God,* the Word from Eternity,—in a wonder-working Christ, in a risen and ascended Jesus, in the living Intercessor and Mediator for the lives of his doomed Brethren?"
>
> He waited, conscious that it was the crisis of his history, and there rose within in him, as though articulated one by one by an audible voice, words of irrevocable meaning.
>
> "Every human soul in which the voice of God makes itself felt, enjoys, equally with Jesus of Nazareth, the divine sonship, and *'miracles do not happen!'* " [63]

If "every man shares divine sonship," and "miracles do not happen," then Elsmere is forced to abandon his beloved church. Robert Elsmere dies eventually of exhaustion and overwork. His trajectory from the ministry through historical criticism and doubt to secular social reform (and death) is repeated in the narrative structure of the historiography of secularization. Historians of secularization trace the development from faith through critical thought to social gospel and the death of religion. The turning point rests on the acceptance of an intrusive supernatural. As the historian Owen Chadwick explained: "this very axiom, *miracles do not happen,* comes near the heart of that elusive shift in the . . . mind that we seek." [64] Major and, apparently, Dougall have crossed the line drawn in the sand; by denying the physical resurrection of Christ they become secular, or at least not Christian, figures.

Many Christians, including members of Dougall's own family, understood modernism to have moved outside the Christian fold.[65] But many liberals felt that they were still faithful Christians. When *Robert Elsmere* was first published, Phillips Brooks argued that Ward had missed the point:

> [*Robert Elsmere*] seems, as Matthew Arnold used to seem, to be entirely unaware of the deeper meanings of Broad Churchmanship, and to think of it only as an effort to believe contradictions, or as a trick by which to hold a living which one ought honestly to resign. It is not good to name a doctrine by a man's name, but there is no sign that this writer has ever heard of the theology of Maurice.[66]

Ward came to share his point of view. She joined the modernist movement and in 1911 published a sequel to *Robert Elsmere, The Case of Richard*

Meynell.[67] Richard Meynell represents the next generation of Anglicans; he courts Elsmere's daughter. Meynell does not leave the church because of his doubts, but stays within Anglicanism, and fights as a modernist to broaden the ancestral church. He is confident of his own reworked faith and only despairing of a church that cannot encompass modern thought. He and his modernist friends are described sympathetically, even heroically, while their opponents are seen as hidebound conservatives. Significantly, Elsmere's wife, the evangelical Catherine, respects Meynell. *The Case of Richard Meynell* never received the attention of *Robert Elsmere* but Mary Ward was closely attuned to intellectual fashion, and the novel suggests that the distinctions regarding miracles laid out in *Robert Elsmere* (and later mooted by historians like Owen Chadwick), had become outdated in the early twentieth century.[68]

We saw above how liberally the key tenets of the church were treated when William Temple was ordained, but theological liberalism was not limited to the Oxford elite. In a small Ontario town, novelist L. M. Montgomery, who appeared to be a devout Presbyterian minister's wife and Sunday School teacher, held strong private doubts about the "essentials" of faith. "I never say much about it to anybody," she wrote a friend in 1906:

> Like you, I *cannot* accept the *divinity* of Christ. I regard him as immeasurably the greatest of all great teachers and as the son of God in the same sense that any man inspired of God is a son of God. Further than this I cannot, at least, go. I believe that He was truly sent from and of God, as are all great teachers. And possibly he may also stand as an emblem of man in his highest and yet-to-be-attained development—the perfect flower of the tree of life blooming before its time as an earnest of what may be.[69]

Nor did Montgomery feel that all ministers believed the essentials:

> By the way, just for the sake of curiosity I read Bob Ingersoll's lectures recently. I expected to be horribly shocked. . . . Well, I was amazed. With the exception of his disbelief in a personal God, Christ's divinity and eternal punishment—and as you know, the last two would not be exceptions with all ministers—everything he states would be admitted openly or tacitly by any minister under 40 years old today.[70]

Montgomery may have been guilty of some exaggeration, but her assessment of the ministry, as a minister's wife in conservative rural Ontario, reveals that the modernist attitude to the miraculous spread far beyond the Oxford elite.

The lack of belief in an intrusive supernatural did not necessarily result in a desacralized world. Dougall's fiction had a running theme of debunking myths of an intrusive supernatural force. Her novels are filled with extraordinary supernatural devices—wailing ghosts, walking corpses, mermaids, glowing lights—that are revealed to be purely natural events. In her first novel a screaming Hell-bound ghost is revealed to be a disturbed but very alive man. The mermaid was a swimmer, the Madonna was a new woman, the corpse rising from the coffin in *What Necessity Knows* was a runaway girl. The flickering light in the mountains was nothing but coal gas. Yet their naturalness does not undermine their power to awake the spiritual nature of the characters. These things were illusions, but Dougall is careful to establish that the higher reality to which they point is real. Caius finds a higher purpose through the woman masquerading as a mermaid. Similarly, the Madonna finds higher truth through the coal gas light, and she, in her false persona as a Madonna, brings about a real redemption in the heart of the rough dwarf. The underlying implication is that the teachings of the church may also have been illusions, myths, and stories with only a faint basis in reality, but that this does not undermine the existence of the higher reality toward which they point. Modernists understood theological dogmas to be the transient symbols of the unchanging religious experience. When the dogmas no longer reflected vital experience, they needed alteration.

In *Voluntas Dei* (1912) Dougall suggests, rather carefully, that the stories of the virgin birth were (like the perception of the mermaid or the sight of the coal gas) a misinterpretation, but the truth they represent is unchanged. Modernists, she argues in *Absente Reo* (1910) do not want to remove mystery, but see mystery in the natural world. "It is more likely that they would urge against the old theology that the whole of life is so impregnated with mystery that it is a pity to retain any artificial mystery if it can be proved to be artificial." [71] "To reject nature in favour of an imaginary super-nature," she argues in *The Practice of Christianity* (1913) "seems to be the last infirmity of spiritually-minded men." [72] God works only through nature, but "we have called [the law of sin and death] 'supernature,' thinking Him to be more honoured in the over riding of His Creation than in its natural fulfilment." [73] If she takes pleasure in debunking miracles, it is because God may be found in the mountains and in the natural order, rather than in miracles that interrupt that order.

In Dougall's fiction, and later more clearly in her religious works, she argues that God works through the natural world and has no need of other miracles. He is not a transcendent figure breaking into this world, but is immanent within the world and working through it. For Dougall, the test of faith is not the intrusive force of the supernatural, but the experience of the spiritual within the natural world. This is the "natural supernatural" of Carlyle's *Sartor Resartus:* the supernatural is now placed within the natural world, the sacred takes part in the secular. One of Dougall's most eloquent religious essays, published first in *Hibbert Journal* as "Miracle Inconsistent with Christianity" and then posthumously in *God's Way with Man,* develops this point.[74] The essay was written in response to the revival of belief in miracles, particularly in the sacraments, in the Anglican Church. Dougall describes the belief in an intrusive supernatural as a primitive theology: "the old pre-Christian faith in a God who at times breaks in and does all that He wills, has grown along with the higher faith, as tares grow up with the wheat."[75] She points out the difficulties in believing in a God who can intervene, but chooses not to: "how can God, while able always to intervene 'easily by a nod,' allow the faithful to call upon Him in vain?"[76] She sorts through the various solutions to this dilemma, and concludes,

> The last, and, as it seems to me, the only answer which is consistent with the Christian revelation, is that God has chosen to work through nature, never performing his own will in spite of natural consequences, but taking upon Himself the whole burden of the universe that in some way emanates from Himself. Such a universe could not be mechanical, and must be thought of as in all its parts alive and interpenetrated with spirit, but with spirit which is not God nor wholly in harmony with the transcendent Spirit of God. This spirit in nature—untamed but tameable— would be everywhere and in all things open in greater or less degree to the influence of God, manifesting His beauty. In this belief all things that have a material nature have, in their own degree, a spiritual nature; and these two natures are not two things but one thing, just as man—spirit and body—is not two but one. The spirit that is in all things and attains personality in every man is not God, but is open to the influence of God, and when yielded to that influence becomes the perfect agent of God. So that although we may speak of God as immanent in man and in all things, and manifest when these are wholesome and good, yet all things are the object of His transcendent love, and He is the object of the love of all things and all men; lover and loved are not one but two.[77]

The passage is a lengthy one, but it serves as an excellent summation of Dougall's mature thought. God does not intervene in the natural world, but is immanent within it. She skirts the dangers of this position, avoiding charges of pantheism by insisting upon the transcendent as well as the immanent nature of God: "lover and loved are not one but two." Michael Brierley identifies Lily Dougall as a panentheist; although he notes that she never used the term in her work, he argues that her theology is compatible with the key tenets of a panentheist position, finding a doctrinal middle path between a transcendent and a pantheist theology.[78] She has more difficulty with the question of church teaching on miracles, arguing that miracles are actual natural processes, or suggesting that they are the product of "reverent imagination." She does not mention the resurrection, and even her discussion of the incarnation is awkward: the incarnation was not a miracle, but a particular historical act of God, not an irruption into nature but "the supreme manifestation of Divine activity on earth." [79]

Dougall argues that those who insist on miracles, "irruptions into the natural order," are looking in the wrong direction for reassurance as to God's existence. Faith in God lies not in the miraculous nature of the incarnation or the sacraments, but in the experience of God. She writes that "it is those who have themselves felt the power of God manifested in Christ and in the Sacraments who believe, in the orthodox sense, in the miraculous nature of the Incarnation or the Sacraments; and we suspect the real belief of such people to be based, not on their belief in miracle, but on *their religious experience, which is incommunicable.*" [80]

Dougall does away with miracles as a test of faith. In their place, she substitutes religious experience. She makes the same point in an essay on her coauthor, Cyril Emmet:

> He had a constant sense of the personal presence of God as revealed in Christ. One day he was in earnest conversation with a friend upon gospel miracles. The other, an eminent Christian, said with eager conviction: "If I did not believe that God had broken through the natural order in the Virgin Birth I could see no reason to believe in Him. What evidence is there? Where is God?" Cyril Emmet looked for a few moments with quiet astonishment and then, with a slight gesture of his hand to indicate the room in which we sat, he said, "God is here. I do not see how you can be unconscious of Him." The slight gesture, made quite unconsciously, conveyed, more than any words could, how real was his constant sense of God. [81]

The political skirmishes of modernism had only strengthened the touchstone of her faith—the personal experience of God.

Conclusion

L<small>ILY</small> <small>DOUGALL DIED OF HEART FAILURE</small> on October 9, 1923, at the age of sixty-five. She died at the height of her career, in the midst of numerous speaking engagements, with several articles underway.[1] Leading Oxford clerics attended her funeral, and a commemorative plaque was placed in her parish church. B. H. Streeter edited her unfinished work for a posthumous volume, *God's Way with Man* (1924), and made plans with Sophie Earp to compile a book of selected letters[2] and build a permanent conference center at Cutts End.[3] Streeter was a busy man, however, and he did not write his contribution to the selected letters before his death in 1937. The center was never established. Apart from the occasional tribute in her friends' memoirs, Dougall was quickly forgotten.

How do we assess her legacy today? Harold Anson suggested in 1938 that the Cumnor Group had been forgotten because "the Church has come to accept as axiomatic many of the truths for which that group fought twenty years ago, and which did appear to be new and revolutionary at that time."[4] He argued that this was in fact the best tribute to the group's influence. As Dougall's young friends moved up the ecclesiastical ranks, their radicalism became the new orthodoxy. William Temple attained the highest position in the church as Archbishop of Canterbury, and while he, like others, may have muted his liberalism, he promoted causes such as the Guild of Health. Young collaborators in the Cumnor Group, including R. G. Collingwood and Leonard Hodgson, became important scholars, and Fellowship member Leonard Elliott-Binns gave a liberal cast to theological history. Tangible evidence of the influence of modernist debates came in 1938 when the Commission on Doctrine of the Church of England, appointed after the controversial Girton Conference of 1921 (and chaired after 1925 by

William Temple), finally reported. Their carefully worded findings vindicated the modernist critique of church doctrine: they suggested that neither miracles nor the Virgin Birth were necessary to faith.[5]

The theological tide, however, had begun to turn. Dougall's optimistic immanent theology sounded naive as the grim reality of the Great War sank in, and the neo-orthodox idea of a sinful humanity presided over by an inscrutable, transcendent God appeared a more fitting theological response. Her posthumous works reveal that she was fighting a rear-guard action against newly popular ideas of transcendence, miracles, and a vengeful God.[6] Even members of the Student Christian Movement, including Cyril Emmet's young daughter Dorothy Emmet, began to find Dougall's benevolent God inadequate.[7] B. H. Streeter's introduction to Dougall's 1924 book started on an apologetic note: he explained her essays as the "glimpses of truth seen by the flashing insight of a free and original mind."[8] In one of a growing number of attacks upon modernism, *Defence of the Faith* (1927), Charles Gardner suggested that Dougall's clerical friends "attach an importance to her utterances which I think must be attributed to their hearts rather than their heads."[9]

The argument has been made by proponents of the secularization thesis that Dougall's generation had a purely negative impact—that they succeeded in destroying the orthodoxy of earlier generations without constructing an adequate alternative to take its place. As the satirical rhyme about modernism went: "Help us all by thy grace, / To teach the whole race, / We know nothing whatever about thee."[10] This argument, however, misses the point. Dougall's generation had not intended to build a new creed. As Dougall wrote, "Modernism is thus a continuous adventure of faith, a way of approach to doctrine, not a doctrinal system."[11] They sought a new method rather than a new set of doctrines, and at the time of her death, Dougall was working toward a different way of incorporating a shared experiential faith through small groups and fellowship with others. This was the method of the Cumnor Group, of the Anglican Fellowship, and of the Student Christian Movement. Dougall's creed was admittedly minimalist. By the measure of many historians of religion, her ideas were essentially secular. She did not, after all, find it necessary to believe in miracles, even central Christian miracles of the virgin birth and the physical resurrection, she took a critical approach to the Bible, and she worked for social reform outside of the Church. This did not mean, however, that she had abandoned faith. For Dougall, the absence of miracles did not mean the absence of God, but rather meant that His presence was felt in the natural world. Biblical criticism did not destroy the Bible, but revitalized it by allowing her to read the Calvinist eschatology out of the Christian past. The realization of the Kingdom of God on earth deepened rather than superseded its mystical dimension: "Thy Kingdom be," Dougall prayed, *"within and around* us." [12] Nor did idealism remove God from her world. Dougall rediscovered the God of her childhood, "the friend close beside me," in the relational world of personal idealism. Even her modernism was more spiritually charged than it appears in most historical accounts. Lily Dougall drew upon a Catholic modernism based on the mystical presence of the Holy Spirit within the living church.

Steve Bruce has argued that the Student Christian Movement lived on the reserve of faith banked by an earlier generation, even as they destroyed the credal basis for that faith. [13] The argument could be applied to Dougall. We might explain her life in terms of the narrative provided by the secularization thesis: in this narrative, her recourse to religious experience becomes another element in the ironic trajectory toward secularization. The experiential core—Dougall's "impregnable rock"—becomes just another unstable transitional idea, religious by past association but inherently secular, that leads, as Jackson Lears has suggested, to an oceanic nothingness. The epilogue suggests one such possible dénouement: the God who communicated through the religious experience was removed from the picture, with a sudden sleight of hand, as the subconscious became the domain of the science of psychology, and the twentieth century was left with the endless subjectivity of the modern subconscious.

But this analysis, with its emphasis on ferreting out the moment of rupture with the religious past does not shed much light on either the current situation or the recent past. The declensionist narrative patterns of the secularization thesis have lost explanatory power, and the debate has resulted in a kind of scholarly paralysis. Rather than trying to trace the elusive dividing line between the "secular" and the "sacred," this study charts the continuities, by examining the development of one woman's understanding of religious experience. The study asks: What are the connections between holiness interiority and liberal theology, mental science, and modernist mysticism? How did the evangelical sense of an abiding relationship with God persist within personal idealism? What are the connections between the theology of the New Woman and today's feminist spirituality? The epilogue suggests that the Christian Holy Spirit shaped the "science" of the subconscious.

In order to identify continuities and develop more nuanced contextual interpretations, we need to move beyond the idea of a single ahistorical spirituality. Experiential faith admits of many variations, from the paradoxical radicalism of Quietist mysticism, to the romantic narrative of Evelyn Underhill's mysticism, to the practical prayerfulness

of the Quaker inner light. We have seen how Lily Dougall made a difficult transition from the submissive holiness piety of her evangelical
childhood to the affirming individualist theology of personal idealism.
Rather than take modern experiential faith at its own essentialist esti-
mation we should place it firmly in context. Dougall's faith did not
arise solely from the depths of her religious experience. The very idea
of a *sui generis* faith was a liberal conceit, with each individual, "alone
in the world with his ideas," breaking from the suffocating embrace of
traditional culture. We have seen how Dougall built her experiential
faith from novels, from her idealist mentors, and from the contemplative elements of her family's holiness faith; she was actively pursuing
an education and an enriched cultural world even as her fictional characters found faith alone in swamps, sunsets, and mountains. The
revival of mysticism was similarly derived from the context of romantic idealism and the modernist rejection of orthodoxy. The "flight of the
alone to the alone" was grounded in a specific cultural location.

Finally, we must be alert to the gendering of this faith. Feminist
theologians, in particular, need to look more critically at the immediate past before building a theology based upon the "life of the Spirit."
The gendered understanding of the experiential has silenced as well as
empowered women. The liberal experiential theologies that informed
Dougall's faith, those of Schleiermacher, F. D. Maurice, and Hannah
Whitall Smith, were deeply gendered. This gendering has, in ways that
we have only begun to explore, distorted women's understanding of
their own spirituality. We have seen how Dougall hid her rational and
her metaphysical interests when she wrote her autobiographical novel,
how conflicted she felt about feminine skepticism and doubt. We have
also seen the lengths to which she went to hide her identity when she
wrote theology, and how a sense of inadequacy undermined her career.
Canon B. H. Streeter wrote an anecdote after Dougall died that reveals
this sense of inadequacy but also her growing sense that her own intellectual world had a value:

> My literary collaborator, the late Miss Lily Dougall, was once arranging for
> a small conference of philosophers and theologians to thresh out a problem
> to which for many years she had given considerable thought, and on which
> she had decided and somewhat original opinions. One of the philosophers
> sent her beforehand a memorandum he had prepared on the question. She
> was delighted to find that this maintained what was virtually her own
> position, but did so with a command of corroboration or refutation from
> other philosophers which she admired but could not emulate. On rereading
> it, however, a misgiving came into her mind as to whether, like as his posi-
> tion was to hers, he had really got what seemed to her to be the true view.

She dreamt that her philosopher friend was showing her round a new house which he had just built. It was of stone of exactly the same kind and colour as her own house at Cumnor; but, whereas this is built on two sides of a square, his formed a quadrangle and was altogether on a grander scale. They went inside; but here although the appointments and conveniences were in general quite to her taste, she yet felt that somehow it would not be so comfortable to live in as her own home.[14]

The quadrangle house of the philosopher represented Oxford learning: of the same color and kind as her education but "altogether on a grander scale." Dougall's Arts and Crafts home, like her command of Greek, was not lacking in sophistication. It was only in comparison with the academic quadrangles below that it, like her learning, was diminished. Dougall appeared to fit neatly into the iconoclastic world of Anglican modernism. Her work was widely accepted and praised. Yet, as she found in her dream about the Oxford quadrangle, the fit was never perfect: "although the appointments and conveniences were in general quite to her taste, yet she felt it would not be so comfortable to live in as her own home." There was, as Streeter observed, "a subtle inward disagreement."[15] This study is, in large part, an exploration of this "disagreement." It is an examination of the difficulties Dougall encountered as she worked along the borders of a masculine theological world, and it is a preliminary attempt to understand the specific contours of female experiential faith, not as an essentialist spirituality, but rather as something specific to the world of educated women at the turn of the century, in the transatlantic world.

Epilogue:
Psychology and Religious Experience

I~n~ L~ily~ D~ougall's~ autobiographical novel, "Lovereen," a young girl explains to her uncomprehending father that her faith had been reduced to its foundations, but that these foundations held firm and were sufficient:

> I cannot go [to be a missionary] because I cannot think as you do. I have tried till I have worn myself out with trying. I know now, looking back, that it was that that made me ill. I was so accustomed to see all religion in your way of seeing it that when I could not see it that way I was afraid it was all untrue; but now I know that was foolish. Then too I thought that perhaps your way was true and that because I thought differently I had deserted God and He me. Now I know better—that God is helping me as he is you.

Her father cannot comprehend this assurance:

> It did not occur to him to ask how she came by the knowledge. He supposed that belief in a helping God went without saying, and was the possession of all sober minds. Such a belief seemed to him no resting place, but only the foundation upon which religion was built. He was like a mariner who, being accustomed only to elaborately constructed steam-engines, could not brook the thought of being in the ocean with only sail and helm; he had never known what it was to be afloat without either.[1]

By grounding her faith in the experience of God, confirmed and reinforced in a renewed Christian fellowship, Dougall appears to have survived the onslaught of biblical criticism. Science had not toppled her faith, as it had that of so many of her peers. Or had it? We turn now to look at the science of psychology. Dougall's interest in psychology had run tandem to her religious work throughout her life, from early spiritualism, to membership in the Society for Psychical Research, to her mature interest in psychotherapeutics. Ann Taves has observed that psychology acted as a mediating tradition, accommodating both natural and supernatural explanations of religious experience. For many years psychology reinforced Dougall's faith, providing a scientific support for her understanding of religious consciousness; it was only in the final years of her life that the potential for psychology to undermine experiential faith became apparent.[2]

Dougall's novels are rife with bizarre supernatural occurrences that are revealed to have natural explanations; mermaids, madonnas, and flickering lights are all revealed to be natural phenomena, but this naturalness does not reduce their spiritual power. The novels appealed to a public whose fascination for the bizarre supernatural paralleled their ebbing faith in Christian supernaturalism. In the Society of Psychical Research (SPR), Dougall found a congenial group of liberals who were similarly interested in natural explanations for supernatural phenomena. Under the presidency of Dougall's mentor, the highly respected Henry Sidgwick, the SPR had attracted an illustrious membership, including eminent academics, rising politicians, and numerous writers. Modernists and personal idealists were well represented: personal idealist A. J. Balfour was president of the SPR from 1893, and the Bishop of Ripon, William Boyd Carpenter, founder of the modernist Ripon College, became the president in 1912 after he retired.

The SPR operated on a number of levels. Although the organization deliberately distanced itself from popular spiritualism, in order to establish its credentials as a professional body, its reports allowed respectable men and women to indulge in the titillation of the supernatural for sound scientific reasons.[3] Dougall had enjoyed the thrill of a haunted house as a young woman, and her novels played to this fascination with spirits. The wide circulation of the SPR reports suggests that their readers were similarly fascinated by accounts of ethereal maidens, sinister mediums, and the thrill of toying with unknown forces. But the work of the SPR also appeased widespread religious anxieties. Janet Oppenheim has argued in *The Other World* that the SPR had an essentially religious purpose: they conducted research into psychic phenomena to provide an empirical base for a renewed universal faith:

> [R]eligion was at the root of their enquiries, for religious yearnings—
> sometimes no more than a vague spiritual malaise—had played a role in
> bringing them together in the study of psychical phenomena. . . .

Although repudiating orthodox Christianity, they longed to find some other basis for the ethical precepts they cherished and some reassurance that all human suffering was not utterly devoid of purpose. Implicitly they sought to use science to disclose the inadequacies of a materialist world view and to suggest how much of cosmic significance scientific materialism failed to explain.[4]

Ann Taves examines the explanations of religious experience informing the SPR and makes a similar point in *Fits, Trances and Visions: Experiencing Religion and Explaining Experience from Wesley to James.*[5] She describes the SPR as the center of a mediating tradition that bridged the scientific and religious worlds. The research of the SPR showed that a religious experience might be both natural and truly religious. Taves argues that American Protestants had distinguished between true religion (which was supernatural and true) and false religion (which was demonstrably natural in origin and therefore false). Religious experiences that were understood to be false, such as mesmerism, or the overwrought enthusiasm of camp meetings, had been simultaneously explained and dismissed as natural phenomena. Members of the SPR, especially William James and Frederic Myers, reconciled the natural and the religious. They drew upon scientific explanations to legitimate, rather than debunk, religious experiences. Lily Dougall understood the SPR to be providing scientific evidence of God's action in the world. She assumed that that the material world was charged with spiritual significance and that the SPR might point to the mechanisms by which this operated. She explained at the end of her life: "We must never forget that God is truth, that all truth is of God and that every scrap of truth that humans can discover helps to educate their souls for the ultimate enjoyment of God. Among the most notable of those who are seeking to discover what truth may underlie spiritualistic phenomena are the leaders of the Psychical Research Society. I have been a member of this society for the last 25 years. . . ."[6]

Dougall probably became involved with the SPR in the 1890s, when she began to incorporate psychological concepts developed by leading SPR members in her work. In the spring of 1895, Dougall sought an interview with a leading member of the SPR, W. H. F. Myers. Myers was best known for developing the concept of telepathy and his theory of the "subliminal self."[7] He told Dougall he had enjoyed *Beggars All* (1891) and *What Necessity Knows* (1893), in spite of his usual dislike of psychical novels, and he encouraged her to write "such an one as was really wanted."[8] He provided her with a list of readings. A year later, she found the ideal subject for such a novel: Joseph Smith, the founder of Mormonism, whose career, Dougall argued, revealed the necessity for "able and unprejudiced research" along the lines conducted by the SPR.[9] Dougall traveled through the United States in the fall of 1896 with her niece, Jean Dougall, and interviewed a number of people involved in the early days of Mormonism, using her connections with the *Montreal Witness* as a reference.[10] The resulting book took nearly three years to complete, and is one of Dougall's most interesting novels. Although Dougall fully exploited the sensational aspects of Mormon history, it is a serious piece of work, and she predicted, "It will be a bigger book in every way, if I can write what is on my mind, than the last four nurselings."[11]

The plot of *The Mormon Prophet* is centered on a young woman, Susannah, who leaves an orthodox adoptive home (Dougall describes it as Calvinism tempered by waves of Methodist revivalism) to join the Mormons.[12] Susannah marries a Quaker convert to Mormonism, the aptly named Angel Halsey, who brings a genuine, if naive, faith into the sect. He dies in the routing of the Mormons, and Susannah suffers under the subsequent persecution of the sect. She stays with the Mormons until they establish themselves in what is described as cheap splendor in Navoo, where, persistently courted by Smith as a second wife, and threatened by his followers, she makes a dramatic escape.

In *The Mormon Prophet*, Dougall invokes the new concepts of the emerging science of psychology to explain the power of Mormonism: "[T]his new sect produced vehement psychical disturbance wherever it touched the surrounding population and many things occurred which might, or might not, be termed miracles, according to the interpretation of the observers."[13] She argues that Smith's visions were delusions: "It appears to me more likely that Smith was genuinely deluded by the automatic freaks of a vigorous but undisciplined brain, and that, yielding to these, he became confirmed in the hysterical temperament which always adds to delusion self-deception, and to self-deception half-conscious fraud."[14] The various effects he produced, such as faith healing and levitation, were the result of his use of natural and psychological forces, "a child playing among awful forces."[15] Susannah was hypnotized by Smith: "[Susannah] had never heard of crystal-gazing; the phrase 'mental automatism' had not then been invented by psychologists; still less could she suspect that she herself might have come partially under the influence of hypnotic suggestion." Without a knowledge of psychology, she is vulnerable to Smith's powers:

> Her gentle intelligence was puzzled, as all the candid historians of this man have since been puzzled. Then, tired of the puzzle, she fell again to contemplating scraps of his speech, which, having a Scriptural sound, suggested piety. . . . How strange if, impossible as it might seem, these words had come to her—to her—direct from the mind of the Almighty![16]

At the end of the novel, hard experience has taught her to make a distinction between the mind of the Almighty and Smith's delusions. When he insists that they marry, she tells Smith: "It is not enough for me that you say the Lord has spoken." [17]

Dougall also describes the cheap psychological tricks employed by sectarian leaders. The holiness revivalist, Charles Grandison Finney, makes an appearance in the novel and sets off sectarian violence, including the tarring and feathering of Susannah's husband.[18] When Susannah attends one of Finney's revivals, she is struck by the similarities to Mormon preaching: "Accustomed as she was to excitement in the meetings of the Saints, her mind easily resisted the infectious influence. Finney's teaching had not differed in any respect from the doctrine which she had heard from her husband daily, a doctrine which she knew by experience did not save men from delusion." When a man falls prostrate, Susannah, accustomed to the nervous affectations among Mormons, is indifferent.[19]

Dougall did not dismiss all religious experience as psychological delusion. Finney and Angel Halsey are both seen to have genuine access to the divine; their weakness lies in taking advantage of the susceptibilities of their audience. More dramatically, in the conclusion of the novel God speaks directly to Susannah: "She felt pressed upon by a spiritual life external to her own. Within her soul from some unknown depth the word arose distinctly as if spoken, 'Pray, You cannot save yourself. Pray.'" She resists. "Susannah had come to class all search for definite and material answer to prayer as one of the superstitions of false religion. In this category stood also the hearing of voices and obedience to monitions from the unseen. Now she reproached herself because she could not immediately silence this fancy of disturbed nerves." [20] She challenges the unseen power to prove itself by saving her. The following morning, in response to an irresistible directive, she makes a miraculous escape. She realizes that God had directed her: "beyond and beneath all this confusion of pain there was for her and for all men an eternal and beneficent purpose." [21]

Here we can see Dougall toying with a psychological interpretation of religious phenomena, but then backing away. On the one hand, she brings psychology to bear upon the visions and illusions of the Mormons, and the enthusiasms of revivalists; but on the other, she acknowledges the eternal and beneficent purpose that informed Halsey's faith, and provided supernatural guidance in Susannah's escape. Letters suggest that writing *The Mormon Prophet* caused Dougall some trouble. After writing a few chapters, she was unable to continue.[22] She was tackling more complex issues than she had in earlier works and it may be that it was difficult to reconcile psychology and faith. Just as she had turned to Edward Caird and William Wallace to work out the idealism informing *The Zeit-Geist,* she now turned to the father of the psychology of religion, William James. James had served as president of the SPR in 1894–1895 and accepted many of Myers's theories about telepathy and the workings of the subliminal mind. He agreed with Dougall about the psychological basis of Smith's visions and illusions. She told Earp,

> He was quite clear that visions that come in answer to prayer—such as the vision of the gold plates to the three witnesses—were the result of "self-suggestion." But when I tried to make him say that "levitation"—of which there is a good case in the Mormon annals—was the result of one man's delusion conveyed by telepathy to a dozen of more spectators, he would not agree. He said twice over, "I think I'd treat that as a miracle; it is simpler." He evidently was not prepared to deny its possibility. When we got on to the subject of Joseph's "revelations," and also the "speaking with tongues," he stood in the middle of the room and imitated a man whom he had known who spoke in an "unknown tongue" like the Irvingites. That, he said, was evidently a clear case of physical automatism.[23]

When they discussed the basis of these phenomena, however, they parted company.

> [H]e believed that the philosophic mind was swinging around to the idea that we lived on the fringes of a reservoir of soul, into which at times we dipped, voluntarily or involuntarily. He said he thought this was the basis of much that I was inclined to call "thought-transference." I can't be sure exactly how he described it, but I think he said, "For instance, it is not that your thought affects mine directly, but that you dip in and agitate some thought-wave there, and I dip in and feel the impression of it." No, that was not what he said, but it was something that gave the impression that the two minds had to take header in. He certainly said, "It is out of this reservoir that all religions come, and by the same method, and we must judge of the value of the revelation by the content and not by the method."

James later developed this reservoir theory using Fechner's image of the "mother-sea."[24] Dougall, however, had two strong reservations. She was concerned with finding new imaginative constructions to replace the punitive Calvinist God of her youth, but this reservoir idea held little resonance: "I said how it was possible to make [the conception of a reservoir] affect my thought or that of others, because it was unimaginable." It was worse than useless, as she said to Earp in the close of her letter: "The only imaginative image that I received from his conversation was that of frogs on the outskirts of a pond." Her second objection lay in the suspension of reason that was involved in "taking a header" into this reservoir. Dougall suggested to William James that the "method" he described was a dangerous form of "automatism," encouraging "a sort of split in consciousness, a numbing of the reasoning faculties, and that there was no proof that a better result would not be produced by the same soul in the full exercise of its conscious powers." She noted in an aside to Earp, "Of course, this is the whole question of quietism, mysticism and all their modern forms."

Dougall suggested to James that his method could produce the worst as well as the best. He agreed and argued that the value of a religious insight must be judged by the content rather than the method, which, as she acerbically noted, "makes the critical powers the standard." Her solution, that the true religion proved itself by progress in righteousness, was met with only a laugh from James. In *The Mormon Prophet*, however, this seems the conclusion she draws. Susannah is only saved when she abandons rational critical thought to follow an inner directive.[25] We can only know the source of the directive by the outcome: Joseph Smith's visions result in the cheap splendor and immoral polygamy of his community, whereas Susannah's faith leads her finally to a learned restraint, the progress in righteousness that Dougall judges the sign of religious truth.

Psychology served to explain religious delusion; its science might be applied to Mormonism without controversy. As Henry Sidgwick said in a complimentary letter on *The Mormon Prophet:* "I have no doubt that [Dougall] is right in thinking that the investigations of the SPR are likely to throw light on the psychological problems presented by the characters and actions of the founders of false religions. . . . [T]he story has the distinction of style and delicacy of spiritual insight which characterise Miss Dougall's other works." [26] Sidgwick did not speculate about the application of these investigations to religions that are not false, but it is a question that hangs unanswered in the conclusion to the novel. What is there to distinguish between the answer to Susannah's final prayer, and the answers Joseph Smith receives in his visions? The science that explains Joseph Smith's delusions might also explain away Susannah's divine guide.

After writing *The Mormon Prophet*, Dougall continued to read William James's work and use psychological terms to understand religious experience. But the fascination with the bizarre manifestations, which characterized James's *Varieties of Religious Experience*, and her own *Mormon Prophet*, was dropped.[27] She became more interested in Myers's concept of the unconscious or subliminal self. "The main progress of [the SPR]," Dougall reported to her family in 1908, "as also in modern psychology, has been in the discovery of the curious and apparently superior powers of the unconscious mind—you may call it the 'sublim-inal self' or the 'subconscious mind' or the 'back of your mind' or what-ever you like." [28] Myers's ideas about the subconscious were powerful because they incorporated pre-existing notions of the soul, the voice of conscience, and the work of the Holy Spirit with the methods and lan-guage of science. As Taves has noted, theories of the subconscious offered a mediating tradition; psychologists of religion avoided defining the source of subconscious inspiration, leaving it open as to whether they were an upwelling *from* the personal subconscious (and natural) or an upwelling *through* the personal subconscious (and so supernatural). [29]

The idea of telepathy was particularly powerful. Myers argued that the subliminal consciousness could receive information through chan-nels, such as telepathy or clairvoyance, inaccessible to the "supralimi-nal self," and then transmit them to the supraliminal self through such psychic phenomena as table rapping, automatic speech, hallucinations, crystal visions, and dreams. [30] His ideas were well received, and although members of the SPR were skeptical about the physical manifestations of spiritualism, they often considered telepathy to be an established fact. [31] "What seems to be abundantly proved," Dougall stated with confidence, "is that the minds of ordinary people on earth have a certain non-sensuous intercourse with one another." [32]

The idea had resonance for a woman like Lily Dougall who had grown up with a strong sense of the living presence of the Holy Spirit. Not only did evangelicals like the Dougalls feel an ever-present "voice of God within the soul," but they felt that this Spirit provided a kind of spiritual conduit among believers. John Dougall had understood him-self to be in contact with Lily's mother through the Spirit: "I have noth-ing special to write but am writing as the only way I can hold intercourse with you except in Spirit and in prayer." [33] In 1883, shortly after the death of her mother, and probably long before she came into contact with Myers or his ideas, Dougall wrote to her old friend Janie Couper, "There is at least one medium through which absent souls may touch one another. That medium is God. Is not this an endless speculation? Think of it for a moment. How near or how far, may two souls be, both coming to God in prayer for the other?" [34] Myers had speculated on the religious implications of telepathy: "that same direct influence of mind upon mind *in minimus* would, if supposed operative *in maximus*, be a form of stating the efficacy of prayer, the communion of saints, or even of the operation of a Divine Spirit." [35]

Myers went further than most members of the SPR in these spec-ulations, and Dougall took his line of reasoning one step further. Not only is our subconscious mind capable of receiving impressions from other minds in the form of "thought transference" or telepathy, but, she argued, it receives impressions from the spiritual world. Her argument was tentative in 1912:

> And all spiritual activities seem to arise from man's consciousness that when he is most alone, in the sense of having retired within himself from the things of sense, he is in company with another spirit and can have distinct dealings with that other, dealings which we may describe by the new word "telepathic" for that is the only word that expresses the communion of two intelligences without sensuous medium.[36]

By 1913, in *The Practice of Christianity,* Dougall described prayer using an odd mix of theological and psychological language: "Prayer is the desire of the whole man, thought, will, feeling, receptivity, and activity, turned Godward in expectation. To have faith is to have the conscious, semi-conscious, and sub-conscious states of mind soaked in the sense of God's goodness, resourcefulness, and power." [37]

By 1917 she was more definite:

> We have then, in what is now commonly called the sub-conscious mind, an organism which, on this hypothesis, is receiving impressions all the time from three sources—from the senses, from the minds of other men, and from the Holy Spirit—perhaps also from evil spirits; and is moreover, assimilating and interpreting these impressions all unknown to us. When, however, we can withdraw our attention from external objects, or internal images, or voluntary trains of thought, there comes a quiet, a lull, a resting place in our mental life. In this state, if we are arrested by no external suggestion, the subconscious mind, in its own slow, quiet, orderly way, puts forward something for our attention, and often puts it forward as such an apparent breach of continuity with the things previously occupying our attention that it seems to come from a source quite external to the self.[38]

The key to the experience, Dougall argues, is the preparation. "If the soul is seeking God, what comes to it in such hours will truly be what the understanding has distilled from the presence of the Spirit of God; and thus it will truly be, as far as that soul can understand, the voice of God." [39] Alternately, the seeker after evil will receive evil counsel, and the seeker after money will learn to make money.

By 1917, then, Dougall had managed to accommodate psychology into a coherent theory of religious experience: even her book titles combined science, psychology, and theology.[40] She invited prominent neurologist James Arthur Hadfield from the Ashhurst Neurological War Hospital to collaborate on the second collection of essays compiled at Cumnor, *Immortality*.[41] Hadfield's essays, written in consultation with Dougall and other members of the Cumnor group, use case studies and medical research to argue essentially theological points.[42] In the first, "The Mind and the Brain: A Discussion of Immortality from the Standpoint of Science," he distinguishes between the physiological attributes of the brain and the psychological attributes of the mind, and uses the distinction to suggest the possibility of immortality.[43] In the second, "The Psychology of Power," he describes patients who drew upon extraordinary powers under conditions of wartime stress or subsequently under hypnosis, and then makes the leap to suggest that these powers reveal hidden channels of energy. "Whether we are to look upon this impulse as cosmic energy, as a life force, or what may be its relation to the Divine immanence in Nature, it is for other investigators to say."[44] In case his readers miss the point, however, Hadfield goes on to draw connections with the power of the Holy Spirit in the Pentecost.[45] Hadfield understood his work to be effecting a reconciliation between science and religion: "the reinterpretation of some of the fundamental beliefs as would make them intellectually possible of acceptance to the modern man."[46] His contribution might be better understood in terms of a transfer of cultural authority. Hadfield had abandoned the clergy for psychology, and he defined his new role as a psychotherapist, as the "physician of the soul."

Dougall had earlier used psychology to explain away Mormon beliefs, and in her contribution to *Immortality* she turned the science upon modern unorthodoxies. Of Theosophy, she argues, "when such claims are honestly put forth they probably owed their origin to the suggestive dreams which occur in any hypnoidal condition and in trance sleep, which after some practice can be easily self-induced and remembered."[47] Spiritualism is also the product of self-hypnosis, in combination with telepathy. The sincere medium is able in a trance to tap the ideas of other people and communicate them as a message from the dead. Dougall reported a test she and a friend conducted: they concocted an imaginary character, complete with details of clothing and manner, before meeting a medium. The medium described this imaginary figure, Dougall assumed, from her telepathic reading of their minds.[48]

Dougall does not entirely rule out communication with the dead. She concludes her 1917 article on the theme of immortality, a vexed subject at that date in the Great War, by holding out some hope for the thousands of bereaved families of soldiers in 1917. She argues that while it is impossible to receive direct communication, it is entirely possible for the bereaved to feel the presence of the dead. In a passage reminiscent of liberal evangelist Henry Drummond in its use of scientific analogy, and more evangelical in terminology than preceding arguments, she writes: "As what the scientists call ether is believed to interpenetrate all things in our universe and is the medium of light between star to star, so the Holy Spirit interpenetrates the universe of living spirits and mediates love between those whose earthly bodies are quick and those we call the dead." [49] Dougall felt she had seen her sister Janet after her death, and argued that Christ's resurrection was the highest example of the telepathic communication of the dead. As Streeter recalled after Dougall's death, "She believed that the souls of the righteous are never far away from those they had loved on earth, and are still able to assist and inspire them by actual personal contact, but not a contact that shows itself through voices and visions." [50]

Dougall's understanding of life after death can be traced to her childhood teachings. Liberal Congregationalists in the 1880s had attempted to mitigate the doctrine of hell with the idea of probationary salvation. Under this scheme, individuals had the opportunity to improve their lot after death. This teaching appears in occasionally in Dougall's work, where it is often at odds with her Anglican liberalism. She suggested in 1912 that evil individuals continue to exert an influence upon humanity after their death, in effect creating a new concept of the devil:

> Thus we may think of individual man on earth as under the attraction, not only of divine Love, but of all those human spirits, in this life and beyond, that have gravitated as it were toward divine Love, and also under the influence of all those spirits which, in this life and beyond, in defiance of divine Love, are sweeping backwards to lose themselves again where the river of life flows in its more elemental condition, and in their sweep exercising their own power of attraction, their own infernal telepathic suction, upon the sons of earth and, for aught we know, upon the immortal whole of humanity.[51]

Dougall gave melodramatic fictional expression to this idea of the "infernal telepathic suction" of the dead, in her unpublished story and novel "Evelyn Vane." The story describes the penalty exacted upon immoral politicians who are required to observe, as ghosts, the effects of their immorality after their death, when they are unable to change anything. "The point about these disembodied [?] is that they began the next life with precisely the same degree of moral insight or blindness as those with which they leave this life and there is only a suggestion of possible progress to good or evil given." The idea was a strange one, and she was probably fortunate that publishers refused these stories.[52]

Dougall developed the psychological interpretation of religious experience along more rational lines in an essay included in her third collaborative work, a book whose subtitle is revealing: *The Spirit: God and His Relation to Man Considered from the Standpoint of Philosophy, Psychology and Art.* She describes religious experience in terms drawn from accounts of mystical experience:

> Under the head of "illumination" I would class all experience of vivid enlightenment which comes to seeking souls, whether as to the nature of sin and holiness or as to the nature of God's personal attitude to the self or to the world. There can be no question as to the extraordinary reality and productiveness of this experience, nor can any believer in God question that, when increased knowledge of truth or of vital virtue is attained in this way, the enlightenment comes from God. On the threshold of the religious life such enlightenment often takes the form of a vivid sense of God's presence, which perhaps for the first time, brings the conviction of His existence to the sceptical or the careless. The conviction of sin, of forgiveness, of vocation, of guidance in perplexity, often comes suddenly as the apparent result of what is figuratively expressed as a flash of light abolishing obscurity. Moments of illumination may become habitual in private prayer, or in participation in the Eucharist or in confession and absolution, or in the pursuit of beauty and truth.[53]

Her explanations, however, are couched in the language of psychology. Citing James's *Varieties of Religious Experience,* she argues that God worked through nature or psychological law. Describing the theories of the subconscious mind, and the power of mental suggestion on the subconscious mind, she then argues that the Spirit works through these channels: "the faculties revealed in suggestible condition, which may be, and are, used by men both for good and evil, are used by the Spirit in the exercise of His beneficent power."[54] Thus the "Creative Spirit" influences the subconscious of the person who appeals to Him in prayer. The apparent miracles that occur as a result of inspiration are, she explains, the result of telepathy. The person thus inspired by the Spirit is, like the evangelist of old, inspired to save the world, not necessarily along the narrow lines of piety but by the broad pursuit of truth, beauty, or righteousness. In a revealing sentence, Dougall argues, "this is not missionary cant, but a psychological fact."[55]

A second essay, "The Language of the Soul: Some Reflections on the Christian Sacraments," explained the psychological power of the sacraments of the Eucharist and baptism. Dougall had earlier explained in *Christus Futurus* the necessity for religious observances in terms of the "life mind" or "unconscious mind":

> It is worth while to pause and reflect upon those powers about which we are all learning to talk so glibly—the unconscious mind or life-mind

which manages us and ours, and our occasional power and frequent powerlessness to direct it. . . . [B]y directing the attention to this or that the conscious will can do very much to control the unconscious mind for good or evil. . . . It thus becomes evident that the voluntary observance of religious acts has a more far-reaching power over him who performs them than he can be consciously aware of. . . . The same is true of the outward observance of any sentiment or principle, such as happy acts, loyal acts, and acts of faith in man or in God. His life mind . . . will eventually become saturated with the sentiments he acts up to, even if at first he experiences almost nothing of the sentiment, and the unconscious life thus acted upon will become a force much greater than the conscious mind, and will accomplish what that could not accomplish.[56]

In this essay, she argued that adult baptism has no supernatural effect, but has a transformative effect because it involves the acceptance of Christian standards worked into the inner consciousness by a suggestive rite.[57] Such an explanation, she argued, does not negate the religious import of the rite: "It is such transforming force that is the mark of the Spirit's working." Similarly, the ceremonies and beauty of the Eucharist are suited to bring about a quiescent state of mind, receptive to the working of suggestion. Dougall had little patience, however, with "extreme sacramentarians"; once again she used psychology to undermine religious beliefs that she did not share.[58] As she had told Maud Petre in 1918, "I believe the real lines of division to be, not any of the more obvious lines, but between those who take a magical view of the sacraments and those who regard them only as poetry, valuable only for what they mean to express and of personal value in accordance with the interpretation given." [59]

Psychology was a double-edged weapon, however, and the arguments that explained away the delusions of Joseph Smith, the claims of theosophists, and the excesses of sacramentarians might also be turned upon Dougall's own experiential faith. Dougall did not see this: she told Earp that her investigations of psychology did not touch the "essentials of religion": "It was a question merely of the methods of the spiritual life, not of the fact. . . ." [60] Besides, as she argued in *The Spirit*, "Whatever is true is God's way of revealing Himself, we may fearlessly seek the fullest knowledge of that way." [61] In a paper, she further defended a psychological interpretation, comparing the impact of psychology to the medieval discovery of gravity:

We must recognise, however, that just as the knowledge of the laws of gravitation was wholly unwelcome to the medieval church because they necessitated a change in outlook which upset many traditional assumptions, so the knowledge of psychological law is today unwelcome to a large class of religious people who desire mystery. . . . it is open to us to either welcome the knowledge they bring in the sure faith that truth, of whatever sort, must always help us in our aspiration toward true Godliness, and that what it may cause us to discard can be no true help in the service or worship of God. Or we can reject such knowledge and endeavour to go on blindly a little longer until we are more rudely awakened.[62]

But she was on the defensive by this time; the issue was clearly a troubling one, for Dougall discussed it again in an article published in 1922, "God and the Subconscious Mind." There she referred to the scientific findings of psychologist Emile Coué, and described the unconscious mind as an instrument that may be used for good or evil, by the atheist or the believer, and concludes, "We must traffic with it for God."[63]

Psychology did undermine the experience of faith. In an early work, Dougall's protagonist had echoed Coleridge's bold assertion of the religious claim to truth, "Just try it":

I believe the Bible . . . not because the Church says it is true, nor because it declares itself to be true, but because it teaches of God what I know to be true. There is not a human soul on the surface of the earth that cannot prove for itself its teaching by experiment. I do not say that one soul can prove it to another, but that each soul can prove it to itself: God thus becomes part of our experience, and *no sane man doubts his own experience.* (Emphasis added)[64]

Psychology, however, provided the means by which believers might doubt their own experience. The telepathic messages of the Holy Spirit could be as easily dismissed as the spiritualist messages of the dead or the insights of theosophical adepts. In a novel published in 1908, Dougall suggested this possibility when she described a conversion with a curious mixture of psychological and mystical language:

At the meeting that afternoon Oriane felt that she learned a secret which lifted her heart to a new level, from which this life wore a different aspect. She was aware that such a sense of change is a common psychical phenomena and was therefore not certain that it might not be a mere fancy; while going out she hugged the new experience, fearing it might not last. . . . [S]he had a curious experience of realising what she had gained—she knew not what it was—made her feel more at home in the common-place of the world. . . .[65]

The language is revealing. A conversion that might only be "common psychical phenomena," a "mere fancy," cannot be trusted. Even conversion, the center of a religious life, can be undermined by the new science. As Dougall herself observed, in an undated typescript: "Religious experiences are now described in psychological terms, religious values are largely psychological values." She noted: "there is a great danger in failing to recognise that subconscious processes are caused by objective experiences, not only the experiences of the earthly and human environment but of the direct touch of God upon the soul." [66]

Dougall, herself, never failed to recognize the subconscious promptings as the "direct touch of God upon the soul." [67] Her religion was built upon the experience of God, and her psychology was simply an investigation into the mechanics of that experience. But the reduction of religion to a matter of religious experience, and the explanation of this experience as a natural phenomenon, prepared the ground for a materialist explanation. What if the unconscious were not simply the conduit for objective experiences but the final ground of those experiences?

Notes

Introduction

1. Records of the Registrar of the Diocese of Oxford indicate that the tablet was installed in 1926, "in accordance with the design of Mr. Eric Gill of Abergaverny." For a description of the design of Dougall's home, see Louise Armstrong, "A House designed by Clough Williams Ellis in Cumnor, Oxfordshire, 1911–1912," A Paper for the Certificate in Historic Conservation, September 1992. Unpublished. Her home was probably within sight of the gravestone; houses have since been built between them.

2. Lily Dougall, "God In Action," in *The Spirit: God and his Relation to Man Considered from the Standpoint of Philosophy, Psychology and Art,* ed. Burnett Hillman Streeter (London: Macmillan, 1919), 28.

3. Psalm 107:9: "For he satisfieth the longing soul, and filleth the hungry soul with goodness."

4. Lily Dougall's papers are held at the Library and Archives Canada (LAC) and the Bodleian Library (BL) at the University of Oxford. The Dougall Family Papers (DFP) at the National Archives include family records and correspondence, with a number of Lily Dougall's letters, and family papers. Dougall's companion, M. S. Earp, collected her personal and publishing papers after her death and compiled a draft biography. A typescript of this biography is at the Library and Archives Canada: M. S. Earp, "Selected Letters of Lily Dougall with Biographical Notes," typescript, LAC, DFP, 5, 9. A number of these papers were then given to B. H. Streeter for his contribution to the biography of Lily Dougall, and are now at the Bodleian Library, in the Lily Dougall Collection (LDP). They have never been organized and are stored loosely in a number of temporary boxes.

The limited critical work on Dougall focuses on her career as a novelist. Lorraine McMullen's unpublished manuscript and two published articles, "Lily Dougall's Vision of Canada," in *A Mazing Space: Writing Canadian Women Writing,* ed. Shirley Neuman and Smaro Kamboureli (Edmonton: Longspoon Press/Newest Press, 1986), 137–47; and "Lily Dougall: The Religious Vision of a Canadian Novelist," *Studies in Religion/Sciences religieuses* 16, no. 1 (Winter 1987): 79–90 are valuable introductions to Dougall's fiction. See also Victoria Walker's introduction to the 1992 reprint of Lily Dougall's *What Necessity Knows* and Simone Vauthier, "Rosemary for Remembrance, A Small Memorial for Lily Dougall," *Études canadiennes* 18 (1985), 51–67. A thoughtful M.A. thesis has been written on three of Dougall's novels: Scott Rothwell Swanson, "Beyond Common Sense: Ideal Love in Three Novels of Lily Dougall" (Master's Thesis, University of Victoria, 1993).

    5. L. Dougall, *Beggars All: A Novel* (London: Longmans, Green and Co., 1891).

    6. [Lily Dougall], *Pro Christo et Ecclesia* (London and New York: Macmillan, 1900).

    7. [Lily Dougall] et al., *The Spirit, God and His Relation to Man Considered from the Standpoint of Philosophy, Psychology and Art* (London: Macmillan, 1919); *Concerning Prayer: Its Nature, Its Difficulties and Its Value* (London: Macmillan, 1916); *Immortality, An Essay in Discovery Co-ordinating Scientific, Psychical, and Biblical Research,* ed. Burnett Hillman Streeter (London: Macmillan, 1917).

    8. Carol P. Christ, "Embodied thinking: Reflections on Feminist Theological Method," *Journal of Feminist Studies in Religion* 5, no. 1 (1989): 14.

    9. [Lily Dougall], *Absente Reo* (London: Macmillan, 1910), 127.

    10. See Ann Taves, "Religious Experience," in *Encyclopedia of Religion,* 2nd ed., edited by Lindsay Jones (Detroit: Macmillan Reference USA, 2005): 7737–7750. See also Robert Sharf, "Experience," in *Critical Terms for Religious Studies,* edited by Mark C. Taylor (Chicago: University of Chicago Press, 2000), 94–116; and Jerome I. Gellman, "Mysticism and Religious Experience," in *The Oxford Handbook of Philosophy of Religion,* ed. William J. Wainwright (Oxford: Oxford University Press, 2005). This attention to phenomena described as "religious experience" reflects growing interest in forms of experience other than mysticism.

    11. Catherine Albanese, "Introduction," *American Spiritualities: A Reader* (Bloomington: Indiana University Press, 2001). David D. Hall describes the interest in experience among historians of religion, in "Review Essay: What Is the Place of 'Experience' in Religious History?" *Religion and American Culture: A Journal of Interpretation* 13, no. 2 (2003): 241–50.

    12. See Sheila Greeve Davaney, "The Limits of the Appeal to Women's Experience," in *Shaping New Vision Gender and Values in American Culture,* The Harvard Women's Studies in Religion Series, ed. Clarissa W. Atkinson et al. (Ann Arbor and London: UMI Research Press, 1987), 48. Nelle Morton, *The Journey Is Home* (Boston: Beacon Press, 1985), 127. "But the private self . . . is only source of authentic experience and this experience can only be stated and understood only by public image . . . *Deep in the experience itself is the source of new imaging.*" (Emphasis in the original)

    13. Steven T. Katz, "Language, Epistemology and Mysticism," in *Mysticism and Philosophical Analysis,* ed. Steven T. Katz (Oxford: Oxford University Press, 1978), 29. Katz argued that the idea of a common core of mystical experience is a form of essentialist reductionism, "reducing all reports of x to one claimed essence y" (p. 24). See also Steven T. Katz, ed., *Mysticism and Language* (Oxford: Oxford University Press, 1992), and *Mysticism and Religious Traditions* (Oxford: Oxford University Press, 1983).

14. Ann Taves's discussion of the terminology of faith, and the emergence of the term "religious experience" from Protestant evangelicalism is very useful. See Taves, "Religious Experience," especially p. 7737.

15. Cited in Earp, "Selected Letters," 66.

16. Ann Taves, *Fits, Trances and Visions: Experiencing Religion and Explaining Experience from Wesley to James* (Princeton: Princeton University Press, 1999).

17. Lily Dougall, "Nature of Religion," undated ts., p. 8, BL, LDP, 1.

18. Carol P. Christ and Judith Plaskow, eds., *Womanspirit Rising: A Feminist Reader in Religion,* 2nd ed. (New York: Harper Collins, 1992), 20.

19. Anne Braude, "Women's History Is American Religious History," in Thomas Tweed, ed., *Retelling U.S. Religious History* (Berkeley: University of California Press, 1997), 87.

20. Katherine M. Faull, "Schleiermacher—A Feminist? Or, How to Read Gender Inflected Theology," in *Schleiermacher and Feminism: Sources, Evaluations and Responses,* ed. Iain G. Nicol (Lewiston, N.Y.: Edwin Mellen Press, 1992), 15. See also Grace Jantzen's criticism of Schleiermacher in *Power, Gender and Christian Mysticism* (Cambridge: Cambridge University Press, 1995), conclusion.

21. Steve Bruce, the most prolific sociologist of secularization, describes the spirituality of the Student Christian Movement as a vestigial remnant of their evangelical origins in *A House Divided: Protestantism, Schism and Secularization* (London and New York: Routledge, 1990). For the most recent explication of Bruce's position, see *God is Dead: Secularization in the West* (Oxford: Blackwell, 2002).

22. Friedrich Schleiermacher, *On Religion, Speeches to Its Cultured Despisers,* translated by John Oman, reprinted with an introduction by Rudolf Otto (1799, trans. 1893; New York: Harper Torchbooks, 1958), 43.

23. Owen Chadwick, *The Secularisation of the European Mind in the Nineteenth Century* (Cambridge: Cambridge University Press, 1975), 13.

24. Ann Braude, *Radical Spirits: Spiritualism and Women's Rights in Nineteenth-Century America,* 2nd ed. (1989; Bloomington: Indiana University Press, 2001), xxii. Ann Douglas set the tone for the dismissal of feminized spirituality, dismissing it in favor of a theological "virility." *The Feminization of American Culture* (New York: Knopf, 1977), 11.

25. Gillian T. Ahlgren, *Teresa of Avila and the Politics of Sanctity* (Ithaca, N.Y.: Cornell University Press, 1997); Jodi Bilinkoff, *The Avila of St. Teresa* (Ithaca, N.Y.: Cornell University Press, 1989); Alison Weber, *Teresa of Avila and the Rhetoric of Femininity* (Princeton, N.J.: Princeton University Press, 1990).

26. Bernard McGinn, "The Letter and the Spirit: Spirituality as an Academic Discipline," *Christian Spirituality Bulletin* 1, 2 (1993): 4. See Bernard McGinn, *The Foundations of Mysticism* (New York: Crossroad, 1991–1994; London: SCM Press, 1992–1995).

27. Bernard McGinn, "The Letter and the Spirit," 6. Similarly, Grace Jantzen argues that we need "[a] theological and social probing of what has been taken to count as the presence of God . . . to develop a history of the theology of the presence of God, rather than to outline a sequence of intense subjective experiences." Grace Jantzen, "Could There Be a Mystical Core of Religion?" *Religious Studies* 29 (1993): 401–411. See also the closely contextual study by Andrew Weeks, *German Mysticism from Hildegard of Bingen to Ludwig Wittgenstein: A Literary and Intellectual History* (Albany: State University of New York Press, 1993).

28. Michel de Certeau, *The Mystic Fable: The Sixteenth and Seventeenth Centuries,* vol. 1, trans. Michael B. Smith (1982; Chicago: University of Chicago Press, 1992).

29. De Certeau, *The Mystic Fable,* 11–13.

30. T. B. Kilpatrick to Lily Dougall, 20 March 1889, 7 Marine Terrace, Aberdeen. BL, LDP, 1.

31. Dorothy Emmet, interview with author, October 6, 1993, Cambridge, England. Emmet had personal as well as theological reasons for discounting Dougall; Emmet was part of a post–World War I generation that turned to neo-orthodoxy; her own father's reputation had been damaged when he published a book with Dougall: Lily Dougall and Cyril W. Emmet, *The Lord of Thought: A Study of the Problems which Confronted Lord Jesus and the Solution He Offered* (London: Student Christian Movement, 1922).

32. Paul Badham has argued that "modernist ideas are now almost universally accepted by mainstream Christians—or at the leading edge of contemporary theology." See Paul Badham, "The Revival of Religious Modernism," in the *The Future of Liberal Theology,* ed. Mark D. Chapman (Burlington, Vt.: Ashgate, 2002), and *The Contemporary Challenge of Modernist Theology* (Cardiff: University of Wales Press, 1998), 7.

1. AN EVANGELICAL CHILDHOOD

1. Dougall's grandfather was John Redpath, who rose from modest origins as a stonemason to become the wealthy owner of Canada's first sugar refinery. He was a prominent citizen in Montreal, a devout Free Church Presbyterian, active in philanthropies and civic organizations. He and his first wife, Janet McPhee, had five children who survived infancy: Elizabeth (married John Dougall), Peter (married Grace Wood), Mary (married Thomas Taylor), Helen (married George Drummond), and John James (married Ada Mills). On her death he married Jane Drummond, the sister of his son-in-law George Drummond, six of whose ten children survived infancy: Margaret Pringle (married Alexander Dennistoun), George Drummond (married Alice Mills, and Anne Savage), Francis (Frank, married Caroline Plimsoll), Augusta Eleanor (married Charles Fleet), Emily Bonar (married Henry Bovey), and William Wood (Willie).

The Dougall family papers include a number of letters from John Redpath's eldest son, Lily's uncle Peter Redpath, who moved with his wife, Grace, to England in 1876 when tariffs on sugar importation were dropped and the refineries temporarily closed. John Redpath's son-in-law George Alexander Drummond, who with Peter Redpath operated the refineries, was also prominent in Montreal affairs and was later made a senator. Family letters refer to the early death of his wife, Helen. He subsequently married Grace Julia Parker, who was prominent as one of Lady Aberdeen's closest collaborators on the National Council of Women.

Lily Dougall's father, John Dougall, was born in Paisley, Scotland in 1808. He immigrated to Canada in 1826, and married Elizabeth Redpath in 1840. Their children included John Redpath, James Duncan (married Laure Emelie Matille), Janet (Jessie), Margaret Jane (Maggie; married Anthony Cochrane), Mary Helen (Polly), Susan (Susie), Arthur, Lily, and Agnes Bertha. Arthur died at the age of four in 1858, Agnes Bertha died at four months in 1861, and Mary Helen died in 1872.

2. For background on John Dougall, see Lorraine Vander Hoef, "John Dougall (1808–1886): Portrait of an Early Social Reformer and Evangelical Witness in Canada," *Journal of the Canadian Church Historical Society*, 43 (2001): 115–145; J. G. Snell, "John Dougall," in *Dictionary of Canadian Biography*, vol. 11 (Toronto: University of Toronto Press, 1982), 270; and Frederick Armstrong, "James Dougall," in *Dictionary of Canadian Biography*, vol. 11, 268. Snell says that John Dougall joined the Congregational Church in 1831, but an obituary published in the family papers reported that he and Elizabeth Dougall had joined in 1840, on the occasion of their marriage, rather than continue in a church that "worshipped rumsellers" (*Northern Messenger and Sunday School Companion*, September 24, 1886, clipping in BL, LDC, 6. This obituary also credits Dougall with starting a temperance society with a "Mr. James Court and another gentleman.").

3. Frederick Armstrong, "James Dougall," 268. Dougall's wealthy brother-in-law, Peter Redpath, joined the two Dougall brothers as a partner in 1840, on the Dougalls' marriage, and pulled out in 1858 after some difficult years. The 1865 bankruptcy was discharged four years later. In her autobiographical manuscript, "Lovereen," Lily Dougall described an evangelical father neglecting his business.

4. LAC, DFP, 1, 2, p. 4. The good causes are identified as abstinence from all intoxicating drinks and tobacco, and promotion of human freedom (interestingly, tobacco was identified and subsequently crossed out); the great religious societies included such nonsectarian organizations as the Evangelical Alliance, the Bible Society, the Religious Tract Society, the Sunday School Union, and the Temperance Society.

5. J. I. Cooper, "The Early Editorial Policy of the *Montreal Witness*," *Canadian Historical Association Report* (Toronto: University of Toronto Press, 1947), 53–62.

6. "Report of the French Canadian Mission Society," The *Montreal Witness*, February 9, 1846.

7. *The Montreal Daily Witness*, July 8, 1868.

8. See Paul Rutherford, *A Victorian Authority: The Daily Press in the Late Nineteenth Century* (Toronto: University of Toronto Press, 1982), 40–50. Rutherford gives the circulation numbers of the *Montreal Witness* at 1872: 23,100; 1880: 42,542; 1891: 46,140, and 1900: 39,250.

9. In 1871, Remington offered a $3,000 loan to start the New York paper, with the promise of further advances if necessary. E. Remington to John Dougall, June 19, 1871, LAC, DFP, 1, 4. Subsequent letters reveal Remington's early enthusiasm and later his growing impatience with the paper's losses. Lorraine Vander Hoef has identified Remington as Eliphalet Remington of Remington Brothers. Vander Hoef, "John Dougall," 130.

10. FED (Frederick Dougall), penciled notation in a 1875 diary by John Dougall, LAC, DFP, 4, 3. A weekly version survived for a number of years.

11. Rutherford attributes their failure to lack of revenue. Their subscription prices were modest, and they had no lucrative liquor ads or political patronage. "Most of all, however, the *Daily Witness* stagnated because the stubbornness of the Dougall family prevented a significant shift to meet changing tastes and

times." Rutherford, *Victorian Authority*, 50. Beyond this oblique reference, he does not note the impact of their religious convictions. The *New York Weekly Witness* continued publication until 1920.

12. M. S. Earp, "Selected Letters of Lily Dougall with Biographical Notes," typescript, LAC, DFP, 5, 9, p. 71.

13. The Dougall Family Papers (DFP) are held in Library and Archives Canada (LAC).

14. "Lovereen," vol. 3, pp. 183–184. See chapters 3 and 4 for a discussion of the autobiographical nature of this manuscript.

15. Emphasis in the original. J. D. Dougall to Elizabeth Dougall, July 1876, Montreal, LAC, DFP, 1, 5.

16. John Redpath Dougall to John Dougall, May 31, 1878, LAC, DFP, 1, 7, p. 5.

17. George R. Scott to John Dougall, New York Witness Offices, New York, July 2, 1882, LAC, DFP, 2, 1. Among his letters are preserved several from emotive evangelicals who seem by their employment and literacy to have been of a lower social standing.

18. Janet suggests in a letter that a visiting minister will have to stay with them, as there was no one else in the church able to entertain a minister. Janet Dougall to Elizabeth Dougall, Montreal June 21, 1876, LAC, DFP, 1, 5.

19. (Punctuation added.) John Redpath Dougall to unknown [judging from the context, the letter was probably written to his mother, Elizabeth Dougall], n.d., LAC, DFP, 1, 2.

20. John Dougall to Elizabeth Dougall, n.d., LAC, DFP, 1, 2.

21. [James Dougall] to my very dear Father [John Dougall], June 26, 1876, LAC, DFP, 1, 5.

22. James Dougall to John Dougall, November 1, 1877, LAC, DFP, 1, 6.

23. James Dougall to my very dear father [John Dougall], November 8, 1877, LAC, DFP, 1, 6.

24. James Dougall to Elizabeth Dougall, November 26, 1877, LAC, DFP, 1, 6; James Dougall to John Dougall, April 26, 1882, postscript, LAC, DFP, 2, 1.

25. October 1, 1870, diary with brown cover, LAC, DFP, 4, 3. Janet also missed school because of illness. See E. Dickinson to Janet Dougall, Cote House, January 3, 1869, LAC, DFP, 1, 3.

26. John wrote in his diary in September 1870 that Janet had taken on Polly's work as editor of the *New Dominion Monthly* to allow her to recuperate: "The latter [Polly] seeking much needed health, I wish her riding tour could have been indefinitely prolonged. I think if she could go with somebody and ride all over Europe she might get well and strong again." Elizabeth and Polly Dougall stayed in Montreal for health after their Christmas visit in 1870. September 16, 1870, December 24, 1870, December 31, 1870, diary with brown cover, LAC, DFP, 4, 3. See "My Daughter, A Brief Memoir of Mary Helen Dougall," *New Dominion Monthly*, May 1872, clipping in LAC, DFP, 4, 3.

27. A letter in 1876 notes the state of Lily's health as if it were a matter of ongoing concern. Janet Dougall to Elizabeth Dougall, Montreal, February 14, 1876, LAC, DFP, 1, 5.

28. Susan Dougall's 1879 letters from Dansville, in LAC, DFP, 1, 8, suggest that tuberculosis is a possibility, as is some form of eating disorder. Family letters lay emphasis on her need to gain weight. Her mother had asked why she

had not been gaining faster, to which Susan replied, "I am not gaining fast in any way, but I am not dying as I was last summer but making just almost imperceptible progress up hill and that only by great care and quiet." She describes the attendants' efforts to entice her to eat various luxuries. Susan Dougall to Elizabeth and John Dougall, [n.d.] LAC, DFP, 1, 8. In another letter, she describes her digestion at some length; noting that she has to lie still all morning in order to digest white bread, gruel, egg, and milk, but says she does not measure her health by digestion but by the state of her nerves. Susan Dougall to Elizabeth Dougall, Dansville, August 7, 1879. LAC, DFP, 1, 8. See also her reference to the plumpness of her own and other patients' arms. Susan Dougall to Elizabeth Dougall and Maggie Cochrane, December 12, 1878, LAC, DFP, 1, 7. Elizabeth Dougall also had chronic health problems. Susan makes reference to nursing her mother in 1872. Susan Dougall to John Dougall, August 17, 1872, LAC, DFP, 1, 4. In 1882 she moved to a rest home, the "Healds Hygeia Home" at Wilmington where Lily cared for her. See the family letters in LAC, DFP, l, 1 and 2, particularly Elizabeth Dougall to John Dougall, Wilmington, April 1882. Lily's description of the death of the mother in her unpublished autobiographical novel, "Lovereen," strongly suggests that she blamed her father's evangelicalism for her mother's health problems. John Dougall's remorse on his wife's death would seem to confirm this.

29. [Probably Janet Dougall] to Elizabeth Dougall, Friday, September 26, 1878, LAC, DFP, 1, 7, p. 6.

30. Lily's father recalled in 1884 that they had "blamed malaria" for her earlier breakdowns. "I now realize you were overtaxed [in 1884] just as you were several years in Brooklyn when we blamed malaria. . . ." John Dougall to Lily Dougall, May 1884. Earp, "Selected Letters," 55.

31. It was the younger women who had the least control over their lives. The relationship between nervous illness and women's confined position in Victorian culture has been examined by Carroll Smith-Rosenberg, "The Hysterical Woman: Sex Roles and Role Conflict in Nineteenth Century America," in her *Disorderly Conduct: Visions of Gender in Nineteenth Century America* (New York: Oxford University Press, 1985); Elaine Showalter, *The Female Malady, Women, Madness and English Culture, 1830–1980* (New York: Pantheon Books, 1985), and Wendy Mitchinson, *The Nature of Their Bodies, Women and Their Doctors in Victorian Canada* (Toronto: University of Toronto Press, 1991), especially chapter 2, "The Frailty of Women." Dougall commented on the gendering of invalidism in "Lovereen"; a doctor commented, in reference to Lovereen: "the commonest product of the bustle and [brain?] and religion, of the nineteenth century—a woman all ideas and fine feelings not diseased but forever ailing." Dougall, "Lovereen," p. 400, BL, LDP, 4.

32. "Lovereen," vol. 3, p. 45, BL, LDP, 4.

33. "Lovereen," vol. 2, 384–85, BL, LDP, 4.

34. "Lovereen," vol. 2, 385, BL, LDP, 4. Lovereen dryly concludes: "I always had a vivid imagination."

35. The conversion of Lily's older sister was more dramatic. For Janet's conversion, see E. Dickinson to Janet Dougall, [n.d.] NAC, DFP, 1, 3. For Lily's, see Earp, "Selected Letters," 128. Dougall's flippancy may also reflect a revisionist approach to her childhood. In her autobiographical novel, Dougall describes Lovereen and Paul as children nervously and uncomfortably acknowledging their commitment to Christ in a revival. They view this

experience differently as adults: Lovereen says, "It does not seem to me that conversion is anything real. Prayer is something; the persistent effort to obey God is something; but I can't think it rational to attach miraculous importance to the first moment that effort is begun in conscious earnest. . . . If conversion is an act, then I was converted dozens of times. . . ." Paul, on the other hand, argues that they gained as childish converts a new "power of spiritual perception": "You cannot look back to our conversion and think that it had no reality. On our part it was a childish resolution to serve Jesus Christ, but many Christian teachers hold that He stands pledged to meet such honest resolution by giving new life in return." "Lovereen," vol. 3, p. 431, 430, BL, LDP, 4.

36. John Dougall to Elizabeth Dougall, n.d., DFP, NAC 1, 1.

37. John Dougall to Lily Dougall, New York, May 28, 1884, BL, LDP, 1.

38. "'At Rest' Calvary Church," *The Montreal Daily Witness*, Monday, August 23, 1886, BL, LDP, 6.

39. Ian C. Bradley, *The Call to Seriousness: The Evangelical Impact on the Victorians* (New York: Macmillan, 1969), 22.

40. "In Memoriam A Sermon preached in the Canada Presbyterian Church, Cote St., Mtl on Sabbath March 14, 1869 on the occasion of the death of John Redpath Esq., Terrace Bank by Rev. Prof. D. H. MacVicar," BL, LDP, 2. Undated clipping.

41. [Elizabeth Dougall] to [John Dougall], n.d., LAC, DFP, 1, 1. (Letter addressed to "my dear old friend" from "your loving wife.") Lily's brother, John, also understood the Devil to be an active presence. See September 24, 1870, April 13, 1875, brown diary, LAC, DFP, 4, 3.

42. John Dougall to Mr. Court, September 28, 1881, LAC, DFP, 1,10.

43. Janet Dougall to Susan Dougall, April 18, 1883, LAC, DFP, 2, 2.

44. Jane Redpath to Elizabeth Dougall, April 30, 1883, LAC, DFP 2, 2.

45. The Evangelical Alliance was one of the movements supported by the *Montreal Witness*. Cooper, "The Montreal Witness," 62. John Redpath Dougall was the vice-president of the Montreal branch of the Evangelical Alliance. See Philip D. Jordan, *The Evangelical Alliance for the United States of America, 1847–1900: Ecumenism, Identity and The Religion of the Republic* (Lewiston, N.Y., and Toronto: Edwin Mellen Press, 1982), 102–113.

46. *The Montreal Witness*, February 9, 1846, p. 42.

47. Jordan, *The Evangelical Alliance*, 112.

48. Lily Dougall to Susan Dougall, October 23, 1887, Cheltenham, England. Earp, "Selected Letters," 77.

49. Frank Hugh Foster, *The Modern Movement in American Theology, Sketches in the History of American Protestant Thought from the Civil War to the World War* (1939: Freeport, N.Y.: Books for Libraries Press, 1969), 14. J. W. Grant was less enthusiastic about similar developments in the British Congregational Churches: he found that new converts had any concept of churchmanship, and were essentially undenominational. *Free Churchmanship in England (1870–1940), with special reference to Congregationalism* (London: Independent Press, 1955).

50. John Dougall appears to have traveled in the same evangelical circles as D. L. Moody. He was enthusiastically received at a YMCA meeting chaired by Moody. See "YMCA Meeting in Detroit," *Montreal Daily Witness*, vol. IX, No. 155, Thursday, July 2, 1868.

51. Lily Dougall's description of the parents in "Lovereen" seems to be drawn from her own family: "He and his wife had always been nominally Presbyterians, but in their new impulse for religious work they found themselves in sympathy with all who appear to be in earnest in religion and Protestantism." "Castoffs of Lovereen," p. 27, BL, LDP, 4.

52. Cooper, "Montreal Witness," 53.

53. The connections between evangelical faith and social reform were first drawn by Timothy L. Smith in *Revivalism and Social Reform in Mid-Nineteenth Century America* (New York: Abingdon Press, 1957) and the subsequent literature is extensive. In Canada, see Richard Allen, *The Social Passion: Religion and Social Reform in Canada, 1914–1928* (Toronto: University of Toronto Press, 1973); and Ramsay Cook, *The Regenerators: Social Criticism in Late Victorian Canada* (Toronto: University of Toronto Press, 1985.

54. Obituaries, BL, LDP, 1. She was also a member of the Women's Boards of the Dominion and Provincial Congregational Missionary Unions.

55. Small black notebook, entry marked Monday, August 15, 1870, NAC, DFP, 4, 3.

56. Small black notebook, page dated November 23, 1869, NAC, DFP, 4, 3. Although this notebook is not signed, it is probably written by John Redpath Dougall. The handwriting looks like that of John Redpath Dougall and the sentiments, particularly a reluctance to proselytize, are his.

57. Undated newspaper clipping, with no masthead. Most likely published in the *Montreal Witness*. BL, LDC, 6.

58. The first reference to "whole consecration" was made on November 19, 1870, further reference was made on a Sunday in April 1873, and then John refers to "whole consecration" and "higher life" in a diary entry on April 19, 1875. Diary with brown cover, NAC, DFP, 4, 3. Miss McPherson lent him *Pathway of Power*, probably *Christian's Pathway of Power*. April 12, 1875. Diary with brown cover, NAC, DFP, 4, 3. Hannah Whitall Smith was publishing articles in this journal, later published as *The Christian's Secret of a Happy Life* (1875; Toronto: Methodist Book and Publishing House, 1889). In 1877 Lily was critical of his "rules for happy living." Lily Dougall to John Dougall, February 23, 1877. Earp, "Selected Letters," 18.

59. Transcribed letter, described as a letter written later to a friend bereaved. Earp, "Selected Letters," 194.

60. *Montreal Daily Witness*, n.d., p. 1, BL, LDP, 1.

61. Sunday, April [n.d.] 1873, diary with brown cover, NAC, DFP, 4, 3.

62. December 17, 1870, diary with brown cover, LAC, DFP, 4, 3.

63. Sunday, April [n.d.] 1873, diary with brown cover, LAC, DFP, 4, 3.

64. Sunday, April [n.d.] 1873, diary with brown cover, LAC, DFP, 4, 3.

65. Monday April 5, 1875, diary with brown cover, LAC, DFP, 4, 3.

66. Sunday, June 27, 1875, diary with brown cover, LAC, DFP, 4, 3.

67. September 17, 1870; July 11, 1875; July 23, 1875; April 21, 30, 1875, and April 18, 1875, diary with brown cover, LAC, DFP, 4, 3.

68. April 12, 1875, diary with brown cover, LAC, DFP, 4, 3.

69. April 12, 1875, diary with brown cover, LAC, DFP, 4, 3.

70. April 19, 1875, diary with brown cover, LAC, DFP, 4, 3.

71. See Benjamin Breckinridge Warfield, *Perfectionism*, vol. 2 (New York: Oxford University Press, 1931). Warfield was one of the original fundamentalists, a contributor to *The Fundamentals*, who made his reputation as the

spokesman for Princeton theology. Salter's biography of Upham includes a full chapter responding to the "Warfield Critique." Darius L. Salter, *Spirit and Intellect: Thomas Upham's Holiness Theology* (Metuchen, N.J.: Scarecrow, 1986). British Anglo-Catholics, including R. A. Knox, were similarly critical of Upham's influence on liberal Anglican theology. R. A. Knox, *Enthusiasm: A Chapter in the History of Religion with Special Reference to the XVII and XVIII Centuries* (Oxford: Clarendon Press, 1950).

72. Warfield, *Perfectionism*, 337, 381.

73. See John Wesley, *An Extract of the Life of Madame Guyon* (London: R. Hawes, 1776). For Quaker influences, see Bebbington, *Evangelicalism*, 156: "The assimilation of Quietist influences by the Evangelicals within the Society of Friends was one of the ways in which alien ideas were sanitized, as it were, before reception by the broader Evangelical community."

74. For a discussion of Thomas Upham, see Salter, *Spirit and Intellect*. See Melvin E. Dieter, *The Holiness Revival of the Nineteenth Century* (Metuchen, N.J.: Scarecrow, 1980), 53–57, for another, brief, assessment of Upham's influence.

The titles of his books suggest the mix of incipient psychology and mysticism in Upham's work: Thomas Upham, *Elements of Mental Philosophy, embracing two departments of the intellect and the sensibilities* (1831; New York: Harper, 1850); *Outlines of Imperfect and Disordered Mental Action* (1840); *Principles of the Interior or Hidden Life* (1843); *Life of Madame Catherine Adorna* (1845) (St. Catherine of Genoa); *The Life of Faith* (1845; New York: Garland, 1984); *Life, Religious Opinions and Experience of Madame Guyon including an account of the personal history and religious opinions of Fénelon, Archbishop of Cambray*, ed. and rev. by an English Clergyman, with a new introduction by W. R. Inge, new ed. (1847; 1905; London: Allenson & Co., 1947); *Treatise on Divine Union: Designed to point out some of the intimate relations between God and Man in the higher forms of religious experience* (1852). They were still being published well into the twentieth century: the modernist Anglican bishop, W. R. Inge, edited a version of Upham's biography of Madame Guyon that was revised as late as 1947.

75. Upham, *Madame Guyon*, 40, 42.

76. (Emphasis in the original.) Upham, *Madame Guyon*, 56.

77. (Emphasis in the original.) Upham, *Madame Guyon*, 56.

78. Warfield, *Perfectionism*, 381. Warfield says he is citing (and presumably translating) Ernest Seillière for this quotation. *Madame Guyon et Fénelon, Precurseurs de Rousseau* (1918), 143 f.

79. Warfield, *Perfectionism*, 431.

80. Warfield, *Perfectionism*, 431.

81. For Stowe, see Dieter, *The Holiness Revival*, 53–57. Hannah Whitall Smith, *The Interior Life* (London: Longley, 1886).

82. Smith, *The Christian's Secret of a Happy Life*, ii–iv.

83. Warfield, *Perfectionism*, 540, 554. Warfield argues that perfectionists reduce God to an instrument of human will. Despite Warfield's criticism, Smith's first book has continued to be influential among fundamentalists.

84. Hannah Whitall Smith to Mrs. Anna Shipley, The Cedars, June 15, 1878. Cited in Logan Pearsall Smith, *Religious Rebel: The Letters of HWS* (London: Nisbet, 1949), 41.

85. Debra Campbell, "Hannah Whitall Smith (1832–1911): Theology of the Mother-Hearted God," *Signs, Journal of Women in Culture and Society* 15 (1989): 88. See David Bebbington, *Evangelicalism in Modern Britain, A History*

from the 1730s to the 1980s (London; Boston: Unwin Hyman, 1989; Grand Rapids, Mich.: Baker Book House, 1992), 171, for a discussion of the liberal nature of the early Broadlands conferences. Georgina Cowper-Temple, for example, who hosted an elite holiness meeting in the summer of 1874, was the wife of prominent Broad Churchman, William Cowper-Temple.

86. Nancy Cott, *The Bonds of Womanhood: Woman's Sphere in New England, 1780–1835* (New Haven, Conn.: Yale University Press, 1977), 78, 140–41.

87. Newspaper clipping, [likely the *Montreal Witness*] n.d., BL, LDP, 6.

88. E. Dickinson to Janet Dougall, LAC, DFP, 1, 3.

2. "Lovereen"

1. [Lily Dougall], *Voluntas Dei* (London: Macmillan, 1912).

2. M. S. Earp, "Selected Letters of Lily Dougall with Biographical Notes," 15, LAC, DFP, 5, 9.

3. Laure Dougall to Elizabeth Dougall, May 22, 1877, LAC, DFP, 1, 6.

4. [Janet Dougall] to "Dear dear Mother" [Elizabeth Dougall], Friday, September 6, 1878, NAC, DFP, 1, 7. The letter is unsigned but the context and handwriting suggest it is written by Janet.

5. Lily Dougall to John Dougall, November 11, [no year], BL, LDP, 1.

6. Lily Dougall to Elizabeth Dougall, Ivy Green, Montreal February 29, [no year], LAC, DFP, 1, 2.

7. Lily Dougall to Elizabeth Dougall, 1878. Earp, "Selected Letters," 20.

8. For Lily's impatience with young preachers, see Lily Dougall to John Dougall, Drummond St. Montreal, Monday Evening, n.d., BL, LDP, 1.

9. M. S. Earp, "Selected Letters of Lily Dougall with Biographical Notes," typescript, LAC, DFP, 5, 9, p. 22.

10. "Rosemary for Remembrance," published in *The Madonna of a Day* (London: Bentley and Son, 1896), 408–409. Lorraine McMullen has suggested that this account reflects a similarly frustrated romance in Dougall's youth. Unpublished ms. See also Simone Vauthier, "Rosemary for Remembrance, A Small Memorial for Lily Dougall," *Études canadiennes* 18 (1985), 51–67.

11. June 13, 1875, black diary, LAC, DFP, 4, 3. For the separatism of the holiness community, see Hannah Whitall Smith, *The Christian's Secret*, chapter 15, which demands the believer turn her back on the world and its amusements.

12. James Dougall to Elizabeth Dougall, January 16, 1877, LAC, DFP, 1, 6. Cunningham notes that the acceptance of fiction generally paralleled the rising education and professional status of members of a particular sect. The Plymouth Brethren continued to be suspicious of the novel late in the nineteenth century, whereas the Congregationalists had by then come to accept fiction. Valentine Cunningham, *Everywhere Spoken Against, Dissent in the Victorian Novel* (Oxford: Clarendon Press, 1975), 50.

13. Several times in his diary, John describes the time lost in reading a book. On one occasion, he wrote that he had been tempted to play croquet with Drummond girls: "the temptation to which I yielded today was like that of reading books a wretched one, but it sufficed to step between me and God for I ought today with a clear hour to have made a step higher than I have

attained this week, instead of which I opened the front door to the way of sin." Thursday, June 10, 1875, diary with brown cover, LAC, DFP, 4, 3.

14. Rev. George H. Bridgman, *Montreal Daily Witness*, Friday, July 3, 1868, p. 3.

15. "Fiction," *The Montreal Witness, Commercial Review and Family Newspaper*, December 27, 1871, p. 4.

16. Lily Dougall to Janie Couper, September 24, 1883. Earp, "Selected Letters," 20.

17. George Eliot, *Letters* i, 65–66. Cited in Elizabeth Jay, *The Religion of the Heart: Anglican Evangelicalism and the Nineteenth Century Novel* (Oxford: Clarendon Press, 1979, 205, 216.

18. Earp, "Selected Letters," 67.

19. Earp, "Selected Letters," 67. Her first story was published under the masculine pseudonym Ernest Duns [Lily Dougall], "Hath Not a Jew Eyes?" *Longman's Magazine* 13, no. 75 (1889).

20. See Earp, "Selected Letters," 97–98. Dougall was safely in Switzerland writing "Lovereen" when her aunt wrote to her.

21. [Janet Dougall] to "Dear dear Mother" [Elizabeth Dougall], Friday, September 6, 1878, LAC, DFP, 1, 7. The letter is unsigned but the context and handwriting suggest it is written by Janet.

22. Elizabeth Dougall's power in the family was in part derived from the moral authority granted an evangelical mother, but was also more materially related to her judicious use of the money she had inherited money from her father. She owned the family home, a gift from her father. *Northern Messenger and Sunday School Companion*, September 24, 1886. Clipping in BL, LDP, 6. Elizabeth Dougall partially financed the expansion of the *Witness* by guaranteeing John Dougall's loans from his children. James Dougall to John Dougall, June 26, 1876, LAC, DFP, 1, 5. She also gave money directly to the children. James used her money to finance the building of a larger house. J. D. Dougall to John Dougall, September 2, 1878, LAC, DFP, 1, 7, and described gifts to all the children in November 23, 1881, LAC, DFP, 1, 5. In 1877, she chastised James for his criticism of his father's business ethics. James Dougall to Elizabeth Dougall, November 26, 1877, LAC, DFP, 1, 6. In 1882, John and James proposed moving to Winnipeg; their mother's response provoked an apologetic letter from her son John. See J. R. Dougall to Elizabeth Dougall, May 1, 1882. LAC, DFP, 2, 1.

23. James Dougall to "my very dear mother," September 20, 1878, LAC, DFP, 1, 7.

24. John Redpath Dougall to John Dougall, [n.d., probably early 1878], LAC, DFP, 1, 7.

25. [John Dougall] to Elizabeth Dougall, Montreal, June 1, 1880, LAC, DFP, 1, 9. His accounting of the expenses suggests he was writing for his mother's financial support.

26. Jane Redpath had lived with the Dougall family when Lily was a child. Her letter to Elizabeth Dougall suggests the intimacy of their relationship and nature of Lily's studies: "Lily has been pretty well since I wrote. She did not go out last Sabbath to church, nor to the School of Design on Monday morning, but since then she has been pretty fully occupied and has joined Masson's class of English literature as well as Calderwood's Moral Philosophy class, so what with attending lectures, studying for them and writing them out she has

not a little on hand but appears to enjoy them all thoroughly. . . . Lily is a great joy to me. How nice and fat her cheeks keep, just as when she was a baby. I feel inclined to kiss them all the time. It is very good of you to do without her I do hope that the climate here will strengthen her." Jane Redpath to Elizabeth Dougall, Saturday, November 13, 1880, 130 Gilmore Place, LAC, DFP, 1, 9. See also Earp, "Selected Letters," 31.

27. For a discussion of higher education for women in Scotland, see Lindy Moore, "The Scottish Universities and Women Students," in *Scottish Universities, Distinctiveness and Diversity,* ed. Jennifer J. Carter and Donald J. Withrington (Edinburgh: John Donald Publishers, 1992).

28. David Masson (1822–1907) was particularly supportive of women's higher education and gave a special course of lectures on English literature to women students under the auspices of the Association for the University Education of Women. G. G. Smith, "Masson, David," *Dictionary of National Biography,* Supplement 1901–1911 (Oxford: Oxford University Press, 1912).

29. Lily Dougall to John Redpath Dougall, August 12, 1885. Earp, "Selected Letters," 68.

30. Lily lived with her mother at a rest home on her return from Edinburgh in 1882. See the family letters in LAC, DFP, l, 1 and 2, particularly Elizabeth Dougall to John Dougall, Wilmington, April 1882. Elizabeth Dougall's complaints about Lily's habit of sketching each morning suggest that Lily sought relief from the confinement of such close quarters. See [Elizabeth to John Dougall] Wilmington, April 24 [no year, probably also 1882], LAC, DFP, 2, 1.

31. See letters in Earp, "Selected Letters," 56–58. Her letter of September 24, 1883, described living with God; in November 1883 she wrote, "How good God was to teach me something about Himself 'before this trouble came' "; and on December 16, 1883, "When I last wrote you [from Brooklyn] I was seeking God with my whole heart. . . . When I sought God with my whole heart, I found Him. . . . Dear, since I found the Lord in this new sense, my life has been transformed. . . ."

32. Earp, "Selected Letters," 61. A subsequent reference to "Mrs. Smith" suggests that "the life [the book] speaks of" was a reference to the holiness movement. The influential book was probably Hannah Whitall Smith's best-seller, *The Christian's Secret of a Happy Life* (1875; Toronto: Methodist Book and Publishing House, 1889). Lily Dougall to J. C. [Janie Couper], Brooklyn, New York, February 1, 1884. Earp, "Selected Letters," 62.

33. Smith, *Christian Secret,* 16.

34. Lily Dougall to J. C. [Janie Couper?], Brooklyn, New York, February 1, 1884. Earp, "Selected Letters," 62.

35. Lily Dougall to J. A. C. [Janie Couper?], Ivy Green, Montreal, December 16, 1883. Earp, "Selected Letters," 59.

36. Lily Dougall to K. D. [Katie Drummond?], July 24, 1886. Earp, "Selected Letters," 74.

37. Lily Dougall to J. A. C. [Janie Couper?], Ivy Green, Montreal, December 16, 1883. Earp, "Selected Letters," 59. For Smith's example of a "life hid with Christ in God," see *The Christian's Secret,* Chapter 3.

38. Lily Dougall, December 6, 1883. Earp, "Selected Letters," 56.

39. Smith, *The Christian's Secret,* 34–35.

40. "What a wonderful thing it must be to die and enter into the beginning of the knowledge of these mysteries. Oh J——I pray again and again that

Christ may take me unto Himself. . . . This [the fact she is tied to housekeeping instead of studying] has been a great heartbreak to me, but God knows far, far better how to make me really happy than I know myself, and He will guide the housekeeping. Oh, yes, dear; He will guide and He will keep, and He will make rich in all happiness; otherwise my heart would break utterly. I am only living by faith, but I know that it is only the lack of faith that makes life seem *in any way* hard to me. The longer I live the more I am quite convinced that *perfect faith is perfect happiness,* under whatever the circumstances." (Emphasis in the original) Lily Dougall to J. A. C. [Janie Couper?], Ivy Green, Montreal, December 16, 1883. Earp, "Selected Letters," 57.

41. Lily Dougall to K. D. [Katie Drummond], Ivy Green, Montreal, December 30, 1883. Earp, "Selected Letters," 60.

42. Significantly, Sophie Earp has edited this letter in her "Selected Letters" (p. 55) and removed John Dougall's apologies. The original is in the Bodleian Library: John Dougall to Lily Dougall, New York, May 28, 1884, BL, LDP, 1.

43. Lily Dougall to J. C. [Janie Couper?], Brooklyn, New York, February 1, 1884. Earp, "Selected Letters," 62.

44. M. S. Earp, "Selected Letters," 25. Dougall describes her difficulties finding time to write in her aunt's household in a letter to John Dougall. Earp, "Selected Letters," 109. Health problems often allowed Lily to retreat from social and family obligations to study. In 1880, Dougall traveled to Edinburgh with the excuse that the bracing climate was good for her health; now she felt it necessary to leave Edinburgh for a more congenial climate.

45. R. N. Smart to Lorraine McMullen, University Library, University of St. Andrews, 5 November 1982. Sophie Earp has transcribed Dougall's letters to her father requesting support for her studies, and his grudging acquiescence. Earp, "Selected Letters," 70–72. John Dougall was supportive of women's independence as an earlier letter (Earp, "Selected Letters," 44) and a passage in his obituary indicates. (*Northern Messenger and Sunday School Companion,* Montreal and New York, September 24, 1886, clipping in BL, LDP, 6.) The financial situation was difficult at this time, however, and he, no doubt, regretted the loss of a favorite daughter as companion and housekeeper.

Dougall first stayed in Ventnor with her sister, Janet, in May 20 of 1885 (Diary, BL, LDP, 1), and then moved there for the 1885–1886, and, it appears, the 1886–1887 school terms. Earp described Dougall "taking lessons in Greek, Latin and Mathematics," (Earp, "Selected Letters," 69) but Dougall described her course of study in Ventnor as including one lesson a week in Greek and unspecified classes in geometry and algebra (Diary, BL, LDP, 1). There is no longer a St. Boniface School in Ventnor, but a building on Mitchell Road near the St. Boniface Downs, built in 1846, operated as a "ladies college" until it was turned into a block of flats. Private correspondence, Mrs. Hart, Hillside Hotel, Ventnor, October 17, 1997. Dougall returned to Ventnor frequently, often in the winter, over the ensuing years. She would have chosen Cheltenham because of its reputation as a health spa, and for the resources of the Cheltenham Ladies College.

46. Earp, "Selected Letters," 41. For an explanation of the L. L. A. see R. N. Smart, "Literate Ladies—a Fifty Year Experiment," in *Alumnae Chronicle* 59 (June 1968), 21–28.

47. Earp, "Selected Letters," 72. Dougall's comments upon the unrealistic expectations that Lovereen could teach without any education herself probably

reflect her own battle for funds for furthering her education; "the old fashioned notion that a woman who could do nothing else could always teach had prevailed among Lovereen's friends and advisors because of their entire inexperience of the changed conditions in the educational world." "Lovereen," vol. 3, p. 400, BL, LDP, 4.

48. Describing students at St. Hugh's College Oxford, Betty Kemp wrote: "Very few students—none in 1886—do not go on to a career, ended by marriage and quite often broken or ended by a period of looking after parents. Teaching of some kind is dominant, including university and training college teaching, and a high proportion of heads of schools and colleges. There is a small but decreasing amount of teaching in private families. There is also a small steady entry into Anglican communities, often teaching or missionary orders. . . . It is true, but peculiarly distorting, to say that teaching was almost the only career open to women students before 1914. Secondary or high school teaching was a new and exciting career. Most of the schools were young—even by 1914, few were as much as thirty or forty years old." See Betty Kemp, "The Early History of St. Hugh's College," in *St. Hugh's: One Hundred Years of Women's Education at Oxford,* ed. Penny Griffin (London: Macmillan Press, 1986), 28–29.

49. B. H. Streeter, "Biographical Note," in Lily Dougall, *God's Way with Man: An Exploration of the Method of the Divine Working Suggested by the Facts of History and Science* (London: Student Christian Movement, 1924), 7. One young contemporary was forced to switch from Greek to French, because her mother feared that no one would marry a girl who read Greek. Margaret W. Nevinson, *Life's Fitful Fever: A Volume of Memories* (London: 1905), 17–18. Cited in Linda Rosenzweig, *The Anchor of My Life: Middle-Class American Mothers and Daughters, 1880–1920* (New York and London: New York University Press, 1993), 143.

50. *The Woman's Bible* (1895; reprint, Coalition Task Force on Women and Religion, 1974), 12.

51. The manuscript is in BL, LDP, 4. Two versions exist: the original manuscript and the early pages of a revised manuscript, presumably the attempts made at revision after the publication of *Beggars All.* The labels are confusing: the revised manuscript is in sheaves marked "Castoffs of Lovereen"; these include some original pages, renumbered, as well as rewritten sections. The manuscript consists of three volumes, with consecutive chapter numbers that run through the entire book, and an independent set of page numbers for each volume. References here are to the volume number and page number. In the case of the revised copy, references are to "Castoffs of Lovereen," and the new page number. Dougall altered the spelling of Lovereen; in the revised manuscript it is altered to Lovreen. The earlier spelling is used here for consistency.

52. Earp, "Selected Letters," 79. See also, T. B. Kilpatrick to Lily Dougall, 20 March 1889, 7 Marine Terrace, Aberdeen. BL, LDP, 1. Kilpatrick's wife, Anna, confirms this in an earlier letter to Lily: "Lovereen is to me most interesting partly because there is so much of you in her." A. Kilpatrick to Lily Dougall, 27 March 1888. BL, LDP, 1.

53. T. B. Kilpatrick to Lily Dougall, 7 Marine Terrace, Aberdeen, April 11, 1889. BL, LDP, 1.

54. T. B. Kilpatrick to Lily Dougall, 7 Marine Terrace, Aberdeen, March 20, 1889. BL, LDP, 1.

55. T. B. Kilpatrick to Lily Dougall, 7 Marine Terrace, Aberdeen, November 19, 1889. BL, LDP, 1.

56. "Lovereen," vol. 2, p. 163, BL, LDP, 4. Elsewhere, Dougall condemned public *ex tempore* prayer as a "gross intrusion." "Lovereen," vol. 3, pp. 373–74, BL, LDP, 4. See also "Lovereen," vol. 2, p. 386, BL, LDP, 4. Public prayer was seen as a duty by the Dougall family. Her brother John, for example, chastised himself for failing to speak directly to others about religion. October 10, 1870, black diary, LAC, DFP, 4, 3.

57. "Lovereen," vol. 2, p. 441, BL, LDP, 4.

58. "Lovereen," vol. 1, p. 258, BL, LDP, 4. Lily left Walford's denominational affiliations vague. She identified a chapel in which he is a visiting preacher as a Dissenting one, then, crossing this out, as Congregational, and finally left it simply as "chapel." "Castoffs of Lovereen," p. 106, BL, LDP, 4. At other times, she suggests he is still, nominally, an Anglican.

59. "Lovereen," vol. 1, p. 213, BL, LDP, 4. Cunningham noted that Scott's work was often an exception to the ban on fiction. Cunningham, *Everywhere Spoken Against,* 48.

60. "Lovereen," vol. 2, p. 137, BL, LDP, 4.

61. "Lovereen," vol. 1, p. 96, BL, LDP, 4.

62. "Lovereen," vol. 2, pp. 114, 292, BL, LDP, 4.

63. "Castoffs of Lovereen," p. 38, BL, LDP, 4.

64. "Castoffs of Lovereen," p. 40, BL, LDP, 4.

65. "Lovereen," vol. 2, p. 7, BL, LDP, 4.

66. "Lovereen," vol. 1, p. 388, BL, LDP, 4.

67. "Lovereen," vol. 1, p. 388, BL, LDP, 4.

68. "Lovereen," vol. 2, p. 97, BL, LDP, 4.

69. Martha Vicinus perceptively concluded that women going through a difficult transition frequently retired into an illness that "permitted a retreat into the self in order to gain the courage and ego strength to break out permanently." Martha Vicinus, *Independent Women, Work and Community for Single Women, 1850–1920* (Chicago and London: University of Chicago Press, 1985), 20. Surprisingly, considering Vicinus's sensitivity to religiosity, she does not mention a religious component to the crisis.

70. "Lovereen," vol. 2, pp. 369, 388, BL, LDP, 4.

71. "Lovereen," vol. 2, pp. 66–67, BL, LDP, 4.

72. Earp, "Selected Letters," 125.

73. Valentine Cunningham, in *Everywhere Spoken Against;* and Jay, *Religion of the Heart.* John Webster Grant also observed that "most writers agreed with Matthew Arnold that dissenters were vulgar." *Free Churchmanship in England (1870–1940) with special reference to Congregationalism* (London: Independent Press, n.d.), 86.

74. Jay, *Religion of the Heart,* 282.

3. GENDERING THE CRISIS OF FAITH

1. Gordon Roper et al., "The Kinds of Fiction, 1880–1920," in *The Literary History of Canada, Canadian Literature in English,* ed. Carl F. Klinck (Toronto: University of Toronto Press, 1965), 306.

2. Gail Twersky Reimer, "Revisions of Labour in Margaret Oliphant's Autobiography," in *Life/Lines: Theorizing Women's Autobiography,* ed. Bella Brodzki

and Celeste Schencke (Ithaca and London: Cornell University Press, 1988), 203–20.

3. M. S. Earp, "Selected Letters of Lily Dougall with Biographical Notes," 15, LAC, DFP, 5, 9, p. 13.

4. Ann Douglas, *The Feminization of American Culture* (New York: Knopf, 1977), 400–405.

5. In 1869, only six years before Lily Dougall's confirmation, her father had gleefully (and erroneously) reported the conversion of Dr. Pusey to Rome. "Editorial Items," *Montreal Daily Witness*, vol. IX, No. 188, August 11, 1868, p. 2.

6. M. S. Earp, "Selected Letters," p. 13.

7. "[The Anglican] congregation was the most fashionable, for there is a certain prestige about the Anglican service in all English speaking communities which is lacking in other forms of worship." "Lovereen," vol. 1, p. 270, BL, LDP, 4.

8. Lily Dougall to John Redpath Dougall, Edinburgh, October 1880. Earp, "Selected Letters," 29–31.

9. Lily Dougall to unknown, November 1, 1879. Earp, "Selected Letters," 23.

10. "I think she was probably influenced in making her choice by the more inclusive character of the Episcopal Communion, for she must always, I think, have depreciated a narrow creed while she sympathised whole-heartedly with the faith which fed on it." Earp, "Selected Letters," 13.

11. Alexander V. G. Allen, *The Life and Letters of Phillips Brooks* (New York: E. P. Dutton, 1901), 207–208.

12. "One Thing Remains Unchanged," *Montreal Witness*, January 4, 1847, p. 4. Cited in Nathan H. Mair, *John Dougall and His Montreal Witness* (Ottawa: The Archives Committee of the Montreal and Ottawa Conference of the United Church of Canada, 1985), 10.

13. S. T. Coleridge, *Confessions of an Inquiring Spirit*, intro. Joseph Henry Green and note by Sara Coleridge, ed. H. St. J. Hart (1853; reprint. London: A. & C. Black, 1956), 41.

14. Coleridge, *Confessions of an Inquiring Spirit*, 42.

15. Lily Dougall to John Redpath Dougall, February 23, 1877. Earp, "Selected Letters," 16–18.

16. Lily Dougall to John Redpath Dougall, March 12, 1877. Earp, "Selected Letters," 18–19.

17. [Probably James Dougall] to my very dear mother, Ivy Green, December 25, 1876, LAC, DFP, 1, 5.

18. Lily Dougall to John Dougall, March 12, 1877. Earp, "Selected Letters," 18.

19. Eternally insecure, he said, "I am by a good way the least educated and worst read man in the [Atheneum] club." John Dougall to Elizabeth Dougall, Nov. 14, 1876, LAC, DFP, 1, 5. He read Kant for meetings at the club, and wrote his mother, "I would have done better to have been writing to you." John R. Dougall to Elizabeth Dougall, December 11, 1876, LAC, DFP, 1, 5.

20. Lily Dougall to John Dougall, February 23, 1877. Earp, "Selected Letters," 18.

21. See H. R. Murphy, "The Ethical Revolt Against Christian Orthodoxy in Early Victorian England," *American Historical Review* 60, no. 4 (1955): 817.

22. Earp, "Selected Letters," 17. See Geoffrey Rowell, *Hell and the Victorians: Study of the Nineteenth Century Theological Controversies Concerning Eternal Punishment and Future Life* (Oxford: Clarendon Press, 1974). Elizabeth Jay describes the quiet abandonment of the doctrine of eternal damnation in M. F. L. Mortimer's popular *Peep of the Day* (1833). Between 1849 and 1873, editors altered only one metaphor in the description of Hell, but in 1891 half the torment was removed, and by 1909 the entire passage was gone. Elizabeth Jay, *The Religion of the Heart: Anglican Evangelicalism and the Nineteenth Century Novel* (Oxford: Clarendon Press, 1979), 87–88.

23. Lily Dougall to John Dougall, March 12, 1877. Earp, "Selected Letters," 18.

24. "As to the particular question of Doctrine most people find eternal torment in the Bible. . . . We have I think wisely, declined to dogmatise or even to discuss it, while giving all scope to the utterances of orthodox teachers on the subject." John R. Dougall to John Dougall, Montreal, May 29, 1876, LAC, DFP, 1, 5. See Joseph C. McLelland, "The Macdonnell Heresy Trial," *Canadian Journal of Theology* 4, no. 4 (1958): 273–84.

25. Dougall's reference is in a letter to her brother, Lily Dougall to J. R. D. [John Dougall], Cutts End, Cumnor, November 12, 1915. Earp, "Selected Letters," 248. Maurice's son came for tea, with Mrs. Caird, and discussed his father and Tennyson. "It was like seeing the mountain peaks of my childhood to hear him talk of the days of his youth." For Maurice's influence in the United States, see also Chorley, *The Episcopal Church*, 289–91, and Hutchison, *Modernist Impulse*, 80.

26. Colin G. Brown "Frederick Denison Maurice in the United States, 1860–1900," *Journal of Religious History* 10 (June 1978): 68.

27. Calderwood was an idealist, influential in the English translation of Schleiermacher's *On Religion*.

28. Lily Dougall to John Dougall, Holy Island, Lindisfarne, October 9, 1880. Earp, "Selected Letters," 28.

29. Lily Dougall to John Dougall, Holy Island, Lindisfarne, October 9, 1880. Earp, "Selected Letters," 28.

30. Andrew Drummond and James Bulloch, *The Church in Late Victorian Scotland, 1874–1900* (Edinburgh: The St. Andrew Press, 1978), 52.

31. Lily Dougall to John Dougall, Edinburgh, May 27, 1881, BL, LDP, 1. Earp, "Selected Letters," 31–38.

32. In 1890, she attended similar cases regarding Marcus Dodd and A. B. Bruce. Notes marked "B's letters," May 13–29, 1890, BL, LDP, 1.

33. T. B. Kilpatrick to Lily Dougall, 20 March 1889, 7 Marine Terrace, Aberdeen. BL, LDP, 1. Kilpatrick's wife, Anna, confirms this in an earlier letter to Lily, "Lovereen is to me most interesting partly because there is so much of you in her." A. Kilpatrick to Lily Dougall, 27 March 1888, BL, LDP, 1. Earp also says, "because it is essentially [Dougall's] own life and her own problems which are depicted, it affords real insight into her girlish character and standpoint." Earp, "Selected Letters," 79.

34. "Lovereen," vol. 2, p. 140, 150, BL, LDP, 4.

35. "Castoffs of Lovereen," p. 256, BL, LDP, 4.

36. "Castoffs of Lovereen," pp. 166–67, BL, LDP, 4.

37. "Lovereen," vol. 3, p. 157, BL, LDP, 4.

38. "Castoffs of Lovereen," p. 86, BL, LDP, 4.

39. "Lovereen," vol. 3, p. 383. See also "Lovereen," vol. 2, p. 400, and "Lovereen," vol. 3, pp. 377–78, BL, LDP, 4.

40. "Castoffs of Lovereen," p. 257, BL, LDP, 4.

41. "Lovereen," vol. 1, pp. 155, 263, 256, vol. 2, p. 107, BL, LDP, 4.

42. See "Lovereen," vol. 1, pp. 253, 254, 283, BL, LDP, 4.

43. Lovereen," vol. 3, p. 272, BL, LDP, 4.

44. T. B. Kilpatrick to Lily Dougall, 7 Marine Terrace, Aberdeen, March 20, 1889. BL, LDP, 1.

45. Mary Ward wrote through Robert Elsmere. Margaret Deland's protagonist is a woman, but she is not permitted to defend her own ideas. Helen Ward rarely debates theology and when she tries, she is told to mend socks. It is her husband who defends orthodox theology, and a brother-in-law provides the philosophic defense of Helen's idealism. Deland, *John Ward,* 413. For Schreiner, see Carol Barash, "Virile Womanhood: Olive Schriener's Narratives of a Master Race," in *Speaking of Gender,* ed. Elaine Showalter (New York: Routledge, 1989), 272.

46. "Castoffs of Lovereen," p. 85, BL, LDP, 4.

47. "Lovereen," vol. 3, p. 379, BL, LDP, 4.

48. "Lovereen," vol. 3, p. 436, BL, LDP, 4.

49. "Lovereen," vol. 3, p. 155, BL, LDP, 4.

50. Earp, "Selected Letters," 81.

51. "Lovereen," vol. 2, p. 326, BL, LDP, 4.

52. T. B. Kilpatrick to Lily Dougall, 7 Marine Terrace, Aberdeen, March 20, 1889. BL, LDP, 1. Kilpatrick was the minister of Ferry Hill Free Church in Aberdeen from 1888 until he joined the faculty of Manitoba College in Winnipeg in 1899. In 1905, he moved to the chair of systematic theology at Knox College. For a description of Kilpatrick's role as a liberal in the Canadian Presbyterian Church, see Brian Fraser, *The Social Uplifters: Presbyterian Progressives and the Social Gospel in Canada, 1875–1915* (Waterloo: Wilfrid Laurier University Press, 1988).

53. The quotation reads in full: "[Lovereen] is no child's play but a serious meditation on the gravest moral and spiritual problems . . . I cannot judge as to its commercial success. . . . It is indeed unfortunate, that Elsmere and John Ward and the African Farm are so recent. But I am persuaded that this is unique enough to claim a place of its own. . . . As yet we have Walford = Evangelicalism, Myers = Anglicanism, Lovereen = The Higher Life. I for one don't admit any of these identifications [but she will be taken to mean this and will be charged with misrepresentation]. . . . I hope we shall have other types further on; for as yet the net result is the despair of Christendom. . . ." T. B. Kilpatrick to Lily Dougall, 7 Marine Terrace, Aberdeen, March 20, 1889, BL, LDP, 1.

54. T. B. Kilpatrick to Lily Dougall, 7 Marine Terrace, Aberdeen, April 11, 1889. BL, LDP, 1.

55. "Lovereen," vol. 1, p. 165, BL, LDP, 4.

56. "Lovereen," vol. 3, pp. 155–60, BL, LDP, 4. He elaborates as to the dangers of her position: "If you go back to the first step of the ladder of knowledge of God, your next neighbour might step off it altogether, and if you do not accept the testimony of the Saints as to *how* they have found God, your position is not so logical as his if he says he does not know if there is any God or not."

57. "Cast-offs of Lovereen," vol. 3, pp. 377–78, 88–95, BL, LDP, 4.

58. "Lovereen," vol. 1, p. 314, BL, LDP, 4.

59. "Lovereen," vol. 1, pp. 243–46, BL, LDP, 4.
60. "Lovereen," vol. 2, pp. 169–72, BL, LDP, 4.
61. "Castoffs of Lovereen," p. 4, BL, LDP, 4.
62. This insight I owe to Sandra Campbell.
63. Brodzki, "Mothers, Displacement and Language in the Autobiographies of Nathalie Sarraute and Christa Wolfe," in *Life/Lines Theorizing Women's Autobiography,* 245–46. Cited in Buss, *Mapping Our Selves,* 17.
64. "Lovereen," vol. 2, p. 310, BL, LDP, 4.
65. "Lovereen," vol. 3, p. 43, BL, LDP, 4. "[H]ow often in the years that were passed had the greatness of the mother's love triumphed over all smallness of theory and yielded to her daughter's desires when such yielding had involved no wrong. All the sternness of her mother's creed had been for herself; toward her child her love had been intense and perfect. But this dear mother was gone. . . ." "Castoffs of Lovereen," p. 128.
66. An excerpt, "Selections," was published in *The Montreal Witness,* February 2, 1846, p. 39. See Ann Taves, "Mothers and Children and the Legacy of Mid-Nineteenth Century American Christianity," *Journal of Religion* 67, 2 (1987): 203–19.
67. Lily Dougall to K. D. [Katie Drummond], December 6, 1883. Earp, "Selected Letters," 56.
68. "Lovereen," vol. 1, p. 206.
69. Earp, "Selected Letters," 54.
70. Lily Dougall, "Lovereen," vol. 1, p. 5, BL, LDP, 4. In *The Zeit-Geist* she wrote: "Was life in the Spring and death in the autumn? Was the power and love of God not resting in the damp fallen things that lay rotting in the ground?" L. Dougall, *The Zeit-Geist* (London: Hutchinson and Co., 1895), 143–44.

4. "She Was Always a Queer Child"

1. Earp, "Selected Letters," 65. See note 22 for a discussion of this quote.
2. Adrienne Rich, "Compulsory Heterosexuality and Lesbian Existence," in *The Lesbian and Gay Studies Reader,* edited by Henry Abelove, Michele Aina Barale, and David M. Halperin (London: Routledge, 1993).
3. M. S. Earp, "Selected Letters of Lily Dougall with Biographical Notes," typescript, LAC, DFP, 5, 9, pp. 88–90. The 1881 British census provides some family background. Mary S. Earp, aged 21, born in Melbourne, lived in Melbourne, Derbyshire "near the Church," with her parents, and a 20-year-old unmarried sister, Annie G. Earp. This is likely Sophie; her full name was Mary Sophia Earp, she was born in Melbourne in 1859, according to her gravestone, and an A. G. Earp is listed in her Visitor Book in 1914 and 1915. (Visitor Book, BL, LDP, 1.)
Mary S. Earp lived with her parents, Henry W. Earp—(Marr. Age 46 yrs. Birthplace—Melbourne, Derby.) and Ann H. Earp (Marr. Age 48 yrs. Birthplace, Algerkirk, Lincoln.) The household included her maternal grandmother, Sophia Bowles (Widow—77 yrs. Birthplace—Little Hall Fen, Lincoln) and a visitor, an elderly male relative, Francis Milns (Widower—71 yrs. Birthplace—Little Hall Fen, Lincoln). They had four servants: Emma Wemham (Unm. Age

33 yrs. Birthplace—Pinchbeck, Lincs.); Eunice Smith (Unm. Age 20 yrs. Birthplace—Staunton); Emma Speed (Unm. Aged 20 yrs. Birthplace—Holbeach, Lincs.) and Ann Pitts (Marr. Age 19 yrs. Birthplace—Old Ningsby, Lincoln.). 1881 British Census, on CD-Rom, from the Church of Jesus Christ and the Latter Day Saints (FHL Film 1341809 Pro ref. RG11 Piece 3386. Folio 60 Page 30). The father, Henry W. Earp, was probably the Henry Webster Earp, a Baptist, b. 1834, in Melbourne, Derby, listed in the International Geneological Index, Church of Jesus Christ and the Latter Day Saints. (Genealogical research courtesy of Edith Friskney.)

4. Earp, "Selected Letters," 89. The *tripos* was the examination at Cambridge, to which women had only been admitted since 1872, unofficially, and 1881 officially.

5. Lewis Carroll, "Hunting the Snark: An Agony in Eight Fits," in *Hunting the Snark and Other Nonsense Verse* (1876; New York: Macmillan, 1891), 82.

6. Lilian Sheldon, "Mary Sophia Earp" in *Newnham College Roll Letter, 1929,* 84. Sheldon was a neighbor for many years.

7. Later, B. H. Streeter credited Earp in the introduction to the joint volume *Immortality, An Essay in Discovery Co-ordinating Scientific, Psychical, and Biblical Research,* ed. Burnett Hillman Streeter (London: Macmillan, 1917), and in the "Biographical Note," in Dougall's posthumous *God's Way with Man,* 18.

8. Earp, "Selected Letters." Dougall acknowledged Earp's assistance in the preface to *What Necessity Knows:* "I would like to take this opportunity to express my obligation to my fellow-worker, Miss M. S. Earp, for her constant and sympathetic criticism and her help in composition." Lily Dougall, *What Necessity Knows* (London: Longmans, 1893; Ottawa: Tecumseh Press, 1992), vii. She dedicated her collection of short stories, *A Dozen Ways of Love,* to M. S. E. without whose aid, I think, none of these stories would have been written." *A Dozen Ways of Love* (London: A. & C. Black, 1897). The editorial notes made on the margins of the manuscript, "Castoffs of Lovereen" (see for example ch. 5, p. 3, BL, LDP, 4) suggest the extent of her involvement. Earp also makes frequent mention in "Selected Letters" to her work on Dougall's books.

For Earp's role, see also her obituary "The Death of Miss Earp," *Oxford Times,* November 23, 1928. Earp is described largely in terms of her role as Dougall's helpmate. "She was best known to some as the colleague of her distinguished friend, Miss Lily Dougall, with whom she lived and worked until Miss Dougall's death in 1923." Although the paper notes her abilities as a writer and speaker, her local activities were those traditionally engaged in by women: "care of the mentally deficient, the village Nursing Association, the Oxford Branch of the British Women's Total Abstinence Association, and matters of local government and public health." She had earlier been involved in local activities, including work with the Liberal party, in Exmouth. Dougall apologized for uprooting Earp from "your works" when they left Exmouth in 1911. Earp, "Selected Letters," 223.

9. Earp, "Selected Letters," 89.

10. Earp described this period: "For ten years Lily had a home with her aunt, the Edinburgh climate always tried her, subject as she was to asthma, and it was not possible, as Miss Redpath grew older, to give her the companionship they both enjoyed and find time for her own work. Her aunt was always

considerate and loving and the upshot was that during these years, Lily paid long visits, wintering with friends at Ventnor, or staying at my home at Melbourne, Derbyshire, and as always up to the end of her life, she periodically visited her Montreal home." "Selected Letters," 90. Diaries reveal the peripatetic nature of her life in Britain: In addition to long stays in Ventnor, Melbourne, and other English destinations, Dougall spent the winter of 1891–1892 at Cannes with her brother and sister (Sophie joined them in the spring), and visited Canada in the summer of 1893, and again in the summer and fall of 1894 and the summer of 1896. Earp lectured at the Midland Institute from 1891 to 1903.

11. Earp probably handled much of the correspondence because of Dougall's frequent changes in address. Her work also freed Dougall to concentrate on writing, as a letter dated October 17, 1893, suggests: "All communication to Miss Earp as Miss Dougall is engaged in getting ready the material [for either *The Mermaid* or *The Madonna of a Day*] she has collected in Canada." BL, LDP, 7. On July 19, 1892, Dougall's literary agent, A. P. Watt, asked where he might find Dougall. On August 9, Earp's role (and some unusual impatience) is revealed in a letter to Dougall: "Dear B. Have Watty's (or rather Watty's juniors) latest attempt at being very civil and well behaved? . . . what shall we say in reply? . . . You never told me how you liked the new edition? You should read my letters *carefully* through when you answer them . . ." BL, LDP, 7.

12. January 2, 1891. Dateline, probably from Dougall's diary, BL, LDP, 1.

13. In her notes titled "B's life," Earp wrote that "Miss Mc began work with B" on November 26, 1893, and then in March 1894 was at Minehead [?] with "B."

14. July 1895, "Lily's letters, 1880–1898," BL, LDP, 1.

15. Jane Redpath left Lily Dougall and her sisters the bulk of her estate. Lily received about 2,500 British pounds. Redpath's house went to her sister, and to Lily after the sister's death. Will of Jane Margaret Redpath, 19 August 1897, Registry of Deeds, vol. 2812, pp. 222–29.

16. April 8, 1898, "Lily's letters, 1880–1898," BL, LDP, 1. Lily Dougall to M. S. Earp, Birch Bay Camp, Georgeville, Quebec, September 1898, Earp, "Selected Letters," 158.

17. Lily Dougall to Hilda Oakeley, Pasadena, California, February 16, 1902. Earp, "Selected Letters," 189. (The dates appear confused in this section of the transcript, and this letter may have been written in 1901.)

18. For her work supervising manuscripts, see note 8, above. Lily Dougall to M. S. Earp, Highlands, Macon Co., North Carolina, June 10, 1898. Earp, "Selected Letters," 154. See also A. P. Watt to Lily Dougall, 2 Paternoster Square, London, October 23, 1894. BL, LDP, 7.

19. "S's Diary, 1904–1911," BL, LDP, 1.

20. Noted on letter to A. P. Watt dated February 11, 1895, BL, LDP, 7.

21. H. Oakeley, cited in Earp, "Selected Letters," 187.

22. Earp, "Selected Letters," 65. Dougall only identifies her hostess as "the younger Miss W." but it appears, from Earp's introduction to the letter, to be Miss M. R. Walker. For her acquaintance with Walker in Edinburgh, see "Diary," October 19, 1884, BL, LDP, 1 and Earp, "Selected Letters," 64. This is almost definitely the Mary Walker whose school is mentioned in "B's Letters," January 7, 1890, BL, LDP, 1.

23. Lily Dougall, *The Spanish Dowry, A Romance* (London: Hutchison, 1906), 269.

24. Access to higher education varied by institution in Britain, and was generally achieved in a piecemeal manner. At Oxford, for example, women were permitted to take "special" women's examinations from 1875, took classes arranged by the Association for the Higher Education of Women from 1878, and could live in a residential hall (either Somerville or Lady Margaret Hall) from 1879. In 1883, the first college lectures were opened to women, and from 1884, women began to take the same examinations as men. In Cambridge, women could not take degrees, but had taken the tripos exam from 1872, unofficially, and 1881 officially. Oxford and Cambridge were more conservative than the older provincial universities. See Rachel Trickett, "Women's Education," and Betty Kemp, "The Early History of St. Hugh's College," in *St. Hugh's: One Hundred Years of Women's Education at Oxford,* ed. Penny Griffin (London: Macmillan Press, 1986), 21. For a discussion of higher education for women in Scotland, see Lindy Moore, "The Scottish Universities and Women Students," in *Scottish Universities, Distinctiveness and Diversity,* ed. Jennifer J. Carter and Donald J. Withrington (Edinburgh: John Donald Publishers, 1992).

25. Alice M. Gordon, "The After-Careers of University Educated Women," *Nineteenth Century* 37 (1895): 958–60. Only about 25 percent of Vassar, Smith, and Wellesley graduates between the ages of twenty-six and thirty-seven were married in 1903. Peter G. Filene, *Her/Him/Self,* 2nd ed. (Baltimore: 1986), 26. Cited in Linda W. Rosenzweig, *The Anchor of My Life: Middle-Class American Mothers and Daughters, 1880–1920* (New York: New York University Press, 1993), 8.

26. See Hilda Oakeley, *My Adventures in Education* (London: Williams and Norgate, 1939).

27. See B. A. Crackanthorpe, "The Revolt of the Daughters," *Nineteenth Century* 35 (1894): 23–31; E. B. Harrison, "Mothers and Daughters," *Nineteenth Century* 35 (1894): 313–22; B. A. Crackanthorpe, "A Last Word on the Revolt," *Nineteenth Century* 35 (1894): 424–36; Alys Pearsall Smith, "A Reply from the Daughters," *Nineteenth Century* 35 (1894): 437–42, and Kathleen Cuffe, "A Reply from the Daughters," *Nineteenth Century* 35 (1894): 443–50. A subsequent debate between Sarah Grande, "The New Aspect of the Woman Question," and Oudia [Louise Rame], "The New Woman," in the *North American Review* 158 (1894): 271–73, 610–19, established the label, the New Woman. See Angelique Richardson and Chris Willis, *The New Woman in Fact and Fiction: Fin-de-Siècle Feminisms* (London: Palgrave, 2001); Sally Ledger, *The New Woman Fiction and Feminism at the Fin de Siècle* (Manchester: Manchester University Press, 1997).

28. See Trisha Franzen, *Spinsters and Lesbians: Independent Womanhood in the United States* (New York: New York University Press, 1996). The figure dropped to 8.7 percent for those born in 1884–1894, and 4.8 percent for those born 1915–1918.

29. Dougall had sent copies of an early story, "The Soul of a Man," to Henry Sidgwick. See "S. Diary, 1887–1895," July and August 1888, October 1888, BL, LDP, 1. See Earp, "Selected Letters," 92, 102, 165.

30. See Earp, "Selected Letters," 133, 139. Miss Keddie also acted as the intermediary when Dougall published her religious writing anonymously.

31. Anna (Mrs. T. B.) Kilpatrick to Lily Dougall, March 27, 1888, 7 Marine Terrace, Aberdeen; an unsigned undated letter addressed to "Dear B.";

226 NOTES TO PAGES 71–73

My Dear Beautiful Clever Beaver from [A-tnoob?] Melbourne, April 13, 1889, BL, LDP, 1.

32. Carroll Smith-Rosenberg, "The Female World of Love and Ritual: 'Relations between Women in Nineteenth Century America.'" *Signs, Journal of Women in Culture and Society* 1 (1975): 1–29; also published with "Discourses of Sexuality and Subjectivity: The New Woman, 1870–1936," in *Disorderly Conduct: Visions of Gender in Victorian America* (New York: Oxford University Press, 1985).

33. Esther Newton, "The Mythic Mannish Lesbian: Radclyffe Hall and the New Woman," in *Hidden from History: Reclaiming the Gay and Lesbian Past*, Martin Bauml Duberman, Martha Vicinus, and George Chauncey, Jr. (New York: New American Library, 1989), 284.

34. Lillian Faderman, *Surpassing the Love of Men: Romantic Friendship and Love between Women from the Renaissance to the Present* (New York: William Morrow, 1981).

35. The concept of two generations of New Women is drawn from Newton, and Smith-Rosenberg, "Discourses of Sexuality and Subjectivity."

36. Smith-Rosenberg, "Discourses of Sexuality and Subjectivity: The New Woman, 1870–1936."

37. Anne Lister, *I Know My Own Heart: The Diaries of Anne Lister (1791–1840)*, ed. Helena Whitbread (London: Virago, 1988). Marylynne Diggs, "Romantic Friends or a 'Different Race of Creatures'? The Representation of Lesbian Pathology in Nineteenth-Century America," *Feminist Studies* 21, no. 2 (1995): 317–40. For more nuanced views of sexology, see Lucy Bland and Laura Doan, eds., *Sexology in Culture* (Chicago: University of Chicago Press, 1998). For the erotics of unnaming, see Harriette Andreidis, "Theorizing Early Modern Lesbianisms: Invisible Borders, Ambiguous Demarcations," in *Virtual Gender: Fantasies of Subjectivity and Embodiment*, ed. Mary Ann O'Farrlee and Lynne Vallone (Ann Arbor: University of Michigan Press, 1999).

38. Terry Castle, *The Apparitional Lesbian: Female Homosexuality and Modern Culture* (New York: Columbia University Press, 1993): 93, 11, 4.

39. Martha Vicinus, "They Wonder to Which Sex I Belong: The Historical Roots of Modern Lesbian Identity," in *The Lesbian and Gay Studies Reader*, p. 436. See also Andreidis, 136.

40. Laura Doan, *Fashioning Sapphism: The Origins of Modern English Lesbian Culture* (New York: Columbia University Press, 2001). In the first chapter, "The Mythic Moral Panic," Doan argues that the initial reaction by critics to *The Well* was accepting.

41. Martha Vicinus, *Intimate Friends: Women Who Loved Women, 1778–1928* (Chicago: University of Chicago Press, 2004): 88–98.

42. Cf. Joan Evans, "An End to *An Adventure*: Solving the Mystery of the Trianon," *Encounter* (October 1976) 47: 34–35. Cited in Castle, 124. Eleanor Jourdain was a guest at Dougall's home on Thursday, March 13, 1913 (Visitor Book, BL, LDP, 1).

43. "Marie Antoinette Obsession," chapter 6 in Castle, *The Apparitional Lesbian*. Charlotte Anne Elizabeth (C. A. E.) Moberly (1846–1937) was the head of St. Hugh's from 1886–1915. With Eleanor Jourdain, a French tutor of St. Hugh's (and the principal after January 1915), she wrote *An Adventure*, which, like *Foundations*, was satirized by R. A. Knox with Charles R. L. Fletcher in *A Still More Sporting Adventure* (London: Basil Blackwell, 1911).

44. See Alison Oram and Annmarie Turnbull, *The Lesbian History Sourcebook, Love and Sex between Women in Britain from 1870–1970* (London: Routledge, 2001). A "Miss Soulsby" is recorded as having visited Dougall from March 3–6, 1905, and on February 7, 1908. BL, LDP, 1.

45. For the proscriptions against overtly sexual behavior, see Diggs. It is difficult to know when or whether Lily and Sophie became aware of the work of Richard von Krafft-Ebing, Havelock Ellis, and Edward Carpenter. Doan has argued that "in the decade after the war lesbianism increasingly became a topic of private and public discussion among educated, upper classes" (Doan, *Fashioning Sapphism*, p. 5. See also pp. 133–35). Earp was active in the Liberal party and in the Oxford suffrage movement and was probably aware of the parliamentary debates in 1921 about predatory lesbian women or "Acts of indecency by females." Dougall's familiarity with the newspaper world makes it likely that she was aware of the sensational stories of lesbian murder that circulated in the American press at this time. See Lisa Duggan, *Sapphic Slashers: Sex, Violence and American Modernity* (Durham: Duke University Press, 2000). There is, of course, knowing and knowing. Would Dougall and Earp have applied this forensic literature to their own relationship?

46. Vicinus, *Intimate Friends*, 230.

47. April 8, 1898, "Lily's letters, 1880–1898," BL, LDP, 1. Lily Dougall to M. S. Earp, Birch Bay Camp, Georgeville, P. Q., September 1898, Earp, "Selected Letters," 158.

48. Lily Dougall to J. C., Edinburgh, July 31, 1888. Earp, "Selected Letters," 90.

49. January 5, 1890, Dateline, BL, LDP, 1.

50. Letter appended to correspondence with publishers, BL, LDP, 7.

51. Scribbled on A. P. Watt letter dated February 11, 1895, BL, LDP, 7.

52. December 31, 1890. Dateline, probably from Dougall's diary. BL, LDP, 1.

53. One reviewer noted that none of the stories in *A Dozen Ways of Love* was a love story. Clipping Book, BL, LDP, 7.

54. Dougall also published a number of short stories in leading journals, often under a pseudonym: Ernest Duns [Lily Dougall], "Hath Not a Jew Eyes?" *Longman's Magazine* 13, no. 75 (January 1889); "Marriage Made in Heaven," *Chambers Journal* 8 (August 1891); "Rosemary for Remembrance," and "The Soul of a Man," *Temple Bar* (1892). *Atlantic Magazine* accepted "Witchcraft," "Face of Death," and "Thrift," in April 1895 (BL, LDP, 1). A number of these early stories were later published in *A Dozen Ways of Love* (London: A. & C. Black, 1897), subsequently reprinted as *Young Love [and other stories]* (A. & C. Black: London, 1904).

55. A. P. Watt to Lily Dougall, September 28, 1891, 2 Paternoster Square London to 130 Gilmour Place Edinburgh, BL, LDP, 7.

56. B. H. Streeter, "Biographical Note," in Dougall, *God's Way with Man*, 12. *Queen* reported in a biographical sketch of Dougall that "Have you read 'BA' is the question that has lately flown from one to another with the rapidity of influenza. . . ." *Queen* 13 II (1892). Clipping Book, BL, LDP, 7. The book was also popular in United States; Dougall describes being lionized in Boston some years later. See Earp, "Selected Letters," 146.

57. L. Dougall, *What Necessity Knows*, 3 vols. (London, New York: Longmans, 1893).

58. *A Question of Faith* might have been published earlier, but Longmans, disappointed at sales of the weighty three-volume *What Necessity Knows*, did not

accept it in early 1894. A. P. Watt to Sophie Earp, February 24, 1894, BL, LDP, 7. It was published serially in *Leisure Hour* and in book form in 1895 by Hutchinson in London and Houghton Mifflin in Boston. *The Mermaid, A Love Story* (after nearly being published in serial form in *Temple Bar*) was published in book form by the *Temple Bar* publisher, Richard Bentley, and by Appleton in New York. *The Madonna of a Day* was published in England by Richard Bentley in both serial form in *Temple Bar* and book form; and by D. Appleton and Co. in New York. See correspondence with A. P. Watt, BL, LDP, 7. *The Zeit-Geist* was published by Hutchinson and Co. and positioned prominently as the first in a new library of pocket books, *The Zeit-Geist Library of Complete Novels*. It was published in New York by D. Appleton and Co.

59. "I am afraid it [*The Mormon Prophet*] will be a fizzle, like the one I wrote last winter. What is the matter with me. I seem to have lost confidence." Lily Dougall to M. S. Earp(?), Montreal, October 12, 1896. Earp, "Selected Letters," 144. Lily Dougall, *The Mormon Prophet* (London: A. & C. Black; New York: Appleton; Toronto: W.J. Gage, 1899).

60. Lily Dougall, *The Earthly Purgatory* (London: Hutchinson and Co., 1904); *Summit House Mystery* (New York: Funk and Wagnalls, 1905). A curious twelve-page manuscript among Dougall's papers, "Synopsis of Earthly Purgatory" which alters the story by marrying off the two couples at the end "to give it a happier ending" was probably written to sell the manuscript in the United States. BL, LDP, 2. The book was popular; one reviewer noted that five editions had been published in a few weeks. *Indianapolis Sentinel*, May 14, 1905. Clippings Book, p. 130, BL, LDP, 7.

61. Lily Dougall, *Spanish Dowry* (London: Hutchinson, 1906; Toronto: Copp Clark, 1906); L. Dougall, *Paths of the Righteous* (London: Macmillan, 1908).

62. See also the young woman in a short-story manuscript: "Gossip said she had a studious disposition, preferred history to novels, and was certainly not shy, and was perhaps passionate, and finally ended with the criticism that she was not pretty but wondrously attractive." "The Common Type," p. 4, BL, LDP, 4.

63. "[Alice] is at her best with Knighton, when only her humility and frankness and lovableness fully appears, with Harvey and Mrs. Ross a sense of what she herself called or rather thought of as her 'superior mind and feeling' is perhaps unavoidably present in her mind and affects her relations with them." A. A. Short to Miss Dougall, December 16, 1895, Montreal, BL, LDP, 1. Kilpatrick notes that Lily's description " 'Lovereen usually felt herself superior to young men,' was deliciously characteristic of the distinguished author herself. . . ." T. B. Kilpatrick to Lily Dougall, 19 November 1889, 7 Marine Terrace, Aberdeen, BL, LDP, 1.

64. Dougall, *What Necessity Knows*, 133, 200. Sophia reflects, "What we need is to think *more* of ourselves—to think so much of ourselves that all aims but the highest are beneath us—are impossible to our own dignity. What we need is ambition" (p. 200). "I tell you there is no such risk for an energetic clever girl as to place her where the rust of unexercised faculties will eat into her soul" (p. 281).

65. "[Eliza] looked larger and stronger than the man with whom she was conversing." Lily Dougall, *What Necessity Knows*, 427. "Any intelligent eye seeing her would have seen large beauty in her figure, which like a Venus in the years when art was young, had no cramped proportions" (p. 24). See also

pp. 10, 96, 117, 121, 205, 384, 389, and 405. Her lover, Bates, was weakened by illness: he looked up at her (p. 389) and was compared to a child, (p. 392) and a boy (p. 391). For Sophia's pistol, see p. 270.

66. Lily Dougall, "A Commercial Traveller," "The Syndicate Baby," *A Dozen Ways of Love,* 165. "The Pauper's Golden Day" features yet another tall strong woman.

67. Henry Sidgwick to Sophie Earp, n.d. Earp, "Selected Letters," 165.

68. "I know it is weak concession to popular taste to make Sophie 28, but I feel she was such a contrast to the ordinary heroine that her love scene at the end might not carry the sympathy of the ordinary mind, unless I made her a little younger." Earp, "Selected Letters," 108.

69. Notebook, BL, LDP, 1.

70. "Lovereen," vol. 3, p. 43, BL, LDP, 4. "All the sternness of her mother's creed had been for herself; toward her child her love had been intense and perfect. But this dear mother was gone . . ." "Castoffs of Lovereen," p. 128.

71. "Lovereen," vol. 2, p. 39, BL, LDP, 4.

72. "Lovereen," vol. 2, p. 390, BL, LDP, 4.

73. "Lovereen," vol. 1, p. 239, BL, LDP, 4.

74. Dougall, *Beggars All,* 13, 117, 353.

75. Dougall, *Beggars All,* 123, 121.

76. Dougall, *Beggars All,* 123.

77. Dougall, *Beggars All,* 123.

78. Dougall, *Beggars All,* 405.

79. Dougall, *Mermaid,* 179–80

80. *National Observer,* May 18, 1895. *Woman,* March 13, 1895. Clipping book, BL, LDP, 7.

81. Clipping book, BL, LDP, 7.

82. Dougall, *What Necessity Knows,* 369. See also the reference to "single blessedness," p. 247.

83. Dougall, *What Necessity Knows,* 403.

84. Dougall's opening description of Caius is typically deflating: "It is a great problem why Nature sets so many young people in the world who are apparently unfitted for the battle of life, and certainly have no power to excell in any direction." She describes in detail his lack of any useful abilities or characteristics. Dougall, *The Mermaid,* pp. 2–3.

85. "Castoffs of Lovereen," p. 325, BL, LDP, 4.

86. Dougall, *Beggars All,* 424.

87. Dougall, *What Necessity Knows,* 396.

88. Dougall, *The Madonna,* 13; *What Necessity Knows,* 245, 264; *Earthly Purgatory,* xx.

89. Dougall, *The Madonna,* 13–14.

90. Dougall, *The Madonna,* 33.

91. Dougall, *The Madonna,* 254.

92. Dougall, *The Madonna,* 260, 267.

93. BL, LDP, 2.

94. "Castoffs of Lovereen," p. 141, BL, LDP, 4.

95. "Castoffs of Lovereen," vol. 3, 477–79, BL, LDP, 4.

96. Patricia Juliana Smith, *Lesbian Panic: Homoeroticism in Modern British Women's Fiction* (New York: Columbia University Press, 1997).

97. Martha Vicinus's work is the exception to this: see "The Gift of Love": Nineteenth-Century Religion and Lesbian Passion," *Nineteenth Century Contexts* 23 (2001): 241–64.

98. Dougall, *The Madonna*, 13–14.

99. M. S. E. [Earp] to the Editor of *The Queen*, [n.d.], BL, LDP, 6.

100. Dougall, *The Madonna*, 260–69.

101. *Manchester Guardian*, November 4, 1893. Clipping file, BL, LDP, 7.

102. "Lovereen," vol. 1, p. 2/8, BL, LDP, 4.

103. "Cast-offs of Lovereen," p. 445, BL, LDP, 4.

104. Dougall, *The Zeit-Geist*, 97.

105. Dougall, *The Zeit-Geist*, 34, 246.

106. Dougall, *The Spanish Dowry*, 62–63.

107. Harold Anson, "Lily Dougall (1858–1923)" in R. S. Forman, ed. *Great Christians* (London: Ivor, Nicolson and Watson, 1933): 204.

108. Lily Dougall, "Thrift," in *A Dozen Ways of Love* (London: Black, 1897), 64, 73–74. First published in *Atlantic Monthly*, 76 (August 1895) 217–23.

109. Joanna E. Wood, *Judith Moore: or, Fashioning a Pipe* (Toronto: The Ontario Publishing Co., 1898), 143, 179. See also the weak minister in Wood's *A Daughter of Witches* (Toronto: W. J. Gage and Co., 1900).

110. See especially, Marshall Saunders, *Deficient Saints: A Tale of Maine* (Boston: L. C. Page and Company, 1899), 95; Alice A. Chown, *The Stairway* (1921; Toronto: University of Toronto Press, 1988), 14. Most of the writers referred to here represent one generation of Canadian women, slightly younger than Lily Dougall: Marshall Saunders (1861–1947), Alice Chown (1866–1949), Flora MacDonald Denison (1867–1921), L. M. Montgomery (1876–1942), Marion Keith [MacGregor, Mary Esther] (1876–1961). Agnes Maule Machar, born in 1837, is older, and Frances Marion Beynon, born in 1884, is younger. For a fuller discussion of anticlericalism among Canadian women writers, see Joanna Dean, "Writing out of Orthodoxy: Lily Dougall, Anglican Modernist (1858–1923)," Ph.D. dissertation, Carleton University, 1999. See Margaret Bendroth, *Fundamentalism and Gender: 1875 to the Present* (New Haven: Yale University Press, 1993), 37–41 for a discussion of the anticlericalism of American feminist and evangelical women.

111. Frances Marion Beynon, *Aleta Day* (1919; London: Virago, 1988), 147, and Flora MacDonald, *Mary Melville, The Psychic* (Toronto: The Austin Publishing Co., 1900), 78.

112. Machar, Saunders, Woods, and Chown were single. Denison and Montgomery were married but had intense relationships with women. Deborah Gorham described Denison's "correspondence with a close female friend in which one woman adopted the persona of a lover, and the other adopted the persona of the beloved." "Flora MacDonald Denison and Walt Whitman," a talk delivered at the Whitman in Ontario Conference, University of Toronto, October 1980. See also Deborah Gorham, "Flora MacDonald Denison: Canadian Feminist," in *A Not Unreasonable Claim: Women and Reform in Ontario*, ed. Linda Keeley (Toronto: The Women's Press, 1979), 47–70. Montgomery is a Canadian icon and debates about homoeroticism in her work have been heated. See Laura M. Robinson, "Bosom Friends: Lesbian Desire in L. M. Montgomery's Anne Books," *Canadian Literature/Littérature canadienne: A Quarterly of Criticism and Review* (Spring 2004): 12–28; and Marah Gubar, " 'Where is the Boy?' The Pleasures of Postponement in the Anne of Green Gables Series," *The Lion and the Unicorn* 25, no. 1 (2001): 47–69.

5. PERSONAL IDEALISM

1. "Cutts End Cumnor, November, 1911," in M. S. Earp, "Selected Letters of Lily Dougall with Biographical Notes," typescript, LAC, DFP, 5, 9, p. 225.

2. Earp, "Selected Letters," 133.

3. Lily Dougall to Hilda Oakeley, Pasadena, California, February 16, 1902. Earp, "Selected Letters," 189. (The dates appear confused in this section of the transcript, and this letter may have been written in 1901.)

4. By the turn of the century, the younger university men were turning away to realism; Caird was brought to Oxford in 1893 in part to reinvigorate idealism. In the wider world, however, and among theologians, idealism held sway until World War I dealt a crushing blow to all optimism and all German ideas as far as the British were concerned.

5. "Lovereen," vol. 3, p. 155, BL, LDP, 4.

6. Lily Dougall to John Dougall, Edinburgh, May 27, 1881, BL, LDP, 1. Earp, "Selected Letters," 31–38.

7. Dougall, "Rosemary for Remembrance," published with *The Madonna of a Day: A Study* (London: R. Bentley and Son, 1895), 436.

8. Dougall, "Rosemary for Remembrance," 402–403. Lorraine McMullen drew my attention to the significance of this story in an unpublished manuscript on Lily Dougall.

9. Dougall, "Rosemary for Remembrance," 424.

10. T. B. Kilpatrick to Lily Dougall, 20 March 1889, 7 Marine Terrace, Aberdeen. BL, LDP, 1.

11. M.R. Walker to [Earp?, probably written after Dougall's death]. Cited in Earp, "Selected Letters," 65.

12. Earp, "Selected Letters," 84.

13. "Masson's long association with Carlyle and his admiration of his friend's genius have to some extent obscured the individuality of his own work; and an alleged physical likeness, more imagined than true, have encouraged the popular notion of discipleship." G. G. Smith, "Masson, David," *Dictionary of National Biography,* Supplement 1901–1911 (Oxford: Oxford University Press, 1912). George Eliot noted Carlyle's influence in 1855: "For there is hardly a superior or active mind of this generation that has not been modified by Carlyle's writings . . . The character of his influence is best seen in the fact that many of the men who have the least agreement with his opinions are those to whom the reading of *Sartor Resartus* was an epoch in the history of their minds." Cited by Peter Sabor and Kerry McSweeney in Thomas Carlyle, *Sartor Resartus,* edited with an introduction by P. Sabor and K. McSweeney (1833–1834; Oxford: Oxford University Press, 987), viii.

14. "Lovereen," vol. 3, p. 158, BL, LDP, 4. Paul later elaborates: "I am not in the least concerned to prove the spiritual truth that underlies our religion [Dougall inserts the phrase 'that rests on religious experience'] but the way in which that must be received and propagated—its dress of words and facts—comes within the province of scientific study and the sciences have only just come into working order." "Lovereen," vol. 3, p. 384, BL, LDP, 4.

15. Carlyle, *Sartor Resartus,* 164.

16. She subsequently prefaced *Beggars All* (1891) with a famous passage from *Sartor Resartus:* "Yes here in this poor hampered Actual where in thou

even now standest, here or nowhere, is thy Ideal." Dougall also referred to Carlyle on the first page of a handwritten book of poetry (BL, LDP, 1), with poems dated as early as 1881.

17. Lily Dougall to Sophie Earp, August 14, 1894, Old Orchard, Maine. Earp, "Selected Letters," 131. It is probable that Dougall was referring to *The Evolution of Religion*, 2 vols., 2nd ed. (Glasgow: MacLehose, 1893; New York: Macmillan, 1894), a book that, first presented as the Gifford Lectures of 1890–1891 and 1891–1892, had been widely read and debated.

18. A letter from Wallace suggests that she was not shy about initiating social events. He wrote, "I find that I can quite as well go up the river on Saturday. Weather permitting. I think to start from the boat house about 3.15." W. Wallace to Lily Dougall, 6 Bradmore Rd., Oxford, June 4, 1896. MS 729, Rare Books Department, McGill University Libraries. Dougall refers in a letter to social visits and excursions: "Afterwards I took supper with the Wallaces. Yesterday we spent the afternoon with Mrs. Caird, seeing the Browning relics." Lily Dougall to M. S. Earp, March 15, 1896. Earp, "Selected Letters," 139.

19. Lily Dougall to Sophie Earp, Oxford, March 15, 1896. Earp, "Selected Letters," 139.

20. Edward Caird to Lily Dougall, Balliol College, Oxford, May 4, 1896. MS 729, Rare Book Department, McGill University Libraries. For John and Edward Caird's efforts on behalf of women's higher education at Glasgow University, see Andrew Drummond and James Bulloch, *The Church in Late Victorian Scotland, 1874–1900* (Edinburgh: The St. Andrew Press, 1978), 252–53.

21. Caird, *Evolution of Religion*, 236.

22. Caird, *Evolution of Religion*, 58.

23. *The Evolution of Religion* was addressed to those who were "alienated from the ordinary dogmatic system of belief but who, at the same time, are conscious that they owed a great part of their spiritual life to the teachings of the Bible and the Christian Church." Caird, *Evolution of Religion*, vii.

24. "Miss Dougall is evidently attempting to put in dramatic form the thoughts of writers like Dr. Caird, to whose book on 'The Evolution of Religion,' we believe she is greatly indebted." Review titled "Musical Gossip," pasted into Clipping Book, p. 63, BL, LDP, 7. Sophie Earp preferred to link Dougall to such eminent philosophers as Caird, but the ideas in *The Zeit-Geist* can also be traced to the liberal evangelist Henry Drummond, a professor of natural sciences at Glasgow, renowned for his evangelism among young men at Edinburgh University whose book, *The Lowell Lectures on the Ascent of Man* (1894), might be considered a popular rendition of Caird's *Evolution of Religion*. Dougall prefaced *The Zeit-Geist* with a quote from Drummond's *Natural Law in a Spiritual World* (1884): "If nature is the garment of God, it is woven without a seam throughout." The main character in *The Zeit-Geist*, Bart Toyner, bears a curious resemblance to Drummond, who was known for the neatness of his dress, for being, as Dougall later describes Bart, dapper, rather dandified. Dougall, *The Zeit-Geist*, 47, 12.

25. Dougall, *The Zeit-Geist*, 142–43.

26. Dougall, *The Zeit-Geist*, 222.

27. Caird, *Evolution of Religion*, 76.

28. Dougall, *The Zeit-Geist*, 206, 207, 143.

29. Dougall, *The Zeit-Geist*, 23.

30. Dougall, *The Zeit-Geist*, 227.

31. Dougall, *The Zeit-Geist,* 202.

32. *The Inquirer,* June 1, 1895. Clipping Book, BL, LDP, 7.

33. One American reviewer wrote, "Setting aside the question of whether it would not have been in better taste to call an English story by an English name, I can't see how the spirit of the book is, in any special sense, 'the spirit of the times.'" Review from *Chicago Interior,* August 1, 1895. Numerous other reviewers were similarly baffled. See the Clipping Book, pp. 53–77, BL, LDP, 7.

34. *The Inquirer.* Clipping Book, BL, LDP, 7.

35. *The Church Times,* August 23, 1895. Clipping Book, BL, LDP, 7. Dougall parodied the Anglican journal in *Paths of the Righteous.*

36. See the reviews compiled in the Clipping Book, pp. 53–77, BL, LDP, 7.

37. *Daily Chronicle,* April 28, 1895. Clipping Book, BL, LDP, 7.

38. *Westminster Gazette,* April 24, 1895. Clipping Book, BL, LDP, 7.

39. *National Observer,* May 18, 1895. Clipping Book, BL, LDP, 7.

40. Scott Rothwell Swanson, "Beyond Common Sense: Ideal Love in Three Novels of Lily Dougall," (Master's Thesis, University of Victoria, 1993).

41. As she explained in "Lovereen," and later in *The Zeit-Geist,* fiction was ideally suited to the presentation of a range of religious opinions. "I do not believe that it belongs to the novel to teach theology but I do believe that religious sentiments and opinions are the legitimate subject of its art, and that perhaps its highest function is to promote understanding by bringing into contact minds that habitually misinterpret each other." Dougall, *The Zeit-Geist,* preface. "Lovereen," vol. 2, pp. 152–53, BL, LDP, 4. Lily Dougall, *The Earthly Purgatory* (London: Hutchinson and Co., 1904); *Summit House Mystery* (New York: Funk and Wagnalls, 1905. The book was popular; one reviewer noted that five editions had been published in a few weeks. *Indianapolis Sentinel,* May 14, 1905. Clippings Book, p. 130, BL, LDP, 7. Lily Dougall, *Spanish Dowry* (London: Hutchinson, 1906; Toronto: Copp Clark, 1906).

42. George Macmillan to Lily Dougall, February 18, 1908, BL, LDP, 6. Dougall blamed poor promotion, but Macmillan said such sales figures were very fair. George Macmillan to Lily Dougall, April 7, 1908, File of letters from publishers, BL, LDP, 6.

43. George Macmillan to Lily Dougall, July 29, 1909, BL, LDP, 3. His firm had sustained considerable losses in the publication of *Paths of the Righteous.* See George Macmillan to Lily Dougall, May 4, 1910, BL, LDP, 3. Dougall's 497-page typescript manuscript, marked "Refused by Macmillan July 30, 1909," is in BL, LDP, 3.

44. Lily Dougall to [?], Edinburgh, November 8, 1893. Earp, "Selected Letters," 120. See "The Instinct of Prayer," from the *Spectator* in *World Wide* IV (September 3, 1904): 723.

45. Lily Dougall to Sophie Earp, [1895]. Earp, "Selected Letters," 128. Dougall wrote of Lovereen, "She had been reared in the atmosphere of daily dependence upon direct providences and although in some things she had of late years crept from under the shelter of her father's creed, her mind still in this respect followed the bent first given to it, especially in times of indecision." "Lovereen," vol. 1, p. 310, BL, LDP, 4.

46. Taken from a list of handwritten notes, apparently consisting of transcribed entries from Dougall's daily diary, probably compiled by Earp. BL, LDP, 1.

47. Dougall to Earp, March 1891. Earp, "Selected Letters," 99. (Earp says the letter was a response to the news that the book was to be published, so it was written after March 13.)

48. Earp had written Dougall, "I incline to be doubtful about expecting to get direct answers to prayer in the shape of definite earthly blessings. I suppose I am too reasonable." Dougall to Earp, Edinburgh, November 11, 1893. Earp, "Selected Letters," 121.

49. Lily Dougall to unknown, Torquay, April 7, 1893. Earp, "Selected Letters," 117.

50. Richard Ostrander, "The Life of Prayer in a World of Science: Protestants, Prayer and American Culture," Ph.D. dissertation, Notre Dame, Indiana, 1996. "[O]ne might expect that liberal Protestants like the German idealists before them, abandoned traditional petitionary prayer altogether. On the contrary, the liberal expurgation of the supernatural element in prayer was a gradual, halting process. Before 1920, a significant element of liberal Protestantism sought to retain the traditional confidence in petitionary prayer even while asserting a devotional element in harmony with modern non-supernaturalistic thought. It was not until the 1920s that a full-fledged ethic of prayer largely stripped of petition began to take prominence within American liberalism" (p. 167).

51. Emphasis in original. Earp, "Selected Letters," 137. She raised this in the novel, speaking through Toyner: "Is it not hard to believe that we may ask and expect forgiveness and gifts from the God who by slow inevitable laws of growth clothes lilies, who ordains the fall of every one of these sparrows, foresees the fall and ordains it—the God whose character is expressed in physical law? The texts of Jesus have become so trite that we forget that they contain the same vision of 'God's mind in all things' that makes it so hard to believe in a personality in God, that makes prayer seem to us so futile." Dougall, *The Zeit-Geist,* 19.

52. See William R. Hutchison, *The Modernist Impulse in American Protestantism* (Cambridge, Mass.: Harvard University Press, 1976), 124–27. For a discussion of the importance of Lotze in the American Social Gospel, see William McGuire King, "'History as Revelation' in the Theology of the Social Gospel" in *Protestantism and Social Christianity,* ed. Martin Marty (Munich: K. G. Saur, 1992), 145–65.

53. [Lily Dougall], *Voluntas Dei* (London: Macmillan, 1912), xi.

54. This definition is drawn from John H. Lavely, "Personalism," in *Encyclopedia of Philosophy* (New York and London: Collier and Macmillan, 1967–1972) 6: 107–110. As C. C. J. Webb put it succinctly, "Individual and mutually exclusive consciousnesses or spirits were ultimately real, and indeed the only ultimate reality, although they are not all alike eternal, one personal God being the cause of the existence of the rest." C. C. J. Webb, "Hastings Rashdall," *Dictionary of National Biography 1922–1930* (London: Oxford University Press, 1937), 708.

55. See Percy Gardner, "Contentio Veritatus," reprinted from the *Hibbert Journal* in *World Wide* 3, no. 6 (February 7, 1903): 92. The article is a review of *Contentio Veritatus* by Six Oxford Tutors (London: J. Murray, 1902).

56. See Phillips Brooks to Arthur Brooks, Berlin, October 29, 1882, in Alexander V.G. Allen, *Life and Letters of Phillips Brooks,* vol. 2 (New York: E. P. Dutton, 1901), 467–69. See pp. 472–82 for Brooks's notes on his changing ideas about religion during his study in Germany, including a section titled "Personality" in which he describes the "personality" as "the essential peculiarity of Christ's teaching." Allen describes the centrality of Lotze's teaching to Brooks's later years. "In his philosophy of life and of religion he had been anticipating what Lotze could teach him" (p. 118). Brooks wrote in 1886: "The New

Testament is always on the brink of pantheism and it is only saved from it by the intense personality of Jesus and His overwhelming injunction of responsibility. Surely [Christ] gives us reason to believe that there is a real possibility of holding both together, the personality of God and the divine life of the universe." Allen, *Phillips Brooks*, 107–109. This was not necessarily a departure from Maurice's theology. See F. D. Maurice's argument that "human relationships are not artificial types of something divine, but are actually the means and the only means through which man ascends to any knowledge of the divine." F. D. Maurice, *Kingdom of Christ*, vol. 1, 280–81. Cited in Prickett, *Romanticism and Religion*, 136.

57. "Lovereen," vol. 3, p. 46, BL, LDP, 4. "how much more *Personal* his love is that we could have any conception of. . . . [Emphasis in the original]" Lily Dougall to M. S. E. [Sophie Earp], October 21, 1892. Earp, "Selected Letters," 112.

58. In Britain, personal idealism was introduced with A. S. Pringle Pattison's *Hegelianism and Personality* in 1887, but became well known through the contributions by J. R. Illingworth (1848–1915) and Henry Scott Holland (1847–1918) to the iconoclastic Anglo-Catholic *Lux Mundi* (1889), Illingworth's Bampton Lectures on *Personality Human and Divine* in 1894, and the collection of essays edited by Henry Sturt, *Personal Idealism, Philosophical Essays by Eight Members of the University of Oxford* (London: Macmillan, 1902). The individuals involved also included Hastings Rashdall, W. R. Sorley, A. C. Fraser, A. S. Pringle-Pattison, J. Cook Wilson, statesman Arthur James Balfour, James Ward, Robert C. Moberly, William Temple, and C. C. J. Webb. Webb identified Illingworth, Moberly, Rashdall, and Temple, all acquaintances of Dougall, in *A Century of Anglican Theology and Other Lectures* (New York: D. Appleton and Co., 1924), 82–83.

59. Dougall had sent copies of an early story, "The Soul of a Man," to James Iverach and Henry Sidgwick. See "S. Diary, 1887–1895," July and August 1888, October 1888, BL, LDP, 1. Their support gave her the confidence to pursue writing fiction on a full-time basis. See Earp, "Selected Letters," 92. James Iverach (1839–1922) was a theologian interested in philosophy, a professor of the Free (later United Free) Church College of Aberdeen who has been described as "among the most perceptive and judicious of commentators on the philosophic-theological frontier." Iverach accepted, with some reservations regarding the loss of personality in God and man, an idealist philosophy. He wrote *Theism in the Light of Present Science and Philosophy* (1900) and was known for articles on T. H. Green and Edward Caird in the *Expository Times*. (See *Expository Times*, IV [1892–1893]: 164; V [1893–1894]: 205.) His advice would have made Dougall sympathetic to the formulations of personal idealism. See Alan P. F. Sell, *The Philosophy of Religion, 1875–1980* (London, Croom Helm, 1988), 3, 15–17, 28, 36.

60. "Dr. and Mrs. Rashdall, Longwall St., Oxford, To tea, Tuesday, November 5, [1912]"; "Professor Royce, Harvard, Mr. and Mrs. Illingworth, Longworth, To tea, Saturday Feb 1st, [1913]." "Mr. and Mrs. Illingworth and Mrs. and Miss Crum.[?] To tea, Thurs April 3, [1913]," Visitor Book, BL, LDP, 1. A. S. Pringle Pattison contributed a chapter, "Immanence and Transcendence" to the joint volume, *The Spirit, God and His Relation to Man Considered from the Standpoint of Philosophy, Psychology and Art* (London: Macmillan, 1919). A copy of his book, inscribed to Dougall, is among her papers, BL, LDP, 8. C. C. J. Webb

wrote an account of Dougall's funeral in Clement Webb Journal, Entry for October 13, 1923, Ms Eng misc. d. 1115, fol 90R, Bodliean Library, C. C. J. Webb Papers.

61. In this she was not unusual: the careful defense of personal faith engaged in by philosophers like Hastings Rashdall and C. C. J. Webb, and the theological arguments of Anglo-Catholics like J. R. Illingworth merged into a blunter statements of faith by figures like Arthur James Balfour. Balfour said in his Gifford Lectures in 1914, "[When I speak of God] I mean something other than an Identity wherein all differences vanish, or a Unity which includes but does not transcend the differences which it somehow holds in solution. I mean a God whom men can love, a God to whom men can pray, who takes sides, who has purposes and preferences, whose attributes, howsoever conceived, leave unimpaired the possibility of a personal relation between Himself and those who He has created." As his remarks indicate, personal idealism for Balfour less a philosophy than an intellectually respectable return to an older form of theism. Arthur James Balfour, *Theism and Humanism. Being the Gifford Lectures Delivered at the University of Glasgow, 1914* (London: Hodder & Stoughton, [1915]), 36. Cited in Oppenheim, *The Other World*, 131.

62. This problem had not been so acute with Caird's idealism. The American personal idealist, Knudson identified both Edward Caird and Josiah Royce as personalistic absolutists, arguing that they ascribed personality to the Absolute, but acknowledging by the designation that personality is secondary to the absolute in their understanding. Knudson, *The Philosophy of Personalism*, 32–35. The editor of the first British work on the subject similarly excused Royce from his criticisms. Sturt, *Personal Idealism*, vii.

63. Lily Dougall, *The Christian Doctrine of Health* (London: Macmillan, 1916), 103. As Rashdall explained, "My toothache is forever my toothache only, and can never become yours; and so is my love for another person, however passionately I desire—to use that metaphor of poets and rhetoricians which imposes upon mystics, and even upon philosophers—to become one with the object of my love: for that love would cease to be if the aspiration were literally fulfilled." Hastings Rashdall, "Personality: Human and Divine," in Sturt, *Personal Idealism*, 384.

64. Lily Dougall, "Orthodox Dualism," [Review of A. S. Pringle-Pattison, *The Idea of Immortality* (Oxford: Clarendon Press, 1923) and Canon O. C. Quick, *Liberalism, Modernism and Tradition* (London: Longmans, 1923)] *The Modern Churchman* 13, no. 1 (1923–1924): 45–53, 50.

65. As Lyman Abbott explained in Dougall's *World Wide*, "the Infinite and Eternal energy from which all things proceed, is an energy that thinks, that feels, that purposes and does; and is thinking and feeling and purposing and doing as a conscious life, of which ours is but a poor and broken reflection." "God in his World" from the recent sermon preached December 18, 1904 by Lyman Abbott at Harvard, from *Outlook,* New York, copy from earlier October 19 sermon to the National Council of Congregational Churches, published in *World Wide* (January 7, 1905): 105.

66. J. R. Illingworth, *The Life and Work of John Richardson Illingworth, as portrayed by his letters and illustrated by photographs* (London: John Murray, 1917), 273.

67. Lily Dougall, *The Christian Doctrine of Health* (London: Macmillan, 1916), 104. "There is an essential difference between learning what we may of

God's character from the best we know of human goodness and having an anthropomorphic conception of God" (p. 100).

68. Dougall, *God's Way*, 67. Illingworth's comments in a letter to friend reveal the central outline of his rather anthropomorphic argument: "I don't think my remarks on personality would repay your perusal, as they are only half finished—they are only a few rather obvious apologetic things strung together. 1. On the personality of man 2. on the inference from it to divine personality 3. on the revelation of a personal God, necessarily culminating in 4. the Incarnation 5. on the way in which a personal God can be known, on the analogy of our knowledge of human personalities." Illingworth, *Life and Work*, 218.

69. [Lily Dougall] *The Practice of Christianity* (London: Macmillan, 1913), xix, 264. F. D. Maurice had anticipated this by arguing that familial relations, especially that between male and female, are routes to God. "They are not artificial types of something divine, but are actually the means, and the only means through which man ascends to any knowledge of the divine. " Frederick Denison Maurice, *The Kingdom of Christ, or Hints to a Quaker, Respecting the Principles, Constitution and Ordinances of the Catholic Church*, 2nd ed. vol. 1, (London: Ribington, 1842), 288.

70. Lily Dougall, *Paths of the Righteous*, 431. [Lily Dougall] "Repentence and Hope," in *Concerning Prayer, Its Nature, Its Difficulties, Its Value*, ed. B. H. Streeter (London: Macmillan, 1916), 137.

71. Webb, "Hastings Rashdall," *DNB*, 708. Reardon argued that the exponents of personal idealism "were not always very rigorous in their arguments, and in retrospect their systems emerge as not much more than individual statements of faith—type products of their time and now chiefly of historical interest." Bernard M. G. Reardon, *From Coleridge to Gore, A Century of Religious Thought in Britain* (London: Longman, 1971).

72. Rashdall, "Personality: Human and Divine," 391.

73. Carol Gilligan, *In a Different Voice, Psychological Theory and Women's Development* (Cambridge, Mass.: Harvard University Press, 1982; 1993), 8. Nancy Choderow, *The Reproduction of Mothering* (Berkeley: University of California Press, 1978).

6. CHRISTIAN SOCIALISM

1. *The Churchman*, November 1910. Clipping file, LDP, BL, 6.

2. L. Dougall, *The Mormon Prophet* (London: A. & C. Black, 1899); *The Earthly Purgatory* (London: Hutchison and Co., 1904); *The Spanish Dowry, A Romance* (London: Hutchison, 1906); *Paths of the Righteous* (London: Macmillan, 1908); [Lily Dougall], *Pro Christo et Ecclesia*, (London: Macmillan, 1900); *Christus Futurus* (London: Macmillan, 1907); *The Christ That Is To Be* (New York: Macmillan, 1907); *Absente Reo* (London: Macmillan, 1910); *Voluntas Dei* (London: Macmillan, 1912), and *The Practice of Christianity* (London: Macmillan, 1913). The American publisher made the decision to translate the title of *Christus Futurus* for the American market. See George Macmillan to Lily Dougall, June 18, 1907, BL, LDP, 6.

3. See comments upon her Christian socialism in *Western Morning News*, April 13, 1914, and *The Daily Express*, March 5, 1914. Clippings file for *The Practice of Christianity*, BL, LDP, 7.

4. [Dougall], *Christus Futurus*, 57. This wording is a fairly free interpretation of the original Greek, albeit one that might be supported by a critical reading of the concept of the Kingdom of God in the New Testament.

5. Earp," Selected Letters," 162.

6. "I am afraid it [*The Mormon Prophet*] will be a fizzle, like the one I wrote last winter. What is the matter with me. I seem to have lost confidence." Lily Dougall to M. S. Earp (?), Montreal, October 12, 1896. Earp, "Selected Letters," 144.

7. The extent of Lily Dougall's editorial role is not clear. Her obituary in *World Wide* notes: "Miss Dougall was the first editor of *World Wide* some twenty-three years ago, and gave it its present shape, a task for which her broad sympathies and vision eminently fitted her" (*World Wide*, October 13, 1923, p. 1). *World Wide* receives no mention in Earp's "Selected Letters," nor is there any reference to it in the papers held at the Bodleian Library. Copies of the review make no reference to the editor, and refer simply to the publishers, Lily's brother and nephew, John and Frederick Dougall. Her editorial control is revealed in the carefully chosen selection of articles on liberal theology, and the number of articles of special interest to highly educated single women, including an article from the *Cheltenham College Magazine*. (See *World Wide*, 1, no. 42.) Lily left Canada in April 1902, but she apparently continued editing the review from Britain. She is described as editor of *World Wide* in *Canadian Men and Women of the Time*, Henry James Morgan, ed., 2nd ed. (Toronto: Wm. Briggs, 1912). See also Carl F. Klinck, ed. *The Literary History of Canada*, 2nd ed. vol. 1 (Toronto: University of Toronto Press, 1976), 333.

8. The statement of purpose on the last page of vol. 1, no. 1 (January 5, 1901) reads: "It is proposed to fill the pages of 'World Wide' with articles and extracts (of permanent and world wide interest) with occasional selections from notable books and scenes from striking stories. An effort will be made to select the articles each week so that due proportion will be given to the various fields of human interest—to the shifting scenes of the world great drama, to letters and science and beautiful things." A quotation from Terence, "So many men, so many minds, / Every man in his own way" was placed on the front page. Articles were chosen so that timeliness was not important, but it appears that it took about three weeks from their initial appearance in British newspapers to publication in *World Wide*. The review appears to have been successful; in the second year a higher grade of paper was used, a cover page with cartoons was introduced, and an annual index created, and the number of advertisements increased. References were made to the growing circulation in appeals for new subscriptions, but as the Dougalls were practiced in the art of newspaper promotion it is difficult to know how to assess these claims.

9. Lily Dougall to M. S. Earp, November 14, 1896; Lily Dougall to [M. S. Earp?], March 1898. Earp, "Selected Letters," 146.

10. Lily Dougall to [M. S. Earp?], March 1898. Earp, "Selected Letters," 153.

11. See Earp's notes, titled "B's Life," in BL, LDP, 1. The entry for September 1898 reads: "First thought of writing theology at the log Hut, Georgeville, Quebec."

12. Lily Dougall to M. S. Earp, Highlands, Macon Co., North Carolina, June 10, 1898. Earp, "Selected Letters," 154.

13. Lily Dougall to M. S. Earp, Birch Bay Camp, Georgeville, P. Q., September 1898. Earp, "Selected Letters," 157.

14. Lily Dougall to Sophie Earp, October 11, 1898. Earp, "Selected Letters," 158.

15. Andrew Martin Fairbairn (1838–1912) was the author of a number of books including the popular *The Place of Jesus Christ in Modern Theology* (1893) and *The Philosophy of the Christian Religion* (1902).

16. *Lincoln's Inn*, 5:191; *Kingdom of Christ*, 2:42. Cited in John McClain, "On Women," in John McClain, Richard Norris, and John Orens, *F. D. Maurice, A Study* (Cambridge, MA: Cowley Publications, 1982), 45–46.

17. *Binghampton Herald*, August 24, 1895. *New York Delineator*, September 1895. BL, LDP, 7.

18. Hannah Whitall Smith, *The Christian's Secret of a Happy Life* (1875; Toronto: Methodist Book and Publishing House, 1889), iv.

19. Dougall, *Paths of the Righteous*, 425.

20. M. S. Earp to George Macmillan, 4 October 1912, Cutts End, Cumnor. University of Reading, Macmillan Papers 61/1. Cited in Lorraine McMullen, unpublished manuscript. See Earp, "Selected Letters," 182.

21. Dougall's papers provide some publishing history for her books but the evidence is incomplete. A chart provided in a letter of April 10, 1913 appears to list the total sales of her religious works. The chart indicates that *Pro Christo et Ecclesia* sold 2,162 copies in Great Britain, and 329 in the United States by June 30, 1912, and a subsequent chart indicates that the sales for the following year, from July 1, 1912 to April 10, 1913, the book sold 85 copies in England and 39 in the United States. By comparison the total sales to April 10, 1913 of *Christus Futurus* were 2,272, *Absente Reo* 1,376 and *Voluntas Dei* 757. George Macmillan to [Lily Dougall] LDP, BL, 6, p. 10. These figures are not entirely reliable, however. Dougall's stature is better measured by the references to her in subsequent reviews. In 1913, Dougall accepted publication of *Pro Christo et Ecclesia* in a shilling Theological Library series. George Macmillan to Lily Dougall, March 27, 1913, LDP, BL, 6.

22. Clipping of review of *Absente Reo* from *The Church Times*, July 29, 1910, BL, LDP, 6.

23. [Lily Dougall], *Pro Christo et Ecclesia*, 3rd ed. (London: Macmillan, 1900; 1913), 142, 32.

24. [Lily Dougall], *Pro Christo et Ecclesia*, 140.

25. Lily Dougall to Hilda Oakeley, Pasadena, California, February 16, 1902. Earp, "Selected Letters," 189. (The dates appear confused in this section of the transcript, and this letter may have been written in 1901.)

26. Canon Scott Holland gave it a long review in *The Commonwealth*, November 1900. See Earp, "Selected Letters," 183. The *Times Literary Supplement* was quoted in an advertisement in the endpapers of Dougall's *God's Way with Man*: "Miss Dougall, whose *Pro Christo et Ecclesia* placed her among the leading religious writers of the day. . . . "

27. [Dougall], *Christus Futurus*, n.p. The reader's comments were included with a letter from George Macmillan to Lily Dougall, March 4, 1907, BL, LDP, 6.

28. George Macmillan to Lily Dougall, December 16, 1907.

29. In 1907, her editor, George Macmillan, said British sales of *Christus Futurus* were surprisingly good (450) considering that the book had not been as favorably reviewed as he had expected. George Macmillan to Lily Dougall, December 11, 1907, BL, LDP, 5.

30. Clipping of review of *Absente Reo* from *The Church Times*, July 29, 1910. Clipping file, BL, LDP, 6.

31. F.W. Maitland, *The Life and Letters of Leslie Stephen* (London: Duckworth and Co., 1906), 240. Cited in McClain et al., *F. D. Maurice,* 61.

32. Torben Christensen, *The Divine Order: A Study in F. D. Maurice's Theology* (Leiden: E. J. Brill, 1973), 53. Christensen, whose interpretation I have drawn on, argues that individuals are already members of the kingdom, and the ordinances of the church mark only the increasing knowledge of, rather than access to, that membership.

33. F. D. Maurice, *Sacrifice,* XLI. Cited in Christensen, *Maurice,* 258.

34. Lily Dougall to M. S. Earp, n.d., 1898. Earp, "Selected Letters," 182.

35. [Dougall], *Pro Christo et Ecclesia,* 124.

36. [Dougall], *Pro Christo et Ecclesia,* 4.

37. The analogy is not a simple one, but the Sadducees, who were the aristocratic and priestly caste in Judaic society, appear to stand for the Tractarians and other conservatives within the Anglican hierarchy. The Pharisees, described by Dougall as progressive but separatist, resemble evangelicals most closely, although Dougall notes similarities to elements in the Anglican, Roman Catholic, and Presbyterian churches. "Briefly, Sadduceeism was characterized by sober reason and a reverence for that part of the national religion which had become historic: in secular matters their judgment was not biased by the enthusiasms of faith; in religion they did not believe in adding to the doctrine of their fathers . . . The Sadducees, in religion, were conservative to a very high degree.

"The Pharisees, practicing the law as interpreted by oral tradition, entered the devout life by choice. Almost all the pious among the common people, and some of the priestly class, were on their side. . . . [T]he legal observances had for their chief aim the dissociation of the pious from the impious." [Dougall], *Pro Christo et Ecclesia,* 23–25.

38. Dougall, *God's Way,* 13.

39. [Dougall], *Pro Christo et Ecclesia,* 72. She identifies Mildmay and Keswick on page 181, and the Salvation Army, Keswick, and the Student Volunteer Movement, in a note on page 132.

40. [Dougall], *Pro Christo et Ecclesia,* 43–44.

41. "What would be our mental attitude towards a being as evidently exalted and powerful who should appear today and contradict what seem to us the obvious tenets of revealed religion, reviling us for our favorite forms of piety. Let us conceive of him, for example, handling our canon of Scripture as roughly as the most destructive of the higher critics, showing himself as indifferent to sacrament and religious service as our modern philosophers, eating the bread and salt of corrupt politicians, receiving gifts from women of doubtful character, and consorting with the ignorant in preference to the clergy." [Dougall], *Pro Christo et Ecclesia,* 43.

42. [Dougall], *Pro Christo et Ecclesia,* 161, 73–74, 180, 80.

43. "Lovereen," vol. 2, pp. 169–72. See also Dougall, *Spanish Dowry,* 62; *Paths of the Righteous,* 10, 246–47, 406.

44. [Dougall], *Pro Christo et Ecclesia,* 187.

45. Review in the *Commonwealth* dated November 1900. Cited in Earp, "Selected Letters," 183. A positive review of *Absente Reo* (London; Macmillan, 1910) from *Commonwealth* is cited in the endpapers of subsequent books, including *The Practice of Christianity* (London: Macmillan, 1913): "Whatever 'our views' are we ought to be glad to have this kindly and keen critic at our

elbow." Scott Holland appears to have assisted in subsequent revisions. See the letter from Dougall's publisher, Macmillan and Co., on November 21, 1900 discussing revisions: "We are glad to hear that Canon Scott Holland has dealt with the point to which we called attention." BL, LDP, 6.

46. See Peter d'A. Jones, *The Christian Socialist Revival, 1877–1914, Religion, Class, and Social Conscience in Late-Victorian England* (Princeton, N.J.: Princeton University Press, 1968), chapter 6. John C. Cort says membership in Great Britain grew to 6,000 at its height, including 16 of 53 bishops. *Christian Socialism, An Informal History* (Maryknoll, N.Y.: Orbis Books, 1988). Edward Pulker has argued that Canadian Anglicans did not share the Christian socialism of the British Anglicans and American Episcopalians; he argued their conservatism on social reform was the product of a more agrarian society. He does not, however, provide a great deal of evidence for this position. *We Stand on their Shoulders: The Growth of Social Concern in Canadian Anglicanism* (Toronto: Anglican Book Centre, 1986).

47. "By 1908, the CSU had thoroughly permeated the Church of England, especially the hierarchy; it was a form of 'socialism' for bishops." Jones, *Christian Socialist Revival*, 217. "We have been having so many visitors lately," she told her brother in 1915. "It is a little difficult to take Christian credit for hospitality, however, as they are one and all solidly rich; but I find the rich are as much in need of spiritual hospitality as the poor." Earp, "Selected Letters," 243.

48. Lily Dougall to A.P. Watt, n.d., BL, LDP, 7.

49. Review cited in the end pages of *Voluntas Dei*.

50. M. S. Earp to George Macmillan, Cutts End, Cumnor, 28 May 1914, MP, 64/282, Reading. Cited in Lorraine McMullen, unpublished manuscript.

51. [Beatrice Webb], *The New Statesman*, 6 June 1914. Clippings Book, BL, LDP, 7.

52. Lily Dougall to George Macmillan, Cutts End, Cumnor, 26 May 1914, MP, 214/291, Reading. M. S. Earp to George Macmillan, Cutts End, Cumnor, 28 May 1914, MP, 64/282, Reading. Lily Dougall to George Macmillan, Cutts End, Cumnor, 2 June 1914, MP, 214/291, Reading. Cited in Lorraine McMullen, unpublished manuscript.

53. *Absente Reo* appears, from the letters from the publisher, to have been accepted quickly for publication (December 10, 1909), received good reviews, sold rather slowly ("fallen rather flat," June 29, 1910) but steadily ("as the sales keep up quite satisfactorily," September 21, 1910). A letter written on April 10, 1913 seems to indicate that the total sales from the time of publication were 1,376 copies, compared to 2,162 copies of *Pro Christo et Ecclesia* and 2,272 copies of *Christus Futurus*. Of these, 159 copies sold in America. George Macmillan to Lily Dougall or Sophie Earp, BL, LDP, 6.

54. *Harrow Gazette*, October 29, 1911. Envelope labeled "Reviews, *Absente Reo*," BL, LDP, 6.

55. [Dougall], *Absente Reo*, 209–210.

56. [Dougall], *Absente Reo*, 67.

57. [Dougall], *Absente Reo*, 45.

58. Earp, "Selected Letters," 219.

59. Lily Dougall to H. D. O. [Hilda Oakeley], Melbourne, Derbyshire, September 7, 1910. Earp, "Selected Letters," 220.

60. See David E. Hall, "On the making and unmaking of monsters: Christian Socialism, muscular Christianity, and the metaphorization of class conflict," *Muscular Christianity, Embodying the Victorian Age*, ed. David E. Hall

(Cambridge: Cambridge University Press, 1994), 45–65; Norman Vance, *The Sinews of the Spirit, The Ideal of Christian Manliness in Victorian Literature and Religious Thought* (Cambridge: Cambridge University Press, 1985), 52.

For the masculinity of the American social gospel, see Janet Forsyth Fishburn, *The Fatherhood of God and the Victorian Family: The Social Gospel in America* (Philadelphia: Fortress Press, 1981); Gail Bederman, " 'The Women Have Had Charge of the Church Work Long Enough': The Men and Religion Forward Movement of 1911–1912 and the Masculinization of Middle-Class Protestantism," *American Quarterly* 41 (September 1989): 432–65. See Michael Gauvreau and Nancy Christie, *A Full-Orbed Christianity* (Montreal: McGill–Queens University Press, 1996), 95–100, for a description of the appeal by Canadian progressives for a more manly and activist faith.

61. Lily Dougall to H. D. O. [Hilda Oakeley]. Earp, "Selected Letters," 218–19.

62. Earp, "Selected Letters," 217. Webb's personal recollections of the summer school were more critical. Beatrice Webb, *The Diary of Beatrice Webb,* vol. 3, *1905–1924 "The Power to Alter Things,"* eds. Norman and Jeanne MacKenzie (London: Virago, 1984), 141–44.

63. [Dougall], *The Practice of Christianity,* 230–31.

64. Lily Dougall to Sophie Earp, October 21, 1892. Earp, "Selected Letters," 112.

65. Dougall, *Paths of the Righteous,* 298.

66. [Dougall], *Christus Futurus,* 328.

67. "The true and only contra-position of the Christian Church is to the world. Her paramount aim and object indeed, is *another* world, not a world *to come* exclusively, but likewise *another world that now is,* and to the concerns of which the epithet spiritual, can without a mischievous abuse of the word be applied." S. T. Coleridge, *On the Constitution of Church and State,* edited by H. N. Coleridge (London: Wm. Pickering, 1839), 127.

68. Lily Dougall to unknown, November 1, 1879. Earp, "Selected Letters," 23.

69. [Dougall], *The Practice of Christianity.*

70. Lily Dougall to Maud Petre, February 25, 1918, Cutts End, Cumnor. The British Library, London, AD 45, 744.

71. Emphasis added. [Dougall], *Christus Futurus,* 16.

72. [Dougall], *Christus Futurus,* 57.

73. Margaret Vaughan, "St. Catherine of Siena, as Seen in her Letters," reprinted from the *Speaker,* London, in *World Wide* (October 21, 1905): 929–30. Review of *St. Catherine of Siena, as Seen in her Letters,* trans. and ed. by Vida D. Scudder (London: J. M. Dent and Sons, 1905). Scudder's first name is given as Viola, but the British Library catalogue identifies the author of this book as Vida Dutton Scudder.

74. Deborah Epstein Nord, *The Apprenticeship of Beatrice Webb* (Ithaca, N.Y.: Cornell University Press, 1985), 92.

75. [Beatrice Webb], "Rational Mysticism," *The New Statesman,* June 6, 1914. Clipping file, BL, LDP, 7.

76. [Dougall], *The Practice of Christianity,* 32.

77. Manuscript letter of 13/9 1852 from Ludlow to Maurice. Cited in Torben Christensen, *Origin and History of Christian Socialism, 1848–54* (Copenhagen: Universistetsforlaget I Aarhus: 1962), 306.

78. Prefaratory note to W. Moore Ede, *The Attitude of the Church to Some of the Social Problems of Town Life* (1896), viii. Cited in Vidler, *Maurice,* 261.

79. [Dougall], *Christus Futurus,* 309.

80. After the war, the CSU merged with the Industrial Christian Fellowship and much of their work was carried on by COPEC. Dougall died before the April 1924 conference.

81. Lily Dougall to Beatrice Webb, November 29, 1917, Cutts End, Cumnor. Earp, "Selected Letters," 259.

82. Scudder wrote in full: "My religious position consigned me again to solitude, among radical comrades to whom I escaped for relief now and then . . . I had not worked out either my socialism or my religion alone, and in the synthesis of the two interests I was a disciple and a learner; yet my fellowship was rather with books than with men, and my union of religious conservatism and of Catholic sympathies with social radicalism was far more unusual then than now." Vida Scudder, *On Journey* (New York: E. P. Dutton, 1937). Cited in Lindley, "Neglected Voices," 83.

83. Beatrice Webb, Diary entry, April 14, 1926. Cited in Nord, *Beatrice Webb,* 237.

84. Beatrice Webb, *My Apprenticeship,* 89. Cited in Nord, *Beatrice Webb,* 92–93.

7. THE MAKING OF A MODERNIST MYSTICISM

1. John Wesley, *An Extract of the Life of Madame Guyon* (London: R. Hawes, 1776). The continuing relevance of Madame Guyon is suggested also by the reference to her work in H. D. A. Major's review of Dougall's later book, *Concerning Prayer.* See *The Modern Churchman* VI (1916–1917), 224. See also Arthur Wollaston Hutton, "The 'Inner Light' Today," from *The Commonwealth* in *World Wide* 2, no. 31 (August 12, 1902): 492–93. Hutton concludes with a quotation from Madame Guyon's spiritual director.

2. Thomas Upham, *A Treatise on Divine Union,* 6th ed., 325. Cited in Benjamin Breckinridge Warfield, *Perfectionism,* vol. II (New York: Oxford University Press, 1931), 392.

3. "Lettres Spirituelles," ii, p. 187. Cited in Warfield, *Perfectionism,* 398.

4. [Lily Dougall], *Absente Reo* (London: Macmillan, 1910), 266.

5. Lily Dougall to John Redpath Dougall, Edinburgh, April 28, 1881. M. S. Earp, "Selected Letters of Lily Dougall with Biographical Notes," typescript, LAC, DFP, 5, 9, p. 42. Although Dougall thought he was a Roman Catholic, Father Ignatius (J. L. Lyne, 1837–1908) was an Anglican who campaigned for the revival of monastic orders in the Church of England.

6. "Do I not spot the paw of the D [Earp] in some of the answers of the priest to Paul and later in the speech of Paul to Mr. Myers about the claims of the Catholic church?" The letter which is undated and unsigned, is addressed to "Dear B" [Beaver, a nickname for Dougall.] BL, LDP, 1. Dorothy Emmet, the daughter of Lily Dougall's collaborator, C. W. Emmet, said that Sophie Earp was Roman Catholic. Private correspondence, Dorothy Emmet to Joanna Dean, April 25, 1993.

7. Lily Dougall, "Lovereen," 21/25, BL, LDP, 4.

8. L. Dougall, *The Mermaid: A Love Tale* (London: R. Bentley and Son, 1895), 41.

9. Dougall, *Mermaid*, 58.

10. L. Dougall, *What Necessity Knows*, 3 vols. (London, New York: Longmans, 1893), 14.

11. Francis Marion Beynon, *Aleta Day* (1919; London: Virago, 1988), 555, 29–30.

12. Joanna E. Wood, *Judith Moore* (Toronto: The Ontario Publishing Co., 1898), 54.

13. Flora MacDonald, *Mary Melville* (Toronto: The Austin Publishing Co., 1900), 99. See also pp. 81, 266.

14. Keith had condemned the modern liberal through the Scottish dialect of an older man: "His societies! Man, wi' his Y.P.S.C.E. and his Y.M.C.A. an his X.Y.Z. fowk's heids are fair turned. Jist sparkin' bees, every ane o'them. An' him the biggest spark o' them a'. A Chreestian Endeavour Society! Man, where's he gaun to get it without the Chreestians?" Marian Keith [MacGregor, Mary Esther], *Duncan Polite: the Watchman of Glenoro* (New York: Hodder and Stoughton, 1905), 163. Dougall ran two separate reviews, in different issues of *World Wide*, dismissing the novel for its derivative characters and outdated theology. The first was merciless: "It's maist s'rprisin' leddy—an it's a leddy we're thinkin' ye'll be by yer name—that when the pioneers went awa' frae Scotland ae Canady they tuk sic'a wheen o' auld releegious notions wi' them." *World Wide* (July 15, 1905): 652. The British review, from the *Outlook*, is more gently dismissive: "Miss Keith has, however, entered on territory which is well occupied already, and if, in doing so, she challenges comparison with great writers she must take the consequences." *World Wide* (June 17, 1905): 571.

15. Keith, *Duncan Polite*, 167, 234–35; 237–38.

16. Agnes Maule Machar, *Roland Graeme: Knight. A Novel of our Times* (Montreal: Drysdale, 1892), 272.

17. L. Dougall, *The Zeit-Geist* (London: Hutchinson, 1895), 222.

18. [Lily Dougall], *Christus Futurus* (London: Macmillan, 1907), 310. (St. John xvii: 20–23.)

19. [Beatrice Webb], "A Rational Mysticism" *The Statesman*, Clipping Book, BL, LDP, 7.

20. Lily Dougall to H. D. O. [Hilda Oakeley], Melbourne, Derbyshire, September 7, 1910. Earp, "Selected Letters," 220.

21. *The Transvaal Leader*, November 1, 1910. Clipping file, p. 11, BL, LDP, 6.

22. W. R. Inge was the Dean of St. Paul's, who wrote numerous books on mysticism as well as columns in the *Evening Standard* (1921–1946). For biographical information, see W. R. Inge, *Diary of a Dean. St. Paul's 1909–1934* (London: Hutchison and Co., 1949); *Vale* (London: Longmans, 1934); Paul Crook, "W. R. Inge and Cultural Crisis, 1899–1920," *Journal of Religious History* 16, 4 (1991): 410, and Robert M. Helm, *Gloomy Dean: The Thought of William Ralph Inge* (Winston Salem, N.C.: John F. Blair, 1962).

Classicist Percy Gardner (1846–1937) was the author of *Exploratio Evanglica: A Brief Exploration of the Basis and Origin of Christian Belief* (London: A. & C. Black, 1899); *The Practical Basis for Christian Belief: An Essay in Reconstruction* (London: Williams and Norgate, 1923); *Modernism in the English Church* (London: Methuen, 1926); *The Interpretation of Religious Experience* (London: Williams and Norgate, 1931), and *Autobiographica* (Oxford: Basil and Blackwell, 1933).

Baron Friedrich von Hugel (1852–1925), dubbed the lay bishop of Roman Catholic modernists, introduced a largely Anglican British audience to mysticism with *The Mystical Element of Religion as Studied in Ste Catherine of Genoa and her Friends* (1908).

Evelyn Underhill (1875–1941) was the author of numerous books on mysticism. See Dana Greene, *Evelyn Underhill, Artist of the Infinite Life* (New York: Crossroads, 1990); and *Evelyn Underhill: Modern Guide to the Ancient Quest for the Holy,* ed. and with an intro. by Dana Greene (Albany: State University of New York Press, 1988). For a more distanced analysis, see Christopher J. R. Armstrong, *Evelyn Underhill (1875–1941): An Introduction to her Life and Writings* (London: Mowbrays, 1975). See also *The Letters of Evelyn Underhill,* ed. Charles Williams (London: Longmans, 1943). Dana Greene notes that Underhill's greatest influence lay among women (*Artist,* p. 148).

Rufus M. Jones (1863–1940), a liberal Quaker, was the author of more than fifty books on mysticism and the Society of Friends. See the compilation in *Rufus Jones Speaks to Our Times: An Anthology,* ed. Harry Emerson Fosdick (New York: Macmillan, 1951). Hal Budges quotes the *American Philosophy of Religion* (1936) by Henry Nelson Wieman and Bernard Eugene Meland: "Rufus Jones may undoubtedly be considered the most eminent American mystic of recent times, if in fact, he is not the American mystic *par excellence.*" *American Mysticism: From William James to Zen* (New York: Harper and Row, 1970), 29. Dougall worked with Jones on the Cumnor volumes (see chapter 9) and stayed with him in the United States in 1914. Lily Dougall to George Macmillan, June 26, 1914, 7 Botanist Place, Flushing, Long Island, Manhattan, Macmillan Papers, 63/33, University of Reading.

23. W. R. Inge, *Christian Mysticism* (London: Methuen and Co., 1899; 7th ed. Meridian, 1956). Evelyn Underhill, *Mysticism, A Study in the Nature and Development of Man's Spiritual Consciousness* (1911; 3rd rev. ed., 1912; 12th rev. ed., 1930; reprint, London: Methuen and Co., 1967).

24. *Light, Life and Love, Selections from the German Mystics of the Middle Ages,* trans. and ed. with an introduction by W. R. Inge (1904).

25. *World Wide* 5, no. 27 (June 3, 1905): 530.

26. T. J. Jackson Lears, *No Place of Grace: Antimodernism and the Transformation of American Culture, 1880–1920* (New York: Pantheon Books, 1981), 223.

27. For Ramsay Cook's dismissal of Bucke, see *The Regenerators: Social Criticism in Late Victorian English Canada* (Toronto: University of Toronto Press, 1985), chapter 6.

28. Michel de Certeau, *The Mystic Fable: The Sixteenth and Seventeenth Centuries,* vol. 1, trans. Michael B. Smith (Chicago: University of Chicago Press, 1992).

29. Eric J. Sharpe, "The Study of Religion in *The Encyclopedia of Religion,*" *Journal of Religion* 70, 3 (July 1990): 347.

30. R. A. Vaughan, *Hours with the Mystics,* 3rd rev. ed. (1856; London: Strahan and Co., 1856).

31. Bertrand Russell, "The Essence of Religion," in *The Collected Papers of Bertrand Russell,* vol. 12, ed. Richard A. Rempel, Andrew Brink, and Margaret Moran (London: George Allen and Unwin, 1985), 114–15.

32. [Lily Dougall], *Absente Reo* (London: Macmillan, 1910), 237.

33. Emphasis added. [Dougall], *Absente Reo,* 127.

34. Emphasis added. Cited in A. M. G. Stephenson, *The Rise and Decline of English Modernism* (London: SPCK, 1984), 73.

35. Inge, *Vale,* 39.

36. Fosdick, ed., *Rufus Jones Speaks to our Time,* v.

37. Paul Badham argues that religious experience, or mysticism, was a foundational element in Anglican modernist theology. See *The Contemporary Challenge of Modernist Theology* (Cardiff: University of Wales Press, 1998), 4.

38. Inge, *Vale*, 55.

39. Inge, *Christian Mysticism*, xiv.

40. Inge, *Christian Mysticism*, 115. Inge's dismissal reveals that he misunderstood the meaning of the *via negativa*—the complex and rich idea that only by negation can the immeasurable power of God be evoked. In his early works, Inge frequently distinguished between the rational forms of mysticism, which he understood to be Greek in origin, and what he saw as the perversions that resulted from "Oriental" influence. This changed when, at the end of his life, Eastern mysticism gained credibility. See his late book *Mysticism in Religion* (Chicago: the University of Chicago Press, 1948), where he says the West has neglected the spirit, and he has been studying the Eastern Orthodox Church for the "wisdom of the East."

41. [Dougall], *Absente Reo*, 270.

42. Emphasis added. Rufus Jones, "Prayer and the Mystic Vision," in *Concerning Prayer, Its Nature, Its Difficulties and Its Value* (1916; 2nd ed., London: Macmillan, 1918), 117. "These mystical experiences in a *perfectly sane and normal fashion* often come over whole groups of persons in times of worship." Jones, *Studies*, xviii, xix, and xx.

43. Inge, *Vale*, 38.

44. Rufus Jones, *Studies in Mystical Religion* (London: Macmillan, 1909), xv.

45. [Dougall], *Absente Reo*, 273.

46. [Dougall], *Christus Futurus*, 60, 309.

47. Lily Dougall to [?] October 22, 1912, Cutts End, Cumnor. Earp, "Selected Letters," 232.

48. W. R. Inge, *Studies of English Mystics, St. Margaret Lectures, 1905* (London: John Murray, 1921), 27–28.

49. See, for example, W. R. Inge's *Christian Mysticism; The Philosophy of Plotinus*, The Gifford Lectures at St. Andrews, 1917–1918 (London: Longmans, 1918); *The Platonic Tradition in English Religious Thought*, The Hulsean Lectures 1925–1926 (London: Longmans, 1926).

50. Inge, *Christian Mysticism*, 290.

51. Inge, *Christian Mysticism*, 139.

52. Inge, *Christian Mysticism*, 150.

53. See Peter van der Veer, *Imperial Encounters: Religion and Modernity in India and Britain* (Princeton, N.J.: Princeton University Press, 2001). Van der Veer's point is that modernity grew out these encounters. The recognition of other traditions also justifies a critical historical approach to Christianity.

54. Max Müller, *Theosophy or Psychological Religion, Gifford Lectures, 1893* (London: Longmans, 1898). Van der Veer points out that Müller was naturalized in Britain.

55. [Dougall], *Voluntas Dei*, 194. See also [Lily Dougall] *The Practice of Christianity* (London: Macmillan, 1913), 271.

56. See Robert Sharf, "Experience," in *Critical Terms for Religious Studies*, ed. Mark C. Taylor (Chicago: University of Chicago Press, 2000), 94–116 for a criticism of these assumptions based on the study of Asian Buddhism.

57. See [Dougall], *Practice of Christianity*, 272. In 1913 when answering a survey, Dougall crossed out the word *finality*, in a phrase arguing that comparative

religion has shown more clearly the supremacy and finality of Christianity. Galley 2, n.p., envelope marked "Free Church Commission," BL, LDP, 1.

58. B. H. Streeter and A. J. Appasamy, *The Message of Sadhu Sundar Singh: A Study in Mysticism on Practical Religion* (New York: Macmillan, 1922), 67.

59. B. H. Streeter, *The Buddha and the Christ, an Exploration of the Meaning of the Universe and the Purpose of Human Life* (London: Macmillan, 1932), 71.

60. R. D. Richardson, *The Gospel of Modernism*, with a foreword by E. W. Barnes (London: Skeffington and Son Ltd., n.d. [1933?]), 53.

61. Underhill continued, "The book is not going to be specifically theological as I want to make a synthesis of the doctrine of Christian and non-Christian mystics, so no 'over-beliefs' are admissible." Evelyn Underhill to Margaret Robinson, [probably] November 1908. See Christopher Armstrong, *Evelyn Underhill*, 104.

62. Evelyn Underhill to Margaret Robinson, November 21, 1908. Cited in *The Letters of Evelyn Underhill*, edited with an introduction by Charles Williams (London: Longmans Green, 1943; Westminster, Md: Christian Classics, 1989), 87. Later, sending a difficult edition of Eckhart, she advised, "there's no need to read it *all* you know, just skip through." Cited in Armstrong, *Evelyn Underhill*, 104.

63. Program of the Church Congress of October 19–20, 1920, LDP, BL, 6. Lily Dougall spoke on "Spirituality: The Things of Sense and Spiritual Communion"; Evelyn Underhill spoke on "The Mystic Experience." Interestingly, Underhill was also moving to a less individualist understanding of spirituality; she finally joined the Anglican Church in 1921.

64. L. Dougall, "The Spirit in the Church," *The Interpreter* 19, 1 (October 1915) in BL, LDP, 6; [Lily Dougall] "The Spirit and the Life" *Present Day Papers* 11, 12 (December 1915): 370–78. Lily Dougall, "Thoughts Preliminary to a Restatement of the Doctrine of the Holy Spirit," unpublished manuscript, 24 pp., BL, LDP, 2. The book she edited with Streeter was the culmination of this work on the Spirit: *The Spirit: God and his Relation to Man Considered From the Standpoint of Philosophy, Psychology and Art,* ed. Burnett Hillman Streeter (1919; 2nd ed., London: Macmillan, 1920).

65. W. R. Inge, *Personal Idealism and Mysticism: The Paddock Lectures for 1906 delivered at the General Seminary, New York* (London: Longmans, 1907), 114.

66. Hastings Rashdall and his wife came to Cutts End for tea in 1912 and the titles of Dougall's subsequent work, as well as their content, indicate his influence upon her thought. For example, in her article, "Conscience and Authority," *The Modern Churchman* 6 (1916–1917): 303–19, Dougall relied heavily upon the arguments made by Rashdall in *Conscience and Christ* (London: Duckworth, 1916).

67. For W. R. Inge's credit to Rashdall, see *Christian Mysticism*, preface. His subsequent alarm is apparent in Inge, *Personal Idealism and Mysticism* (London: Longmans and Green, 1907): "Oxford has produced a band of 'Personal Idealists' some of whom proclaim the virtues of pragmatism and subjectivism with an almost blatant persistency and assurance" (p. 120). He is, as he notes later in *Vale*, referring to the authors of *Personal Idealism, Philosophical Essays by Eight Members of the University of Oxford,* ed. Henry Sturt (London: Macmillan, 1902) including Rashdall.

Percy Gardner's review of Rashdall's contribution to the liberal manifesto *Contentio Veritatus* (London: J. Murray, 1902)—published by Dougall in *World Wide*—reveals the collegial attitude. Gardner praised the book but noted: "Certainly St. Paul makes that appeal [to reason] but the founder of

Christianity does not make his appeal to reason, at all events not to the philosophic faculty of man. He appeals to the conscience, to feeling, experience. . . ." Percy Gardner, "Contentio Veritatus," reprinted from the *Hibbert Journal* in *World Wide* 3, no. 6 (February 7, 1903): 91. Gardner identified Inge as a personal idealist for his contribution to *Contentio Veritatus* and accused Inge and Rashdall of creating a "new orthodoxy." Gardner, "Contentio Veritatus," *World Wide*, 92.

68. Inge, *Vale.*

69. The strength of Rashdall's disavowal of mysticism and the emphasis placed on explaining this by his biographers, P. E. Matheson and the philosopher C. C. J. Webb, suggest that his was a minority position among modernists. Matheson concludes his biography with a defense of Rashdall's personal faith, arguing: "Suspicious as he was of anything which could be called mysticism he had in reality, along with a strong conviction of the necessity of a rational faith, two qualities which are characteristic of a mystic—a profound belief in the presence of God in the world and a humility of spirit which enabled him to lose himself in worship and prayer and contemplation of the life of Christ. . . ." Matheson, *The Life of Hastings Rashdall* (Oxford: Oxford University Press, 1928), 255. Webb contributed a chapter on Rashdall's philosophy and theology to this biography, a chapter that circles around his rejection of mysticism. The division between the mystics and personal idealists is one that warrants further study.

70. Hastings Rashdall to Professor Gardner, The Deanery, Carlisle, July 17, 1923. Cited in Matheson, *The Life of Hastings Rashdall*, 227. See also 241–44, 251.

71. [Dougall], *Absente Reo*, 274.

72. [Dougall], *Voluntas Dei*, 51, 92, xiii, xiv.

73. In "Conscience and Authority," Dougall described two definitions of conscience: Rashdall's ethical concept and Inge's emphasis upon "the actual touch with living God." She argued for a more explicit mysticism: "If on the other hand conscience is in any real sense 'the voice of God within the individual soul,' we need to make such doctrine comprehensive and welcome by a more liberal doctrine of the Holy Ghost, an explicit conception of the indwelling of God as being as universal to humanity as the moral consciousness is universal." Lily Dougall, "Conscience and Authority," manuscript, p. 4, BL, LDP, 2. The article was published in 1916/17 in *The Modern Churchman.*

74. "Dr. and Mrs. Rashdall, Longwall St., Oxford, To tea, Tuesday, November 5, [1912]"; "Professor Royce, Harvard, Mr. and Mrs. Illingworth, Longworth, To tea, Saturday Feb 1st, [1913]." "Mr. and Mrs. Illingworth and Mrs. and Miss Crum.[?] To tea, Thurs April 3, [1913]" Visitor Book, BL, LDP, 1. The visit of the Illingworths and Royce was memorable enough for Earp to comment on it in her "Selected Letters." She suggests they met for the first time at Cutts End: "One of our earliest visitors was Professor Royce, of Harvard, who was lecturing in Oxford in the Lent Term of 1913, and who here met Mr. Illingworth, the author of *Personality Human and Divine*, at whose house in the neighbouring village of Longworth the group met who had lately written *Foundations*" (p. 234).

75. See A. S. Peake to Lily Dougall, May 12, 1913, Gairloch, Freshfield, nr. Liverpool, BL, LDP, 1. He says he does not mind her consulting with Illingworth for her contributions to the Free Church Commission.

76. Lily Dougall to W. F. Lofthouse, June 15, 1914, Cumnor Oxford. BL, LDP.

8. FELLOWSHIP

1. A large new wing was added to the small cottage, creating bedrooms for several guests, as well as servants, and large rooms to facilitate discussions. One small downstairs room was labeled "business" on the plans, and the drawing room and parlor were connected to create a forty-two-foot space suitable for entertaining large groups of people. A central component of Dougall's plans from the start was a spacious upstairs room with large windows. Local tradition says that the room was designed for prayer meetings and retreats. See Louise Armstrong, "A House Designed by Clough Williams Ellis in Cumnor, Oxfordshire, 1911–1912," A Paper for the Certificate in Historic Conservation, September 1992. Unpublished paper.

It appears Dougall could house four guests: when she invited the Anglican Fellowship to meet in Cumnor, minutes read, "Miss Dougall . . . can put up 4 members at her house and rooms can be got near by for others, and we can meet and have meals at the house." Anglican Fellowship Minutes of the Committee which met at Annandale, Golders Green, on April 10, 1916, BL, LDP, 8. Dougall's will and an obituary in the family review suggest that she subsequently purchased other nearby houses to accommodate guests. *World Wide*, October 13, 1923, p. 1.

2. Anonymous [Canon E. W. Barnes], "A Woman Modernist: Lily Dougall," *Times* (London) October 13, 1923, p. 14.

3. [Dougall, Lily], *Immortality, An Essay in Discovery Co-ordinating Scientific, Psychical, and Biblical Research*, ed. B. H. Streeter (London: Macmillan, 1917), 367.

4. C. A. Anderson Scott, "What Happened at Pentecost," in *The Spirit, God and His Relation to Man Considered from the Standpoint of Philosophy, Psychology and Art* (London: Macmillan, 1919), 142, 153. See chapter 9 for Dougall's attempt to rename the Guild of Health "The Fellowship of Faith and Health."

5. Scott, "Pentecost," 146.

6. See F. D. Maurice, *The Kingdom of Christ, or Hints to a Quaker, respecting the principles, constitution and ordinances of the Catholic Church*, 2nd ed., vol. 2, (London: Rivington, 1842), 416–20, for his discussion of Christian fellowship: "there is a fellowship larger, more irrespective of outward distinctions, more democratical, than any which you can create; but it is a fellowship of mutual love, not mutual selfishness, in which the chief of all is the servant of all. . . .' "

7. B. H. Streeter had been central to the "Doubts and Difficulties" conference, and it may be through her relationship with him that she became involved with the SCM.

8. Tissington Tatlow, *The Story of the Student Christian Movement of Great Britain and Ireland* (London: SCM Press, 1933), 435–36.

9. See Tatlow, *The Student Christian Movement*. Tissington Tatlow was a key figure in the early SCM, the General Secretary of the Student Volunteer Missionary Union from 1898–1900 and 1903–1929, and the editor of *The Student Movement* from 1900–1902 and 1904–1933. D. S. Cairns, an SCM leader and friend of Lily Dougall, wrote: "[Drummond's] ideal and spirit are working through the country in the Student Christian Movement. This has been reinforced by other streams, but the movement, as a whole, is exactly the kind of thing he would have delighted in and rejoiced to serve." D. S. Cairns, "Recollections of Henry Drummond" *The North American Student* (November 1913). Cited in Tatlow, *Student Christian Movement*, 14–15.

For Drummond, see Cuthbert Lennox, *Henry Drummond, A Biographical Sketch with Bibliography* (Toronto: William Briggs, 1901); George Adam Smith, *The Life of Henry Drummond* (Toronto: Revell Co., 1899), and Henry Drummond, *The Ideal Life: Addresses Hitherto Unpublished with Memorial Sketches by Ian McLaren and W. Robertson Nicoll* (Toronto: William Briggs, n.d.). For his liberalism, see D. S. Cairns, *David Cairns, An Autobiography* (London: SCM Press, 1950), 112–16. For his influence in Canada, see Brian Fraser, *The Social Uplifters: Presbyterian Progressives and the Social Gospel in Canada, 1875–1915* (Waterloo: Wilfrid Laurier University Press, 1988) and Barry Mack, who suggests that Drummond's liberal evangelicalism is so unorthodox as to be unworthy of the label, in "From Preaching to Propaganda to Marginalization: The Lost Centre of Twentieth Century Presbyterianism," in *Aspects of the Canadian Evangelical Experience,* ed. George A. Rawlyk (Montreal and Kingston: McGill–Queen's University Press, 1997), 137–53.

10. Saunders described his preaching in her diaries for 1876: "Almost beyond description even the girls who are not professors of religion were quite charmed with it." Diary of Margaret Saunders dated December 3, 1876, Acadia University Archives, Wolfville, Nova Scotia. Margaret Marshall Saunders Papers 1, Number 2. See also her autobiographical *Esther de Warren: The Story of a Mid-Victorian Maiden* (New York: George H. Doran, 1927), 109, and the sketch in *The Junior Book of Authors,* ed. Stanley Kunitz and Howard Haycraft (New York: H. W. Wilson, 1934): "Henry Drummond was our clergyman, and we fairly worshipped him." I am indebted to Paul MacKenzie for these citations.

11. Henry Drummond, *Natural Law in the Spiritual World* (New York: James Pott and Co., 1884), and *The Lowell Lectures on the Ascent of Man* (1894; New York: James Potter, 1895). Dougall paraphrased the central theme of the later book: "And what of man rising through the ages from beast to sainthood, rising from the mere dominion of physical law which works out its own obedience into the moral region, where a perpetual choice is ordained of God, and the consequences of each choice ordained." Dougall, *The Zeit-Geist,* 151.

12. Like Drummond, Toyner has a magnetic personality and a slight dapper appearance. Dougall, *The Zeit-Geist,* 12, 17, 47.

13. Tatlow, *Student Christian Movement,* 387.

14. Tatlow, *Student Christian Movement,* 386.

15. Tatlow, *Student Christian Movement,* 387. Steve Bruce, *A House Divided: Protestantism, Schism and Secularization* (London and New York: Routledge, 1990). Others have described the shift in more positive terms. Kenneth Hylson-Smith referred to the "growing together of the Anglo-Catholic with the SCM thread in Anglican life." Kenneth Hylson-Smith, *High-Churchmanship in the Church of England from the Sixteenth Century to the Late Twentieth Century* (Edinburgh: T. & T. Clark, 1993), 268.

16. Arthur Mayhew, "The Student Christian Movement Camp 1912," *The Modern Churchman* 2, no. 6 (September 1912): 271–75. See *The Modern Churchman* 12, no. 7 for the SCM advertisement; Dougall's book, *The Lord of Thought,* is at the top of the list, and was reviewed in this issue.

17. Tatlow, *Student Christian Movement,* 427–28. See also 620, and 213–14, where Tatlow distinguishes between the women's intellectual debates about Christianity at Oxford and Cambridge, compared to the spiritual and moral problems of the men. Men dominated the leadership, and, according to Tatlow, women took a subordinate position until 1909 when Zoë Fairfield became assistant to the general secretary. Tatlow, *Student Christian Movement,* 235–36.

18. See Donald L. Kirkey, " 'Building the City of God': The Founding of the Student Christian Movement in Canada," M.A. thesis, McMaster University, 1983, 46–50. Canadian artist Doris McCarthy described the combination of SCM spirituality with an intense female culture, a "fellowship with God and my friends" in *A Fool in Paradise: An Artist's Early Life* (Toronto: MacFarlane, Walter and Ross, 1990), especially 58, 147. Marjorie Agnes Powles described SCM involvement as "a liberating experience, both intellectually and socially" in *To a Strange Land: The Autobiography of Marjorie Agnes Powles* (Dundas, Ont.: Artemis Enterprises, 1993), 28, 32.

19. D. S. Cairns visited on September 8, 1912. Visitor Book, BL, LDP, 1.

20. *The Student Movement,* June 14, 1914. Clippings Book, BL, LDP, 7. M. S. Earp to George Macmillan, Cutts End, Cumnor, 15, September 1913, MP, 217/131, Reading; M. S. Earp to George Macmillan, Cutts End, Cumnor, 26 August [1914?] MP, 217/131, Reading. Cited in Lorraine McMullen, unpublished manuscript.

21. Earp, "Selected Letters," 255.

22. The tie to the SCM is clear: see Tatlow, *The Story of the Student Christian Movement,* 463–64, 729–30, 737; and Lily Dougall, "English Modernism," 13, manuscript in BL, LDP, 8. *The Anglican Fellowship Bulletin* described the SCM perspective as "a large part of the impulse which brought us into being." *The Anglican Fellowship Bulletin* 1 (December 1913): 10. Although it was still in existence in 1933, when Tatlow wrote his history of the SCM, he wrote that it had done little to recruit younger members. Tatlow, *Student Christian Movement,* 730. The organizing committee included a number of men who subsequently became Dougall's friends and associates: William Temple and Neville S. Talbot, Anglo-Catholic contributors to *Foundations,* and two men who later contributed to Dougall's group books, E. R. Bevan and A. C. Turner. Talbot is identified in Dougall's guest book at Cutts End, February 1, 1913. B. H. Streeter identified A. C. Turner as "the" founder of the Fellowship in his "Biographical Note," in Lily Dougall, *God's Way with Man: An Exploration of the Method of the Divine Working Suggested by the Facts of History and Science* (London: Student Christian Movement, 1924), 14.

23. There is no record of the Anglican Fellowship in the Church of England Record Centre or the National Register of Archives. Lambeth Palace Library has some records including a program and membership list of the 1913 Swanwick conference, but there is no reference to Dougall. The discussion here is based on the records in Dougall's papers, which consist of an incomplete run of the *Anglican Fellowship Bulletin* from 1913 to 1920, incomplete minutes from 1915 and 1916, and assorted printed documents and lists, as well as copies of the *Bulletin* from the Ripon College Library.

24. Carbon copy titled "The Anglican Fellowship," 4 pp., BL, LDP, 8.

25. *The Anglican Fellowship Bulletin* I (December 1913): 3.

26. The following members on the Anglican Fellowship List of Members, August 1914, are identified by Stephenson as modernists: Baron Barclay, editor of *The Challenge;* Rev. E. A. Burroughs, Oxford tutor; L. W. Grensted, vice principal of Egerton Hall, a theological college; H. D. A. Major; Rev. C. H. S. Matthews; Rev. R. G. Parsons; Rev. C. E. Raven, a Cambridge Fellow; Rev. T. G. Rogers; A. M. Royden; Rev. H. R. L. Sheppard; Canon V. F. Storr, a writer on theology; B. H. Streeter; Rev. William Temple; A.C. Turner, and Rev. C. S. Woodward. A. M. G. Stephenson, *The Rise and Decline of English Modernism* (London: SPCK, 1984).

27. *The Anglican Fellowship Bulletin* III (December 1914): 14–15. "The Anglican Fellowship Notes, March, 1919," p. 2. BL, LDP, 8. Lily Dougall, "English Modernism," n.d., BL, LDP, 2. See also Mr. Raven's comments in *The Anglican Fellowship Bulletin* XIII (December 1920).

28. Dougall, "English Modernism," 11. By January 1916, broader membership criteria had been established, with the creation of a small groups and a circle of "group leaders." "Minutes of the Committee," January 12, 1916. BL, LDP, 8.

29. Lily Dougall, "English Modernism," *The Contemporary Review* (1923) 123: 477.

30. A member of the Free Church Fellowship (which had initially excluded women) commented on the equal cooperation of men and women at the 1916 Anglican Fellowship conference. *Anglican Fellowship Bulletin* VII (January 1917). See Brian Heeney, *The Women's Movement in the Church of England, 1850–1930* (New York and Toronto: Clarendon Press, 1988), for Mrs. Creighton's work. She was a member of the Fellowship at least until 1916, when her name appears on a list of those attending a retreat at Swanwick from May 9–13. BL, LDP, 8.

31. Members included three members of St. Hugh's College, Oxford: Ann (C. A. E.) Moberly, the head of the College 1886–1915, Miss C. M. Ady, History tutor, and Miss C. B. Firth, vice principal after 1923; two members of University of London: Miss E. M. Almond, assistant lecturer in Latin, and Miss F. R. Shields, assistant lecturer in Philosophy at Bedford College (University of London), and Mrs. Wilmot Brook, from the Ladies' Committee in connection with the Archbishop's Diploma in Theology (for women). A "Miss Toynbee" offered her home for Fellowship meetings in 1919 and 1920. It is likely, given St. Hugh's involvement in the Fellowship, that this was the Jocelyn Toynbee, a tutor in Classics at St. Hugh's College, Oxford. A "Miss Toynbee" visited Dougall March 19–25, 1917, when Dougall was in the middle of her year on the Fellowship Committee. Mrs. H. L. Paget, a 1914 A.F. member, was also linked to St. Hugh's, as the wife of the Bishop of Stepney, who as Bishop of Oxford was on the Council as the Visitor of St. Hugh's from 1901 to 1910, and through her sister-in-law, Catherine.

There were also several men with progressive views on women's education, such as B. H. Streeter, Percy Dearmer, and Rev. E. A. Burroughs, a tutor at Oxford who was a Member of Council of Lady Margaret Hall, Oxford. The Anglican Fellowship List of Members, June 1914. BL, LDP, 8.

32. *Anglican Fellowship Bulletin* VI (July 1916).

33. Miss B. M. Legge filled one of the positions; the other was left open. *The Anglican Fellowship Bulletin* I (December 1913): 38.

34. Anglican Fellowship, Minutes of Committee that met at Annandale, Golders Green on March 20, 1916. (Miss Fairfield [Chair], Miss Dougall, Miss Talbot, Miss E. M. Barton, A. C. Turner, and Miss Knowles.) BL, LDP, 8.

35. "The Facts of the Modern Situation," *The Anglican Fellowship Bulletin* 1 (December 1913): 10–11.

36. Heeney, *The Women's Movement.* See the discussion of "The Church and the Woman's Movement," in *The Anglican Fellowship Bulletin* I (December 1913): 18–19. The report is vague and avoids taking any position, beyond saying that the Church should "face the situation." In comparison, the preceding discussion of "The Church and Labour" is pragmatic and conclusive.

37. The first *Bulletin* proposed limiting membership. Rules were subsequently relaxed, although debate continued through to 1915. See *The Anglican Fellowship Bulletins* for December 1913, 1914, and 1915. For the creation of local groups, see "The Anglican Fellowship, Nature and Function," [1919?] BL, LDP, 8, and "The Anglican Fellowship Notes, March 1919."

38. *The Anglican Fellowship Bulletin* I (December 1913): 4. A number of commissions were established: Christian Ethics; The Presentation of Christianity; the Recruiting and Training of Clergy; the Gospel of Christ and the Church; Religious Unity; The Position of Lay Men and Women; A Missionary Commission, and the pre-existing commission, The Church and the Workpeople. The first commission, on Christian ethics, was subdivided into 1. The relations between the sexes; 2. Christianity and Property; 3. Christianity and War. Membership included Maude Royden, Zoë Fairfield, William Temple, and C. H. S. Matthews.

39. *The Anglican Fellowship Bulletin* I (December 1913): 6.

40. *The Anglican Fellowship Bulletin* III (December 1914): 6, 9.

41. See *The Anglican Fellowship Bulletin* I (December 1913): 4 and Dougall, *God's Way with Man,* ed. B. H. Streeter (London: SCM, 1924), 120. I am indebted to Michael Brierley for these references in his unpublished paper: "Lily Dougall's Doctrine of God."

42. M. S. Earp does not describe Dougall's role in the Fellowship in her "Selected Letters." This may simply reflect the fact that she had left the later years of Dougall's life up to B. H. Streeter. The presence of copies of the *Anglican Fellowship Bulletin* among her papers to 1920 suggests that she continued to take an interest in the organization at least until this date. The last one, *The Anglican Bulletin* XIII (December 1920) includes Dougall's *Practice of Christianity* on a short list of twelve recommended works.

43. "One of the results of these Fellowships is certainly that the tie becomes almost as close as that of kindred, because the outlook of the Group becomes so homogeneous." Lily Dougall to John Dougall, June 20 [1916 or 1917—Earp is unsure of the date]. Earp, "Selected Letters," 250.

44. *Anglican Fellowship Bulletin* III (December 1914): 7.

45. Dougall's connections with St. Hugh's may have played a role. Eleanor Jourdain, a French tutor of St. Hugh's (and the principal after January 1915) was her guest on Thursday, March 13, 1913. (Visitor Book, BL, LDP, 1). Subsequently, Miss Toynbee visited on March 19– 25, 1917 and Miss Firth was a visitor on December 16–18, 1917. B. H. Streeter, who was working with her on *Concerning Prayer,* may also have brought Dougall into the AF.

46. The additional women were C. B. Firth, Nan Knowles (who subsequently married Percy Dearmer) and L. C. Talbot. The committee was also included H. K. Archdall, E. R. Bevan, E. C. Dewick, Geoffrey Gordon, J. Hanaghan, H. F. Houlder, J. L. Johnston, and J. H. Kidd.

47. F. A. Iremonger cited in the *Dictionary of National Biography,* Supp. 1951–1960, 856. For background on Royden, see Sheila Fletcher, *Maude Royden* (London: Basil Blackwell, 1989); for insight into her personal life, see Maude Royden, *A Three Fold Cord* (London: Victor Gollancz, 1947); for general background on women in the Anglican Church, including Royden, see Heeney, *The Women's Movement in the Church of England.* Royden spoke at the 1922 Modern Churchman's Association conference and is included in the list of modernists in Stephenson's *English Modernism,* 211, 269.

48. Among Dougall's papers is an autographed copy of Royden's pamphlet, *Women and the Church of England* (London: George Allen Unwin, n.d.).

49. Fairfield was a graduate of Slade School of Art and worked as the secretary of the Guild of Helpers of the YWCA, from 1907 to 1909, as the assistant general secretary of the SCM from 1909–1929, and the general secretary of the Auxiliary Movement from 1929. In his history of the SCM, Tatlow repeatedly paid tribute to her intellectual and leadership abilities: "[On her appointment as assistant, people] thought of Miss Fairfield at first as someone who was going to help to bear the burden of day-to-day business in the office, and she certainly bore this burden year after year, but soon people realized that a first-class mind was being brought to bear upon the problems of the Movement." Tatlow, *Student Christian Movement*, 337. *Some Aspects of the Woman's Movement*, ed. Zoë Fairfield (London: SCM, 1915). Fairfield had supported Royden when she preached at City Temple. Fletcher, *Maude Royden*, 154.

50. *Anglican Fellowship Bulletin* IV (August 1915): 27.

51. Lily Dougall to E. W. Barnes [Early October 1915] Cumnor. Earp, "Selected Letters," 247.

52. Harold Anson, *Looking Forward* (London: William Heinemann Ltd., 1938), 201. A. C. Turner signed Dougall's guest book from September 23–27, 1915, January 17–20, 1916. BL, LDP, 1.

53. "Anglican Fellowship Minutes of the Committee," October 15, 1915, January 12, March 20, and April 10, 1916, *The Anglican Fellowship Bulletin* VI (July 1916). There is no record of a Fellowship meeting in May of 1916 in Dougall's Visitor Book. BL, LDP, 1.

54. *The Anglican Fellowship Bulletin* XI (December 1919).

55. *The Anglican Fellowship Bulletin* III (December 1914): 13.

56. L. Dougall, "The Spirit in the Church," *The Interpreter* 19 (1922): 32–39.

57. Dougall, "Thoughts Preliminary," 6. Spirituality is "that which results from the operation of the Spirit of God upon man's higher nature." The Holy Spirit is "God Himself in His present and unceasing relation to the souls of men" (pp. 7, 13).

58. Lily Dougall, "Thoughts Preliminary" 14. BL, LDP, 2.

59. Lily Dougall, "The Spirit in the Church," *The Interpreter* 19–20 (1922–1924): 36.

60. *The Anglican Fellowship Bulletin* VIII (July 1917).

61. *The Anglican Fellowship Bulletin* VIII (July 1917).

62. Dougall, "English Modernism." Review cited by B. H. Streeter in *In Memorium Lily Dougall, A Sermon preached at Cumnor Church on Sunday Evening*, October 21, 1923. BL, LDP, 1. See also the reference in *The Modern Churchman* XI,1 (April 1921): 1. "The student world finds its theology in the writings of men often quite out of touch with Catholic Christianity and in all cases definitely opposed to the position taken up (say) by the Anglo-Catholic Congress. Books like Grove's *Jesus of History*, Fosdick's *Manhood of the Master*, Gray's *Christian Adventurer*, and on the more definitely theological side, the works of the Cumnor School and of the Dean of Carlisle [Hastings Rashdall] are being very widely read—more so than any other religious writing of the time. . . . [The student] is simply asking that the Christian experience of the ages be given to him in a form and in a language he can understand."

63. Earp says they met on January 22, 1915. "Mr. Streeter (Queen's) came up at 4.30. Stayed till 10. A very long talk on the proposed book on

Prayer." Earp, "Selected Letters," 251. Streeter, however, says they first met in November 1914, in "Biographical Note," in *God's Way with Man,* 16.

64. Streeter, "Biographical Note," in *God's Way with Man,* 16.

65. Canon E. W. Barnes also credits Dougall with organizing the conferences: "She best deserves to be remembered, however, for the skill and sympathy with which she gathered in her house at Cumnor, near Oxford, groups of men and women interested in religious problems. These gatherings had a charm peculiar to themselves, because of Miss Dougall's personal charm and religious insight." Anonymous [Canon E. W. Barnes] "A Woman Modernist: Lily Dougall," *Times* (London), October 13, 1923, p. 14.

66. Earp, "Selected Letters," 237, 251. According to Earp, *Concerning Prayer* was Dougall's idea (p. 251). Dougall herself described Streeter as "the chairman" of the group. Lily Dougall to E. W. Barnes [early October 1915] (p. 247).

67. Anson, "Lily Dougall," 200.

68. Earp, "Selected Letters," 264. Anson, *Looking Forward,* 201.

69. The British Library lists Streeter as the principal author or editor. In fact, Streeter is identified as editor only in *The Spirit;* in the other books all the authors, including Dougall, are listed as coauthors, and no one editor is identified. When Dougall contributed a chapter to *The Interpreter* for early publication, she is identified as a coeditor. (See *The Interpreter* 13, no. 4 (1916–1917), p. 128.) Streeter wrote the introductions to *Immortality* and *The Spirit,* though the fact that he wrote them both at Cutts End suggests Dougall was involved. (To each of Streeter's introductions is appended a date, October 1, 1917, and September 9, 1919, and a place, Cutts End, Cumnor.) Dougall wrote the introduction to *Concerning Prayer.*

70. Personal section entitled "Minutes of Committee," October 15, 1915. Personal correspondence from Dr. Dorothy Emmet, Emeritus Professor of Philosophy, University of Manchestor, April 25, 1993, and June 7, 1993. Emmet said that while Dougall fostered the intellectual debate, and made contributions, these were "not very tightly thought—in a way she let her zeal for a liberal loving view of Christianity, take control of her critical judgment. Which is not to say she was not an able writer . . . a sympathetic populariser rather than first-rate thinker."

71. Anson, *Looking Forward,* 201.

72. We can trace some of the meetings for *Concerning Prayer* through Dougall's correspondence and Visitor Book. Various contributors had stayed individually with Dougall prior to the conference on the book. Harold Anson and B. H. Streeter were regular visitors, both having stayed with Dougall in early March. Collingwood and Anson stayed several nights in late July, and Turner stayed for four days in September, when he was writing his contribution. In early October, various contributors met at Cutts End with other progressive Anglicans to discuss the book. Harold Anson, Maude Royden, and a Miss Campbell appear in Dougall's visitor book. Other contributors, like Streeter and Collingwood may have cycled up from Oxford for the day. Dougall sent Rufus Jones a copy of her manuscript in late October, presumably for his comments. (Lily Dougall, "Spirit and Life," BL, LDP, 2. The manuscript is marked, "Duplication sent to Dr. Rufus Jones, October 28, 1915.") Then in January 1916, Turner, Campbell, and Streeter stayed several days for an unspecified "conference." M. S. Earp participated in the conferences and also assisted with the editorial work. As a number of the entries in the Visitor Book

are made in the same hand—possibly Earp's—and probably after the event, it is not an entirely reliable record of the visits to Cutts End. There appear to be a number of omissions. Visitor Book, BL, LDP, 1. Campbell is probably the May Campbell who stayed in 1916, and the Miss M. E. Campbell acknowledged in *Immortality* for the compilation of the index; she may have played a similar role in *Concerning Prayer*. See also Lily Dougall to E. W. Barnes [Early October 1915] in Earp, "Selected Letters," 247. She describes Turner's stay in September and mentions plans for a group meeting at her house from October 11–16, 1915.

73. *Immortality: An Essay in Discovery Co-ordinating Scientific, Psychical, and Biblical Research* (London: Macmillan, 1917), xi–xiii.

74. Clipping of a review of *Immortality* from *The Christian Commonwealth*, March 6, 1918, in BL, LDP, 6.

75. B. H. Streeter acknowledged the contributions of Barnes, Rev. W. S. Bradley, tutor of Mansfield College, Rev. C. H. S. Matthews, Vicar of St. Peter's, Captain W. H. Moberly, Fellow of Lincoln College, and Sophie Earp to *Immortality*. "Introduction," *Immortality*, xii. See the clipping of the review of *Immortality* from *Challenge* January 18, 1918, BL, LDP, 6.

76. Anson, "Lily Dougall (1858–1923)," 201.

77. Lily Dougall, "What is English Modernism?" *Contemporary Review* (1923) 123: 477.

78. See J. R. Illingworth, *The Life and Work of John Richardson Illingworth, as portrayed by his letters and illustrated by photographs* (London: John Murray, 1917), 156 for this method. See also 33–35 for the origins of this group, and the centrality of personal idealism.

79. See W. F. Lofthouse to Lily Dougall, Endcliffe Cottage, Friary Rd, Handsworth, June 13, 1914; Lily Dougall to Mr. Lofthouse, June 15, 1914, BL, LDP, 1. Another unsigned letter suggests the religious gulf that Dougall was crossing in working with men like Lofthouse. Unknown to Lily Dougall, Links Hotel, April 16, 1914. "I think Mrs. Lofthouse was at Swanwick last month, how is she? Did she not come to our Guild of Health talk in Room 3? I do not remember her. Perhaps we shall cease to be 'fatally churchy' soon, and then all the good, nice people who will be such a strength will come in to help us." Lofthouse visited Cutts End with his wife in early 1914; alone for lunch on April 16, 1914; July 27, 1914, and July 27 to August 3, 1914. Visitor Book, BL, LDP, 1.

80. Clipping of the review of *Immortality* from *Challenge*, January 18, 1918, BL, LDP, 6.

81. *Anglican Liberalism*, by Twelve Churchmen (New York: G. P. Putnams, London: Williams and Norgate, 1908).

82. Hodgson's new membership is noted in the Anglican Fellowship Minutes of the Committee, April 10, 1916. BL, LDP, 8.

83. Harold Anson, *Looking Forward* (London: William Heinemann, 1938).

84. Collingwood read an early version of his essay before Streeter's Eranos Group in 1908, and it was later reprinted. See R. G. Collingwood, *An Autobiography* (London: Oxford University Press, 1939), 43, and James Patrick, *The Magdalen Metaphysicals, Idealism and Orthodoxy at Oxford, 1901–1945* (Macon, Ga.: Mercer University Press, 1985), 87–89.

85. H. D. A. Major, *The Modern Churchman* VI (1916–1917): 223–25.

86. Harold Anson said the book was still selling in 1938 when he wrote his memoirs. Anson, *Looking Forward*, 201.

87. Lily Dougall to K. D., J. A. C. and E. B., October 1, 1917, Cutts End, Cumnor. Earp, "Selected Letters," 260. The Visitor Book records a number of visits likely associated with *Immortality:* Mr. and Mrs. Clutton-Brock, August 8–10, 1916; E. W. Barnes and his wife, October 9–12; R. C. Emmet from October 9–13; B. H. Streeter, November 4–6 and 11–13; May [Mary?] Campbell, November 21–22; B. H. Streeter, November 25–27; Mr. and Mrs. J.H. Oldham, December 12–19; Miss C. B. Firth (from the Fellowship), December 16–18, with Miss Graveson; Clutton-Brock, C. H. Matthews, W. R. Bradley, C. W. Emmet, W. H. Moberley, and B. H. Streeter from Monday, January 15, to Friday, January 19, 1917. (There are no records from May 1917 to 1925.)

88. The publisher noted that sales had been good—2,000 of 3,000 copies having been sold—although "reviews have, with some exceptions, not been very satisfactory." George Macmillan to Lily Dougall, March 11, 1918, BL, LDP, 5.

89. B. H. Streeter, "Introduction," in *The Spirit*, xii.

90. Randall Canterbury [The Archbishop of Canterbury] to Miss Dougall, Old Palace, Canterbury [no date], BL, LDP, 1: "I have already in the interstices of some overcrowded days read a good many bits of it and I see how valuable a contribution it has made to the sober consideration of many large questions. But it is not a book for 'interstices,' [He says he hopes to give it consecutive study.]"

91. J. A. Hadfield, "The Psychology of Power," *Immortality*, 115.

92. "This book is only a series of successive efforts to think what the gospel of Jesus really is. Each line of thought is unfinished, and there is very much in what is said that, in a mature work, would be more carefully guarded from misconstruction." The Author of *Pro Christo et Ecclesia* [Lily Dougall] *Christus Futurus* (London: Macmillan, 1907), n.p.

93. Handwritten note appended to a carbon copy of a manuscript, "Conscience and Authority," BL, LDP, 2.

94. Typescript, "The Purpose of the Church," 5 pp., BL, LDP, 2.

95. Typescript, "Creation," 7 pp., BL, LDP, 2.

96. Lily Dougall to Griffith Jones, January 6, 1914, 294 Drummond St., Montreal, BL, LDP, 1. Dougall apologized to Dr. Ridgeway, the Bishop of Salisbury: "I am fully aware [*The Christian Doctrine of Health*] has many weaknesses, but it was written in response to a real demand, and had to be produced amid a conflict of duties." Lily Dougall to the Bishop of Salisbury, November 1916, Cumnor, Oxford. Earp, "Selected Letters," 256–57.

97. See, for example, her references to a friend who is archbishop and to an unnamed "distinguished continental theologian" in her article, "The Meaning of Paul for Today," BL, LDP, 2.

9. Body and Soul

1. Lily Dougall to Susan Dougall, October 23, 1887, Cheltenham, England. Earp, "Selected Letters," 77.

2. See pp. 23–24 and pp. 34–40 for a discussion of these illnesses.

3. Susan Dougall to John and Elizabeth Dougall, Dansville, June 8, 1879, LAC, DFP, 1, 1.

4. Elizabeth (Lizzie) Dougall to John Dougall, April 12 [probably 1882], LAC, DFP, 1, 1.

5. William E. Boerdman, *Faithwork under Dr. Cullis, in Boston* (Boston: Willard Tract Company, 1874). Charles Cullis, *More Faith Cures* (Boston: Willard Tract Depository, 1881); Charles Cullis, *Other Faith Cures; or, Answers to Prayers in the Healing of the Sick* (Boston: Willard Tract Depositary, 1885), Carrie Judd, *The Prayer of Faith* (Boston: Willard Tract Depository, 1880).

6. James Opp, *The Lord for the Body* (Montreal and Kingston: McGill-Queens Press, 2005), 29.

7. Lily Dougall to John Dougall [her father], June 15, 1885 [year penciled on original], 36 Beresford Rd., Highbury New Park, London, BL, LDP, 1.

8. The logic of the holiness healing movement led to some disturbing conclusions: as Elizabeth Dougall was aware, her chronic ill health could be interpreted as a sign of her imperfect faith.

9. See Opp, *The Lord for the Body*, for a history of faith healing in Canada.

10. Andrew Murray, *Divine Healing* (New York: Christian Alliance, 1900). For other examples, see David D. Bundy, *Keswick: a Bibliographic Introduction to the Higher Life Movements* (Wilmore, Ky: Asbury Theological Seminary, 1975), 63.

11. As she wrote in the autobiographical novel, "Lovereen": "No one pressed her to study for they thought she was not strong enough for regular school work. They saw her idle and were satisfied that she was having the consideration which her health required, while all the time there went on within her a mental travail to which the enforced work of lessons would have been rest and play." "Lovereen," p. 95, BL, LDP, 4. "I have been missing a good many of my lectures, and I am a good deal discouraged about it. I battled against a cold as long as I could, but had to give in. It is nearly gone now, and the pain in my side, which I believe I mentioned, also." Lily Dougall to Susan Dougall, February 12, 1881. Earp, "Selected Letters," 41. "I do hope that the climate here will strengthen her," Jane Redpath to Elizabeth Dougall, Saturday, November 13, 1880, 130 Gilmore Place, LAC, DFP, 1, 9.

12. Susan later qualified as a doctor in Edinburgh, Quebec, and New York, but after a few years' practice turned instead to evangelical "rescue work." "Dr. S. G. Dougall Dead: Devoted Life to Philanthropic and Evangelical Work," *Montreal Gazette*, Monday December 7, 1914, and "Tribute to Deceased," in the *Montreal Weekly Witness*, December 15, 1914. A diploma from the Woman's Medical College, stating that she has been entered in the Register of Physicians and Surgeons by the Clerk of New York County, is dated 1889. LAC, DFP, 2, 3.

13. Lily Dougall to Susan Dougall, Weltham House, Suffolk Road, Cheltenham, October 23, 1887. Earp, "Selected Letters," 76–78.

14. See Heather D. Curtis's discussion of S. A. Hanscombe in "Faith Healing, Christian Science and Kindred Phenomona": Women and Healing in Late-Nineteenth-Century Boston Symposium on Religious Healing in Boston: First Findings, Harvard Divinity School, 8 May 2001. Hanscombe's healing narrative is in Charles Cullis, *Other Faith Cures or Answers to Prayer in the Healing of the Sick* (Boston: Willard Tract Depository, 1885), 51–59.

15. "Evangelicalism had the power to transform into gruesome spectres all the beautiful things of God's creation." Lily Dougall, "Lovereen," p. 102, BL, LDP, 4.

16. "I'll never face the melting of the snow again in Montreal if I can help it," Lily Dougall to Sophie Earp, Washington [April 1898]. Earp, "Selected Letters," 153. She spent the following spring with Earp in England.

17. Earp, "Selected Letters," 191, 192.

18. Harold Anson, "Lily Dougall: 1858–1923," in R. S. Forman, ed. *Great Christians* (London: Ivor, Nicolson and Watson, 1933), 193–207.

19. [Lily Dougall], "The Salvation of the Body by Faith," *Hibbert Journal* 4, 3 (1906): 606–23. The article was later published in [Lily Dougall] *Christus Futurus* (London: Macmillan, 1907). See also a series of apparently unpublished manuscripts by Dougall in BL, LDP, 2: "Body and Soul"(written after 1914); "The Church and Christian Science"; "The Relation of the Church to Faith Healing" (labeled as a "memorandum submitted [possibly to the Guild of Health] by Miss Dougall, the author of *Pro Christo et Ecclesia*") and "Wanted: A Wholesome Faith," 19 pp. (written after 1918).

20. John R. Illingworth to MCL, May 16, 1906. Cited in J. R. Illingworth, *The Life and Work of John Richardson Illingworth, as Portrayed by His Letters and Illustrated by Photographs* (London: John Murray, 1917), 245. See also J. R. Illingworth to M. S., December 28, 1909 (p. 253).

21. "The Problem of Pain," in *Lux Mundi: A Series of Studies in the Religion of the Incarnation.* Gore, Charles, ed. (London: John Murray, 1889).

22. J. R. Illingworth, *Divine Immanence: An Essay on the Spiritual Significance of Matter* (London: Macmillan, 1898), 97, 98.

23. [Dougall], *Christus Futurus,* xiii.

24. [Dougall], *Christus Futurus,* 268.

25. Lily Dougall to Dougall family, May 21, 1908, BL, LDP, 1. She was reporting on the speech of the first woman president of the SPR, Mrs. Sidgwick.

26. Paul Dubois, *The Psychic Treatment of Nervous Disorders (The Psychoneuroses and their Moral Treatment),* trans. and ed. Smith Ely Jelliffe and William A. White, 7th ed. (1905; New York: Funk and Wagnalls, 1909). Dubois argued that he had moved beyond hypnosis and suggestion to a form of persuasion or affirmation in "rational psychotherapeutics" (p. ix). Dougall does not explore these subtleties, but uses his work to affirm the power of the mind over the body.

27. [Dougall], *Christus Futurus,* 222.

28. Dresser, *New Thought,* 309.

29. See Beryl Satter, *Each Mind a Kingdom: American Women, Sexual Purity, and the New Thought Movement, 1875–1920.* Berkeley: University of California Press, 1999.

30. Lily Dougall to Dougall family, London, May 15, May 16, 1908, LDP, BL, 1.

31. Lily Dougall to Dougall family, May 15, May 16, 1908, BL, LDP, 1. Although she includes these letters in her biography of Lily Dougall ("Selected Letters," 211). Sophie Earp neglects to describe the extent of Dougall's interest, perhaps because of the directions taken by mental science by the time of Dougall's death.

32. Lily Dougall to John Dougall, May 16, 1908, BL, LDP, 1.

33. Lily Dougall to John Dougall, May 19, 1908, BL, LDP, 1.

34. Lily Dougall to "My own dearest people," May 19, 1908, BL, LDP, 1.

35. Lily Dougall to Dougall family, May 15, 1908 BL, LDP, 1.

36. Lily Dougall to Dougall family, London, May 21, 1908. BL, LDP, 1.

37. Lily Dougall to Dougall family, London, May 21, 1908, BL, LDP, 1. She later referred to the mental science movement as the "New American School of Psychology." Lily Dougall, "The Spirit in the Church," *The Interpreter* 19–20 (1922–1924): 38–39.

38. Lily Dougall to Dougall family, 181 Cromwell St., South Kensington, May 22, 1908, p. 7, BL, LDP, 1.

39. Lily Dougall to Dougall family, May 16, 1905. Earp, "Selected Letters," 214.

40. Lily Dougall, "The Church and Christian Science," Unpublished [?] manuscript. BL, LDP, 2. For a similar assessment, see Gaius Glenn Atkins, *Modern Religious Cults and Movements* (New York: Fleming H. Revell, 1923), 8.

41. Lily Dougall to Dougall family, May 22, 1908, BL, LDP, 1.

42. [Dougall], *Absente Reo,* 181, 184–86.

43. Douglas W. Frank has analyzed the many similarities between the Mind Cure movements and the twentieth-century permutations of higher life in the Victorious Life Movement. Douglas W. Frank, *Less Than Conquerors: How Evangelicalism Entered the Twentieth Century* (Grand Rapids, Mich.: Eerdmans, 1986).

44. [Dougall], *Absente Reo,* 185–86.

45. Earp, "Selected Letters," 255. For a critique of Christian Science, see Dougall's paper, "The Church and Christian Science," typescript, no date, BL, LDP, 2, where she argues that the strength of Christian Science is "due to neglect by the church of one part of the Apostolic Commission."

46. Lily Dougall, "The Spirit in the Church," *The Interpreter* 19–20 (1922–1924): 38–39. "[T]he truth underlying the claims of its votaries is that in hypnoidal states—by practice easily induced—certain powers of the human mind are discovered which, so far, have never been thoroughly explored or utilized."

47. [Dougall], *Immortality,* 369.

48. Lily Dougall, "Conscience and Authority," manuscript, p. 4, BL, LDP, 2.

49. Lily Dougall, *God's Way with Man, An Exploration of the Method of the Divine Working suggested by the Facts of History and Science,* with an introduction and biographical note by Canon B. H. Streeter (London: Student Christian Movement Press, 1924), 55.

50. Dougall, *God's Way,* 56.

51. Cited without attribution, probably from personal correspondence, in Dearmer, *Percy Dearmer,* 187.

52. Details on the early organization are included in the "Letter to the Members of the Guild of Health," printed sheet, June 11, 1918, BL, LDP, 5. A short history is published by the Guild of Health: Geoffrey C. Harding, "The First 75 Years of the Guild of Health" (London: The Guild of Health, 1983). Dearmer's involvement is described in Nan Dearmer, *The Life of Percy Dearmer* (Oxford: Alden Press, 1941). Details differ. The letter describes Lombard as the leader, but Nan Dearmer identifies Percy Dearmer as chairman, Lombard as honorary secretary, and Noel as a third member of the organizing committee (p. 187). Percy Dearmer (1867–1936) was a Christian socialist and modernist. Dougall was critical of his early theology for neglecting evil, in "Our Conception of God," *The Interpreter* 11, no. 4 (July 1915): 396–407. Harold Anson was a Christian Socialist, editor of *The Commonwealth,* and active in other progressive church movements, like the Anglican Fellowship. See Harold Anson, *Looking Forward* (London: William Heinemann Ltd., 1938).

53. LD to [?], July 5, 1913, Melbourne Derbyshire. Earp, "Selected Letters," 234. (See also p. 251.) It is possible that Dougall was a member of the early guild; however, Earp makes no mention of any affiliation before 1913.

54. Participants included Miss Reed, Miss Hewit, Mme. Maseryk, Mrs. Alexander Whyte, Dr. David Cairns, Rev. Harold Anson, Rev. Maurice Richmond, and Dr. Ash. Dr. Ash is no doubt the Dr. Edwin Ash, formerly of St. Mary's Hospital, London, and author of *Mental Self Help* and *Dorothy Kernin,* whose assistance is acknowledged in a note in the ensuing handbook, Lily Dougall's *Christian Doctrine of Health.* Entries in Dougall's Visitor Book describe one visit, Monday, March 19 to Friday, March 25, with Miss Sturger, Mrs. Barclay, B. H. S. [Streeter], Miss Toynbee, Dr. Gillett, Dr. MacDougall, and a second visit July 28–August 4, with Mrs. Whyte, Miss Hill [?] Harrison, Mrs. Hewitt, Miss Reid, Miss Haley, Miss Pattison, Olga Maseryk, Dr. Ash and Dr. Cairns.

55. Lily Dougall, *The Christian Doctrine of Health, A Handbook on the Relation of Bodily to Spiritual and Moral Health* (London: Macmillan, 1916; 3d ed. rev. London: Guild of Health, 1921). Citations are from the 1916 edition. She also wrote the Guild's first pamphlet, "The Functions of the Guild of Health," as well as promotional articles for liberal journals, such as Lily Dougall, "Christianity and Psychic Healing," *The Modern Churchman* 9 (1919–1920): 360–68. In his article, Harold Anson called upon religious teachers to cooperate with psychologists and psychotherapists in their researches "without forgetting that religion should aim at something more fundamental than providing a contented and healthy mind." Anson, "Prayer and Bodily Health," in *Concerning Prayer* (London: Macmillan, 1916), 332.

56. Mary Baker Eddy had launched Christian Science officially in Britain when she sent the first lecturer in 1897, and in 1908, the Lambeth conference discussed spiritual healing at the request of American bishops who wanted to coordinate their response to Christian Science. J. M. Hickson founded the Society of Emmanuel, an evangelical healing group, in 1905, one year after the Guild. See Stuart Mews, "The Revival of Spiritual Healing in the Church of England, 1920–1926," in *The Church and Healing,* ed. W. J. Shiels (Oxford: Basil Blackwell, 1982), 311. The phrase *miracle-mongering,* was coined by modernist W. R. Inge. Mews, "Spiritual Healing," 304, 311. The origin of the Guild of St. Raphael is less clear. Mews says that it was started by disaffected High Church members of the Anglican Guild of Health *after* that Guild became ecumenical. Mews, "Spiritual Healing," 311. A printed letter among Dougall's papers, advocating ecumenicism, and referring to the existence of the Guild of St. Raphael, suggests that this organization already existed, although its membership may have been increased subsequently by disaffected members (see note 63). Geoffrey C. Harding also says that the Guild of St. Raphael was started, earlier, in 1915, three years before the Guild became ecumenical, by a group of High Churchmen who felt that the Guild did not represent Catholic values.

In 1922, John Maillard, who had taken over the work of J. M. Hickson in the Spiritual Healing Fellowship, suggested that the Guild unite with his organization and the Guild of St. Raphael. The Guild of St. Raphael refused. For Anson's description of the differences between the Guild of Health and the other movements, see *Looking Forward,* 177.

See Mullin, "Religion and Healing," for a sensitive discussion of the theological differences between the healing movements in the Protestant Episcopal Church of the United States. Closest theologically to the Anglican Guild of Health was the American Emmanuel Movement led by Elwood Worcester and the Oxford-educated cleric, Samuel McComb. McComb contributed to the

British debate through his article, "Christianity as Healing Power," *Hibbert Journal* 8 (1909): 10–27. Mullin says that the Emmanuel Movement was succeeded by the American Guild of Health, presumably an offshoot of the British Guild of Health. Mullin, "Religion and Healing," 220–21. Ann Taves's description of Samuel McComb's Emmanuel Movement reveals many parallels with Dougall's understanding of healing, including the reliance upon Dubois. Ann Taves, *Fits, Trances and Visions: Experiencing Religion and Explaining Experience from Wesley to James* (Princeton, N.J.: Princeton University Press, 1999), chapter 8. It is not clear whether the Guild of Health endorsed the Anglican ritual of anointing with oil. Stuart Mews says that Harold Anson and the Guild used oil, and Robert Mullin says that Dearmer did. Dougall, however, explained at length in a letter why the Guild did not endorse it. Mews, "The Revival of Spiritual Healing," 324. Robert Bruce Mullin, "The Debate over Religion and Healing in the Episcopal Church: 1870–1930," *Anglican Episcopal History*, 60, 2 (1991): 228. Lily Dougall to the Bishop of Salisbury, Dr. Ridgeway, November 1916. Earp, "Selected Letters," 256–59.

57. Lily Dougall to Katie Drummond, The Church House, Melbourne, Derby, January 7, 1912. Earp, "Selected Letters," 226. For Underhill and Von Hugel, see Harding, "The Guild of Health," unpaginated.

58. Earp, "Selected Letters," 255.

59. Lily Dougall to John R. Dougall, Cumnor, Oxford, July 27, 1915. Cited in Earp, "Selected Letters," 243.

60. Dr. Gore to Lily Dougall, January 16, 1917, Cuddesdon, Wheatley. Earp, "Selected Letters," 258.

61. See also two apparently unpublished articles in BL, LDP, 2: Lily Dougall, "Wanted: A Wholesome Faith," 19 pp., in which Dougall suggests that the church was losing its more progressive members by neglecting bodily healing, and "The Relation of the Church to Faith Healing, a memorandum submitted by Miss Dougall, author of *Pro Christo et Ecclesia.*"

62. [Dougall], *Christus Futurus*, xiv.

63. Lily Dougall, *Paths of the Righteous* (London: Macmillan, 1908).

64. Harold Anson gives Dougall credit for the change. Anson, *Looking Forward*, 206, and "Lily Dougall (1858–1923)," 203. A printed letter among Dougall's papers presents the arguments for becoming ecumenical: it says that Nonconformists would welcome the Guild, and argues that the work needs broadening, but the Anglican clergy are too busy, and inclined to turn to Guild of St. Raphael "which can afford a centre for all who wish to work on a strictly church basis." In a toughly worded conclusion, the letter warns of the potential loss of progressive members if the Guild did not change. This proposal was implemented. (As Dougall put it, the Guild "once merely Anglican, [is] now nondenominational." Lily Dougall, "Wanted: A Wholesome Faith," 19-page manuscript, BL, LDP, 2.) But an additional suggestion in this letter, that the name be changed to the Fellowship of Faith and Health to avoid confusion with Guild of Help, was not acted upon.

65. Sophie Earp to W. H. Murray, July 12, 1923, BL, LDP, 6. Earp's comments were made as part of an argument for a new British edition of *The Christian Doctrine of Health*: "The Guild paid for an edition which had been printed and sold it out very quickly and at good profit. The Guild is not a publishing house it prints privately and is managed by a large committee with frequent reversals of policy. It decided to organise Study Circles everywhere

hence the breaking up of my book into pamphlet form. It then gave up the plan of study circles and thus had no interest in publishing the pamphlet. It has no capital and finds the outlay for larger book difficult. It is quite possible that there is not further demand for this or any book of its kind in England. I have no means of knowing that. But certainly there is no proof in what has occurred that the book will not sell."

66. See Mews, "Spiritual Healing," for a discussion of the operations of the committee and its findings. For a good contemporary discussion of the issues, see, the Bishop of Durham, "Spiritual Healing," *Hibbert Journal* 24 (1925): 385–401, and the response by Harold Anson, "Spiritual Healing— What is it? A Reply to the Bishop of Durham," *Hibbert Journal* 24 (1925): 101–11.

67. For the efforts by the Guild of Health to circulate the book, including the distribution of free copies to all overseas Anglican bishops and to study circles, see Lily Dougall to George Macmillan, 11 October 1916, Macmillan Papers, 213/253, University of Reading.

68. [Dougall], *Christian Doctrine of Health*, 54, n.1; 74, n.1, 92. Psychologists include Edwin L. Ash, Hudson, author of *The Law of Mental Medicine*, and Bernard Hart, author of *The Psychology of Insanity*. Jane Walker (1859–1938) was a specialist in tuberculosis, and was one of the members of the Guild who met at Dougall's home.

69. [Dougall], *Christian Doctrine of Health*, 142.

70. [Dougall], *Christian Doctrine of Health*, 173. See also p. 142. She reiterated these ideas in a promotional article for *The Modern Churchman* in 1919: "The faith that God is the God of health, that the indwelling Spirit can, and will, enhance the bodily and mental powers in response to faith, makes all work easier, makes all leisure more delightful." The article was intended to recruit members. She describes the Guild as a society "endeavouring to form study circles for the devout consideration of this whole subject," and calls upon readers to join, or at least apply the teachings to their lives. Lily Dougall, "Christianity and Psychic Healing," *The Modern Churchman* 9 (1919–1920): 360–68.

71. Dougall, *Christian Doctrine of Health*, 120.

72. LD to Bishop of Salisbury, November 1916, Cumnor, Oxford. Earp, "Selected Letters," 256–57.

73. George Macmillan to Lily Dougall, February 10, 1917, and February 11, 1918, BL, LDP, 6.

74. W. H. Murray, Religious Books Dept., Macmillan Publishing, New York to Lily Dougall, July 11, 1923; and Sophie Earp to W. H. Murray, July 12, 1923, BL, LDP, 6. He refers to plans to publish a revised American edition. She had evidently pressed for a revised British edition as well. Percy Dearmer, *Body and Soul, An Enquiry into the Effects of Religion on Health with a Description of Christian Works of Healing from the New Testament to the Present Day* (London: Sir Isaac Pitman and Sons, 1909; New York: E. P. Dutton and Co., 1923). Harold Anson, *Spiritual Healing: A Discussion of the Religious Element in Physical Health* (London: University Press, 1923). Percy Dearmer also contributed several pamphlets: "Christian Science and Spiritual Healing," "The Inner Health Movement," and "The Thorn in the Flesh."

75. The Guild continued to operate in 2005 from St. Paul's Church Centre, 3 Rossmore Road, London.

10. ANGLICAN MODERNISM

1. J. R. Illingworth to "MCL," April 1907. Cited in *The Life and Work of John Richardson Illingworth, as portrayed by his letters and illustrated by photographs* (London: John Murray, 1917), 246.

2. Prayer written by Ronald Knox. Cited in Alan M. G. Stephenson, *The Rise and Decline of English Modernism, The Hulsean Lectures 1979–80* (London: SPCK, 1984), 3–4. Knox appears to have been a satirical thorn in the modernist side; see earlier references to his critical work on Thomas Upham, *Enthusiasm: A Chapter in the History of Religion with Special Reference to the XVII and XVIII Centuries* (Oxford: Clarendon Press, 1950), and his condemnation of B. H. Streeter's edited volume, *Some Loose Stones, Being a consideration of certain tendencies in modern theology illustrated by reference to a book called "Foundations"* (London: Longmans, Green, 1914).

3. Alan M. G. Stephenson, *The Rise and Decline of English Modernism, The Hulsean Lectures 1979–80* (London: SPCK, 1984). W. R. Hutchison's *The Modernist Impulse in American Protestantism* (Cambridge, Mass.: 1976) is a history of the American Protestant variant of the movement. Several biographical articles are useful: Norman W. Pittenger, "James Matthew Thompson: The Martyr of English Modernism," *Anglican Theological Review* 39, no. 4 (1957): 291–96; "The Christian Apologetic of James Franklin Bethune-Baker," *Anglican Theological Review* 37, no. 4 (1955): 260–77; "Modernism," *Theology* 67, no. 535 (1965): 53–60; 55–56, and Paul Avis, "Charles Gore and Modernism: A Half-Centenary Exercise in 'Corporate Believing,'" *Theology* 85, no. 703 (1982): 269–77.

For recent work see: Michael W. Brierley, "Ripon Hall, Henry Major and the Shaping of English Liberal Theology," in *Ambassadors of Christ: Commemorating 150 Years of Theological Education in Cuddesdon, 1854–2004*, edited by M. D. Chapman (Aldershot: Ashgate, 2004); Paul Badham, *The Contemporary Challenge of Modernist Theology* (Cardiff: University of Wales Press, 1998); Adrian Hastings, "On Modernism: Centenary Lecture, given at Lambeth Palace 10 November, 1998," *Modern Believing* 40, no. 2 (1999); C. R. Pearson, "H. D. A. Major and English Modernism, 1911–1948." Ph.D. thesis, University of Cambridge, 1989.

Memoirs and autobiographies also provide some insight into the movement and the period: W. R. Inge, *Vale* (London: Longmans, 1934); W. R. Inge, *Diary of a Dean, St Paul's 1911–1934* (London: Hutchison and Co., 1949); Herbert Hensley Henson, *Retrospective of an Unimportant Life*, vol. 1, 1863–1920 (Oxford: Oxford University Press, 1942); P. E. Matheson, *The Life of Hastings Rashdall* (Oxford: Oxford University Press, 1928); Nan Dearmer, *The Life of Percy Dearmer* (Oxford: The Religious Book Club/Alden Press, 1941); Harold Anson, *Looking Forward* (London: William Heinemann Ltd., 1938), and Maude Royden, *A Three Fold Cord* (London: Victor Gollancz, 1947).

Contemporary accounts of the movement also provide a perspective, if usually a partial one: H. D. A. Major, "The Biographical Record of the Modern Churchman's Movement, 1898–1957," *The Modern Churchman* 46, no. 3 (March 1956); H. D. A. Major, *English Modernism: Its Origin, Methods, Aims*, (Cambridge, Mass.: n.p., 1927); J. F. Bethune-Baker, *The Way of Modernism and Other Essays* (Cambridge: Cambridge University Press, 1927); Alfred Fawkes, *Studies in Modernism* (London: Smith. Elder and Co., 1913); Percy Gardner, *Modernism in the English Church* (London: Methuen, 1926); R. Gladstone Griffiths, *The Necessity of Modernism,* Modernist Series (London, Skeffington and Son, Ltd., n.d. [post 1932]); R. D. Richardson, *The Gospel of Modernism,* Modernist Series (London: Skeffington and Son, Ltd, n.d. [1933?]); Leonard J. Dunne, *The Heart of Modernism or the Morals of a Modernist. A Startling Disclosure of the Truth Concerning the Modern Churchman's Union* (1936); Edmund McClure, *Modernism and Traditional Christianity,* 2nd ed. rev. (London: SPCK, 1914); C. H. S. Matthews, ed., *Faith and Freedom. Being Constructive Essays in the Application of Modern Principles to the Doctrine of the Church* (London: Macmillan, 1918; contributors included Alfred Fawkes, W. Scott Palmer, Charles E. Raven, A. Clutton-Brock, and Harold Anson); W. Pryke, *Modernism as a Working Faith* (Cambridge: W. Heffer and Sons, 1925); H. P. V. Nunn, *What is Modernism* (London: SPCK, 1932); Herbert Leslie Stewart, *Modernism: Past and Present* (London: John Murray, 1932), and T. Wigley, *The Necessity of Christian Modernism,* with a fore-word by H. D. A. Major (London: James Clarke and Co., [1939]). Lily Dougall's account of the movement is also useful: Lily Dougall, "English Modernism," *Contemporary Review* 123 (1923): 472–79.

For the American movement, see Leighton Parks, *What is Modernism?* (New York, London: Charles Scribner Sons, 1924); Shailer Mathews, *The Faith of Modernism* (New York: Macmillan, 1925); Frank Hugh Foster, *The Modern Movement in American Theology: Sketches in the History of American Protestant Thought from the Civil War to the World War* (1939; reprint, Freeport, New York: Books for Libraries Press, 1969), and E. Clowes Chorley, *Men and Movements in the Episcopal Church* (New York: Scribner, 1946).

4. Temple's authorized biographer, F. A. Iremonger, said that "from B. H. Streeter, with whom he was in closer spiritual contact than with any other member of the University, Temple acquired most of his views on New Testament criticism." Scott Holland, he said, taught Temple to see his faith as a whole, so that the truth of certain parts might carry the others. F. A. Iremonger, *William Temple, Archbishop of Canterbury, His Life and Letters* (London: Oxford University Press, 1948), 126. See also Joseph Fletcher, *William Temple: Twentieth Century Christian* (New York: Seabury Press, 1963).

5. "[Temple] could explain neither Christian or European history if he did not firmly believe that our Lord was in visible tangible personal contact with the Disciples as Teacher and Guide after His Death and Resurrection, and he regards the evidence in favour of what you and I believe true as being in his judgment far stronger than the difficulties which beset it. I believe him *in all essential particulars* an orthodox believer in the Virgin Birth of Our Blessed Lord and His Resurrection." Randall Davidson to Francis Paget, March 22, 1908. Cited in Iremonger, *William Temple,* 116. The precarious nature of Temple's orthodoxy is suggested in the bishop's request that Temple be ordained by the archbishop.

6. William Temple to R. A. Knox, October 29, 1913. Cited in Iremonger, *William Temple,* 163.

7. Cited in Chorley, *Episcopal Church,* 284–85.

8. Dougall included an article on Loisy's *L'évangile et l'église* in *World Wide* III,15 (April 11, 1903): 247–48, and two on Loisy himself: "The Abbé Loisy," (no author cited) *World Wide* 2, no. 8 (February 21, 1903): 122; "M. Loisey and His Work," A.L. Lilley, *World Wide,* IV (December 17, 1904): 95.

9. For membership numbers see Pearson, p. 79. For Ripon Hall, see Brierley, "Ripon Hall." Stephenson cites membership at 281 in 1901, 484 in

1908. *English Modernism*, 65, 75. *The Modern Churchman* reported concern at low membership in 1911, although it was noted that 1,000 copies of the journal circulated. *The Modern Churchman*, 1, 5 (August 1911): 283.

10. Stephenson, *English Modernism*, 7. Adrian Hastings points out that the term "modern" identified the movement well before it was formally assumed in 1928. He suggests the delay was caused by the Anglican fear of associating too closely the Roman Catholic modernists. Hastings, 5, 9.

11. Dougall's Visitor Book documents a series of visits from key modernists: Kirsopp Lake visited with his family, see Visitor Book on July 30, 1912, and August 17, 1912. Dr. and Mrs. Rashdall came to tea on Tuesday, November 5, 1912. Other modernist guests include Dr. Skrine, September 8, 1912, Harold Anson, (repeatedly), B. H. Streeter, R. J. Collingwood, and Mr. and Mrs. Clutton-Brock, who stayed for two days in 1916. The Student Christian Movement Secretary visited on September 8, 1912 with Dr. Skrine. Eleanor Jourdain, the vice principal, and shortly after, the principal of the women's college, St. Hugh's College, came to lunch on March 13, 1913. Visitor Book, BL, LDP, 1. For a description of Streeter's group and brief reference to Dougall, see James Patrick, *The Magdalen Metaphysicals, Idealism and Orthodoxy in Oxford, 1901–1945* (Macon, Ga.: Mercer University Press, 1985), xxvi.

12. Major, "Biographical Record," 207. The conference venues were: 1914, The Spa Hotel, Ripon; 1915, The Laurels Girls School, Rugby; 1916, Lady Margaret Hall, Oxford; 1917, Girton College, Cambridge; 1918, Girton College, Cambridge; 1919, London; 1920, Somerville College, Oxford; 1921, Girton College, Cambridge; 1922, Somerville College, Oxford; 1923, Girton College, Cambridge; 1924, Somerville College and St. Hugh's College, Oxford; 1925, Somerville College and St. Hugh's College, Oxford; 1926, Girton College, Cambridge; 1927, Selly Oak, Birmingham; 1928, Girton College, Cambridge; 1929, Girton College, Cambridge; 1930, Somerville College and St. Hugh's College, Oxford. They continued to be held largely in women's colleges in the 1930s and 1940.

13. He recalled in 1956 that the women's section had been responsible for venue, "domestic and social arrangements," and finances: "what our conferences owe to the self-sacrificing competency of our women's section year after year cannot be over-estimated." Major, "The Biographical Record," 28.

14. Major's bibliography includes three of Dougall's religious works, *Pro Christo et Ecclesia, The Lord of Thought,* and *Christus Futurus.*

15. Dougall, "Conscience and Authority," *The Modern Churchman* V, no. 7/8 (1916), 318–19. Her argument reveals her new friendship with A. Clutton-Brock, whose recently published book, *The Ultimate Belief* (London: Constable, 1916), had dwelt on the triumvirate of truth, love and beauty, and Hastings Rashdall, whose latest book, *Conscience and Christ* (London: Duckworth: 1916), covered similar ground.

16. Her paper went unpublished, but a typescript among her papers, titled "Religious Experience in Maturity" and dated July 1918 is almost certainly a draft of her contribution.

17. *The Modern Churchman* 12, nos. 6 and 7 (October 1922). Other articles in *The Modern Churchman* included "The Lay Section of the Churchman's Union" (1917), "Christianity and Psychic Healing" (1919), "Spiritualism and Science"(1920), and "The Theology of Mr. Clutton-Brock" (1920).

18. Later he cited her, with Maude Royden and Alice Gardner, as defenders of the faith versus secularist materialists. H. D. A. Major, *English Modernism: Its Origin, Methods, Aims, Being the William Belden Noble Lectures delivered in Harvard University, 1925–6* (London: Oxford University Press; Cambridge, Mass.: Harvard University Press, 1927), 224.

19. Hutchison, *The Modernist Impulse*, 2, 6, 14. See also Steve Bruce's definitions of liberalism, "A Sociological Account of Liberal Protestantism," *Religious Studies* 20, 3 (September 1984): 401–15. "Liberalism is a tendency within Protestantism which recognizes as paramount human reason, and which accepts as primary the agenda of the secular world. It thus appears as a continual impulse to modernize the faith, to abandon the confines of the old creeds and to accommodate the thought and practice of the churches to that of the secular world" (p. 401). Edmund McClure, writing for the Society for the Propagation of Christian Knowledge in 1914, described modernism in terms of accommodation: "[Modernism] represents a far spreading attempt to accommodate Christianity to the assumed demands of modern science, philosophy and criticism." McClure, *Modernism*, 147.

20. Lily Dougall, "Lovereen," vol. 3, p. 75, BL, LDP, 4.

21. His description of their doctrinal position is closest of recent scholars to the modernists' own understanding: "the self-conscious acknowledgement of the historical tentativeness of all theological formulations; thus freeing modern theology from the grip of tradition." William McGuire King, "Liberalism," in *Encyclopedia of American Religious Experience,* ed. Charles H. Lippy (New York: Scribner, 1988), 1139.

22. In *Christus Futurus,* for example, Dougall compared the canonical scriptures to old garments: "If the Christian Church, by upholding the authority of all the canonical Scriptures, has determinedly put a new patch on an old garment, the ever-increasing rent cannot be charged to Jesus." [Lily Dougall], *Christus Futurus* (London: Macmillan, 1907), 138. For other uses of this metaphor, see 183, 307, 343–45.

23. Lily Dougall, "Lovereen," vol. 1, chapter 1, p. 5, BL, LDP, 4. Edwin Abbott, *The Kernel and the Husk: Letters on Spiritual Christianity* (London: Macmillan, 1886).

24. L. M. Montgomery, *The Selected Journals of L. M. Montgomery, 1889–1910,* vol. 1, edited by Mary Rubio and Elizabeth Waterston (Toronto: Oxford University Press, 1885), 197.

25. Stephenson, *English Modernism,* 59.

26. Sermon delivered October 6, 1899, St. Peter's Parish Room, Bayswater. Described by Philip Henry Bagenall in H. D. A. Major, "The Biographical Record." See also Stephenson, *English Modernism,* 61.

27. F. M. Szasz makes a similar observation of American liberalism: "[Harold] Bolce noted that the crucial issues of the time [1909] rested not on the conflict between science and religion but on vital faith versus antiquated creeds." Ferenc Morton Szasz, *The Divided Mind of Protestant America* (Tuscaloosa: University of Alabama Press, 1982).

28. For the comparison with the Reformation, see Hastings Rashdall's review of *The New Theology* in *Hibbert Journal* 7, no. 4 (1909): 922. See also Michael Glazebrook's paper for the first Conference of the Churchman's Union, in 1914, "The Second Reformation."

29. Badham, 3.

30. Richardson, *Modernism*, 11.

31. Cited in Chorley, *Episcopal Church*, 294. For an account of some of the debates, see Keith W. Clements, *Lovers of Discord: Twentieth-Century Theological Controversies in England*. London: SPCK, 1988.

32. Brierley, "Ripon Hall," 115.

33. E. W. Barnes, Foreword, in Richardson, *Modernism*, 17.

34. See Pittenger, "Modernism," 53–60. American theologian Newman Smythe, who was deeply affected by Catholic modernism, was an exception (p. 59). For a further discussion of the distinctions between a Catholic modernism and Protestant liberalism, see H. D. A. Major, *English Modernism*; Stephenson, *Modernism*, especially 150–54, and Norman W. Pittenger, "The Christian Apologetic of James Franklin Bethune-Baker." Protestant modernism also had an incarnational element: W. R. Hutchison, in his definitive study of modernism, describes the central theme of New Theology as God's presence in the world and in human culture. W. R. Hutchison, *The Modernist Impulse in American Protestantism* (Cambridge, Mass: Harvard University Press, 1976).

35. Hastings, 11. In her 1922 paper, "English Modernism," Lily Dougall described two groups, the early Broad Churchmen and a younger generation, "many of whom belonged to what was called 'the High Church party.'" Dougall, "English Modernism," 3, BL, LDP, 2. H.D.A. This was subsequently published in *Contemporary Review* 123 (1923): 472–79. Major described two wings, Liberal Protestant and Liberal Catholic, in the modernist movement, and argued that the Catholic was the stronger one. Major, "The Biographical Record of the Modern Churchman's Movement, 1898–1957," *The Modern Churchman* 46, no. 3 (March 1956), 198. (Hastings suggests that H. D. A. Major had "almost a fundamentalist streak" and steered the modernism closer to liberal Protestantism in later years. Hastings, 11.) Percy Gardner described both the liberal Protestantism influenced by Harnack and the French modernism coexisting in England. Gardner, *Modernism in the English Church* (London: Methuen, 1926), 12. As Walter Matthews, later a president of the MCU, recalled in *The Spectator* in 1937: "The Modernist movement in England is to a large extent, though not entirely, derived from two different and partly incompatible sources—Harnack and late nineteenth century thought on the one hand, and the Catholic modernists on the other."

36. Kirsopp Lake, *The Stewardship of Faith. Our Heritage from Early Christianity* (London: Christophers, 1915), 43f. Cited in Stephenson, *English Modernism*, 110.

37. Pearson argues that Girton was intended to distance the MCU from Lake and Foakes-Jackson. See Pearson, chapter 4.

38. *Hibbert Journal* (January 1922): 205.

39. Lily Dougall and Cyril W. Emmett, *The Lord of Thought. A Study of the Problems Which Confronted Lord Jesus and the Solution He Offered* (London: Student Christian Movement, 1922). The title dates back to Dougall's first religious book, *Pro Christo et Ecclesia*. When she identified the "Dramatis personae" (the book had been written as a drama) she identified Jesus as "The Lord of Thought." [Dougall], *Pro Christo et Ecclesia* (London: Macmillan, 1900), 4. Cyril William Emmet (1875–1923), was the vice principal of Ripon College and an active modernist vicar. Lily Dougall's respect and feeling for Emmet are apparent in a memoir published posthumously in *God's Way with Man*. Streeter suggested that Emmet's early death in 1923 hastened her own death three months later.

Streeter, "Biographical Note" in *God's Way,* 9. Emmet had written *Eschatological Question in the Gospels* (1911) and *Conscience, Critics and Creeds* (1918), as well as a number of commentaries and translations of biblical texts. He had contributed an article, "The Bible and Hell," to Dougall's group book *Immortality,* in which he argued that the doctrine of eternal punishment was not taught in the New Testament; and two articles, "The Psychology of Grace: How God Helps," and "The Psychology of Inspiration: How God Teaches," to her book on *The Spirit.*

40. For sales totals, see BL, LDP, 6. See the critical review of *The Lord of Thought,* "Eschatology Rearranged," by W. Maurice Pryke, in *The Modern Churchman* 12, no. 8 (1922–1923): 475–80. Emmet's brief response is in the following issue, p. 526.

41. See Claude J. Montefiore to Cyril Emmet, dated Feb 16, [probably 1923]. Letter in the possession of Dorothy Emmet. His criticism was well founded: Dougall credits Judaism with the "priceless contribution" of the highest existing idea of God, but then refers to "the Jewish thirst for retributive punishment for the unrighteous," and argues: "In Christendom all instances of persecution and exclusiveness would seem to be due to the acceptance of, and emphasis on, Jewish eschatology." Dougall, *Lord,* 210–12. Claude Montefiore was a student of Broad Church leader Benjamin Jowett, and his Hibbert Lectures, "The Origin and Development of the Religion of the Ancient Hebrews," published in 1892, had been influential on the development of English Modernism. Stephenson, *English Modernism,* 87.

42. Lily Dougall, "Orthodox Dualism," *The Modern Churchman,* XIII, 1 (1923–1924): 50–52.

43. Keith W. Clements, *Lovers of Discord,* 49.

44. J. M. Thompson, *Miracles in the New Testament,* 217. Cited in Stephenson, *English Modernism,* 89. See Pittenger, "James Matthew Thompson."

45. B. H. Streeter, ed., "The Historic Christ," *Foundations* (1912) (rpt., New York: Books for Libraries Press, 1971), 132–33. Streeter replaces the doctrine of the atonement and physical resurrection with the idea of the incarnation and continuing mystical presence of Christ: "Shortly after the appearances which convinced His disciples that He was still alive, there came upon them an immense influx of spiritual power. They had been men, they now were giants, and the secret of the change in them was not merely that they believed the Master *had* risen, but that He was *still and now* their constant though unseen companion" (p. 143; Emphasis in the original).

46. See R. B. Mullin's discussion of this debate in *Miracles and the Modern Religious Imagination* (New Haven, Conn.: Yale University Press, 1996), 162–64. See also William Sanday, *Bishop Gore's Challenge to Criticism* (London: Longmans, 1914), H. M. Gwatkin, *The Bishop of Oxford's Open Letter* (London: Longmans, 1914), J. F. Bethune Baker, *The Miracle of Christianity* (London: Longmans, 1914), B. H. Streeter, *A Plea for Liberty: A Letter to the Bishops in Reference to Dr. Gore's Pronouncement* (London: 1914), and Cyril W. Emmet, *Conscience, Creeds and Critics, A Plea for Liberty of Criticism within the Church of England* (London: Macmillan, 1918).

47. See Pearson, 79; Clements, 67.

48. See Pearson, 80–89.

49. Hastings Rashdall, *Doctrine and Development, University Sermons* (London: Methuen, 1898).

50. See C. C. J. Webb, "Hastings Rashdall," *Dictionary of National Biography,* 1921–1930 (Oxford: Oxford University Press, 1937).

51. [Dougall], *Christus Futurus* (London: Macmillan, 1907), 22.

52. [Dougall], *Voluntas Dei* (London: Macmillan, 1912), xvi. See also her equivocations on pp. 113, 116. On p. 105, she suggested that Christ's divinity came about only after his birth, when God recognized his spiritual powers.

53. [Dougall], *Voluntas Dei,* 200, 195.

54. [Dougall], *Voluntas Dei,* 203, 272.

55. Lily Dougall, "Orthodox Dualism," *The Modern Churchman* 13, no. 1 (1923–1924): 45–53, 53.

56. Dougall, *The Lord of Thought,* 3.

57. Dougall, *Lord of Thought,* 218.

58. Emphasis added. See also an earlier article in which she argues that Christ did not share the belief in corporeal resurrection. "The Quick and the Dead," *The Interpreter* 13, 4 (1916–1917): 133–34. A. M. Fairbairn, her mentor for *Pro Christo et Ecclesia,* had written an article defending the Resurrection, on the grounds of its historical influence and wide acceptance, rather than written evidence. A. M. Fairbairn, "Evidences of the Resurrection," *World Wide* (April 14, 1906): 392–93.

59. Lily Dougall speculated about a limited resurrection for the faithful in a letter to "a friend bereaved," n.d. Earp, "Selected Letters," 190. See also *Voluntas Dei,* 233.

60. Lily Dougall, "The Undiscovered Country," in *Immortality,* 361.

61. Lily Dougall, "What is English Modernism?" *Contemporary Review* (1923) 123: 477.

62. These ideas are also central to the Apostle's Creed, a creed Dougall would have recited on a regular basis in church services. Robert Bruce Mullin discusses the debate around the virgin birth in *Miracles,* 151–78.

63. Mary Augusta Ward, *Robert Elsmere,* vol. II (London: Smith and Elder, 1888), 291. He later tells his anguished wife, "Miracle is the natural product of human feeling and imagination; and God was in Jesus—pre-eminently, as He is in all great souls, but not otherwise in kind than He is in me or you."

64. Owen Chadwick, *The Secularization of the European Mind in the Nineteenth Century* (Cambridge: Cambridge University Press, 1975), 6. Chadwick's own knowledge of the intellectual history of the church forces him to acknowledge that it is possible for a Christian to deny the existence of miracles. For a similar argument by a Canadian historian, see David Marshall, *Secularizing the Faith, Canadian Protestant Clergy and the Crisis of Belief, 1850–1940* (Toronto: University of Toronto Press, 1992), 7, 21, 24.

65. A letter from James Dougall to his son in 1911 reveals his hostility: "The good Lord can preserve my health until he sees fit to appoint a successor. I am sure He would not wish to see the *Witness* and *Sabbath Reading* preaching the 'modern' gospel, which is no gospel." James Dougall to Frederick Dougall, July 12, 1911, LAC, DFP, 2, 12. He defined modernism in terms of unbelief in a literal Bible.

66. Phillips Brooks to Miss Meredith, September 1, 1888. Cited in Alexander V. G. Allen, *The Life and Letters of Phillips Brooks* (New York: E.P. Dutton and Co., 1901), 276–77.

67. Ward is described as a member of the Union in *The Modern Churchman,* 10, no. 1 (April 1920): 14, but she probably joined earlier. She was booked to speak to the Union on "Church Membership" in December of 1903 but was not

able to do so. Stephenson, *English Modernism*, 70. In her reminiscences, Ward wrote, "Like Mr. Jowett, [Matthew Arnold] would have liked to see the Church slowly reformed and 'modernized' from within. . . . And in the course of years—as I showed in a later novel written 24 years after *Robert Elsmere*—I feel have very much come to agree with him." Cited, from *The Cornhill*, in *The Modern Churchman* 8, no. 2 (May 1918): 52. Alfred Fawkes described the novel as the romance of Anglican liberalism. Fawkes, *Studies in Modernism*, 461. *The Modern Churchman* reported that the novel, "seems to represent correctly with few exceptions, the attitude and aspect of the liberal churchman." "The Case of Richard Meynell," *The Modern Churchman* 1, no. 12 (March 1912), 667.

68. James Livingston is one of the only historians to acknowledge this shift, which he dates to the 1890s. He argues that the new emphasis on the nobility of those who stayed within the church was due to a pragmatic concern about moral decline with reduced church attendance. James C. Livingston, *The Ethics of Belief, An Essay on The Victorian Religious Conscience* (Tallahassee, Fla.: American Academy of Religion, 1974).

69. L. M. Montgomery, *The Green Gables Letters, from L. M. Montgomery to Ephraim Weber, 1905–1909*, ed. Wilfred Eggleston (Ottawa: Borealis Press, 1981), 35.

70. L. M. Montgomery to Ephraim Weber, April 5, 1908. *Green Gables Letters*, 65–69.

71. [Lily Dougall], *Absente Reo* (London: Macmillan, 1910), 117. See also p. 161.

72. [Dougall], *The Practice of Christianity* (London: Macmillan, 1913), 42.

73. [Dougall], *The Practice of Christianity*, 282.

74. The later version is titled "Providence and Miracle"; the book was published posthumously by B. H. Streeter, and he may have substituted the more cautious title. Miss Dougall, "Miracle Inconsistent with Christianity," *Hibbert Journal* 9, no. 2 (January 1921): 296–307. Lily Dougall, *God's Way with Man. An Exploration of the Method of Divine Working suggested by the Facts of History and Science* with introduction and biographical noted by Canon B. H. Streeter (London: Student Christian Movement, 1924).

75. Dougall, *God's Way*, 43.

76. Dougall, *God's Way*, 28.

77. Dougall, *God's Way*, 33–34.

78. See Michael W. Brierley, "Lily Dougall's Doctrine of God: A Ph.D. Paper for Professor Gareth Jones" (unpublished), and "Naming a Quiet Revolution: The Panentheist Turn in Modern Theology," in *In Whom We Live and Move and Have Our Being: Panentheistic Reflections on God's Presence in a Scientific World*, edited by Philip Clayton and Arthur Peacocke (Grand Rapids, Mich.: William B. Eerdmans, 2004).

79. Dougall, *God's Way*, 33–34.

80. (Emphasis added.) Dougall, *God's Way*, 27.

81. Dougall, "Cyril William Emmet," *God's Way*, 121.

CONCLUSION

1. *World Wide*, October 13, 1923, p. 1.

2. Dougall left all of her Cumnor property and motor car to Earp with the proviso that she take the advice of B. H. Streeter or Dougall's nephew Frederick Eugene Dougall, in the bequeathing or giving of this property. She noted that

obtaining their permission was not legally binding, but that if any part of the property be sold that the proceeds go to her nephew and nieces who also received the remainder of her estate, after Earp was given 400 pounds per year from the estate, and Streeter was given a lump sum of 100 pounds. Her estate was calculated on February 6, 1924 to have a gross value of 3,248 pounds and a net value of her personal estate was 1,467 pounds. Last will and testament, Lily Dougall, Cutts End, May 24, 1923.

It appears from Earp's will that Dougall had intentions for Cutts End that were not expressed in her own will. Earp left the properties to B. H. Streeter and his wife, "in the hope but without creating any legal obligation so to do that they will deal with the same in accordance with what they know to have been the wishes of the late Miss Lily Dougall as expressed by her to them with reference thereto." Last Will and Testament, Mary Sophia Earp, Oxford, March 9, 1927.

A codicil to the will, dated Cumnor, June 25, 1928, alters it, by changing the bequest to her sisters to an allowance, and granting all income in excess of that sum "for the furtherance of the wishes of the late Miss Lily Dougall in regard to Cutts End which are referred to in the aforementioned will." If the property were to be sold before the death of her sisters she directs the executors (Streeter and her nephew) to apply their discretion having consideration to the needs of the Earp family and the Student Christian Movement. In her unpublished manuscript, Lorraine McMullen makes reference to an earlier will by Earp, Last Will and Testament, Mary Sophia Earp, Somerset House, London, March 1, 1927, which refers to a conference center.

Streeter's will makes no reference to Cutts End or Cumnor properties. Cutts End was occupied after 1932 by the writer Grace James. It is now divided into two properties and is privately owned.

3. B. H. Streeter, *God's Way With Man, An Exploration of the Method of Divine Working Suggested By the Facts of History and Science*, with an introduction and biographical note by Canon B. H. Streeter (London: Student Christian Movement, 1924). He and Earp attempted one more Cumnor group book, *Adventure: The Science of Faith and the Faith of Science* (London: Macmillan, 1928). The papers now held in the Bodleian Library in the Lily Dougall Collection had been in Streeter's possession.

4. Harold Anson, *Looking Forward* (London: William Heinemann Ltd., 1938), 202–203.

5. See Alan M. G. Stephenson, *The Rise and Decline of English Modernism*, The Hulsean Lectures 1979–80 (London: SPCK, 1984), 155–60. On miracles, Temple wrote: "On the question of whether or not events occur which are strictly miraculous, the Commission is divided; but the reluctance of some to admit miraculous events, or the strictly miraculous character of events admitted, is based on the supposition, not that God *could* not do such works, but that he *would* not." On the Virgin Birth, the report concluded: "There are, however, some among us who hold that a full belief in the historical Incarnation is more consistent with the supposition that Our Lord's birth took place under the normal conditions of human generation. In their minds the notion of a Virgin Birth tends to mar the completeness of the belief that in the Incarnation God revealed Himself at every point in and through human nature."

6. Essay I, "Providence and Miracle," incorporates a transcendent God. Yet her language is still that of the immanent God who works through nature, rather than miracle, and "should be universally invading the universe

everywhere, at all times, with the constant pressure of his inspiration." In "Forgiveness," "The Worship of Wrath," and "Beyond Justice," she preaches against punitive settlements against the Germans. Finally, an essay on Emmet provides an opportunity to reiterate a theology of religious experience. Dougall, *God's Way with Man.*

7. Dorothy Emmet recalled the theological shift among SCM members during her youth. Interview with Dorothy Emmet, October 6, 1993, Cambridge, England.

8. B. H. Streeter, "Introduction," in *God's Way With Man,* 7. "Miss Dougall had a rare faculty for seeing things religious from a point of view quiet different from that which strikes the ordinary mind. Critics said this made her do insufficient justice to accepted views. Perhaps it sometimes did. But for accepted views in religion there is never any lack of doughty advocates; the case for them runs no risk of going by default. Hence, if her essays are read, not as presenting 'the conclusion of the whole matter,' but as glimpses of truth seen by flashing insight of a free and original mind, Orthodox and Modernist alike will find in them valuable food for reflection."

9. Cited in *A Standard Dictionary of Canadian Biography,* vol. 1, Charles D.G. Roberts and Arthur L. Tunnell, ed. (Toronto: TransCanada Press, 1934), 157.

10. Prayer written by Ronald Knox. Cited in Stephenson, *English Modernism,* 3–4.

11. Lily Dougall, "What is English Modernism?" *Contemporary Review* (1923) 123: 472–79.

12. [Dougall], *Christus Futurus* (London: Macmillan, 1907), 57.

13. Bruce argues that liberalism was "parasitic" on evangelicalism: "I will argue that the appeal of liberalism was that of a release from a conservative strait-jacket, and that it was the years in the strait-jacket which gave liberalism its shape and delayed its collapse." *A House Divided: Protestantism, Schism and Secularization* (London and New York: Routledge, 1990), 110. This argument is based on his thesis: Steve Bruce, "The Student Christian Movement and the Inter-Varsity Fellowship: A Sociological Analysis of the Two Student Movements" (Ph.D. dissertation, Stirling University, 1980).

14. B. H. Streeter, *Reality, A New Correlation of Science and Religion* (London: Macmillan, 1927), 322.

15. Streeter, *Reality,* 322.

EPILOGUE

1. Lily Dougall, "Lovereen: A Canadian Novel," vol. 2, pp. 66–67, BL, LDP, 4.

2. Ann Taves, *Fits, Trances and Visions: Experiencing Religion and Explaining Experience from Wesley to James* (Princeton, N.J.: Princeton University Press, 1999).

3. Roger Lockhurst describes it as a professionalizing body. See Roger Luckhurst, *The Invention of Telepathy, 1870–1871* (Oxford: Oxford University Press, 2002), 52.

4. Janet Oppenheim, *The Other World, Spiritualism and Psychical Research in England, 1850–1914* (London: Cambridge University Press, 1985), 52.

5. Taves, *Fits, Trances and Visions.*

6. Lily Dougall, "The Life Beyond, The Relation of the Mortal to the Immortal Life," typescript, 16 pp., BL, LDP, 2, p. 10. Although this remark is not dated, it places her membership in the late 1890s at the earliest. Her meetings with Myers, described below, suggest she was a well-established member by 1895. Dougall's papers originally included broken sets of the Proceedings (1900–1923) and the Journal (1899–1919) of the Society of Psychical Research. The frequent inclusion of articles about SPR or by Oliver Lodge in *World Wide* also reflect Dougall's interest in the organization.

7. For an introduction to Myers's work, see Oppenheim, *The Other World;* F. M. Turner, *Between Science and Religion: The Reaction to Scientific Naturalism in Late Victorian England* (New Haven, Conn.: Yale University Press, 1974); Alan Gauld, *The Founders of Psychical Research* (New York: Schocken Books, 1968), and Roger Luckhurst, *The Invention of Telepathy, 1870–1901* (Oxford: Oxford University Press, 2002).

8. Letter quoted in Earp, "Selected Letters," 142. (No addressee, or date.) She visited Myers on April 18, 1895. Diary, BL, LDP, 1.

9. L. Dougall, *Mormon Prophet* (London: A. & C. Black, 1899), ix.

10. "Taking necessary liberty with incidents, I have endeavoured to present Smith's character as I found it in his own writings, in the narratives of contemporary writers, and in the memories of the older inhabitants of Kirtland." Dougall, *Prophet,* vi.

11. Lily Dougall to Sophie Earp, October 25, 1896, Montreal. Earp, "Selected Letters," 145.

12. Dougall, *Prophet,* 4.

13. Dougall, *Prophet,* 93.

14. Dougall, *Prophet,* vii.

15. Dougall, *Prophet,* 211.

16. Dougall, *Prophet,* 49.

17. Dougall, *Prophet,* 361.

18. "Of all the human beings she had ever met, this remarkable evangelist [Finney] most impressed her as a man who had intimate dealing, awful yet friendly, with an unseen power." Dougall, *Prophet,* 158. For Halsey's spirituality, see pp. 74, 133.

19. Dougall, *Prophet,* 169–71.

20. Dougall, *Prophet,* 391.

21. Dougall, *Prophet,* 406.

22. Lily Dougall to Sophie Earp, October 12, 1896, Montreal. Earp, "Selected Letters," 144. The difficulties were prolonged. She put the novel aside as she nursed her aunt until her death in August 1897. Dougall continued to struggle with depression and ill health, before revising the manuscript in June 1898, and finally publishing it in 1899.

23. L. Dougall to M. S. Earp, November 14, 1896, Cambridge, Mass. Earp, "Selected Letters," 147–48.

24. Taves, *Fits, Trances and Visions,* p. 290.

25. Susannah muses on "the history of her inward life" after her escape: "With what strong protest against the obvious evils attendant upon unreasoning faith had she resisted through many years the infectious influences of belief in an interfering spiritual world. Now she had defied Smith with a faith in the ideal marriage unsupported by any conscious reason, and when she had looked to the interference of Providence, not even in meekness, but in desperate

challenge, she had strong impression of being encompassed by invisible power and protection" (Dougall, *Prophet*, 406). Similarly, Susannah's cousin Ephraim was a scholar, yet even he found religion through a knowledge that was "past belief," but was also past rational argument: "he knew God with a knowledge that passed belief. He could argue no more, but he *knew*. This I think is the sort of knowledge which guides unerringly" (Dougall, *Prophet*, 267).

26. Henry Sidgwick to Sophie Earp. Earp, "Selected Letters," 165.

27. For a reference to James's *Will To Believe* (1897), see Louise Chandler Moulton to Lily Dougall, July 22 [no year], London, BL, LDP, 1.

28. Lily Dougall to Dougall family, May 21, 1908, BL, LDP, 1. She was reporting on the speech of the first woman president of the SPR, Mrs. Sidgwick.

29. Taves, *Fits, Trances and Visions*, p. 286.

30. See Luckhurst, *The Invention of Telepathy*; Gauld, *The Founders of Psychical Research*, and Oppenheim, *The Other World*, 253–64.

31. See Oppenheim, *The Other World*, especially p. 249, and R. Laurence Moore, *In Search of White Crows, Spiritualism, Parapsychology and American Culture* (New York: Oxford University Press, 1977), Chapter 5, for a discussion of the wide acceptance of telepathy. As Edward S. Reed has noted, historians of psychology rarely acknowledge the contributions of psychic phenomena and the occult to their science. Edward S. Reed, *From Soul to Mind, The Emergence of Psychology from Erasmus Darwin to William James* (New Haven: Yale University Press, 1997). See also Percy Gardner, *The Interpretation of Religious Experience* (London: Williams and Norgate, 1931), Chapter IX, "Thought Transference."

32. [Lily Dougall] "The Quick and the Dead, Part II," *The Interpreter* 14, 1 (1917–1918), 63. In 1908, she wrote: "Whatever be the truth of any theory of intelligible vibrations in the ether set agoing by the motion of thought in the brain, it is certain that one man's force of thought and feeling knocks at the door of another man's brain in many ways that are not perceptible to conscious sense." L. Dougall, *Paths of the Righteous* (London: Macmillan 1908), 429.

33. John Dougall to Elizabeth Dougall, n.d., DFP, LAC 1, 1.

34. Lily Dougall to J. A. C. [Janie Couper], December 16, 1883. Earp, *Selected Letters*, 57. Oppenheim says that Myers first coined the word telepathy in 1882 (Oppenheim, *The Other World*, 142) so it is possible, but unlikely, that Dougall knew of the theory. Although the SPR *Proceedings* had published from 1882, the first pioneering work on mental telepathy, *Phantasms of the Living*, by Myers, Edmund Gurney and Frank Podmore, was only published in 1886. Oppenheim, *The Other World*, 141.

35. F. W. H. Myers, "Science and a Future Life," in *Science and a Future Life, with Other Essays* (London: Macmillan, 1893), 40. Cited in Oppenheim, *The Other World*, 154. As Janet Oppenheim has observed, these ideas served an essentially religious purpose. Oppenheim, *The Other World*, 111.

The essentially religious purpose of Myers's work is demonstrated in his somewhat contradictory attempts to prove personal immortality; his posthumous magnum opus, *Human Personality and its Survival of Bodily Death* (1903), was an attempt to prove the continuation of the integrated personality after death. (Ironically, as Oppenheim observes, Myers's proof of immortality through the concepts of telepathy had involved the disintegration of the unitary personality into multiple shifting components. His final work emphasised the integration of this personality.) Toward the end of his life, when the interest in mysticism was growing, Myers explored the idea of a universal oneness, an *anima mundi* or world soul, but like the personal idealists, he resisted the implications of this for the dissolution of a unitary personality. Dougall included a review of this book in the review she edited, *World Wide;* the reviewer noted that Myers's "special sense was that mystic's sixth sense, the vivid consciousness of supersensuous realities." "Survival of Bodily Death," excerpted from *Christian World,* London in *World Wide* 3, no. 9 (February 28, 1902): 139.

36. [Dougall], *Voluntas Dei,* 92.

37. [Dougall], *The Practice of Christianity,* 228.

38. [Dougall], "The Quick and the Dead, Part II," 60.

39. [Dougall], "The Quick and the Dead, Part II," 60.

40. *Immortality, An Essay in Discovery Coordinating Scientific, Psychical, and Biblical Research; The Spirit: God and His Relation to Man Considered from the Standpoint of Philosophy, Psychology and Art,* and *God's Way with Man: An Exploration of the Method of the Divine Working Suggested by the Facts of History and Science.*

41. See *Who's Who in British Science* (London: L. Hill, 1953). By this date Hadfield was a lecturer in Psychopathological and Mental Hygiene at London University, and a consultant in psychological medicine on Harley Street. His publications include, in addition to the numerous editions of *Psychology and Morals* (London: Methuen and Co., 1923; 1964), *Psychology and Mental Health* (London: George Allen & Unwin, 1950), and *Introduction to Psychotherapy, Its History and Modern Schools* (London: George Allen & Unwin, 1967). For his early career as a minister, see Stuart Mews, "Spiritual Healing," 318.

42. J. A. Hadfield, "The Mind and the Brain," in *Immortality;* "The Psychology of Power," in *The Spirit.* The second essay was also published separately as a pamphlet, *The Psychology of Power* (London: Macmillan, 1933).

43. Immortality, he concludes, "is not only not contradictory to science but . . . science points to this supremacy and liberation of the mind as the goal to which nature is pointing." J. A. Hadfield, "The Mind and the Brain," 71. "[W]e have now crossed the great gulf between the physiological and the psychological, and have set our feet firmly on that shore where the higher faculties of the mind, reason and abstract thought, are subsequently developed. These higher powers serve only to point us further along the road that delivers us from bondage to the flesh, and leads us to anticipate the complete emancipation of the mind from the body. The mind may henceforth become indifferent to the disasters which in the course of nature are bound to overtake the body, and may hope to survive its destruction and decay—and perhaps thereafter to find or create for itself a "spiritual body" adapted to a different sphere of existence and to other modes of life" (p. 70).

44. Hadfield, "The Psychology of Power," 112.

45. A series of lectures delivered in Oxford in 1920 were published in his most widely read work, *Psychology and Morals,* the purpose of which was to argue that the "new Psychology" was consistent with moral principles. See the "Preface to the Sixteenth Edition," *Psychology and Morals, An Analysis of Character* (1923; London: Methuen and Co., 1964), vii.

46. Hadfield, "The Psychology of Power," 113.

47. [Dougall], "The Quick and the Dead, Part II," 62.

48. Harold Anson, "Lily Dougall (1858–1923), 202.

49. [Dougall], "The Quick and the Dead, Part II," 64.

50. Streeter, "Biographical Note," in *God's Way,* 23.

51. [Dougall], *Voluntas Dei,* 112.

52. "Got Corchestor off to Macmillans July 15; Macmillans refused Corchestor July 30, 1909," BL, LDP, 1. See outline of plot of in "Sketch of Evelyn Vane," in BL, LDP, 4.

53. Lily Dougall, "God in Action," in *The Spirit God and His Relation to Man Considered from the Standpoint of Philosophy, Psychology and Art* (London: Macmillan, 1919), 36.

54. [Lily Dougall], 42.

55. Lily Dougall, "God in Action," 58. Dougall continued to draw upon psychology. An article published the year before her death discussed the impact of Emile Coué's work on the interaction of psychology and religion. Lily Dougall, "God and the Subconscious Mind," *The Road: A Quarterly Journal* 3, 9 (1922): 325.

56. [Dougall], *Christus Futurus,* 224.

57. For another application of this example and this argument, see the manuscript: "Definition of Religion and Godliness," typescript, BL, LDP, 2.

58. See Dougall, "English Modernism," 9. Dougall recognizes the value of the sacraments in appealing to the "child that is in us all" and the "racial sub-consciousness," but condemns the denial of reason implicit in the emotional dependence upon sacraments of the "extreme sacramentarians" in the Anglican and Roman Catholic churches.

59. Lily Dougall to Maud Petre, February 25, 1918, Cutts End, Cumnor. The British Library, London, AD 45, 744.

60. Lily Dougall to Sophie Earp, November 14, 1896. Cited in Earp, "Selected Letters," 146.

61. Dougall, "God in Action," 28.

62. "Definition of Religion and Godliness," n.p. [page numbers are omitted in the manuscript after page 20. This is in the section with the subtitle, "Psychological Knowledge and Tradition."] BL, LDP, 2.

63. Lily Dougall, "God and the Subconscious Mind," *The Road: A Quarterly Journal* 3, no. 9 (January 1922): 325.

64. Cited in Earp, "Selected Letters," 66.

65. Dougall, *Paths,* 268. The expression "she knew not what" is a common mystical one, originating in the work of St. John of the Cross.

66. Lily Dougall, "Nature of Religion," undated ts., p. 8, BL, LDP, 1.

67. Even William James retained a belief in some form of "cosmic consciousness"—the kind of consciousness named and explored by Canadian psychologist and mystic, R. M. Bucke. James, while he said he had never experienced it, believed it was possible for the individual to have some sort of communion with the supernatural. But this attenuated form of communion was a far cry from the direct personal relationship that Dougall felt with a personal God.

Bibliography

PRIMARY SOURCES

Manuscript Collections

Dougall Family Papers. Library and Archives Canada.
Dougall, Lily Papers. Department of Western Manuscripts, Bodleian Library, Oxford.
Dougall, Lily. Correspondence. Department of Rare Books and Special Papers, McLennan Library, McGill University.
Dougall, Lily. Correspondence. British Library.
Dougall, Lily. Correspondence. Rare Books, The Templeman Library, University of Kent.
Macmillan Papers, University of Reading.
Montefiore, Claude J. Correspondence to Cyril Emmet, in the possession of Dorothy Emmet.
Webb, C. C. J. Papers. Department of Western Manuscripts, Bodleian Library, Oxford.

Interviews and Personal Communications

Emmet, Dorothy. Correspondence with Author. April 25, 1993 and June 7, 1993.
Emmet, Dorothy. Interview with Author. October 6, 1993. Cambridge, England.

Newspapers and Periodicals

Hibbert Journal. Vols. 1–10.
The Modern Churchman Vols. 1–10.
World Wide: A Weekly Reprint of Articles from Leading Journals and Reviews Reflecting the Current Thought of Both Hemispheres.

Books and Articles by Lily Dougall

Lily Dougall's work was published in multiple revised editions in Britain, United States, and Canada. This list identifies the first edition of her works. Later editions are identified only in cases where the page references in the text refer to those editions. Eight of her novels are currently available online through Early Canadiana Online at www.canadiana.org.

Lily Dougall published some of her short fiction under a pseudonym, Ernest Duns, most of her novels as L. Dougall, and most of her religious writing anonymously; from 1900 her books and articles are attributed to "the author of *Pro Christo et Ecclesia.*" With the publication of *Immortality* in 1917, she is also identified by name. This list does not include the numerous short stories published in periodicals, nor is it necessarily a comprehensive listing of her religious writings.

Published Work

Dougall, L. *Beggars All: A Novel.* London: Longmans, Green and Co., 1891. 6th ed. London: Longmans, 1892.

———. *What Necessity Knows.* 3 vols. London, New York: Longmans, 1893. Reprint with an intro. by Victoria Walker. Ottawa: Tecumseh, 1992.

———. *The Madonna of a Day: A Study.* London: R. Bentley and Son, 1895. Published as *The Madonna of a Day* in the United States. New York: Appleton, 1895.

———. *The Mermaid: A Love Tale.* London: R. Bentley and Son, 1895. New York: Appleton, 1895.

———. *A Question of Faith.* London: Hutchinson, 1895. Boston, New York: Houghton Mifflin, 1895.

———. *The Zeit-Geist.* London: Hutchinson, 1895.

———. "When I Was a Little Girl." *City Sparrows,* no. 21 (January 1896): 12–17.

———. *A Dozen Ways of Love.* London: A. & C. Black, 1897.

———. "The Concord of Clofield," in *The Dome: a Quarterly Containing Examples of All the Arts* Number 1 (London: Unicorn Press, 1897): 13–31.

Dougall, Lily. *The Mormon Prophet.* London: A. & C. Black; New York: Appleton; Toronto: W.J. Gage, 1899.

———. "Willie and I." *City Sparrows,* no. 58 (February 1899).

———. "Home and Social Life." In *Women of Canada, 1900: Their Life and Work.* With an introduction by Lady Aberdeen. Ottawa: National Council of Women of Canada, 1900.

[Dougall, Lily]. *Pro Christo Et Ecclesia.* London and New York: Macmillan, 1900. 2nd ed. 1913.

———. "The Protestantism of Jesus." *Monthly Review* (May 1901).

Dougall, L. *The Earthly Purgatory: A Novel.* London: Hutchinson and Co., 1904. Published in United States as *The Summit House Mystery.* New York: Funk and Wagnalls, 1905.

———. *Young Love (and Other Stories).* London: A. & C. Black, 1904. Reprint from *A Dozen Ways of Love.*

[Dougall, Lily]. "The Alleged Indifference of Laymen to Religion." *Hibbert Journal* 2 (1904): 596–602.

[Dougall, Lily]. "The Salvation of the Body by Faith." *Hibbert Journal* 4, no. 3 (1906): 606–623.

Dougall, L. *The Spanish Dowry. A Romance.* London: Hutchinson, 1906.

[Dougall, Lily]. *Christus Futurus.* London: Macmillan, 1907; 2nd ed. 1909; 3rd ed., 1914. Published in the United States as *The Christ That Is To Be.* New York/London: Macmillan, 1907.

———. "Christus Futurus—excerpt." *Monthly Review* (1907).

Dougall, L. *Paths of the Righteous.* London: Macmillan, 1908.

———. *Modern Journalism: Every Woman's Responsibility Towards It.* Toronto: International Council of Women, 1909.

[Dougall, Lily]. "To a Correspondent, III: The Summer School at the Cloisters, Letchworth, August 14, 1909." *The City, A Monthly Magazine Written and Printed in the First Garden City* 1, no. 9 (September 1909).

———. *Absente Reo.* London: Macmillan, 1910.

———. "A Vision of Unity." *Hibbert Journal* 9: 76–81.

———. *Voluntas Dei.* London: Macmillan, 1912.

———. *The Practice of Christianity.* London: Macmillan, 1913.

———. "Reading Summer School: Impression by Members, by an Onlooker." *The Friend, a Religious Literary and Miscellaneous Journal* III, no. 38 (19 September 1913): 609–10.

———. "Book for Everyman, Part II." *The Commonwealth, A Christian Social Magazine* XIX, no. 224 (August 1914): 247–48.

———. "On Human Goodness" *Present Day Papers* (1914).

———. Review of N. S. Talbot. "The Mind of the Disciples," *Commonwealth* 19: 247–48.

———. "Our Conception of God." *The Interpreter, A Quarterly Magazine of Bibical and Theological Study* II, no. 4 (July 1915).

[Dougall, Lily]. *The Removing of Mountains.* London, Toronto: H Milford, Oxford University Press, 1915.

———. "The Spirit in the Church." *The Interpreter, A Quarterly Magazine of Biblical and Theological Study* 19, no. 1 (October 1915).

———. "The Spirit and the Life." *Present Day Papers* 11, no. 12 (December 1915): 370–78.

Dougall, Lily. "The Function of the Guild of Health." Pamphlet no. 1, Anglican Guild of Health, 1916.

[Dougall, Lily], B. H. Streeter, W. F. Lofthouse, Harold Anson, Rufus M. Jones, Edwyn Bevan, Leonard Hodgson, C. H. S. Matthews, N. Micklem, A. C. Turner and R. G. Collingwood. *Concerning Prayer: Its Nature, Its Difficulties and Its Value.* London: Macmillan, 1916. 2nd ed. 1918.

Dougall, Lily. *The Christian Doctrine of Health: A Handbook On the Relation of Bodily to Spiritual and Moral Health.* London: Macmillan, 1916; 3rd. rev. ed. London: Guild of Health, 1921.

———. "Veni Creator Spiritus!" *Hibbert Journal* (1916) 14: 528–37.

———. "Conscience and Authority." *The Modern Churchman* V, no. 7/8 (1916).

———. "The Quick and the Dead, Part I." *The Interpreter, A Quarterly Magazine of Biblical and Theological Study* 13, no.3 (1916–1917): 128–36.

[Dougall, Lily], B. H. Streeter, A. Clutton-Brock, C. W. Emmett, J. A. Hadfield. *Immortality, An Essay in Discovery Co-ordinating Scientific, Psychical, and Biblical Research.* Edited by Burnett Hillman Streeter. London: Macmillan, 1917.

[Dougall, Lily]. "The Quick and the Dead." *The Interpreter, A Quarterly Magazine of Biblical and Theological Study* 13, no. 4 (July 1917): 128–36.

————. "The Quick and the Dead, Part II." *The Interpreter, A Quarterly Magazine of Biblical and Theological Study* 14, no. 1 (October 1917): 52–65.

[Dougall, Lily]. "The Lay Section of the Churchman's Union." *The Modern Churchman* VII, no. 8 (November 1917): 432–34.

Dougall, Lily, B. H. Streeter, J. Arthur Hadfield, A. Seth Pringle-Pattison, C. A. Anderson Scott, Cyril W. Emmet, and A. Clutton-Brock. *The Spirit: God and His Relation to Man Considered From the Standpoint of Philosophy, Psychology and Art.* Edited by B. H. Streeter. 1919; 2nd ed. London: Macmillan, 1920.

Dougall, Lily, B. H. Streeter, and Archbishop of Dublin. *God and the Struggle for Existence.* London: Student Christian Movement, 1919.

Dougall, Lily. "Christianity and Psychic Healing." *The Modern Churchman* IX, no. 8 (November 1919): 360–67.

————. "Christianity and the Power of Physical Healing," *The Interpreter: A Quarterly Magazine of Biblical and Theological Study.* 16: 39–50.

————. "Liberty to the Captive." *Commonwealth* 24: 323–25.

————. "Spiritualism and Science." *The Modern Churchman* IX, no. 12 (March 1920): 565–74.

————. "The Theology of Mr. Clutton Brook." *The Modern Churchman* X, no. 2 (May 1920): 57–65.

————. Letter to the editor. *The Modern Churchman.* X: 100.

————. "The Meaning of Paul for Today." *The Modern Churchman* (1920–21): 640.

————. "Miracle Inconsistent with Christianity." *Hibbert Journal* XIX, no. 2 (January 1921): 296–307. Reprinted as "Providence and Miracle" in *God's Way with Man.*

————. "The Salvation of Nations." *The Hibbert Journal* (1921) 20: 113–23.

Dougall, Lily, and Cyril W. Emmet. *The Lord of Thought. A Study of the Problems Which Confronted Lord Jesus and the Solution He Offered.* London: Student Christian Movement, 1922.

Dougall, Lily. "Conscience and Authority." *The Modern Churchman* XII, no. 6/7 (1922).

————. "God and the Subconscious Mind." *The Road, A Quarterly Journal* 3, no. 9 (January 1922): 325.

————. "Christianity and the Western World." *The Modern Churchman* (1922) XII: 327–39.

————. "What is the Holy Spirit?" *Interpreter* (1922) 19: 113.

————. "Orthodox Dualism." *The Modern Churchman* XIII, no. 1 (1923–24): 45–53.

————. Letter to the editor. *Jewish Guardian* February 9, 1923: 6.

————. "Faith and the World's Future." *The Interpreter, A Quarterly Magazine of Biblical and Theological Study* (July 1923). Reprint for the Anglican and Free Church Fellowships.

————. "What is English Modernism?" *Contemporary Review* (1923) 123: 472–79.

————. "The Worship of Wrath." *Hibbert Journal* (1923) 22: 168–77. Reprinted in 1924: 75–91.

————. *God's Way With Man, An Exploration of the Method of Divine Working Suggested By the Facts of History and Science.* With an introduction and biographical note by Canon B. H. Streeter. London: Student Christian Movement, 1924.

————. *What We May Expect of God* National Mission Pamphlet E. (London: SPCK) n.d.

Dougall, Lily, and Gilbert Sheldon. *Arcades Ambo: Verse.* Oxford: B. H. Blackwell, 1919.

Unpublished Material

Dougall, Lily. Lovereen, A Canadian Story. (c.1888.) Unpublished manuscript, 465 pp. Bodleian Library, Lily Dougall Papers, Temporary Box 4.

————. Body and Soul. Unpublished (?) manuscript. Bodleian Library, Lily Dougall Papers, Temporary Box 2.

————. The Church and Christian Science. Unpublished (?) manuscript. Bodleian Library, Lily Dougall Papers, Temporary Box 2.

————. The Common Conviction of Immortality. Unpublished (?) manuscript, 4 pp. Bodleian Library, Lily Dougall Papers, Temporary Box 2.

————. Concerning Punishment. Unpublished (?) manuscript. 8 p. Bodleian Library, Lily Dougall Papers, Temporary Box 2.

————. Corchestor of the Future, A Phantasy. Unpublished manuscript, 497 pp. Bodleian Library, Lily Dougall Papers, Temporary Box 3.

————. Creation. Unpublished (?) manuscript, 7 pp. Bodleian Library, Lily Dougall Papers, Temporary Box 2.

————. The Diary of a Canadian Woman in England. Unpublished (?) manuscript. Bodleian Library, Lily Dougall Papers, Temporary Box 2.

————. The Dilemma About God, Part I. Unpublished (?) manuscript, 14 pp. Bodleian Library, Lily Dougall Papers, Temporary Box 2.

————. The Editor and the Angel, Myths of the After Life I. Unpublished (?) manuscript. Bodleian Library, Lily Dougall Papers, Temporary Box 2.

Dougall, Lily. English Modernism. Manuscript. Bodleian Library, Lily Dougall Papers, Temporary Box 2.

————. Ethics. Unpublished (?) manuscript, 18 pp. Bodleian Library, Lily Dougall Papers, Temporary Box 2.

————. Ettal Is. Unpublished (?) manuscript. Bodleian Library, Lily Dougall Papers, Temporary Box 2.

————. The Eucharist—How We Feel. Unpublished (?) manuscript, 11pp. Bodleian Library, Lily Dougall Papers, Temporary Box 2.

————. The Face of Death. Unpublished (?) manuscript. Bodleian Library, Lily Dougall Papers, Temporary Box 2.

————. Genius. Unpublished (?) manuscript, 8 pp. Bodliean Library, Lily Dougall Papers, Temporary Box 2.

————. The Giant Infant and Its Golden Spoon (A Study of Southern California). Unpublished (?) manuscript, Bodleian Library, Lily Dougall Papers, Temporary Box 2.

————. Impressions of the World Missionary Conference, First Sketch of Article. Unpublished (?) manuscript, 5 pp. Bodleian Library, Lily Dougall Papers, Temporary Box 2.

————. Introduction. Unpublished (?) manuscript, 10 pp. Bodleian Library, Lily Dougall Papers, Temporary Box 2.

————. Introduction. Unpublished (?) manuscript, 4 pp. Bodleian Library, Lily Dougall Papers, Temporary Box 2.

————. The Land Of Kingsley and King Arthur. Unpublished (?) manuscript and photographs. Bodleian Library, Lily Dougall Papers, Temporary Box 2.

————. The Land of the Free. Unpublished (?) manuscript, 6 pp. Bodleian Library, Lily Dougall Papers, Temporary Box 4.

———. The Life Beyond, The Relation of the Mortal to the Immortal Life. Unpublished (?) manuscript. Bodleian Library, Lily Dougall Papers, Temporary Box 2.

———. Life. Unpublished (?) manuscript. Bodleian Library, Lily Dougall Papers, Temporary Box 2.

———. A Modern Ghost Story. Unpublished (?) manuscript, 21 pp. Bodleian Library, Lily Dougall Papers, Temporary Box 4.

———. Noblesse Oblige. Unpublished (?) manuscript, 25 pp. Bodleian Library, Lily Dougall Papers, Temporary Box 4.

———. On Immanence. Unpublished (?) manuscript. Bodleian Library, Lily Dougall Papers, Temporary Box 2.

———. The Pain of Love. Unpublished (?) manuscript. Bodleian Library, Lily Dougall Papers, Temporary Box 4.

———. The Peace Angel. Unpublished (?) manuscript, 2 pp. Bodleian Library, Lily Dougall Papers, Temporary Box 2.

———. Prayer. Unpublished (?) manuscript. Bodleian Library, Lily Dougall Papers, Temporary Box 2.

———. The Purpose of the Church. Unpublished (?) manuscript, 5 pp. Bodleian Library, Lily Dougall Papers, Temporary Box 2.

———. Questions of Sin and Holiness. Unpublished (?) manuscript, 20 pp. Bodleian Library, Lily Dougall Papers, Temporary Box 2.

———. The Relation of the Church to Faith Healing. Unpublished (?) manuscript. Bodleian Library, Lily Dougall Papers, Temporary Box 2.

———. "Religious Experience in Maturity: Relation of Religious Experience to the Total of Experience." Unpublished (?) manuscript, 14 pp. Bodleian Library, Lily Dougall Papers, Temporary Box 2.

———. Religious Union. Unpublished (?) manuscript. Bodleian Library, Lily Dougall Papers, Temporary Box 2.

———. A Reminiscence of Wartime. Unpublished (?) manuscript. Bodleian Library, Lily Dougall Papers, Temporary Box 2.

———. [Northwest] A Reminiscence of Wartime. Unpublished (?) manuscript. Bodleian Library, Lily Dougall Papers, Temporary Box 2.

———. The Ruling Passion. Unpublished (?) manuscript, 9 pp. Bodleian Library, Lily Dougall Papers, Temporary Box 4.

———. Sketch of a Story called 'Evelyn Vane.' Unpublished manuscript. Bodleian Library, Lily Dougall Papers, Temporary Box 4.

———. Spirit and Life. Unpublished (?) manuscript, 10 pp. Bodleian Library, Lily Dougall Papers, Temporary Box 2.

———. The Success of Francis Vane. Unpublished manuscript, 643 pp. Bodleian Library, Lily Dougall Papers, Temporary Box 3.

———. Synopsis of The Earthly Purgatory. Unpublished manuscript, 12 pp. Bodleian Library, Lily Dougall Papers, Temporary Box 2.

———. Thoughts Preliminary to a Restatement of the Doctrine of the Holy Spirit. Unpublished (?) manuscript, 24 pp. Bodleian Library, Lily Dougall Papers, Temporary Box 2.

———. Transmuting Earthly Ideals. Unpublished (?) manuscript, 9 pp. Bodleian Library, Lily Dougall Papers, Temporary Box 2.

———. The Truth Once Given. Unpublished (?) manuscript, 11 pp. Bodleian Library, Lily Dougall Papers, Temporary Box 2.

————. Upon Immanence. Unpublished (?) manuscript, 6 pp. Bodleian Library, Lily Dougall Papers, Temporary Box 2.

————. Wanted: A Wholesome Faith. Unpublished (?) manuscript, 19 pp. Bodleian Library, Lily Dougall Papers, Temporary Box 2.

————. What Happened to Jones After He Died. Unpublished (?) manuscript. Bodleian Library, Lily Dougall Papers, Temporary Box 2.

————. What is the Soul? Here and Hereafter. Unpublished (?) manuscript, 20 pp. Bodleian Library, Lily Dougall Papers, Temporary Box 2.

————. What is Truth? Unpublished (?) manuscript. Bodleian Library, Lily Dougall Papers, Temporary Box 2.

Books and Articles

Allen, Alexander V. G. *The Life and Letters of Phillips Brooks.* 2 vols. New York: E. P. Dutton and Co., 1901.

Anson, Harold. *Spiritual Healing: A Discussion of the Religious Element in Physical Health.* London: University Press, 1923.

————. "Lily Dougall." *The Modern Churchman.* XIII (1924): 550–54.

————. "Spiritual Healing—What is it? A Reply to the Bishop of Durham." *Hibbert Journal* 24 (1925): 101–11.

————. "Lily Dougall: 1858–1923." In R. S. Forman, ed., *Great Christians.* London: Ivor, Nicolson and Watson, 1933. 193–207.

————. *Looking Forward.* London: William Heinemann, 1938.

Ash, Edwin. *Faith and Suggestion: Including an Account of the Remarkable Experiences of Dorothy Kerin.* London: Herbert and Daniel, 1912.

————. *Mental Self Help: A Practical Handbook.* London: Mills and Boon, 1912.

Atkins, Gaius Glenn. *Modern Religious Cults and Movements.* New York: Fleming H. Revell, 1923.

Bethune-Baker, J. F. *The Way of Modernism and Other Essays.* Cambridge: Cambridge University Press, 1927.

Beynon, Francis Marion. *Aleta Day.* 1919. Reprint with an introduction by Anne Hicks. London: Virago, 1988.

Bishop of Durham. "Spiritual Healing." *Hibbert Journal* 24 (April 1925): 385–401.

Bucke, Richard Maurice. *Cosmic Consciousness: A Study in the Evolution of the Human Mind.* 1901. Reprint. New York: Penguin, 1991.

Buckham, John Wright. *Progressive Religious Thought in America: A Survey of the Enlarging Pilgrim Faith.* Boston: Houghton Mifflin Co., 1919.

Caird, Edward. *The Evolution of Religion.* 2 vols. 2nd ed. New York: Macmillan, 1894.

————. *Essays on Literature and Philosophy.* 2 vols. Glasgow: Maclehose, 1892.

Chown, Alice A. *The Stairway.* 1921. Reprint with an introduction by Diana Chown. Toronto: University of Toronto Press, 1988.

Clutton-Brock, Arthur. *Thoughts on War* [From the Times Literary Supplement]. London: Methuen and Co., 1914.

————. *More Thoughts on War.* London: Methuen, 1915.

————. *The Ultimate Belief.* London: Constable, 1916.

————. *What is the Kingdom of Heaven?* London: Methuen, 1919.

Coleridge, S. T. *Confessions of an Inquiring Spirit*. Introduced by Joseph Henry Green and with the note by Sara Coleridge. 1853. Reprint edited by H. St. J. Hart. London: A.& C. Black, 1956.

Dearmer, Nan. *The Life of Percy Dearmer*. Oxford: The Religious Book Club/Alden Press, 1941.

Dearmer, Percy. *Body and Soul, An Enquiry into the Effects of Religion On Health With a Description of Christian Works of Healing from the New Testament to the Present Day*. London: Sir Isaac Pitman and Sons, 1909; New York: E. P. Dutton, 1923.

Deland, Margaret. *John Ward, Preacher*. 1888. Reprint Ridgewood, N.J.: Gregg Press, 1967.

Dresser, Horatio W. *A History of the New Thought Movement*. New York: Thomas Y. Crowell, 1919.

Drummond, Henry. *Natural Law in the Spiritual World*. New York: James Pott, 1884.

———. *The Lowell Lectures On the Ascent of Man*. 1894. 5th ed. New York: James Pott, 1895.

———. *The Ideal Life: Addresses Hitherto Unpublished With Memorial Sketches By Ian McLaren*. Toronto: Revell, 1898.

Dubois, Paul. *The Psychic Treatment of Nervous Disorders (The Psychoneuroses and Their Moral Treatment)*. 7th ed. Translated and edited by Smith Ely Jelliffe and William A. White. New York and London: Funk and Wagnalls, 1909.

Emmet, Cyril W. *Conscience, Creeds and Critics: A Plea for Liberty of Criticism within the Church of England*. London: Macmillan, 1918.

Fairbairn, A. M. *Catholicism, Roman and Anglican*. London: Hodder and Stoughton, 1899.

Fawkes, Alfred. *Studies in Modernism*. London: Smith, Elder, 1913.

Fosdick, Harry Emerson, *The Living of these Days: An Autobiography*. New York: Harper and Brothers, 1956; London: SCM Press, 1957.

Foster, Frank Hugh. *The Modern Movement in American Theology, Sketches in the History of American Protestant Thought from the Civil War to the World War*. 1939. Reprint. Freeport, N.Y.: Books for Libraries Press, 1969.

Froude, J. A. *The Nemesis of Faith*. Chicago: Bedford, Clarke, 1849.

Gardner, Alice. *Within Our Limits: Essays On Questions Moral, Religious and Historical*. London: T. Fisher Unwin, 1913.

Gardner, Charles. *In Defense of the Faith*. Oxford: Blackwell, 1927.

Gardner, Percy. *Exploratio Evangelica, A Brief Examination of the Basis and Origin of Christian Belief*. London: A. & C. Black, 1899.

———. *Exploratio Evangelica: A Survey of the Foundations of Christianity*. London: A. & C. Black, 1907.

———. *The Practical Basis of Christian Belief: An Essay in Reconstruction*. London: Williams and Norgate, 1923.

———. *Modernism in the English Church*. London: Methuen, 1926.

———. *The Interpretation of Religious Experience*. London: Williams and Norgate, 1931.

———. *Autobiographica*. Oxford: Basil Blackwell, 1933.

Gordon, Alice M. "The After-Careers of University-Educated Women." *Nineteenth Century* 37 (June 1895): 958–60.

Gore, Charles, ed. *Lux Mundi: A Series of Studies in the Religion of the Incarnation*. London: John Murray, 1889.

————. *The Basis of Anglican Fellowship in Faith and Organization:* An open letter to the clergy of the diocese of Oxford. London, Oxford: A. R. Mowbray, 1914.

Gosse, Edmund. *Father and Son: A Study of Two Temperaments.* London: Heineman, 1907.

Grant, James B. "Salvation of the Body by Faith." *Hibbert Journal* 4, no. 4 (1906): 908–909.

Griffiths, R. Gladstone. *The Necessity of Modernism.* Modernist Series. London: Skeffington and Sons, n.d.

Hadfield, J. A. *Introduction to Psychotherapy: Its History and Modern Schools.* London: George Allen and Unwin, 1967.

————. *Psychology and Morals: An Analysis of Character.* London: Methuen, 1923.

————. *The Psychology of Power.* London: Macmillan, 1933.

Henson, Herbert Hensley. *Retrospective of an Unimportant Life.* Oxford: Oxford University Press, 1942.

Illingworth, J. R. *Divine Immanence: An Essay On the Spiritual Significance of Matter.* London: Macmillan, 1898.

————. *The Life and Work of John Richardson Illingworth, As Portrayed By His Letters and Illustrated By Photographs.* London: John Murray, 1917.

Inge, W. R. *Christian Mysticism.* 1899. 7th ed. New York: Meridian Books, 1956.

————. *Faith and Knowledge: Sermons.* Edinburgh: T. & T. Clarke, 1905.

————. *Personal Idealism and Mysticism: The Paddock Lectures for 1906 Delivered At General Seminary, New York.* London: Longmans Green, 1907.

————. "Review of *Studies in Mystical Religion,*" *Hibbert Journal* VIII (1909–10): 208–10.

————. *The Church and the Age.* London: Longmans, 1912.

————. *Studies of English Mystics.* St. Margaret Lectures, 1905. London: John Murray, 1921.

————. *The Platonic Tradition in English Religious Thought.* New York: Longmans, Green, 1926.

————. "Harnack and Liberal Protestantism." *Hibbert Journal* VI (July 1928): 633–46.

————. *Vale.* London: Longmans, 1934.

————. *Mysticism in Religion.* Chicago: University of Chicago Press, 1948.

————. *Diary of a Dean, St Paul's 1911–1934.* London: Hutchison, 1949.

————, ed. *Radnakrishnan: Comparative Studies in Philosophy Presented in Honour of His Sixtieth Birthday.* London: George Allen and Unwin, 1951.

James, William. *The Varieties of Religious Experience.* Edited and with an introduction by Martin Marty. 1902. Reprint. New York: Penguin Books Ltd., 1985.

Jones, R. Tudor. *Congregationalism in England, 1662–1962.* London: Independent Press Ltd., 1962.

Jones, Rufus M. *Studies in Mystical Religion.* 1909. London: Macmillan, 1927.

————. *Spiritual Reformers in the 16th and 17th Centuries.* London: Macmillan, 1914.

————. *New Studies in Mystical Religion.* The Ely Lectures. London: Macmillan, 1927.

————. *Duncan Polite: The Watchman of Glenoro.* New York: Hodder and Stoughton, 1905.

Keith, Marian. [MacGregor, Mary Esther]. *The Bells of St. Stephens.* Toronto: McClelland and Stewart, 1922.

Knox, R. A. *Some Loose Stones, Being a Consideration of Certain Tendencies in Modern Theology Illustrated By Reference to a Book Called "Foundations."* London: Longmans, Green, 1914.

―――. *Enthusiasm: A Chapter in the History of Religion With Special Reference to the XVII and XVIII Centuries.* Oxford: Clarendon Press, 1950.

Knudson, Albert C. *The Philosophy of Personalism: A Study in the Metaphysics of Religion.* 1927. Reprint. New York: Krause Reprint, 1969.

Lathbury, Bertha. "Agnosticism and Women." *Nineteenth Century* 7 (April 1880): 619–27.

Leighton, Parks. *What Is Modernism?* New York and London: Charles Scribner and Sons, 1924.

Lennox, Cuthbert. *Henry Drummond: A Biographical Sketch With Bibliography.* Toronto: William Briggs, 1901.

Lizars, Robina, and K. M. Lizars. *Committed to His Charge.* Toronto: George N. Morang, 1900.

MacDonald, Flora. *Mary Melville The Psychic.* Toronto: Austin, 1900.

Machar, Agnes Maule. *Roland Graeme: Knight. A Novel of Our Times.* Montreal: Drysdale, 1892.

Major, H. D. A. *English Modernism: Its Origin, Methods, Aims.* Being the William Belden Noble Lectures delivered in Harvard University, 1925–26. London: Oxford University Press; Cambridge, Mass.: Harvard University Press, 1927.

―――. "The Biographical Record of the Modern Churchman's Movement, 1898–1957." *The Modern Churchman* XLVI, no. 3 (March 1956).

Matheson, P. E. *The Life of Hastings Rashdall.* Oxford: Oxford University Press, 1928.

Mathews, Shailer. *The Faith of Modernism.* New York: Macmillan, 1924.

Maurice, Frederick Denison. *The Kingdom of Christ, or Hints to a Quaker, Respecting the Principles, Constitution and Ordinances of the Catholic Church.* 2nd ed. 2 vols. London: Ribington, 1842.

McClure, Edmund. *Modernism and Traditional Christianity.* 2nd rev. ed. London: SPCK, 1914.

McComb, Samuel. "Christianity as Healing Power." *Hibbert Journal* 8 (October 1909): 10–27.

"Members of the Church of England." *Liberal Evangelicalism: An Interpretation.* London: Hodder and Stoughton, n.d. [after 1922].

―――. *The Inner Life: Essays in Liberal Evangelicalism.* London: Hodder and Stoughton, 1925.

Montgomery, L. M. *My Dear Mr. M.: Letters to G. B. Macmillan.* Edited by Francis W. P. Bolger and Elizabeth R. Epperly. Toronto: McGraw-Hill Ryerson, 1980.

―――. *The Green Gables Letters, from L. M. Montgomery to Ephraim Weber, 1905–1909.* Edited by Wilfred Eggleston. Ottawa: Borealis Press, 1981.

―――. *The Selected Journals of L. M. Montgomery.* Vols. 1–4. Edited by Mary Rubio and Elizabeth Waterston. Toronto: Oxford University Press, 1885–1992.

Müller, Max. *Theosophy or Psychological Religion,* Gifford Lectures, 1893. London: Longmans, 1893.

Murray, Andrew. *Abide in Christ: Thoughts On a Blessed Fellowship With the Son of God.* New York: Fleming H. Revell, 1895.

―――. *Divine Healing.* New York: Christian Alliance, 1900.

Murry, John Middleton. *God: Being an introduction to the Science of Metabiology.* London: Jonathon Cape, 1929.

Oakeley, Hilda. *My Adventures in Education.* London: Williams and Norgate, 1939.

Otto, Rudolf. *The Idea of the Holy (Das Heilige).* Translated by John W. Harvey. London: Humphrey Milford, 1923.

———. "How Schleiermacher Rediscovered the Sensus Numinis." In *Religious Essays: A Supplement to "The Idea of the Holy."* Translated by Brian Lunn. London: Oxford University Press, 1931.

Parks, Leighton. *What Is Modernism?* New York, London: Charles Scribner's Sons, 1924.

Rashdall, Hastings. *Doctrine and Development.* University Sermons. London: Methuen, 1898.

———. "Clerical Liberalism." In *Anglican Liberalism* by Twelve Churchmen. London: William and Norgate, 1908.

———. *Christus in Ecclesia.* Sermons on the Church and Its Institutions. Edinburgh: T.T. Clark, 1912.

———. *Conscience and Christ.* Six Lectures on Christian Ethics. London: Duckworth, 1916.

———. *The Idea of Atonement in Christian Theology.* Being the Bampton Lectures for 1915. London: Macmillan, 1919.

[Rashdall, Hastings et al.]. *Contentio Veritatus,* by Six Oxford Tutors. London: J. Murray, 1902.

Richardson, R. D. *The Gospel of Modernism.* Foreword by E. W. Barnes. Modernist Series. London: Skeffington and Sons, n.d. [1933?].

Royden, Maude. *Women and the Church of England.* London: George Allen Unwin Ltd., [1916].

———. *A Three Fold Cord.* London: Victor Gollancz, 1947.

Saunders, Margaret Marshall. *The House of Armour.* Philadelphia: A. J. Rowland, 1897.

———. *Deficient Saints: A Tale of Maine.* Boston: L. C. Page and Co., 1899.

Schleiermacher, Friedrich. *On Religion: Speeches to Its Cultured Despisers, 1799.* Translated by John Oman, 1893. Reprint with an introduction by Rudolf Otto. New York: Harper Torchbooks, 1958.

[Schreiner, Olive] Iron, Ralph. *The Story of an African Farm.* 1883. Reprint. London: Penguin, 1971.

Scott Holland, Henry. *A Bundle of Memories.* London: Wells, Gardner, Darton, 1915.

Scudder, Vida D. *Social Ideals in English Letters.* Boston: Houghton Mifflin, 1898.

Scudder, Vida, ed. *Saint Catharine of Siena, As Seen in Her Letters.* Translated with an introduction by Vida Scudder. London: J. M. Dent, 1905.

———. *Socialism and Character.* London: J. M. Dent and Sons, 1912.

Sheldon, Lilian. "Mary Sophia Earp." *Newnham College Roll Letter* (1929): 84.

Smith, George Adam. *The Life of Henry Drummond.* Toronto: Revell, 1899.

Smith, Hannah Whitall. *The Christian's Secret of a Happy Life.* 1875; Toronto: Methodist Book and Publishing House, 1889.

———. *The Interior Life.* London: Longley, 1886.

———. *Religious Fanaticism: Extracts from the Papers of Hannah Whitall Smith.* Edited and with an introduction by Ray Strachey. London: Faber and Gwyer, 1928.

———. *The Religious Rebel: The Letters of "H. W. S." (Mrs. Pearsall Smith).* Edited by her son, Logan Pearsall Smith. With a Preface and Memoir by Robert Gathorne-Hardy. London: Nisbet, 1949.

Strachey, Ray. *Frances Willard: Her Life and Work.* London: T. Fisher Unwin, 1912.

————. *A Quaker Grandmother.* New York: Revell, 1914.

Streeter, B. H., ed. *Foundations.* 1912. Reprint. New York: Books for Libraries Press, 1971.

————. *Reality: A New Correlation of Science and Religion.* London: Macmillan, 1927.

————. *Adventure: The Science of Faith and the Faith of Science.* London: Macmillan, 1928.

————. *The Buddha and the Christ. An Exploration of the Meaning of the Universe and of the Purpose of Human Life.* Bampton Lectures 1932. 1932: Reprint. Pt. Washington, N.Y., London: Kennikat Press, 1970.

————. *The God Who Speaks.* Warburton Lectures, 1933–1935. New York: Macmillan, 1937.

Streeter, B. H., and A. J. Appasamy. *The Message of Sadhu Sundar Singh: A Study in Mysticism or Practical Religion.* New York: Macmillan, 1922.

Streeter, B. H., and Edith Picton-Turbervill. *Woman and the Church.* London: T. Fisher Unwin, 1917.

Sturt, Henry, ed. *Personal Idealism.* Philosophical Essays By Eight Members of the University of Oxford. London: Macmillan, 1902.

Tatlow, Tissington. *The Story of the Student Christian Movement of Great Britain and Ireland.* London: SCM Press, 1933.

Temple, William. *Studies in the Religion of the Incarnation.* Repton School Sermons. London: Macmillan, 1913.

Tulloch, John. *Movements of Religious Thought in Britain in the Nineteenth Century.* 1885; New York: Humanities Press, 1971.

Underhill, Evelyn. *Mysticism: A Study in the Nature and Development of Man's Spiritual Consciousness.* London: Methuen, 1911. 3rd ed. 1912. 12th rev.ed.1930.

[Underhill, Evelyn] John Cordelier. *The Spiral Way, Being Meditations Upon the Fifteen Mysteries of the Soul's Ascent.* London: J. M. Watkins, 1912.

Underhill, Evelyn. *The Mystic Way: A Psychological Study in Christian Origins.* London: J. M. Dent, 1913.

————. *Practical Mysticism.* London: J. M. Dent, 1914.

————. *The Essentials of Mysticism and Other Essays.* London: J. M. Dent, 1920.

————. *The Life of the Spirit and the Life of Today.* Lectures Delivered in Oxford in 1921. London: Methuen, 1922.

————. *Mystics of the Church.* London: James Clark, 1925.

————. *Concerning the Inner Life.* London: Methuen, 1926.

————. *The Golden Sequence: A Four-Fold Study of the Spiritual Life.* New York: Harper Brothers, 1932.

————. *Worship.* London: Nisbet, 1936.

————. *The Letters of Evelyn Underhill.* Edited with an introduction by Charles Williams. 1943. Westminster, Md.: Christian Classics, 1989.

Upham, Thomas. *Elements of Mental Philosophy, embracing two departments of the intellect and the sensibilities.* 1831. Reprint. New York: Harper, 1850.

————. *The Life of Faith.* 1845. Reprint. New York: Garland, 1984.

————. *Life, Religious Opinions and Experience of Madame Guyon Including an Account of the Personal History and Religious Opinions of Fénélon, Archbishop of Cambray.* 1847. Edited and revised by "an English Clergyman" with a new introduction by W.R. Inge, 1905. New ed. London: Allenson, 1947.

Vaughan, R.A. *Hours with the Mystics: A contribution to the history of religious opinion.* 1856. 3rd rev. ed. 2 vols. London: Strahan, 1880.

[Ward, Mary Augusta] Mrs. Humphrey Ward. *Robert Elsmere.* 3 vols. London: Smith, 1888.

———. *The Case of Richard Meynell.* London: Smith, 1911.

———. *Helbeck of Bannisdale.* 9th ed. London: John Murray, 1911.

Warfield, Benjamin Breckinridge. *Perfectionism.* 2 vols. New York: Oxford University Press, 1931.

Webb, Beatrice. *"The Power to Alter Things": The Diary of Beatrice Webb.* Vol. 3, 1905–1924. Edited by Norman and Jeanne MacKenzie. London: Virago, 1984.

Webb, Clement C. J. *Problems in the Relations of God and Man.* London: Nisbet, 1911.

———. *A Century of Anglican Theology and Other Lectures.* New York: D. Appleton, 1924.

———. *A Study of Religious Thought in England From 1850.* Being the Olaus Petri Lectures Delivered at Uppsala in 1932. Oxford: Clarendon, 1933.

———. *Religious Experience:* A Public Lecture Delivered in the Hall of Oriel College on Friday 19 May, 1944. Oxford: Oxford University Press, 1945.

Wigley, T. *The Necessity of Christian Modernism.* With a foreword by H. D. A. Major. London: James Clarke, n.d.

Wood, Joanna E. *Judith Moore: Or, Fashioning a Pipe.* Toronto: Ontario Publishing, 1898.

———. *A Daughter of Witches.* Toronto: W. J. Gage, 1900.

"The Case of Richard Meynell." *The Modern Churchman* 1, no. 12 (March 1912): 667.

"The Death of Miss Earp," *Oxford Times,* November 23, 1928.

Secondary Sources

Albanese, Catherine. *American Spiritualities: A Reader.* Bloomington: Indiana University Press, 2001.

Allen, Alexander V. G. *The Life and Letters of Phillips Brooks.* New York: E. P. Dutton, 1901.

Allen, Richard. "The Social Gospel and the Reform Tradition in Canada, 1890–1928," *Canadian Historical Review* 49, 4 (December 1968): 381–99.

———. *The Social Passion. Religion and Social Reform in Canada, 1914–1928.* Toronto: University of Toronto Press, 1971.

———, ed. *The Social Gospel in Canada.* Ottawa: National Museums of Canada, 1975.

Altholz, Josef, ed. *The Mind and Art of Victorian England.* Minneapolis: University of Minnesota Press, 1976.

———. "The Mind of Victorian Orthodoxy: Anglican Responses to Essays and Reviews, 1860–1864." *Church History* 51 (June 1982): 186–97.

Andreidis, Harriette. "Theorizing Early Modern Lesbianisms: Invisible Borders, Ambiguous Demarcations." In *Virtual Gender: Fantasies of Subjectivity and Embodiment.* Edited by Mary Ann O'Farrlee and Lynne Vallone. Ann Arbor: University of Michigan Press, 1999.

Anson, Harold. *Looking Forward.* London: William Heinemann, 1938.

Armstrong, Christopher J. R. *Evelyn Underhill (1875–1941): An Introduction to Her Life and Writings.* London and Oxford: Mowbrays, 1975.

Armstrong, Louise. A House Designed by Clough Williams Ellis in Cumnor, Oxfordshire, 1911–12. Unpublished paper written for the Certificate in Historic Conservation, September, 1992.

Ashley, Matthew. "The Turn to Spirituality? The Relationship Between Theology and Spirituality." *Christian Spirituality Bulletin* 3, no. 2 (Fall 1995): 13–18.

Ashton, Rosemary. "Doubting Clerics: From James Anthony Froude to Robert Elsmere via George Eliot." In *The Critical Spirit and the Will to Believe: Essays in Nineteenth Century Literature and Religion*. Edited by David Jasper. London: St. Martins Press, 1989.

Averill, Lloyd J. *American Theology in the Liberal Tradition*. Philadelphia: Westminster Press, 1967.

Avis, Paul. "Charles Gore and Modernism: A Half-Centenary Exercise in 'Corporate Believing'." *Theology* LXXXV, no. 703 (January 1982): 269–77.

Badham, Paul. *The Contemporary Challenge of Modernist Theology*. Cardiff: University of Wales Press, 1998.

———. "The Revival of Religious Modernism." In the *The Future of Liberal Theology*. Edited by Mark D. Chapman. Burlington, Vt.: Ashgate, 2002.

Bagger, Michael. "Critical Notice": Ecumenicalism and Perennialism Revisited." *Religious Studies* 27 (1991): 399–412.

Barash, Carol. "Virile Womanhood: Olive Schreiner's Narratives of a Master Race." In *Speaking of Gender*. Edited by Elaine Showalter. New York: Routledge, 1989.

Barker, Eileen et al. *Secularization, Rationalism and Sectarianism: Essays in Honour of Bryan Wilson*. New York: Oxford University Press, 1993.

Baym, Nina. *Novels, Readers and Reviewers: Responses to Fiction in Antebellum America*. Ithaca, N.Y.: Cornell University Press, 1984.

Beattie, M. E. *A Brief History of the Student Christian Movement of Canada, 1821–1974*. Toronto: SCM, 1975.

Bebbington, David W. *Evangelicalism in Modern Britain: A History from the 1730s to the 1980s*. 1989. Reprint, Grand Rapids, Mich.: Baker Book House, 1992.

———. "Baptism and Fundamentalism in Inter-war Britain." In *Protestant Evangelicalism: Britain, Ireland, Germany and America, c. 1750–c. 1950, Essays in Honour of W. R. Ward*. Edited by Keith Robbins. Oxford: Basil Blackwell, 1990.

———. "Canadian Evangelicalism: A View from Britain." In Aspects of the Canadian Evangelical Experience. Edited by George A. Rawlyk. Montreal and Kingston: McGill-Queen's University Press, 1997.

Beeson, T. R. *Rebels and Reformers: Christian Renewal in the Twentieth Century*. London: Student Christian Movement Press, 1999.

Bendroth, Margaret L. "Millenial Themes and Private Visions: The Problem of 'Women's Place' in Religious History." *Fides Et Historia* 20 (June 1988): 24–31.

———. *Fundamentalism and Gender: 1875 to the Present*. New Haven: Yale University Press, 1993.

Bland, Lucy, and Laura Doan (eds.). *Sexology in Culture*. Chicago: University of Chicago Press, 1998.

Bouyer, Louis, Jean Leclerq et al. *A History of Christian Spirituality*. 3 vols. London: Burns and Oats, 1968.

Bradley, Ian C. *The Call to Seriousness: The Evangelical Impact on the Victorians*. New York: Macmillan, 1969.

Brainard, Samuel F. "Defining 'Mystical Experience.'" *Journal of the American Academy of Religion* 64, no. 2 (1996): 359–93.

Braude, Ann D. "Spirits Defend the Rights of Women." In *Women, Religion and Social Change*. Edited by Yvonne Yazbeck Haddad and Ellision Banks Findly. Albany: State University of New York Press, 1985.

———. *Radical Spirits, Spiritualism and Women's Rights in Nineteenth Century America*. Boston: Beacon Press, 1989.

Brereton, Virginia Lieson. *From Sin to Salvation: Stories of Women's Conversions, 1800 to the Present*. Bloomington: Indiana University Press, 1991.

Brierley, Michael W. "Ripon Hall, Henry Major and the Shaping of English Liberal Theology," in *Ambassadors of Christ: Commemorating 150 Years of Theological Education in Cuddesdon, 1854–2004*. Edited by M. D. Chapman. Aldershot: Ashgate, 2004.

———. "Naming a Quiet Revolution: The Panentheistic Turn in Modern Theology." In *In Whom We Live and Move and Have Our Being: Panentheistic Reflections on God's Presence in a Scientific World*. Edited by Philip Clayton and Arthur Peacocke. Grand Rapids, Mich: William B. Eerdmans, 2004.

———. "Lily Dougall's Doctrine of God." Unpublished paper. 2005.

Briggs, Sheila. "Schleiermacher and the Construction of the Gendered Self." In *Schleiermacher and Feminism: Sources, Evaluations and Responses. Schleiermacher: Studies and Translations*. Edited by Iain G. Nicol. Lewiston: Edwin Mellen Press, 1992.

Brodzki, Bella, and Celeste Schenck, eds. *Life/Lines:Theorizing Women's Autobiography*. Ithaca, N.Y., and London: Cornell University Press, 1988.

Brose, Olive J. *Frederick Denison Maurice: Rebellious Conformist*. Athens: Ohio University Press, 1971.

Brouwer, Ruth Compton. "The 'Between-Age' Christianity of Agnes Machar." *Canadian Historical Review* 65, no. 3 (1984): 347–70.

———. "Transcending the 'Unacknowledged Quarantine': Putting Religion into English-Canadian Women's History," *Journal of Canadian Studies* 27, 3 (Fall 1992): 47–61.

Brown, Colin G. "Frederick Denison Maurice in the United States, 1860–1900." *Journal of Religious History* 10 (June 1978): 68.

Bruce, Steve. "A Sociological Account of Liberal Protestantism." *Religious Studies* 20, no. 3 (September 1984): 401–15.

———. *A House Divided: Protestantism, Schism and Secularization*. London and New York: Routledge, 1990.

———, ed. *Religion and Modernization: Sociologists and Historians Debate the Secularization Thesis*. Oxford: Clarendon Press, 1992.

Budges, Hal. *American Mysticism: From William James to Zen*. New York: Harper and Row, 1970.

Buss, Helen M. *Mapping Our Selves: Canadian Women's Autobiography in English*. Montreal and Kingston: McGill-Queens University Press, 1993.

Caine, Barbara. *Victorian Feminists*. Oxford: Oxford University Press, 1992.

———. "Feminist Biography and Feminist History." *Women's History Review* 3, no. 32 (1994): 247–61.

Campbell, Debra. "Hannah Whitall Smith (1832–1911): Theology of the Mother-Hearted God." *Signs: Journal of Women in Culture and Society* 15 (Autumn 1989): 70–101.

Campbell, Ted A. *The Religion of the Heart: A Study of European Religious Life in the Seventeenth and Eighteenth Centuries*. Columbia, S.C.: University of South Carolina Press, 1991.

Carr, Ann E. *Transforming Grace: Christian Tradition and Women's Experience*. San Francisco: Harper and Row, 1988.

————. "On Feminist Spirituality." In *Horizons in Catholic Feminist Theology*. Edited by Joann Wolski Conn and Walter E. Conn. Washington: Georgetown University Press, 1992.

Carrington, Philip. *The Anglican Church in Canada: A History*. Toronto: Collins, 1963.

Carter, Jennifer J., and Donald J. Withrington, eds. *Scottish Universities: Distinctiveness and Diversity*. Edinburgh: John Donald Publishers Ltd., 1992.

Castle, Terry. *The Apparitional Lesbian: Female Homosexuality and Modern Culture*. New York: Columbia University Press, 1993.

Cauthen, Kenneth. *The Impact of American Religious Liberalism*. 1962. 2nd ed. Lanham: University Press of America, 1983.

Certeau, Michel de. *The Writing of History*. Translated by Tom Conley. New York: Columbia University Press, 1988.

————. *The Mystic Fable: The Sixteenth and Seventeenth Centuries*. Vol. 1. Translated by Michael B. Smith. Chicago: University of Chicago Press, 1992.

Chadwick, Owen. *The Victorian Church*. London: Oxford University Press, 1970.

————. *The Secularization of the European Mind in the Nineteenth Century*. The Gifford Lectures in the University of Edinburgh for 1973–74. Cambridge: Cambridge University Press, 1975.

————. *From Bossuet to Newman: The Idea of Doctrinal Development*. 2nd ed. New York: Cambridge University Press, 1987.

Chopp, Rebecca. "Feminism's Theological Pragmatics: A Social Naturalism of Women's Experience." *Journal of Religion* 67 (1987): 239–56.

Chorley, E. Clowes. *Men and Movements in the Episcopal Church*. New York: Scribner's, 1946.

Chown, Alice A. *The Stairway*. Boston: Cornhill, 1921. Reprint with an introduction by Diana Chown. Toronto: University of Toronto Press, 1988.

Christ, Carol P. "Embodied Thinking: Reflections on Feminist Theological Method." *Journal of Feminist Studies in Religion* 5, no. 1 (Spring 1989): 7–15.

————. *Rebirth of the Goddess: Finding Meaning in Feminist Spirituality*. Reading, Mass.: Addison-Wesley, 1997.

Christ, Carol P., and Judith Plaskow, eds. *Womanspirit Rising: A Feminist Reader in Religion*. 2nd ed. New York: Harper Collins, 1992.

Christensen, Torben. *The Origin and History of Christian Socialism, 1848–1854*. Copenhagen: Universistetsforlaget I Aarhus, 1962.

————. *The Divine Order: A Study in F. D. Maurice's Theology*. Leiden: E. J. Brill, 1973.

Christian, William. "George Grant and Religion: A Conversation Prepared and Edited by William Christian." *Journal of Canadian Studies/Revue d'études canadiennes* 26, no. 1 (Spring 1991): 42–63.

Clark, Elizabeth, and Herbert Richardson. *Women and Religion: A Feminist Sourcebook*. New York: Harper and Row, 1977.

Clements, Keith W. *Lovers of Discord: Twentieth Century Theological Controversies in England*. London: SPCK, 1988.

Clowes-Chorley, E. *Men and Movements in the American Episcopal Church*. New York: Scribners, 1946.

Coakley, Sarah. "Gender and Knowledge in Western Philosophy: The 'Man of Reason' and the 'Feminine' 'Other' in Enlightenment and Romantic

Thought." In *The Special Nature of Women?* Edited by Ann Carr and Elisabeth Schüssler Fiorenza. London: SCM Press, 1991.

Conn, Joann Wolski. "Toward Spiritual Maturity." In *Freeing Theology: The Essentials of Theology in Feminist Perspective.* Edited by Catherine Mowry LaCugna. San Francisco: Harper, 1993.

Cooey, Paula M. *Religious Imagination and the Body.* Oxford: Oxford University Press, 1994.

Cook, Ramsay. "Francis Marion Beynon and the Crisis of Christian Reformism." In *The West and the Nation: Essays in Honour of W. L. Morton.* Edited by Carl Berger and Ramsay Cook. Toronto: McClelland and Stewart, 1976.

———. "Spiritualism, Science of the Earthly Paradise." *Canadian Historical Review* 65 (1984).

———. *The Regenerators: Social Criticism in Late Victorian English Canada.* Toronto: University of Toronto Press, 1985.

Cook, Sharon. *Through Sunshine and Shadow: The Women's Christian Temperance Union, 1874–1930.* Montreal and Kingston: McGill-Queen's University Press, 1995.

Coon, Lynda L., Katherine J. Haldane, and Elisabeth W. Sommer, eds. *That Gentle Strength: Historical Perspectives On Women in Christianity.* Charlottesville and London: University Press of Virginia, 1990.

Cooper, J. I. "The Early Editorial Policy of the Montreal Witness." In *Canadian Historical Association Report.* Toronto: University of Toronto Press, 1947.

Cort, John C. *Christian Socialism: An Informal History.* Maryknoll, N.Y.: Orbis Books, 1988.

Cott, Nancy F. *The Bonds of Womanhood: Woman's Sphere in New England, 1780–1835.* New Haven: Yale University Press, 1977.

Cox, Jeffrey. *The English Churches in a Secular Society: Lambeth, 1870–1930.* Oxford: Oxford University Press, 1982.

Crook, Paul. "W. R. Inge and Cultural Crisis, 1899–1920." *Journal of Religious History* 16, no. 4 (December 1991): 410.

Cunningham, Raymond J. "From Holiness to Healing: The Faith Cure in America." *Church History* 43 (1974): 499–513.

Cunningham, Valentine. *Everywhere Spoken Against: Dissent in the Victorian Novel.* Oxford: Clarendon Press, 1975.

Curtis, Susan. "The Son of God and God the Father: Social Gospel and Victorian Masculinity." In *Meanings for Manhood: Constructions of Masculinity in Victorian America.* Edited by Mark C. Carnes and Clyde Griffen. Chicago and London: University of Chicago Press, 1990.

Davaney, Sheila Greeve. "The Limits of the Appeal to Women's Experience." In *Shaping New Vision Gender and Values in American Culture.* Edited by Clarissa W. Atkinson et al. Ann Arbor and London: UMI Research Press, 1987.

———. "Problems with Feminist Theory: Historicity and the Search for Sure Foundations." In *Embodied Love: Sensuality and Relationship as Feminist Values.* Edited by Paula M. Cooey. San Francisco: Harper and Row, 1987.

Davies, Horton. *Worship and Theology in England: The Ecumenical Century, 1900–1965.* Princeton: Princeton University Press, 1965.

Dayton, Donald W., and Robert K. Johnston. *The Variety of American Evangelicalism.* Knoxville, Tenn.: University of Tennessee Press, 1991.

Deat, Paul, and Carol Robb, eds. *The Boston Personalist Tradition in Philosophy, Social Ethics and Theology.* Macon, Ga.: Mercer, 1986.

DeBerg, Betty A. *UnGodly Women: Gender and the First Wave of American Fundamentalism*. Minneapolis: Fortress Press, 1990.

DeVries, Dawn. "Schleiermacher's Christmas Eve Dialogue: Bourgeois Ideology or Feminist Theology." *Journal of Religion* 69 (1989): 169–83.

Dieter, Melvin E. *The Holiness Revival of the Nineteenth Century*. Metuchen, N.J.: Scarecrow, 1980.

Diggs, Marylynne. "Romantic Friends or a 'Different Race of Creatures,' The Representation of Lesbian Pathology in Nineteenth Century America." *Feminist Studies* 21, 2 (1995): 317–40.

Donovan, Mary Sudman. *A Different Call: Women's Ministries in the Episcopal Church, 1850–1920*. Wilton, Conn.: Morehouse-Barlow, 1999.

Douglas, Ann. *The Feminization of American Culture*. New York: Knopf, 1977.

Dreyer, Elizabeth A. "Spirituality as a Resource for Theology: The Holy Spirit in Augustine." *Christian Spirituality Bulletin* 4, no. 2 (Fall 1996): 1–12.

———. "The Spirit Blows in the Academy: The Theological Spirituality of Walter H. Principe, CSB (1922–1996)." *Christian Spirituality Bulletin* 4, no. 2 (Fall 1997): 7–8.

Drummond, Andrew, and James Bulloch. *The Church in Late Victorian Scotland, 1874–1900*. Edinburgh: St. Andrew Press, 1978.

Duggan, Lisa. *Sapphic Slashers: Sex, Violence and American Modernity*. Durham, N.C.: Duke University Press, 2000.

Eastman, Annis F. F. "The Influence of Religion on Women." In *The Dawn of Religious Pluralism: Voices from the World's Parliament of Religions*. Edited by Richard Hughes Seager. LaSalle, Ill.: Open Court, 1993. Reprint from Walter R. Hough, *Neely's History of the Parliament of Religions*. Chicago: Neely Publishing House, 1894.

Edwards, David L. *Leaders of the Church of England, 1828–1944*. London: Oxford University Press, 1971.

Edwards, Elizabeth. "Homoerotic Friendship and College Principals, 1880–1960." *Women's History Review* 4, no. 2 (1995): 149–63.

Eller, Cynthia. "Relativizing the Patriarchy: The Sacred History of the Feminist Spirituality Movement." *History of Religions* 30, no. 3 (February 1991): 279–95.

———. *Living in the Lap of the Goddess: The Feminist Spirituality Movement in America*. Boston: Beacon Press, 1995.

Ellis, Ievan. "Schleiermacher in Britain." *Scottish Journal of Theology* 33, no. 4 (1982): 417–42.

Evans, Donald. "Can Philosophers Limit What Mystics Can Do? A Critique of Steven Katz." *Religious Studies* 25 (1989): 53–60.

Evans, R. J. W. *St Michael's Church, Cumnor: A Short History With Description of Church*. Chapel Place, Ramsgate: The Church Publishers, 1981.

Faderman, Lillian. *Surpassing the Love of Men: Romantic Friendship and Love between Women from the Renaissance to the Present*. New York: William Morrow, 1981.

Faull, Katherine M. "Schleiermacher—A Feminist? Or, How to Read Gender-Inflected Theology." In *Schleiermacher and Feminism: Sources, Evaluations and Responses*. Edited by Iain G. Nicol. Lewiston: Edwin Mellen Press, 1992.

Ferm, Vergilius, ed. *An Encyclopedia of Religion*. New York: The Philosophical Library, 1945.

Fessenden, Tracy. " 'Woman' and the 'Primitive' in Paul Tillich's Life and Work: Some Implications for the Study of Religion." *Journal of Feminist Studies in Religion* 14, no. 2 (Fall 1998): 45–76.

Fishburn, Janet Forsyth. *The Fatherhood of God and the Victorian Family: The Social Gospel in America*. Philadelphia: Fortress Press, 1981.

Fletcher, Joseph. *William Temple: Twentieth Century Christian*. New York: Seabury Press, 1963.

Fletcher, Sheila. *Maude Royden*. London: Basil Blackwell, 1989.

Flew, R. Newton. *The Idea of Perfection in Christian Theology: An Historical Study of the Christian Ideal for the Present Life*. London: Oxford University Press, 1934.

Flint, Kate. *The Woman Reader, 1837–1914*. Oxford: Clarendon Press, 1993.

Forman, Robert, ed. *The Problem of Pure Consciousness*. Oxford: Oxford University Press, 1990.

Foster, Frank Hugh. *The Modern Movement in American Theology: Sketches in the History of American Protestant Thought from the Civil War to the World War*. 1939. Reprint. Freeport, New York: Books for Libraries Press, 1969.

Fox-Genovese, Elizabeth. "Two Steps Forward, One Step Back: New Questions and Old Models in the Religious History of American Women." *Journal of the American Academy of Religion* LIII, no. 3 (September 1985): 465–71.

———. "Culture and Consciousness in the Intellectual History of European Women." *Signs: Journal of Women in Culture and Society* 12, no. 3 (1987): 529–47.

Frank, Douglas W. *Less Than Conquerors: How Evangelicalism Entered the Twentieth Century*. Grand Rapids, Mich: Eerdmans, 1986.

Fraser, Brian J. "The Progress in Theology Debate (1882): Consensus and Conflict in North Atlantic Presbyterianism." *Proceedings of the Canadian Society of Church History*, McMaster University, Hamilton, Ontario, June 3–4, 1987.

———. *The Social Uplifters: Presbyterian Progressives and the Social Gospel in Canada, 1875–1915*. Waterloo: Wilfrid Laurier University Press, 1988.

———. "Christianizing the Social Order: T. B. Kilpatrick's Theological Vision of the United Church of Canada." *Toronto Journal of Theology* 12, no. 2 (1996): 189–200.

Freeman, Ruth, and Patricia Klaus. "Blessed or Not? The Spinster in England and the United States in the Late Nineteenth and Early Twentieth Centuries." *Women's History Review* 9, no. 4 (Winter 1984): 394–414.

Gagan, Rosemary. *A Sensitive Independence: Canadian Methodist Women Missionaries in Canada and the Orient, 1881–1925*. Kingston and Montreal: McGill-Queen's University Press, 1992.

Gauld, Alan. *The Founders of Psychical Research*. New York: Schocken Books, 1968.

Gauvreau, Michael. "The Taming of History: Reflections on the Canadian Methodist Encounter with Biblical Criticism, 1830–1900." *Canadian Historical Review* 65, no. 3 (1984): 315–46.

———. *The Evangelical Century: College and Creed in English Canada from the Great Revival to the Great Depression*. Montreal and Kingston: McGill–Queen's University Press, 1991.

Gauvreau, Michael, and Nancy Christie. *A Full-Orbed Christianity: The Protestant Churches and Social Welfare in Canada, 1900–1914*. Montreal: McGill–Queen's University Press, 1996.

Gilbert, Alan D. *Religion and Society in Industrial England: Church, Chapel and Social Change, 1740–1914*. Edited by J. Stevenson. London and New York: Longman, 1976.

Gilbert, Sandra, and Susan Gubar. *The Madwoman in the Attic*. New Haven, Conn.: Yale University Press, 1979.

Gilligan, Carol. *In a Different Voice: Psychological Theory and Women's Development.* 1982; Cambridge: Harvard University Press, 1993.

Godard, Barbara. "A Portrait with Three Faces: The New Woman in Fiction by Canadian Women, 1880–1920." *The Literary Criterion* 19, no. 3–4 (1984): 72–92.

Gordon, Alice M. "The After-Careers of University-Educated Women," *Nineteenth Century* 37 (1895): 958–60.

Gorham, Deborah. "Flora MacDonald Denison and Walt Whitman." Paper presented at the "Whitman in Ontario" Conference, Erindale College, University of Toronto, October, 1980.

Gorrell, Donald K. *The Age of Social Responsibility: The Social Gospel in the Progressive Era, 1900–1920.* Macon,Ga: Mercer University Press, 1988.

Grant, John Webster. *Free Churchmanship in England (1870–1940) With Special Reference to Congregationalism.* London: Independent Press, n.d.

———. *The Church in the Canadian Era.* Rev. ed. 1972; Burlington, Ont.: Welch Publishing Co., 1988.

———. *A Profusion of Spires: Religion in Nineteenth Century Ontario.* Toronto: University of Toronto Press, 1988.

Greene, Dana. *Evelyn Underhill: Modern Guide to the Ancient Quest for the Holy.* Edited and with an introduction by Dana Greene. Albany: State University of New York Press, 1988.

———. *Evelyn Underhill: Artist of the Infinite Life.* New York: Crossroads, 1990.

Griffin, Nicholas. "Bertrand Russell as a Critic of Religion." *Studies in Religion/Sciences religieuses* 24, no. 1 (1995): 47–58.

Griffin, Penny, ed. *St. Hugh's: One Hundred Years of Women's Education At Oxford.* London: Macmillan, 1986.

Gubar, Marah. " 'Where is the Boy?' The Pleasures of Postponement in the Anne of Green Gables Series." *The Lion and the Unicorn* 25, no. 1 (2001): 47–69.

Guenther-Gleason, Patricia. "Schleiermacher's Feminist Impulses in the Context of his Later Work." In *Schleiermacher and Feminism: Sources, Evaluations and Responses.* Edited by Iain G. Nicol. Lewiston, N.Y.: Edwin Mellen Press, 1992.

Gundersen, Joan R. "The Local Parish as a Female Institution: The Experience of All Saints Episcopal Church in Frontier Minnesota." *Church History* 55, no. 3 (September 1986): 307–22.

Hackett, David G. "Gender and Religion in American Culture, 1870–1930." *Religion and American Culture* 5, no. 2 (Summer 1995): 127–58.

Hall, David D. "Review Essay: What is the Place of 'Experience' in Religious History?" *Religion and American Culture: A Journal of Interpretation* 13, no. 2 (2003): 241–50.

Hall, Donald., ed. *Muscular Christianity: Embodying the Victorian Age.* Cambridge: Cambridge University Press, 1994.

Hallman, Diane M. "Religion and Gender: The Writing and Work of Agnes Maule Machar." Ph.D. dissertation, Ontario Institute for Studies in Education, 1994.

Hamilton, Michael S. "Women, Public Ministry and American Fundamentalism, 1920–1950." *Religion and American Culture* 3 (1993): 171–96.

Hamm, Thomas D. *The Transformation of American Quakerism: Orthodox Friends, 1800–1907.* Bloomington: Indiana University Press, 1988.

Hampson, Daphne. *Theology and Feminism.* Basil Blackwell: Oxford, 1990.

Handy, Robert T. "Christianity and Socialism in America, 1900–1920." In *Protestantism and Social Christianity.* Edited by M. E. Marty. Munich: K. G. Saur, 1996.

Hardesty, Nancy. *Your Daughters Shall Prophesy: Revivalism and Feminism in the Age of Finney.* Brooklyn: Carlsen, 1991.

Hardesty, Nancy, Lucille Sider Dayton, and Donald W. Dayton. "Women in the Holiness Movement: Feminism in the Evangelical Tradition." In *Women of Spirit: Female Leadership in the Jewish and Christian Traditions.* Edited by Rosemary Ruether and Eleanor McLaughlin. New York: Simon and Schuster, 1979.

Hassey, Janette. *Not Time for Silence: Evangelical Women in Ministry Around the Turn of the Century.* Grand Rapids, Mich.: Zondervan, 1986.

Hastings, Adrian. "On Modernism: Centenary Lecture, given at Lambeth Palace 10 November, 1998." *Modern Believing* 40, no. 2 (1999): 5–15.

Hatch, Nathan O. *The Democratization of American Christianity.* New Haven, Conn.: Yale University Press, 1989.

Headon, Christopher. "Women and Organized Religion in Mid and Late Nineteenth Century Canada." *Journal of Canadian Church Historical Society* 20, nos. 1–2 (March–June 1978): 3–18.

Heeney, Brian. *The Women's Movement in the Church of England, 1850–1930.* New York and Toronto: Clarendon Press, 1988.

Helm, Robert M. *Gloomy Dean: The Thought of William Ralph Inge.* Winston-Salem, N.C.: John F. Blair, 1962.

Helmstadter, Richard J., and Bernard Lightman, eds. *Victorian Faith in Crisis: Essays On Continuity and Change in Nineteenth-Century Religious Belief.* London: Macmillan, 1990.

Henderson, Heather. *The Victorian Self: Autobiography and Biblical Narrative.* Ithaca and London: Cornell University Press, 1989.

Hunt, Mary. *Fierce Tenderness: A Feminist Theology of Friendship.* New York: Crossroad, 1991.

Hunter, Jane. *The Gospel of Gentility: American Women Missionaries in Turn-Of-The-Century China.* New Haven: Yale University Press, 1984.

Hutchison, William R., ed. *American Protestant Thought: The Liberal Era.* New York: Harper and Row, 1968.

———. *The Modernist Impulse in American Protestantism.* Cambridge, Mass: Harvard University Press, 1976.

Hylson-Smith, Kenneth. *High-Churchmanship in the Church of England from the Sixteenth Century to the Late Twentieth Century.* Edinburgh: T. & T. Clark, 1993.

Iremonger, F. A. *William Temple, Archbishop of Canterbury: His Life and Letters.* London: Oxford University Press, 1948.

Jantzen, Grace. *Power, Gender and Christian Mysticism.* Cambridge: Cambridge University Press, 1995.

Janz, Bruce. "Mysticism and Understanding: Steven Katz and his Critics." *Studies in Religion/Sciences Religieuses* 24, no. 1 (1995): 77–94.

———. "Response to Robert K.C.Forman." *Studies in Religion/Sciences Religieuses* 25, no. 2 (1996): 209–13.

Jay, Elizabeth. *The Religion of the Heart: Anglican Evangelicalism and the Nineteenth Century Novel.* Oxford: Clarendon Press, 1979.

———. "Doubt and the Victorian Woman." In *The Critical Spirit and the Will to Believe: Essays in Nineteenth Century Literature and Religion.* Edited by David Jasper. London: St. Martins Press, 1989.

Jones, Peter d' A. *The Christian Socialist Revival, 1877–1914: Religion, Class and Social Conscience in Late Victorian England.* Princeton, N.J.: Princeton University Press, 1968.

Jones, R. Tudor. *Congregationalism in England, 1662–1962.* London: Independent Press Ltd., 1962.

Jones, S. "Women's Experience: Between a Rock and a Hard Place: Feminist, Womanist and Mujerista Theologies in North America." *Religious Studies Review* 21, no. 3 (1995): 171–78.

Jordan, Philip D. *The Evangelical Alliance of the United States of America, 1847–1900: Ecumenicism, Identity and the Religion of the Republic.* New York: Edwin Mellen Press, 1982.

Judah, J. Stillson. *The History and the Philosophy of the Metaphysical Movements in America.* Philadelphia: The Westminster Press, 1967.

Katz, Steven T., ed. *Mysticism and Philosophical Analysis.* Oxford: Oxford University Press, 1978.

———. *Mysticism and Religious Traditions.* Oxford: Oxford University Press, 1983.

———. *Mysticism and Language.* Oxford: Oxford University Press, 1992.

Kelly, Rosemary Skinner, Ann Braude, Maureen Ursenbach Beecher, and Elizabeth Fox-Genovese. "Forum: Female Experience in American Religion." *Religion and American Culture* 5, no. 1 (Winter 1995): 7.

Kemp, Betty, ed. *St. Hughes: One Hundred Years of Women's Education At Oxford.* London: Macmillan, 1986.

King, Ursula. *Women and Spirituality: Voices of Protest and Promise.* London: Macmillan, 1989.

———. "Voices of Protest and Promise: Women's Studies in Religion: The Impact of the Feminist Critique on the Study of Religion." *Studies in Religion/Sciences religieuses* 23, no. 3 (1994): 315–29.

King, William McGuire. " 'History as Revelation' in the Theology of the Social Gospel." In *Protestantism and Social Christianity.* Edited by Martin Marty. Munich: K. G. Saur, 1992.

Kirkey, Donald L., Jr. "The Student Christian Movement in Canada: Religion and Intellectuals between the Two World Wars." Ph.D. thesis, McMaster University, 1981.

———. " 'Mediating the Religion of Jesus': Henry Burton Sharman and the Student Christian Movement of Canada." Paper presented to the joint meeting of the Canadian and American Societies of Church History, Hamilton, Ont., 1987.

———. "The Decline of Radical Liberal Protestantism: The Case of the Student Christian Movement of Canada." Paper presented to the Canadian Historical Association, Windsor, Ontario, June 1988.

Klinck, Carl F., ed. *The Literary History of Canada.* 2nd ed. Vol. 1. Toronto: University of Toronto Press, 1976.

Knudson, A. C. *The Philosophy of Personalism: A Study in the Metaphysics of Religion.* New York: The Abingdon Press, 1927; New York: Krause Reprint, 1969.

LaCugna, Catherine, ed. *Freeing Theology: The Essentials of Theology in Feminist Perspective.* San Francisco: HarperCollins, 1993.

Langford, Thomas A. *In Search of Foundations: English Theology, 1900–1920.* New York, Nashville: Abingdon Press, 1969.

Lears, T. J. Jackson. *Fables of Abundance: A Cultural History of Advertising in America.* New York: Basic Books, 1994.

————. *No Place of Grace: Antimodernism and the Transformation of American Culture, 1880–1920*. New York: Pantheon Books, 1981.

Lelwica, Michelle M. "From Superstition to Enlightenment to the Race for Pure Consciousness: Antireligious Currents in Popular and Academic Feminist Discourse." *Journal of Feminist Studies in Religion* 14, no. 2 (Fall 1998): 108–23.

Lennox, Cuthbert. *Henry Drummond: A Biographical Sketch With Bibliography.* Toronto: William Briggs, 1901.

Leonard, Ellen. "Experience as a Source for Theology: A Canadian and Feminist Perspective." *Studies in Religion/Sciences religieuses* 19, no. 2 (1990): 143–62.

Lightman, Bernard. "Robert Elsmere and the Agnostic Crises of Faith." In *Victorian Faith in Crisis: Essays On Continuity and Change in Nineteenth-Century Belief.* Edited by Richard J. Helmstadter and Bernard Lightman. London: Macmillan, 1990.

Lindley, Susan H. "Women and the Social Gospel Novel." *Church History* 54 (March 1985): 56–73.

————. "Neglected Voices and Praxis in the Social Gospel." *Journal of Religious Ethics* 18/1 (1990): 75–102.

Lippy, Charles, ed. *Encyclopedia of American Religious Experience: Studies of Traditions and Movements.* New York: Scribner, 1988.

Livingston, James C. *The Ethics of Belief: An Essay On the Victorian Religious Conscience.* Tallahassee, Fla.: American Academy of Religion, 1974.

Lloyd, Roger. *The Church of England, 1900–1965.* London: SCM Press Ltd., 1966.

Loades, Ann, ed. *Feminist Theology: A Reader.* London: SPCK, 1990.

Luckhurst, Roger. *The Invention of Telepathy, 1870–1871.* Oxford: Oxford University Press, 2002.

Mack, Barry. "From Preaching to Propaganda to Marginalization: The Lost Centre of Twentieth Century Presbyterianism." In *Aspects of the Canadian Evangelical Experience.* Edited by George A. Rawlyk. Montreal and Kingston: McGill–Queen's University Press, 1997.

Macquarrie, John. *Twentieth-Century Religious Thought.* 1963. 3rd. ed. London: SCM Press Ltd., 1988.

Maitland, Sara, and Jo Garcia, eds. *Walking On the Water: Women Talk about Spirituality.* London: Virago, 1983.

Marsden, George M. *Fundamentalism and American Culture: The Shaping of Twentieth-Century Evangelicalism 1870–1925.* New York and Oxford: Oxford University Press, 1980.

Marshall, David B. *Secularizing the Faith: Canadian Protestant Clergy and the Crisis of Belief, 1850–1940.* Toronto: University of Toronto Press, 1992.

Marty, M. E. *Protestantism and Social Christianity.* Munich: K. G. Saur, 1996.

Massey, Marilyn Chapin. *The Feminine Soul: The Fate of an Ideal.* Boston: Beacon Press, 1985.

McCarthy, Doris. *A Fool in Paradise: An Artist's Early Life.* Toronto: MacFarlane, Walter and Ross, 1990.

————. *The Good Wine: An Artist Comes of Age.* Toronto: MacFarlane, Walter and Ross, 1991.

McClain, Frank Mauldin. *Maurice: Man and Moralist.* London: SPCK, 1972.

McClain, Frank, Richard Norris, and John Orens. *F. D. Maurice: A Study.* Cambridge, Mass.: Cowley Publications, 1982.

McDannell, Colleen. *The Christian Home in Victorian America, 1840–1900.* Bloomington: Indiana University Press, 1986.

McGinn, Bernard. *The Presence of God: A History of Western Christian Mysticism.* Vol. 1, *The Foundations of Mysticism.* New York: Crossroads, 1991. London: SCM Press, 1992.

———. "The Language of Love in Christian and Jewish Mysticism." In *Mysticism and Language.* Edited by Steven D. Katz. Oxford: Oxford University Press, 1992.

———. "The Letter and the Spirit: Spirituality as a Academic Discipline." *Christian Spirituality Bulletin* 1, no. 2 (Fall 1993): 1–9.

———. *The Presence of God: A History of Western Christian Mysticism.* Vol. 2, *The Growth of Mysticism: From Gregory the Great to the Twelfth Century.* New York: Crossroad, 1994. London: SCM Press, 1995.

———. *The Presence of God: A History of Western Christian Mysticism.* Vol. 3, *The Flowering of Mysticism: Men and Women in the New Mysticism (1200–1350).* New York: Crossroad, 1994. London: SCM Press, 1995.

McKillop, A. B. *A Critical Spirit: The Thought of William Dawson LeSueur.* Toronto: University of Toronto Press, 1977.

———. *A Disciplined Intelligence: Critical Inquiry and Canadian Thought in the Victorian Era.* Montreal: McGill–Queen's University Press, 1979.

———. "Moralists and Moderns." *Journal of Canadian Studies/Revue d'études canadiennes* 14 (Winter 1979–80): 144–50.

———, ed. *Contours of Canadian Thought.* Toronto: University of Toronto Press, 1987.

———. *Matters of Mind: The University in Ontario, 1791–1951.* Toronto: University of Toronto Press, 1994.

McLean, Ken. "Evangelical and Ecclesiastical Literature." *Journal of Canadian Fiction* 21 (1977–1978): 105–19.

McLelland, Joseph C. "The Macdonnell Heresy Trial." *Canadian Journal of Theology* IV, no. 4 (1958): 273–84.

McMullen, Lorraine. "Lily Dougall's Vision of Canada." In *A Mazing Space: Writing Canadian Women Writing.* Edited by Shirley Neuman and Smaro Kamboureli. Edmonton: Longspoon Press/Newest Press, 1986.

———. "Lily Dougall: The Religious Vision of a Canadian Novelist." *Studies in Religion/Sciences Religieuses* 16, no. 1 (Winter 1987): 79–90.

———, ed. *Re(Dis)Covering Our Foremothers: Nineteenth-Century Canadian Women Writers.* Ottawa: University of Ottawa Press, 1989.

McQuarrie, John. *Twentieth-Century Religious Thought.* 1963; London: SCM Press, 1988.

Mews, Stuart. "The Revival of Spiritual Healing in the Church of England, 1920–1926." In *The Church and Healing.* Edited by W. J. Shiels. Oxford: Basil Blackwell, 1982.

Mitchinson, Wendy. *The Nature of Their Bodies: Women and Their Doctors in Victorian Canada.* Toronto: University of Toronto Press, 1991.

Moore, R. Laurence. *In Search of White Crows: Spiritualism, Parapsychology and American Culture.* New York: Oxford University Press, 1977.

Moore, Lindy. "The Scottish Universities and Women Students." In *Scottish Universities: Distinctiveness and Diversity.* Edited by Jennifer J. Carter and Donald J. Withrington. Edinburgh: John Donald Publishers, 1992.

Morton, Nelle. *The Journey Is Home.* Boston: Beacon Press, 1985.

Mair, Nathan H. *John Dougall and His Montreal Witness.* Ottawa: The Archives Committee of the Montreal and Ottawa Conference of the United Church of Canada, 1985.

Mullin, Robert Bruce. "The Debate over Religion and Healing in the Episcopal Church: 1870–1930." *Anglican Episcopal History* 60, no. 2 (June 1991): 213–34.

———. *Miracles and the Modern Religious Imagination.* New Haven: Yale University Press, 1996.

Murphy, H. R. "The Ethical Revolt in Against Christian Orthodoxy in Early Victorian England." *American Historical Review* 60, no. 4 (July 1955): 800–17.

Newton, Esther. "The Mythic Mannish Lesbian: Radclyffe Hall and the New Woman." In *Hidden from History: Reclaiming the Gay and Lesbian Past.* Edited by Martin Bauml Duberman, Martha Vicinus, and George Chauncey, Jr. New York: New American Library, 1989.

Nicol, Iian G., ed. *Schleiermacher and Feminism: Sources, Evaluations and Responses.* Lewiston: Edwin Mellen Press, 1992.

Nord, Deborah Epstein. *The Apprenticeship of Beatrice Webb.* Ithaca, N.Y.: Cornell University Press, 1985.

Opp, James. *The Lord for the Body: Religion, Medicine, and Protestant Faith Healing in Canada, 1880–1930.* Montreal and Kingston: McGill-Queens University Press, 2006.

Oppenheim, Janet. *The Other World: Spiritualism and Psychical Research in England, 1850–1914.* London: Cambridge University Press, 1985.

Oram, Alison, and Annmarie Turnbull. *The Lesbian History Sourcebook: Love and Sex between Women in Britain from 1870–1970.* London: Routledge, 2001.

Orsini, G. N. G. *Coleridge and German Idealism: A Study in the History of Philosophy with Unpublished Materials from Coleridge's Manuscripts.* Carbondale, Ill.: Southern Illinois University Press, 1969.

Ostrander, Richard. "The Life of Prayer in a World of Science: Protestants, Prayer and American Culture." Ph.D. dissertation, Notre Dame University (Indiana), 1996.

———. "The Battery and the Windmill: Two Models of Protestant Devotionalism in Early-Twentieth-Century America." *Church History* 65, no. 1 (March 1996): 42–61.

Outler, Albert C. "Pietism and Enlightenment: Alternatives to Tradition." In *Christian Spirituality: Post-Reformation and Modern.* Vol. 18 of *World Spirituality: An Encyclopaedic History of the Religious Quest.* Edited by Louis Dupre and Don E. Saliers. New York: Crossroads, 1996.

Owen, Alex. *The Darkened Room: Women, Power and Spiritualism in Late Victorian England.* London: Virago Press, 1989.

Ozment, Steven. *Mysticism and Dissent: Religious Ideology and Social Protest in the Sixteenth Century.* New Haven and London: Yale University Press, 1973.

Patrick, James. *The Magdalen Metaphysicals: Idealism and Orthodoxy at Oxford, 1901–1945.* Macon, Ga.: Mercer University Press, 1985.

Pearson, C. R. "H. D. A. Major and English Modernism, 1911–1948." Ph.D. thesis, University of Cambridge, 1989.

Pederson, Diana L. "The YWCA in Canada, 1870–1920, 'A Movement to Meet a Spiritual, Civic and National Need.'" Ph.D. dissertation, Carleton University, 1987.

Pellauer, Mary D. *Toward a Tradition of Feminist Theology: The Religious Social Thought of Elizabeth Cady Stanton, Susan B. Anthony, and Anna Howard Shaw.* Brooklyn, N.Y.: Carlsen Publishing, 1991.

Peterson, Linda H. *Victorian Autobiography: The Tradition of Self-Interpretation.* New Haven and London: Yale University Press, 1986.

———. "Gender and the Autobiographical Form: The Case of the Spiritual Autobiography." In *Studies in Autobiography*. Edited by James Olney. New York and Oxford: Oxford University Press, 1988.

Pike, Nelson. *Mystic Union: An Essay on the Phenomenology of Mysticism*. Ithaca, N.Y.: Cornell University Press, 1992.

Pittenger, Norman W. "The Christian Apologetic of James Franklin Bethune-Baker." *Anglican Theological Review* XXXVII, no. 4 (October 1955): 260–77.

———. "James Matthew Thompson: The Martyr of English Modernism." *Anglican Theological Review* XXXIX, no. 4 (October 1957): 291–96.

———. "Modernism." *Theology* VLXVII, no. 535 (1965): 53–60.

Plaskow, Judith. *Sex, Sin and Grace: Women's Experience and the Theologies of Reinhold Niebuhr and Paul Tillich*. Washington, D.C.: University Press of America, 1980.

———. "We Are Also Your Sisters: The Development of Women's Studies in Religion." *Women's Studies Quarterly* 1–2 (1993): 9.

Plaskow, Judith, and Carol P. Christ, eds. *Weaving the Visions: New Patterns in Feminist Spirituality*. San Francisco: Harper and Row, 1989.

Pourat, Pierre. *Christian Spirituality*. 4 vols. Translated by W. R. Mitchell and S. P. Jacques. Westminster: Neuman, 1953–55.

Prickett, Stephen. *Romanticism and Religion: The Tradition of Coleridge and Wordsworth in the Victorian Church*. Cambridge: Cambridge University Press, 1976.

Principe, Walter H. "Toward Defining Spirituality," *Studies in Religion/Sciences religieuses* 12, no. 2 (1983): 127–41.

———. "Broadening the Focus: Context as a Corrective Lens in Reading Historical Works in Spirituality." *Christian Spirituality Bulletin* 2, no. 1 (Spring 1994): 1–5.

Proudfoot, Wayne. *Religious Experience*. Boston: Berkeley, 1985.

Pulker, Edward. *We Stand On Their Shoulders: The Growth of Social Concern in Canadian Anglicanism*. Toronto: Anglican Book Centre, 1986.

Rabinovitz, Richard. *The Spiritual Self in Everyday Life: The Transformation of Personal Religious Experience in Nineteenth Century New England*. Boston: Northeastern University Press, 1989.

Raphael, Melissa. "Feminism, Constructivism and Numinous Experience." *Religious Studies* 30 (1994): 511–26.

———. *Champions of Truth: Fundamentalism, Modernism and the Maritime Baptists*. Montreal and Kingston: McGill–Queen's University Press, 1990.

———, ed. *The Canadian Protestant Experience, 1760–1990*. Burlington, Ont.: Welch Publishing Co., 1990.

———, ed. *Aspects of the Canadian Evangelical Experience*. Montreal and Kingston: McGill-Queen's University Press, 1997.

Rawlyk, George, David Bebbington, and Mark Noll. *Amazing Grace: Evangelicalism in Australia, Great Britain, Canada and the United States*. Montreal and Kingston: McGill–Queens University Press, 1994.

Reardon, Bernard M. G. *Religious Thought in the Victorian Age: A Survey from Coleridge to Gore*. London: Longman, 1971. 2nd rev. ed., 1995.

Reed, Edward S. *From Soul to Mind: The Emergence of Psychology from Erasmus Darwin to William James*. New Haven: Yale University Press, 1997.

Reimer, Chad. "Religion and Culture in Nineteenth-Century English Canada." *Journal of Canadian Studies/Revue d'études canadiennes* 25, no. 1 (Spring 1990): 192–203.

Reimer, Gail Twersky. "Revisions of Labour in Margaret Oliphant's Autobiography." In *Life/Lines: Theorizing Women's Autobiograph*. Edited by Bella Brodzki and Celeste Schencke. Ithaca, N.Y., and London: Cornell University Press, 1988.

Reynolds, David S. "The Feminization Controversy: Sexual Stereotypes and the Paradoxes of Piety in Nineteenth-Century America." *New England Quarterly* 53 (1980): 96–106.

Rich, Adrienne. "Compulsory Heterosexuality and Lesbian Existence." In *The Lesbian and Gay Studies Reader*. Edited by Henry Abelove, Michele Aina Barale, and David M. Halperin. London: Routledge, 1993.

Ridout, Katherine. " 'A Woman of Mission': The Religious and Cultural Odyssey of Agnes Wintemute Coates." *Canadian Historical Review* 71, no. 2 (June 1990): 208–44.

Robbins, Keith. *History, Religion and Identity in Modern British History*. London: The Hambledon Press, 1993.

Roberts, Ruth. *Thomas Carlyle and Comparative Religion*. Berkeley: University of California Press, 1988.

Robinson, Laura M. "Bosom friends: Lesbian desire in L. M. Montgomery's Anne books." *Canadian Literature/Littérature canadienne: a quarterly of criticism and review* (Spring 2004): 12–28.

Rosenzweig, Linda W. *The Anchor of My Life: Middle-Class American Mothers and Daughters, 1880–1920*. New York and London: New York University Press, 1993.

Ross, Susan A., and Elizabeth A. Johnson. "Feminist Theology: A Review of the Literature." *Theological Studies* 56, no. 2 (1995): 327–52.

Rowell, Geoffrey. *Hell and the Victorians: A Study of the Nineteenth-Century Theological Controversies Concerning Eternal Punishment and Future Life*. Oxford: Clarendon Press, 1974.

Royden, Maude. *A Three-Fold Cord*. London: Victor Gollancz, 1947.

Reuther, Rosemary Radforth. *Sexism and God-Talk: Towards a Feminist Theology*. Boston: Beacon Press, 1983.

———. "The Future of Feminist Theology in the Academy." *Journal of the American Academy of Religion* 53 (1985): 709.

———. *Womanguides: Readings Toward a Feminist Theology*. Boston: Beacon Press, 1985.

———. "Feminist Spirituality and Historical Religion." *Harvard Divinity Bulletin* 16, no. 3 (1986): 11.

Ruether, Rosemary Radford, and Eleanor McLaughlin, eds. *Women of Spirit: Female Leadership in the Jewish and Christian Traditions*. New York: Simon and Schuster, 1979.

Ruether, Rosemary Radford, and Rosemary Skinner Keller, eds. *Women and Religion in America*. Vol. 1, *The Nineteenth Century*. San Francisco: Harper and Row, 1981.

Rutherford, Paul. *A Victorian Authority: The Daily Press in the Late Nineteenth Century*. Toronto: University of Toronto Press, 1982.

Saiving, Valerie. "A Conversation with Valerie Saiving." *Journal of Feminist Studies in Religion* 4, no. 2 (Fall 1988): 99–115.

———. "The Human Situation: A Feminine View." In *Womanspirit Rising: A Feminist Reader*. Edited by Carol P. Christ and Judith Plaskow. San Francisco: Harper Collins, 1992.

Salter, Darius L. *Spirit and Intellect: Thomas Upham's Holiness Theology*. Metuchen, N.J.: Scarecrow Press, 1986.

Sandeen, Ernest. *The Roots of Fundamentalism: British and American Millenarianism, 1800–1930.* Chicago: University of Chicago Press, 1970.

Sanders, Valerie. *The Private Lives of Victorian Women: Autobiography in Nineteenth-Century England.* New York: Harvester Wheatsheaf, 1989.

Sanders, Charles Richard. *Coleridge and the Broad Church Movement: Studies in S. T. Coleridge, Dr. Arnold of Rugby, J. C. Hare, Thomas Carlyle and F. D. Maurice.* Durham, N.C.: Duke University Press, 1942.

Satter, Beryl. *Each Mind a Kingdom: American Women, Sexual Purity and the New Thought Movement, 1875–1920.* Berkeley and Los Angeles: University of California Press, 1999.

Schneider, Sandra M. "Spirituality in the Academy." *Theological Studies* 50, no. 4 (1989): 684–87.

———. "Spirituality as an Academic Discipline: Reflections from Experience." *Christian Spirituality Bulletin* 1, no. 2 (Spring 1993): 10–15.

———. "The Cost of Interpretation: Sacred Texts and Ascetic Practice in Desert Spirituality." *Christian Spirituality Bulletin* 3, no. 1 (Spring 1994): 9–14.

Scott, Joan Wallach. *Gender and the Politics of History.* New York: Columbia University Press, 1988.

Sell, Alan P. F. *The Philosophy of Religion.* London: Croom Helm, 1988.

Sharpe, Eric J. "The Study of Religion in *Encyclopedia of Religion.*" *Journal of Religion* 70, no. 3 (July 1990): 347.

Sheils, W. J., and Diana Wood, eds. *Women in the Church. Papers Read at the 1989 Summer Meeting and the 1990 Winter Meeting of the Ecclesiastical History Society.* Oxford: Basil Blackwell for the Ecclesiastical History Society, 1990.

Sheldrake, Philip F. "Spirituality and the Process of History." *Christian Spirituality Bulletin* 1, no. 1 (Spring 1993): 1–4.

———. "Some Continuing Questions: The Relationship Between Spirituality and Theology." *Christian Spirituality Bulletin* 2, no. 1 (Spring 1994): 15–17.

———. *Spirituality and History: Questions of Interpretation and Method.* 1991. Rev. ed. Maryknoll, N.Y.: Orbis Books, 1995.

Showalter, Elaine. *A Literature of their Own: British Women Authors from Brontë to Lessing.* Princeton, N.J.: Princeton University Press, 1977.

———. *The Female Malady: Women, Madness and English Culture, 1830–1980.* New York: Pantheon Books, 1985.

———, ed. *Speaking of Gender.* New York: Routledge, 1989.

Sinclair-Faulkner, Tom. "Theory divided from practice: The Introduction of the Higher Criticism into Canadian Protestant Seminaries." *Studies in Religion/ Sciences religieuses* 10, no. 3 (Summer 1981): 321–43.

Sklar, Kathryn Kish. *Catharine Beecher: A Study in American Domesticity.* New Haven and London: Yale University Press, 1973.

———. "The Last Fifteen Years: Historians' Changing Views of American Women in Religion and Society." In *Women in New Worlds: Historical Perspectives On the Wesleyan Tradition.* Edited by Hilah F. Thomas and Rosemary Skinner Keller. Nashville: Abingdon Press, 1981.

Smith, Patricia Juliana. *Lesbian Panic: Homoeroticism in Modern British Women's Fiction.* New York: Columbia University Press, 1997.

Smith, Timothy L. *Revivalism and Social Reform in Mid-Nineteenth Century America.* New York: Abingdon Press, 1957.

Smith, Wilfred Cantwell. *Faith and Belief: The Difference Between Them.* 1979. Reprint. Oxford: Oneworld, 1998.

Smith-Rosenberg, Caroll. "The Female World of Love and Ritual: 'Relations between Women in Nineteenth-Century America.'" *Signs: Journal of Women in Culture and Society* 1 (1975): 1–29.

———. *Disorderly Conduct: Visions of Gender in Victorian America.* New York: Oxford University Press, 1985.

Sommerville, C. John, and John Edwards. "Debate: Religious Faith, Doubt and Atheism." *Past and Present* 128 (1990): 152–61.

Spretnak, Charlene. *The Politics of Women's Spirituality: Essays On the Rise of Spiritual Power Within the Feminist Movement.* New York: Anchor Books, 1982.

Stephenson, Alan M. G. *The Rise and Decline of English Modernism.* The Hulsean Lectures 1979–80. London: SPCK, 1984.

Stoeffler, Ernest F. *The Rise of Evangelical Pietism.* Leiden: E. J. Brill, 1965.

Streeter, Robert F. "Romanticism and the Sensus Numinous in Schleiermacher." In *The Interpretation of Belief: Coleridge, Schleiermacher and Romanticism.* Edited by David Jasper. London: Macmillan, 1986.

Swanson, Scott Rothwell. "Beyond Common Sense: Ideal Love in Three Novels of Lily Dougall." M.A. Thesis, University of Victoria, 1993.

Sweet, Leonard I. *The Minister's Wife: Her Role in Nineteenth-Century American Evangelicalism.* Philadelphia: Temple University Press, 1983.

———. "Wise as Serpents, Innocent as Doves: The New Evangelical Historiography." *Journal of the American Academy of Religion* LVI, no. 3 (1988): 397–416.

Szasz, Ferenc Morton. *The Divided Mind of Protestant America.* University: University of Alabama Press, 1982.

Taves, Ann. "Mothers and Children and the Legacy of Mid-Nineteenth Century American Christianity." *Journal of Religion* 67, no. 2 (1987): 203–19.

———. "Women and Gender in American Religion(s)." *Religious Studies Review* 18, no. 4 (October 1992): 263.

———. *Fits, Trances, and Visions: Experiencing Religion and Explaining Experience from Wesley to James.* Princeton: Princeton University Press, 1999.

———. "Religious Experience." In *Encyclopedia of Religious Experience.* 2nd ed. Gale: 2005.

Tennyson, G. B. *Sartor Called Resartus: The Genesis, Structure and Style of Thomas Carlyle's First Major Work.* Princeton: Princeton University Press, 1965.

Thayne, Gail Parker. *Mind Cure in New England: From the Civil War to World War I.* Hanover, N.H.: University Press of New England, 1973.

Tillich, Paul. *Perspectives On Nineteenth- and Twentieth-Century Protestant Theology,* edited and introduced by Carl E. Braaten. London: Harper and Row, 1967.

Tompkins, Jane. *Sensational Designs: The Cultural Work of American Fiction, 1790–1860.* New York: Oxford University Press, 1985.

Tulloch, John. *Movements of Religious Thought in Britain in the Nineteenth Century.* 1885. Reprint. New York: Humanities Press, 1971.

Turner, Elizabeth Hayes. "Episcopal Women as Community Leaders: Galveston, 1900–1989." In *Episcopal Women: Gender, Spirituality, Commitment in an American Mainline Congregation.* Edited by Catherine M. Prelinger. Oxford: Oxford University Press, 1992.

Turner, Frank M. *Between Science and Religion: The Reaction to Scientific Naturalism in Late Victorian England.* New Haven and London: Yale University Press, 1974.

————. "The Victorian Crisis of Faith and the Faith that was Lost." In *Victorian Faith in Crisis: Essays On Continuity and Change in Nineteenth-Century Belief.* Edited by Richard J. Helmstadter and Bernard Lightman. London: Macmillan, 1990.

————. *Contesting Cultural Authority: Essays in Victorian Intellectual Life.* Cambridge: Cambridge University Press, 1993.

Turner, James. *Without God, Without Creed: The Origins of Unbelief in America.* Baltimore and London: Johns Hopkins University Press, 1985.

————. "Forward," in *Reckoning with the Past.* Edited by D. G. Hart. Grand Rapids: Baker, 1995.

Vance, Norman. *The Sinews of the Spirit: The Ideal of Christian Manliness in Victorian Literature and Religious Thought.* Cambridge: Cambridge University Press, 1985.

Vander Hoef, Lorraine. "John Dougall (1808–1886): Portrait of an Early Social Reformer and Evangelical Witness in Canada." *Journal of the Canadian Church Historical Society* 43 (2001): 115–45.

Van der Veer, Peter. *Imperial Encounters: Religion and Modernity in India and Britain.* Princeton: Princeton University Press, 2001.

Van Die, Marguerite. *An Evangelical Mind: Nathanael Burwash and the Methodist Tradition in Canada, 1839–1918.* Kingston and Montreal: McGill–Queen's University Press, 1989.

————. "Recovering Religious Experience: Some Reflections on Methodology." *Historical Papers: Canadian Society of Church History* (1992): 155–69.

Vicinus, Martha. *Independent Women: Work and Community for Single Women, 1850–1920.* Chicago and London: University of Chicago Press, 1985.

————. "They Wonder to Which Sex I Belong: The Historical Roots of Modern Lesbian Identity." In *The Lesbian and Gay Studies Reader,* p. 436. See also Andreidis, 136. Edited by Henry Abelove, Michele Aina Barale, and David M. Halperin. London: Routledge, 1993.

————. "The Gift of Love": Nineteenth-Century Religion and Lesbian Passion." *Nineteenth-Century Contexts* 23 (2001): 241–64.

Vidler, Alex R. *F. D. Maurice and Company.* London: SCM Press, 1966.

Vipond, Mary. "Bestsellers in English Canada, 1899–1918: An Overview." *Journal of Canadian Fiction* 24: 96–119.

Viller, Marcel. *Dictionnaire de spiritualité ascétique et mystique:Doctrine et histoire.* 20 vols. Paris: Beauchesne, 1932.

von Arx, Jeffrey. "The Victorian Crisis of Faith as a Crisis of Vocation." In *Victorian Faith in Crisis: Essays On Continuity and Change in Nineteenth-Century Belief.* Edited by Richard J. Helmstadter and Bernard Lightman. London: Macmillan, 1990.

Wainwright, William. *Mysticism: A Study of its Nature, Cognitive Value, and Moral Implications.* Brighton, England: Harvester Press, 1981.

Wakefield, Gordon. "Anglican Spirituality." In *Christian Spirituality: Post Reformation and Modern.* Vol. 18 in *World Spirituality: An Encyclopedic History of the Religious Quest.* Edited by Louis Dupré and Don E. Saliers. New York: Crossroad, 1996.

Ward, W. R. "Faith and Fallacy: English and German Perspectives in the Nineteenth Century." In *Victorian Faith in Crisis: Essays on Continuity and Change in Nineteenth-Century Belief.* Edited by Richard J. Helmstadter and Bernard Lightman. London: Macmillan, 1990.

Warfield, Benjamin Breckinridge. *Perfectionism.* Vol. 2. New York: Oxford University Press, 1931.

Warne, Randi R. *Literature as Pulpit: The Christian Social Activism of Nellie L. McClung.* Waterloo, Ont.: Wilfrid Laurier University Press, 1993.

————. "Double Discourse or Straight Talking: Whither Women in Canadian Religious History?" Paper presented at the Annual Meeting of the Canadian Historical Association, Victoria, 1990.

Webb, R. K. "The Faith of Nineteenth-Century Unitarians: A Curious Incident." *In Victorian Faith in Crisis: Essays On Continuity and Change in Nineteenth-Century Belief.* Edited by Richard J. Helmstadter and Bernard Lightman. London: Macmillan, 1990.

Weeks, Andrew. *German Mysticism from Hildegard of Bingen to Ludwig Wittgenstein: A Literary and Intellectual History.* Albany: State University of New York Press, 1993.

Welch, Claude. *Protestant Thought in the Nineteenth Century, 1870–1914.* New Haven, Conn.: Yale University Press, 1985.

Welter, Barbara. "The Feminization of American Religion, 1800–1860." In *Clio's Consciousness Raised.* Edited by Mary Hartman and Lois Banner. New York: Harper Torchbooks, 1973.

————. "Defenders of the Faith: Women Novelists of Religious Controversy in the Nineteenth Century." In *Dimity Convictions: The American Woman in the Nineteenth Century.* Edited by Barbara Welter. Athens, Ohio: Ohio University Press, 1976.

Westfall, William. *Two Worlds: The Protestant Culture of Nineteenth-Century Ontario.* Kingston: McGill–Queen's University Press, 1989.

Whelen, Gloria. "Maria Grant, 1854–1937: The Life and Times of an Early Twentieth-Century Christian." In *In Her Own Right: Selected Essays On Women's History in B.C.* Edited by Barbara Latham and Cathy Kess. Victoria, B.C.: Camosun College, 1980.

Whiteley, Marilyn Fardig and Elizabeth Gillan Muir, eds. *Changing Roles of Women in the Christian Church in Canada.* Toronto, University of Toronto Press, 1995.

Willey, Basil. *More Nineteenth-Century Studies: A Group of Honest Doubters.* London: Chatto and Windus, 1963.

Williams, Daniel Day. *Andover Liberals: A Study in American Theology.* 1941; New York: Octagon, 1970.

Williams, Peter. *Popular Religion in America: Symbolic Change and the Modernization Process in Historical Perspective.* Eaglewood Hills, N.J.: Prentice-Hall, 1980.

Wilson, Bryan. *Religion in a Secular Society.* London: C.A. Watts, 1966.

Wolffe, John. "The End of Victorian Values? Women, Religion and the Death of Queen Victoria." In *Women in the Church.* Edited by W. J. Sheils and Diana Wood. Oxford: Basil Blackwell for the Ecclesiastical History Society, 1990.

Wright, T. R. "Middlemarch as a Religious Novel, or Life without God." *Images of Belief in Literature.* Edited by David Jasper. New York: St. Martin's Press, 1984.

Wuthnow, Robert. *After Heaven: Spirituality in America After the 1950s.* Berkeley: University of California Press, 1998.

Young, Pamela Dickey. *Feminist Theology/Christian Theology.* Minneapolis, Minn.: Fortress, 1990.

310	BIBLIOGRAPHY

—————. "Feminist Theology: From Past to Future." In *Gender, Genre and Religion: Feminist Reflections.* Edited by Morny Joy and Eva K. Neumaier-Dargyay. Waterloo, Ont.: Wilfrid Laurier University Press, 1995.

Zikmunk, Barbara Brown. "The Feminist Thrust of Sectarian Christianity." In *Women of Spirit: Female Leadership in Jewish and Christian Traditions.* Edited by Rosemary Reuther and Eleanor McLaughlin. New York: Simon and Schuster, 1979.

Dictionary of National Biography. Supplement, *1901–11; 1921–1930; 1931–1940.* Oxford: Oxford University Press, 1912; 1937; 1949.

World Spirituality: An Encyclopedic History of the Religious Quest, 25 vols. New York: Crossroad, 1985.

Index

109, 110–11; influence of H. Drummond, 136–37; influence of J. R. Illingworth, 133; LD's opinion of her writing, 45–46, 102, 104, 163, 190, 228n59; lists of published work, 3–5, 74–76, 102; poems, 77; portrayal of intellectual development, 48, 53–54; portrayals of heterosexual violence, 74, 75–76, 79–80, 83; portrayals of same-sex relationships, 78, 82, 83; portrayals of single women, 77–78; portrayals of strong women, 54–55, 74, 76–77, 79, 80; portrayals of the supernatural, 178–81, 188, 190–91, 199; on psychology, 151–64; on religious topics in fiction, 233n41; S. Earp's role in, 42, 67, 69, 70, 73, 104, 123; sexual themes, 77, 79, 81–83; social reform in writings, 56, 85, 102, 112–15; use of metaphors, 91–92, 169; using men to represent women's thoughts, 55, 56, 58–59, 70, 93

written works: *The Christian Doctrine of Health,* 160, 161–62, 162–64, 262–63n65; "Conscience and Authority," 168; "Corchester of the Future," 76, 96, 277n52; *A Dozen Ways of Love,* 79, 103, 223n8, 227n54; *The Earthly Purgatory: A Novel,* 76, 82, 95; "Evelyn Vane," 197; *God and the Struggle for Existence,* 138; "God and the Subconscious Mind," 200; *God's Way with Man,* 138, 180, 182, 268n39, 273nn6,8; *The Lord of Thought,* 138, 172, 175–76; "Orthodoxy Dualism," 172; *A Question of Faith,* 75; *Rosemary for Remembrance,* 36, 88–89, 227n54; "The Salvation of the Body by Faith," 154–55; "The Selected Letters of Lily Dougall," 73; *The Spanish Dowry,* 76, 84–85, 96, 110; *The Summit House* Mystery, 76, 95; "Synopsis of *Earthly Purgatory*", 81; "Thoughts Preliminary to the Restatement of the Doctrine of the

Holy Spirit," 143, 144; "Thrift," 85; *Voluntas Dei,* 102, 108, 133, 174, 179, 239n21. *See also Absente Reo; Beggars All: A Novel; Christus Futurus; Concerning Prayer; Immortality;* "Lovereen: A Canadian Story"; *The Madonna of a Day; The Mermaid: A Love Tale; The Mormon Prophet; Paths of the Righteous; The Practice of Christianity; Pro Christo et Ecclesia; The Spirit; What Necessity Knows*

Dougall, Mary Helen "Polly" (LD's sister), 23

Dougall, Susan "Susie" (LD's sister): and mental science meeting, 157; religious influence on, 26; sickness, 23, 24, 35, 151–52, 152

Dougall family: attitude toward fiction writing, 36–37; belief in faith healing, 152; and Congregational Church, 27–28; evangelicalism in, 17, 18, 22, 24–26, 154; and holiness theology, 17; illness in New York, 23–24; LD's ambivalence toward, 34; and prayer, 151–52; sense of God's presence among, 24, 25. *See also* individual members of Dougall family

Drummond, Agnes, 69

Drummond, Henry, 136–37, 196, 232n24

Drummond, Katie, 69, 161

Dubois, Paul, 156

Earp, Sophie: background, 66, 222n3; career, 67, 70, 106; comment on LD's books, 83, 105, 113, 232n24; and Cumnor School, 144–45, 149, 254–55n63, 255n72, 256n75; death and obituary, 1, 65, 223n8, 272n2; on LD's character, 87, 89; and LD's death, 271–72n2; on LD's health, 154; LD's letters to, 91, 97, 103–104, 192–93; on LD's religion, 48, 49, 259n31; and LD's role in Guild of Health, 262–63n65; picture, *68;* relationship with LD, 65–67, 69, 70, 72, 73–74, 103, 106; religious beliefs, 97, 114, 123;

JOANNA DEAN is Assistant Professor in the Department of History at Carleton University, Ottawa, Canada, and teaches women's and gender history. She is co-author of *Guide to Women's Archives/Guides des Archives sur les Femmes.*